Kazunari Kakei

I got so much help from my readers and the members of my staff! Thank you very much! I hope we can meet again soon...

NORA: The Last Chronicle of Devildom is Kazunari Kakei's first manga series. It debuted in the April 2004 issue of *Monthly Shonen Jump* and eventually spawned a second series, *SUREBREC: NORA the 2nd*, which premiered in *Monthly Shonen Jump*'s March 2007 issue.

THE LAST CHRONICLE OF DEVILDOM

VOL. 9

SHONEN JUMP ADVANCED
Manga Edition

STORY AND ART BY
KAZUNARI KAKEI

English Adaptation/Park Cooper & Barb Lien-Cooper
Translation/Nori Minami
Touch-up Art & Lettering/Annaliese Christman
Design/Sam Elzway
Editor/Shaenon K. Garrity

VP, Production/Alvin Lu
VP, Sales & Product Marketing/Gonzalo Ferreyra
VP, Creative/Linda Espinosa
Publisher/Hyoe Narita

Published by VIZ Media, LLC
P.O. Box 77010
San Francisco, CA 94107

10 9 8 7 6 5 4 3 2 1
First printing, February 2010

www.viz.com

THE WORLD'S MOST
CUTTING-EDGE MANGA

www.shonenjump.com

SHONEN JUMP ADVANCED
Manga Edition

NORA
THE LAST CHRONICLE OF DEVILDOM

Volume 9:
Null and Void

Kazunari Kakei

OUR FIENDISH

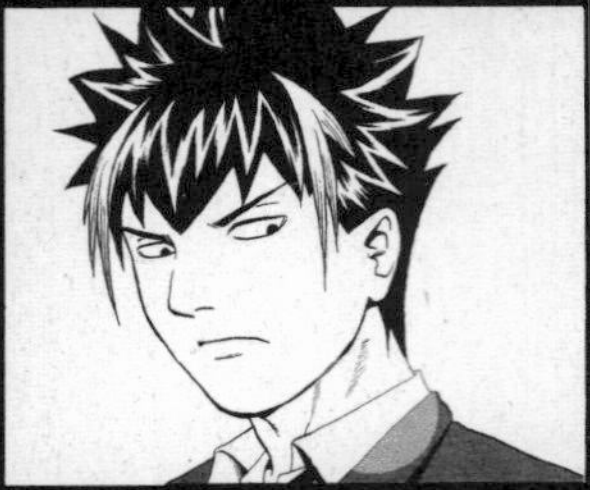

KAZUMA (KAZUMA MAGARI)

KAZUMA SEEMS TO HAVE IT ALL. HE'S THE PRESIDENT OF THE STUDENT COUNCIL AS WELL AS A CLEVER GUY WHO'S GOOD AT SPORTS. HE'S ALSO NORA'S MASTER. DESPITE SEEMING CALM AND COMPOSED, KAZUMA'S GOT QUITE A TEMPER. AS A RESULT, OTHER STUDENTS FEAR HIM. VERDICT: HE'S MORE DEVILISH THAN ANY DEMON.

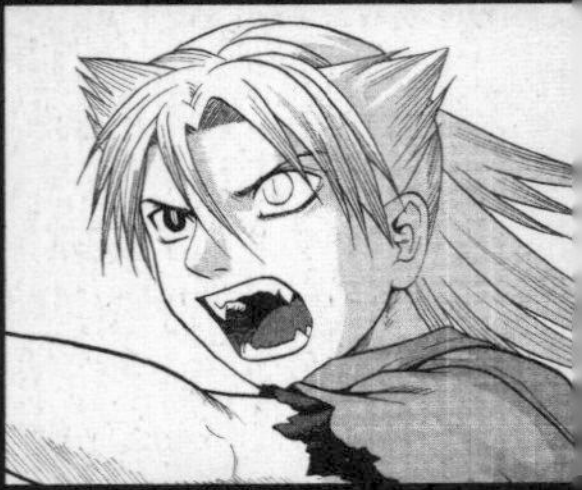

NORA

THE DEMON WORLD'S PROBLEM CHILD, NORA'S FOUL TEMPER IS SUR PASSED ONLY BY HIS STUPIDITY. NORA IS BETTER KNOWN AS THE VICIOUS DOG OF DISASTER, THE LEG ENDARY DEMON CERBERUS. HIS POWER IS SAID TO SURPASS THAT O THE DARK LIEGE HERSELF.

DARK LIEGE AR

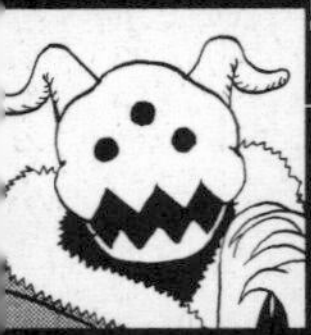

HER INFERNAL MAJESTY,
THE DARK LIEGE

THE COMMANDER IN CHIEF OF THE DARK LIEGE ARMY AS WELL AS THE ONE WHO EXILED NORA TO THE HUMAN WORLD. WHEN SHE WEARS HER GLAMOUR SPELL, SHE'S ONE SMOKIN' HOTTIE.

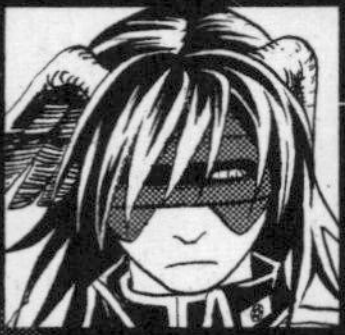

KAIN

A GOVERNOR-GEN AIDE AND RIGHT-H MAN TO THE DARK IN ADDITION TO BE COMMANDER, HE' DARK LIEGE'S MOS TRUSTED CONFIDA

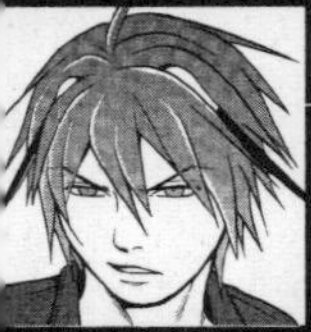

NAVAL FLEET GENERAL
RIVAN

LAID BACK AND SEEM-INGLY LAZY, ONCE RIVAN SNAPS, NOBODY CAN HOLD HIM DOWN. HE'S INTO FISHING.

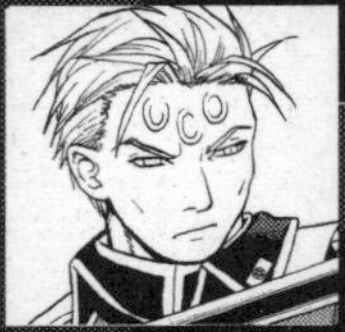

LAND CORPS GENERAL
LEONARD

THE DEMON WORL NUMBER ONE GO-GUY. DEDICATED A SERIOUS, LEONAR ALWAYS WORRYING LEADING TO STRE RELATED MALADIE

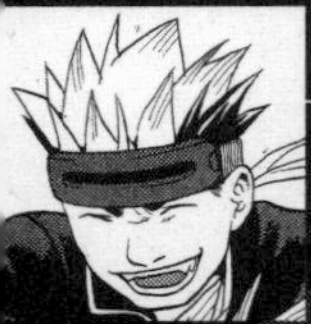

WIND DIVISION GENERAL
BAJEE

THE WIND DIVISION GENERAL AND THE STRON-GEST, TOUGHEST SON OF A GUN IN THE DARK LIEGE ARMY. HE COMES OFF AS A BIT OF A JERK, BUT A FUN ONE. HE'S LIKE A BIG BROTHER TO NORA.

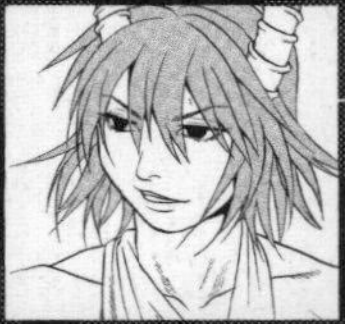

FIRE BRIGADE GENERAL
MELFIA

DESPITE HER TOUG LOOKS, SHE'S A CA FIGHTER WHO USES BRAINS MORE THA FISTS. SHE TRAINED KAZUMA TO CONTR MAGICAL STREAM.

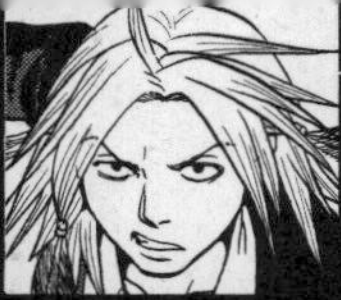

NICKS

ANOTHER FORMER BIG-WIG IN THE RESISTANCE. ALTHOUGH HE POSSESSES POWERFUL ABILITIES, HE'S OFTEN HESITANT TO FIGHT.

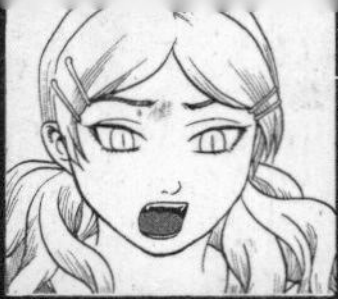

KEINI

A FORMER MEMBER OF THE RESISTANCE AND A TERROR WHEN SHE'S MIFFED. SHE HAD A STRONG ATTACHMENT TO FALL, THE LEADER OF THE RESISTANCE, WHICH ONLY PROVES THERE'S NO ACCOUNTING FOR TASTE.

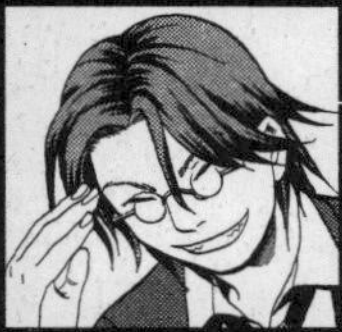

KNELL

YET ANOTHER FORMER MEMBER OF THE RESISTANCE, KNELL CONSIDERS HIMSELF A LADIES' MAN, ALTHOUGH "SOCIOPATH" IS CLOSER TO THE TRUTH. THE ONLY SIDE HE'S REALLY ON IS HIS OWN. HE VANISHED AFTER LOSING A BIG FIGHT AGAINST NORA, BUT YOU KNOW WHAT THEY SAY ABOUT BAD PENNIES...

TENRYO ACADEMY MIDDLE SCHOOL, STUDENT COUNCIL

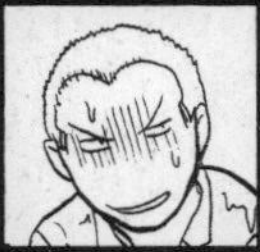

FUJIMOTO

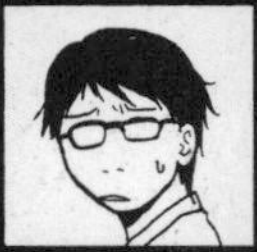

YANO

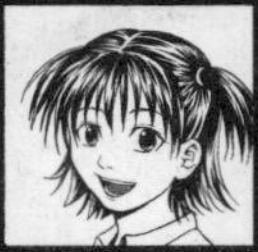

KOYUKI HIRASAKA

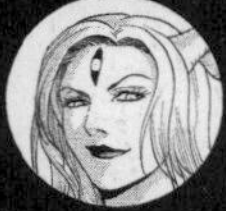

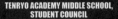

LISTEN TO TEACHER! ♥
THE DARK LIEGE EXPLAINS IT ALL

HELLO, BELOVED READERS! IT'S THE DEMONESS WITH THE MOSTEST ONCE AGAIN! ♥

LET'S RECAP ONCE MORE JUST FOR OLD TIMES' SAKE. MY FAVORITE PET, NORA, WAS ONCE A BAD, BAD PUPPY DEMON. AND THERE I WAS WITH THAT WHOLE RESISTANCE THING AND THOSE PESKY OUTLAW DEMONS TO DEAL WITH. FINALLY I DECIDED ENOUGH WAS TOO MUCH!

BECAUSE I'VE GOT A SMOKIN' BRAIN UNDER THAT FANTASTIC HEAD OF HAIR, I SENT MY STRAY DOG TO THE HUMAN WORLD. I TOLD NORA IT WAS HIS JOB TO TAKE CARE OF THE OUTLAW DEMONS THAT HAD TRESPASSED INTO THE HUMAN WORLD, THUS KILLING TWO BIRDS WITH ONE STONE! AREN'T I A GENIUS?

THEN I CHOSE DEVIOUS SCHOOLBOY KAZUMA MAGARI TO BE IN CHARGE OF NORA'S "OBEDIENCE TRAINING." NAUGHTY ME!

I FORCED NORA INTO A MASTER AND SERVANT CONTRACT WITH KAZUMA, MAKING NORA A "FAMILIAR SPIRIT." MY PUPPY CAN LONGER USE MAGIC OR RELEASE HIS SEAL SPELL AND BECOME A DEMON DOG AGAIN WITHOUT HIS NEW MASTER'S APPROVAL.

WAR, AS THEY SAY, IS HELL. OH, BUT EVER SO EXCITING! THE ALL-OUT WAR BETWEEN THE RESISTANCE AND MY DARK LIEGE ARMY FINALLY CAME DOWN TO A DECISIVE BATTLE AGAINST FALL, THE LEADER OF THE BAD GUYS. FALL HELD A LOT MORE POWER THAN WE IMAGINED, SO IT LOOKED LIKE WE WERE DONE FOR. WE MANAGED TO FIGHT ON, BUT FALL UNLEASHED EVERYTHING AGAINST NORA. KAZUMA TRIED SACRIFICING HIMSELF (HOW GALLANT!) TO PROTECT MY PUPPY AND SUFFERED A GRAVE INJURY! WELL, NORA GOT SO PEEVED THAT HE REALLY LET FALL HAVE IT! OH MY! EVEN AFTER NORA WAS ABSORBED BY FALL, HE SOMEHOW MANAGED TO RETURN AND DEFEAT THE LEADER OF THE RESISTANCE. PEACE HAS RETURNED TO BOTH WORLDS... BUT THERE'S MORE TO THE STORY! READ ON!

NORA

THE LAST CHRONICLE OF DEVILDOM

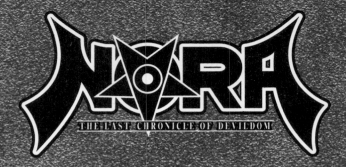

CONTENTS

Volume 9: Null and Void

Story 33: The Next Generation

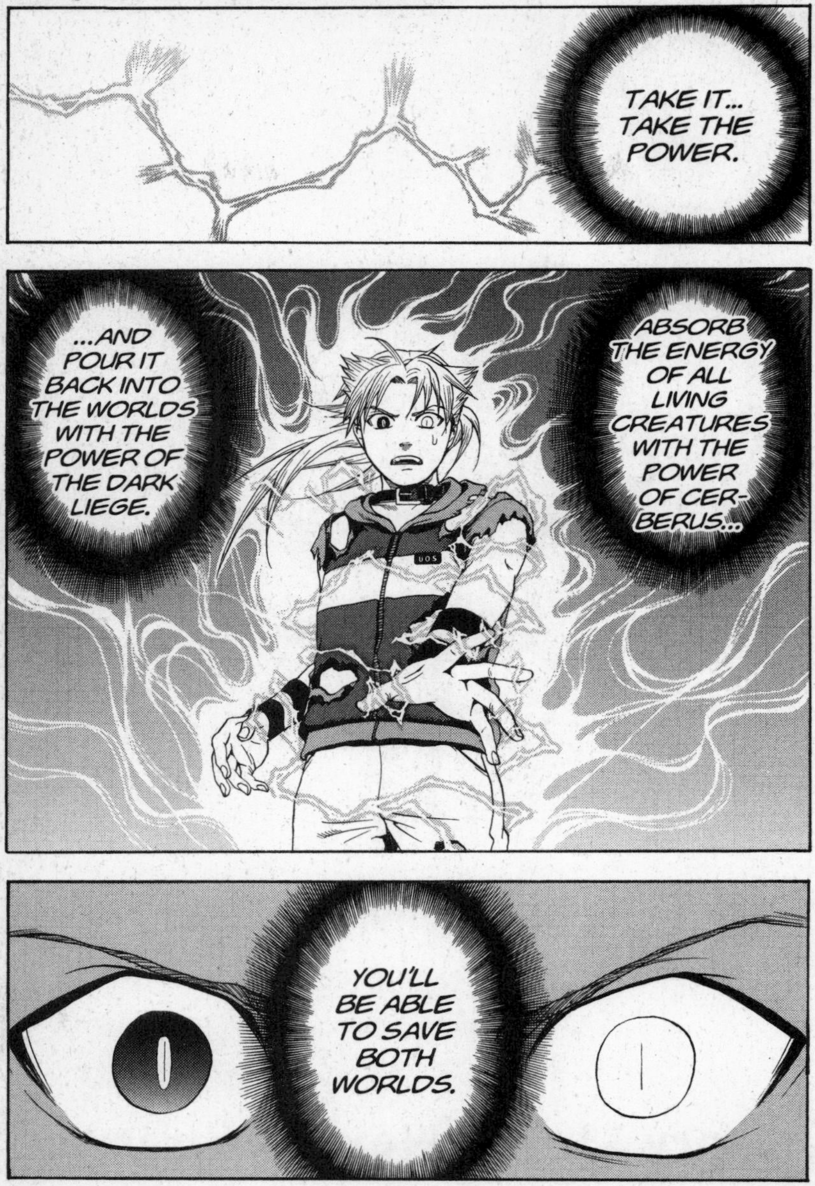

TAKE IT... TAKE THE POWER.
ABSORB THE ENERGY OF ALL LIVING CREATURES WITH THE POWER OF CER-BERUS...
...AND POUR IT BACK INTO THE WORLDS WITH THE POWER OF THE DARK LIEGE.
YOU'LL BE ABLE TO SAVE BOTH WORLDS.

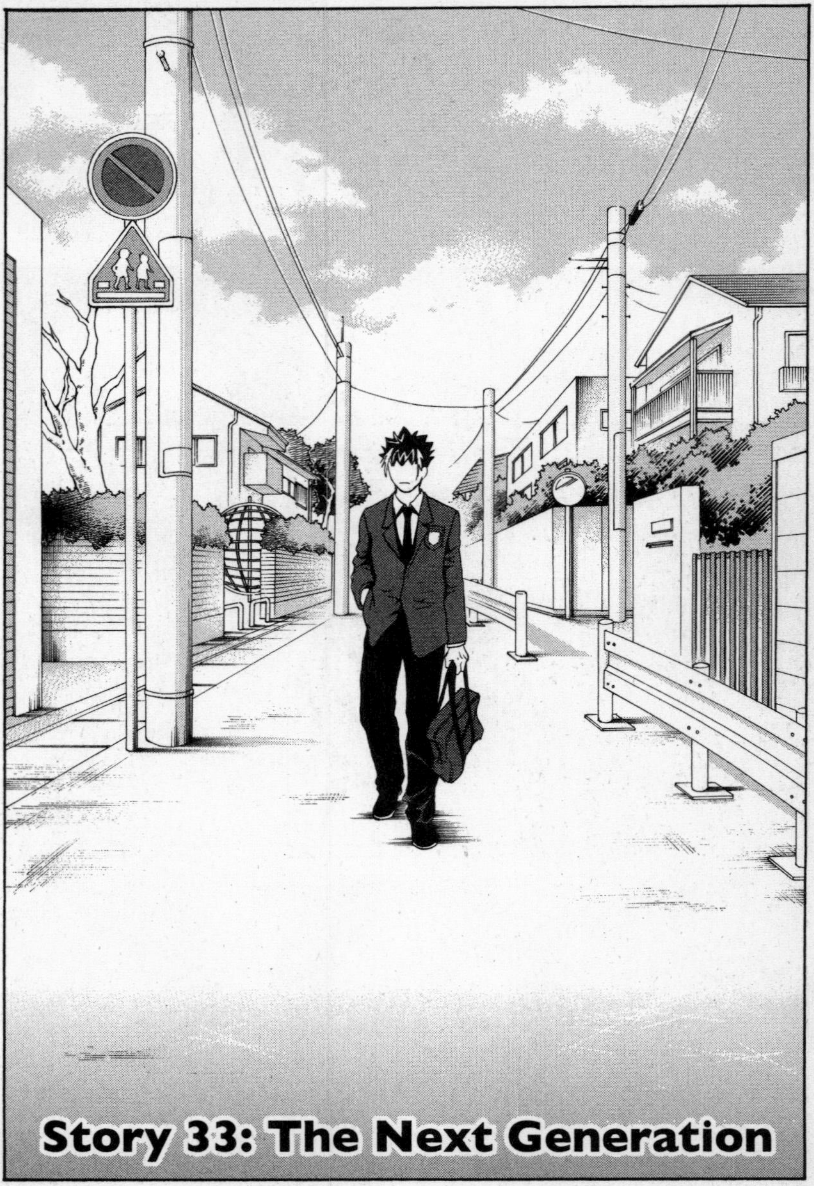
Story 33: The Next Generation

READ THIS WAY

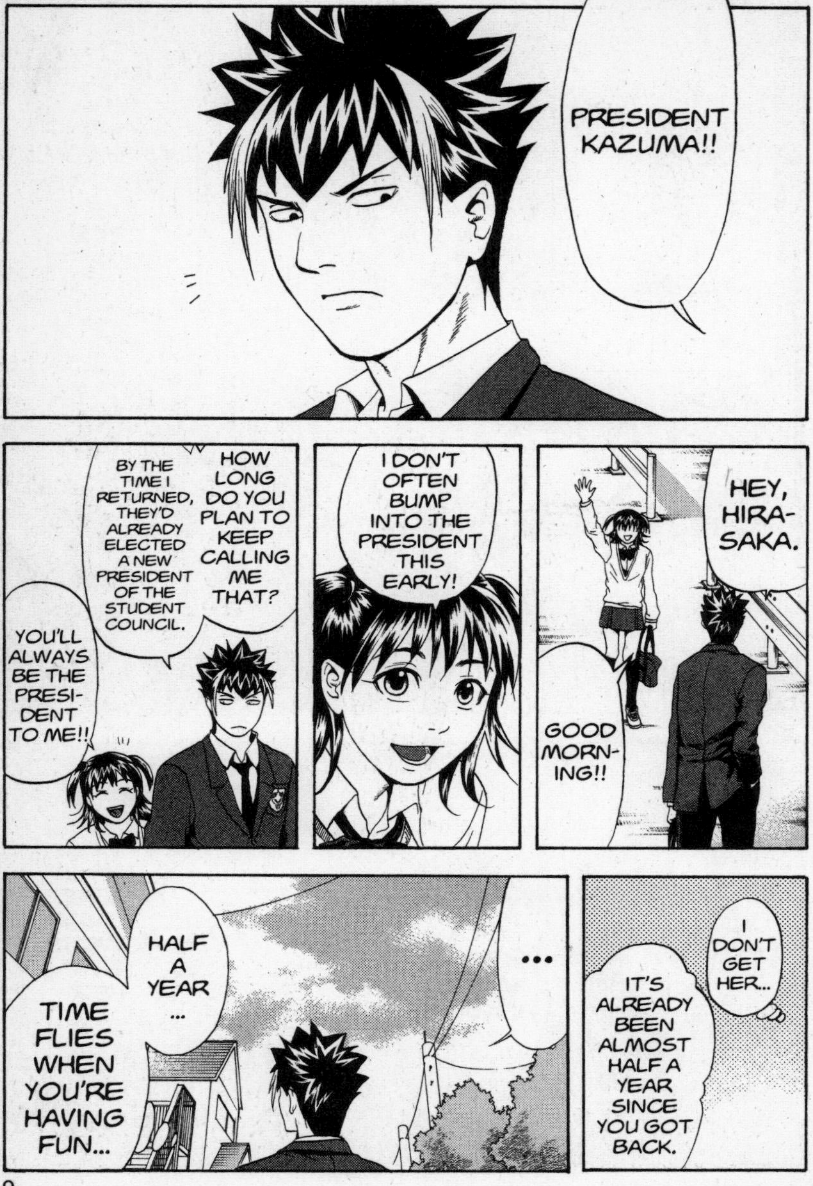

PRESIDENT KAZUMA!!
HEY, HIRA-SAKA.
GOOD MORNING!!
I DON'T OFTEN BUMP INTO THE PRESIDENT THIS EARLY!
HOW LONG DO YOU PLAN TO KEEP CALLING ME THAT?
BY THE TIME I RETURNED, THEY'D ALREADY ELECTED A NEW PRESIDENT OF THE STUDENT COUNCIL.
YOU'LL ALWAYS BE THE PRESI-DENT TO ME!!
I DON'T GET HER...
IT'S ALREADY BEEN ALMOST HALF A YEAR SINCE YOU GOT BACK.
...
HALF A YEAR ...
TIME FLIES WHEN YOU'RE HAVING FUN...

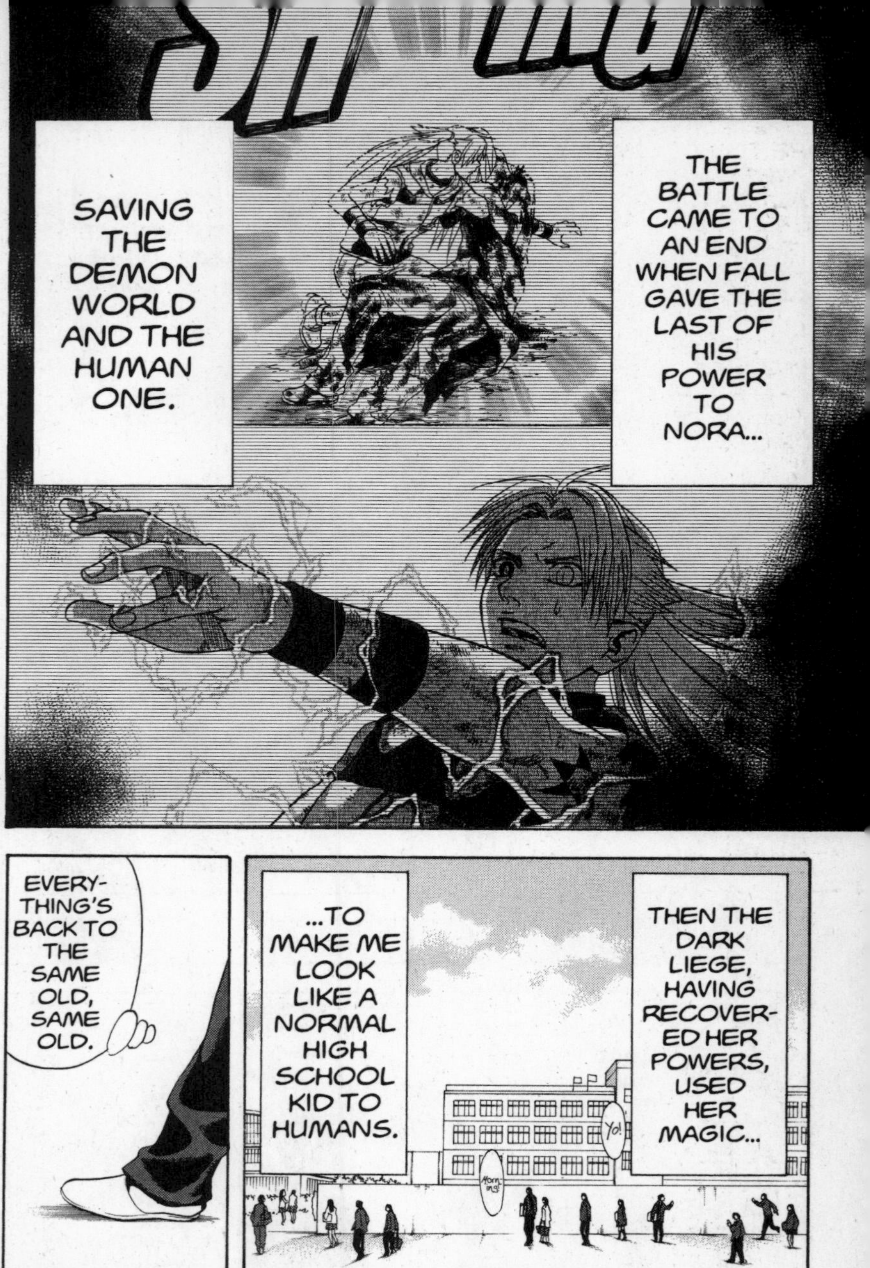
THE BATTLE CAME TO AN END WHEN FALL GAVE THE LAST OF HIS POWER TO NORA...
SAVING THE DEMON WORLD AND THE HUMAN ONE.
THEN THE DARK LIEGE, HAVING RECOVERED HER POWERS, USED HER MAGIC...
...TO MAKE ME LOOK LIKE A NORMAL HIGH SCHOOL KID TO HUMANS.
Yo!
Morning!
EVERYTHING'S BACK TO THE SAME OLD, SAME OLD.

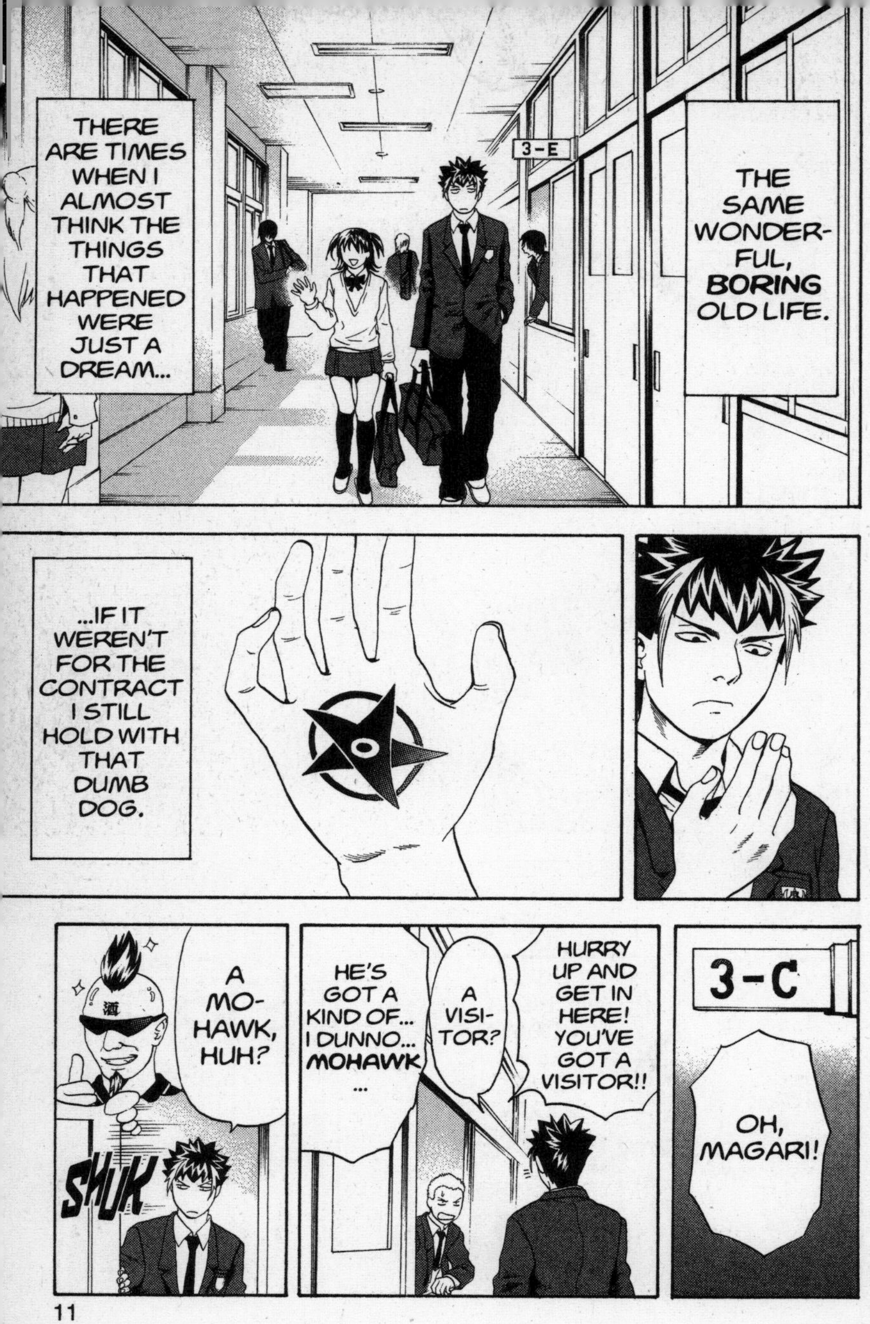
THE SAME WONDERFUL, BORING OLD LIFE.
3-E
THERE ARE TIMES WHEN I ALMOST THINK THE THINGS THAT HAPPENED WERE JUST A DREAM...
...IF IT WEREN'T FOR THE CONTRACT I STILL HOLD WITH THAT DUMB DOG.
3-C
OH, MAGARI!
HURRY UP AND GET IN HERE! YOU'VE GOT A VISITOR!!
A VISITOR?
HE'S GOT A KIND OF... I DUNNO... MOHAWK...
A MOHAWK, HUH?
SHUK

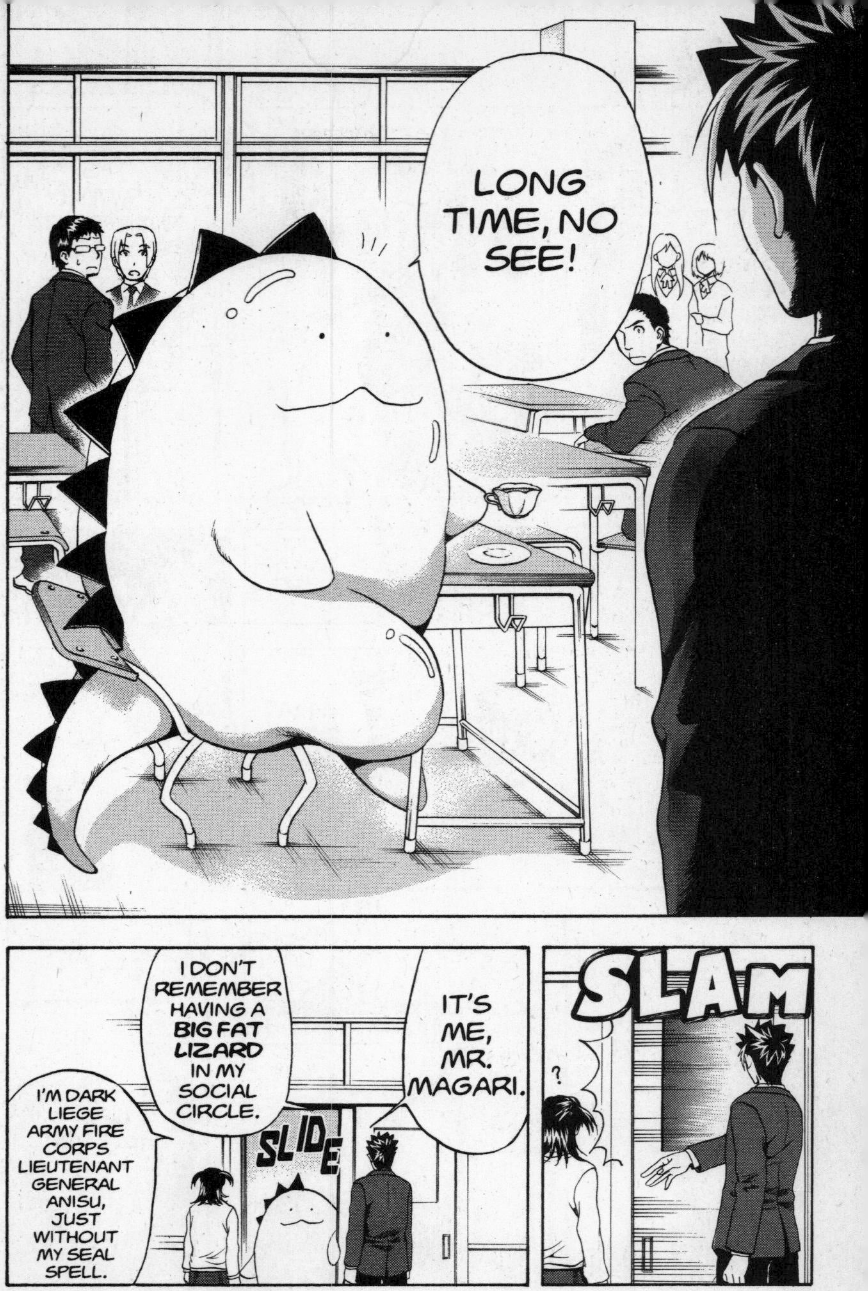
LONG TIME, NO SEE!
SLAM
?
IT'S ME, MR. MAGARI.
I DON'T REMEMBER HAVING A BIG FAT LIZARD IN MY SOCIAL CIRCLE.
SLIDE
I'M DARK LIEGE ARMY FIRE CORPS LIEUTENANT GENERAL ANISU, JUST WITHOUT MY SEAL SPELL.

READ THIS WAY

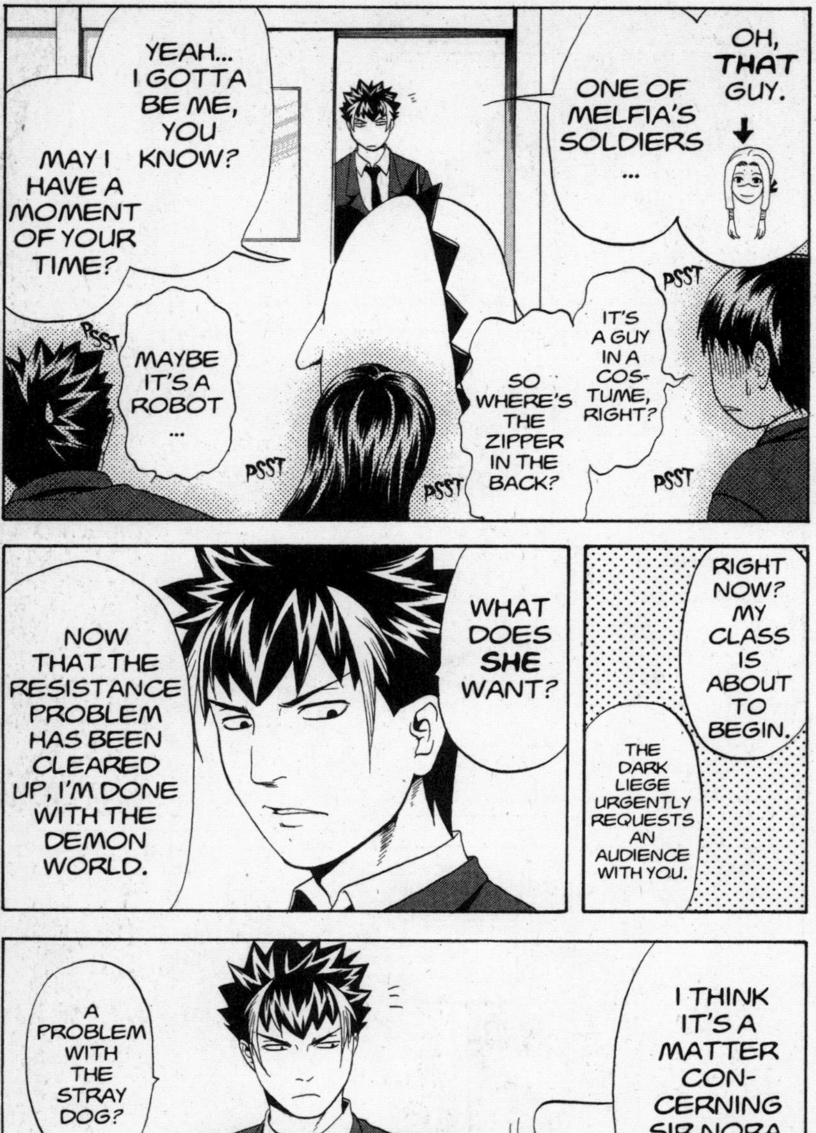

OH, THAT GUY.
ONE OF MELFIA'S SOLDIERS ...
YEAH... I GOTTA BE ME, YOU KNOW?
MAY I HAVE A MOMENT OF YOUR TIME?
PSST
IT'S A GUY IN A COSTUME, RIGHT?
SO WHERE'S THE ZIPPER IN THE BACK?
PSST
PSST
PSST
MAYBE IT'S A ROBOT ...
PSST
RIGHT NOW? MY CLASS IS ABOUT TO BEGIN.
THE DARK LIEGE URGENTLY REQUESTS AN AUDIENCE WITH YOU.
WHAT DOES SHE WANT?
NOW THAT THE RESISTANCE PROBLEM HAS BEEN CLEARED UP, I'M DONE WITH THE DEMON WORLD.
I THINK IT'S A MATTER CONCERNING SIR NORA.
A PROBLEM WITH THE STRAY DOG?

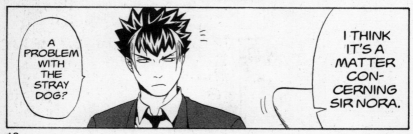

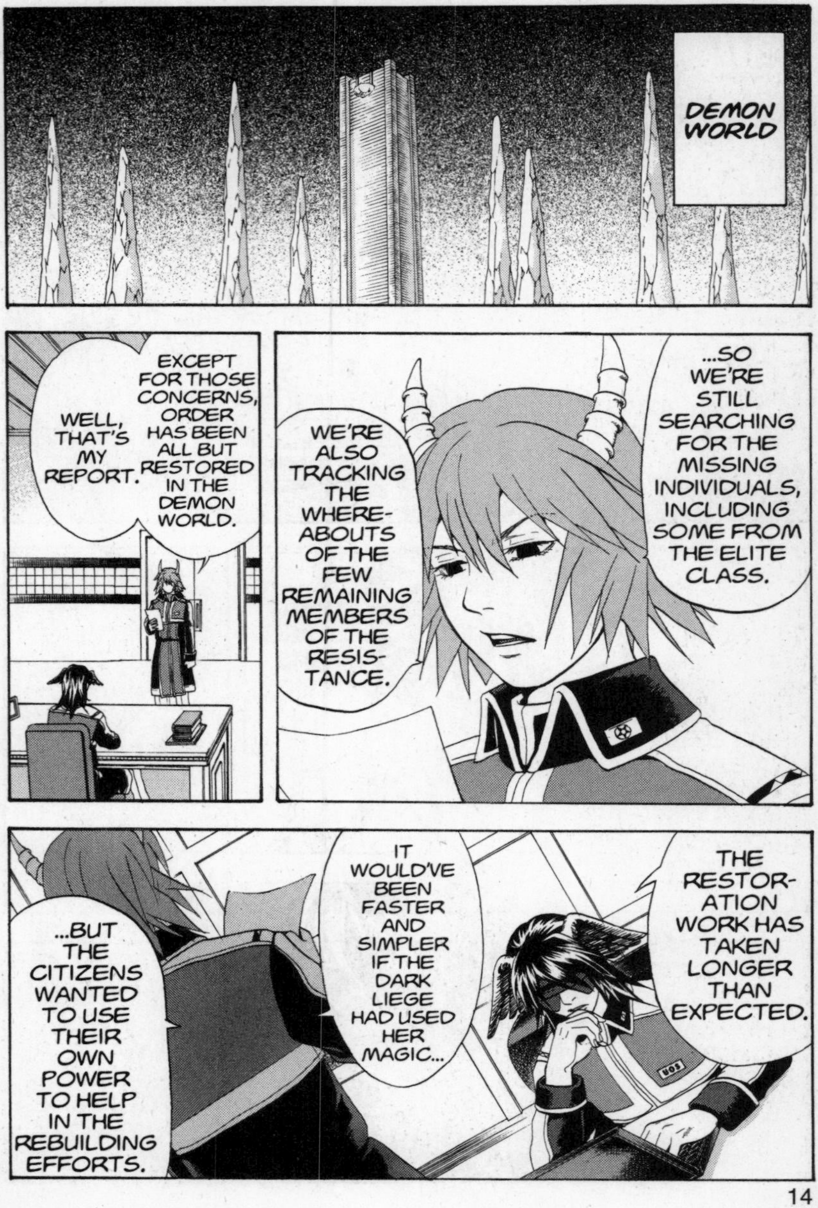
DEMON WORLD
...SO WE'RE STILL SEARCHING FOR THE MISSING INDIVIDUALS, INCLUDING SOME FROM THE ELITE CLASS.
WE'RE ALSO TRACKING THE WHERE-ABOUTS OF THE FEW REMAINING MEMBERS OF THE RESIS-TANCE.
EXCEPT FOR THOSE CONCERNS, ORDER HAS BEEN ALL BUT RESTORED IN THE DEMON WORLD.
WELL, THAT'S MY REPORT.
THE RESTOR-ATION WORK HAS TAKEN LONGER THAN EXPECTED.
IT WOULD'VE BEEN FASTER AND SIMPLER IF THE DARK LIEGE HAD USED HER MAGIC...
...BUT THE CITIZENS WANTED TO USE THEIR OWN POWER TO HELP IN THE REBUILDING EFFORTS.

READ THIS WAY

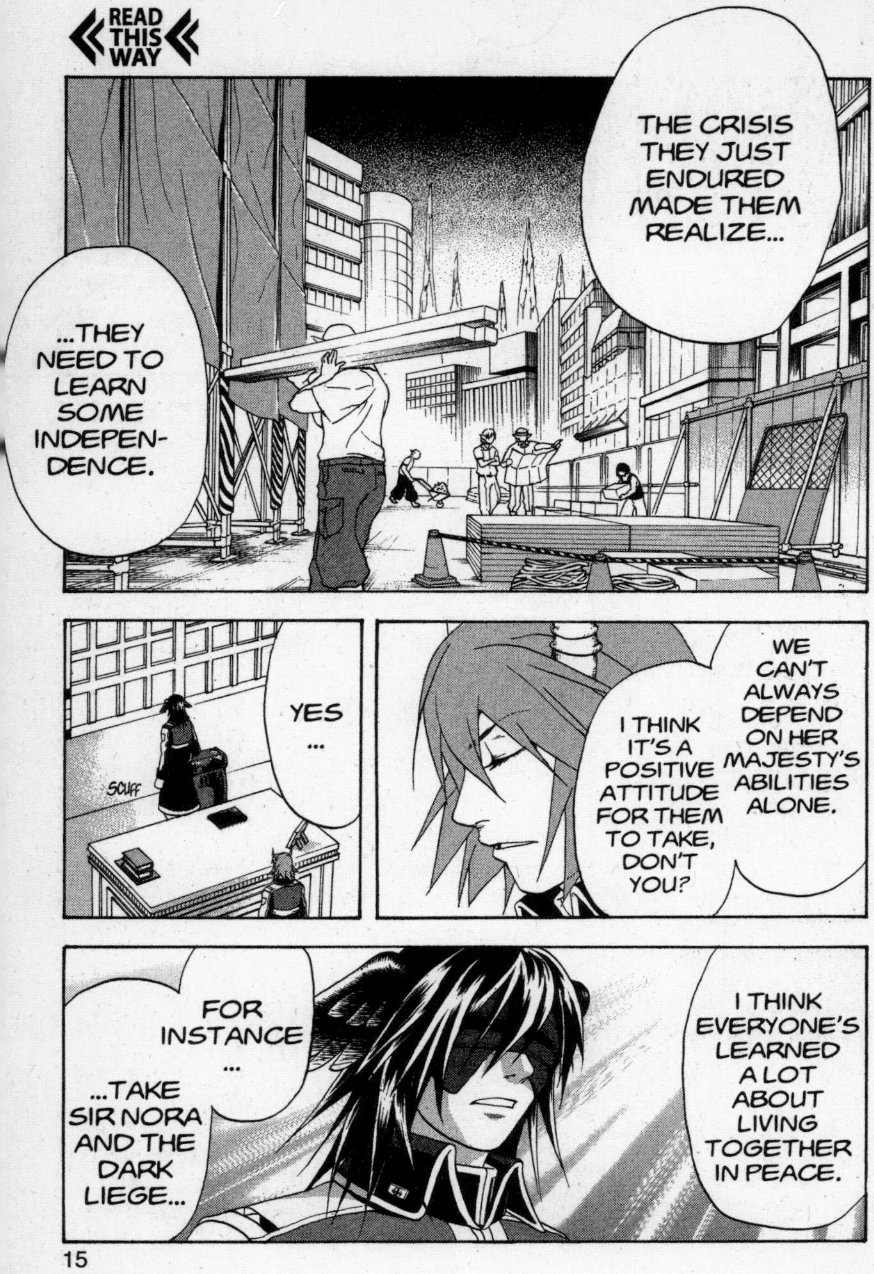
THE CRISIS THEY JUST ENDURED MADE THEM REALIZE...
...THEY NEED TO LEARN SOME INDEPEN-DENCE.
WE CAN'T ALWAYS DEPEND ON HER MAJESTY'S ABILITIES ALONE.
I THINK IT'S A POSITIVE ATTITUDE FOR THEM TO TAKE, DON'T YOU?
YES ...
SCUFF
I THINK EVERYONE'S LEARNED A LOT ABOUT LIVING TOGETHER IN PEACE.
FOR INSTANCE ...
...TAKE SIR NORA AND THE DARK LIEGE...

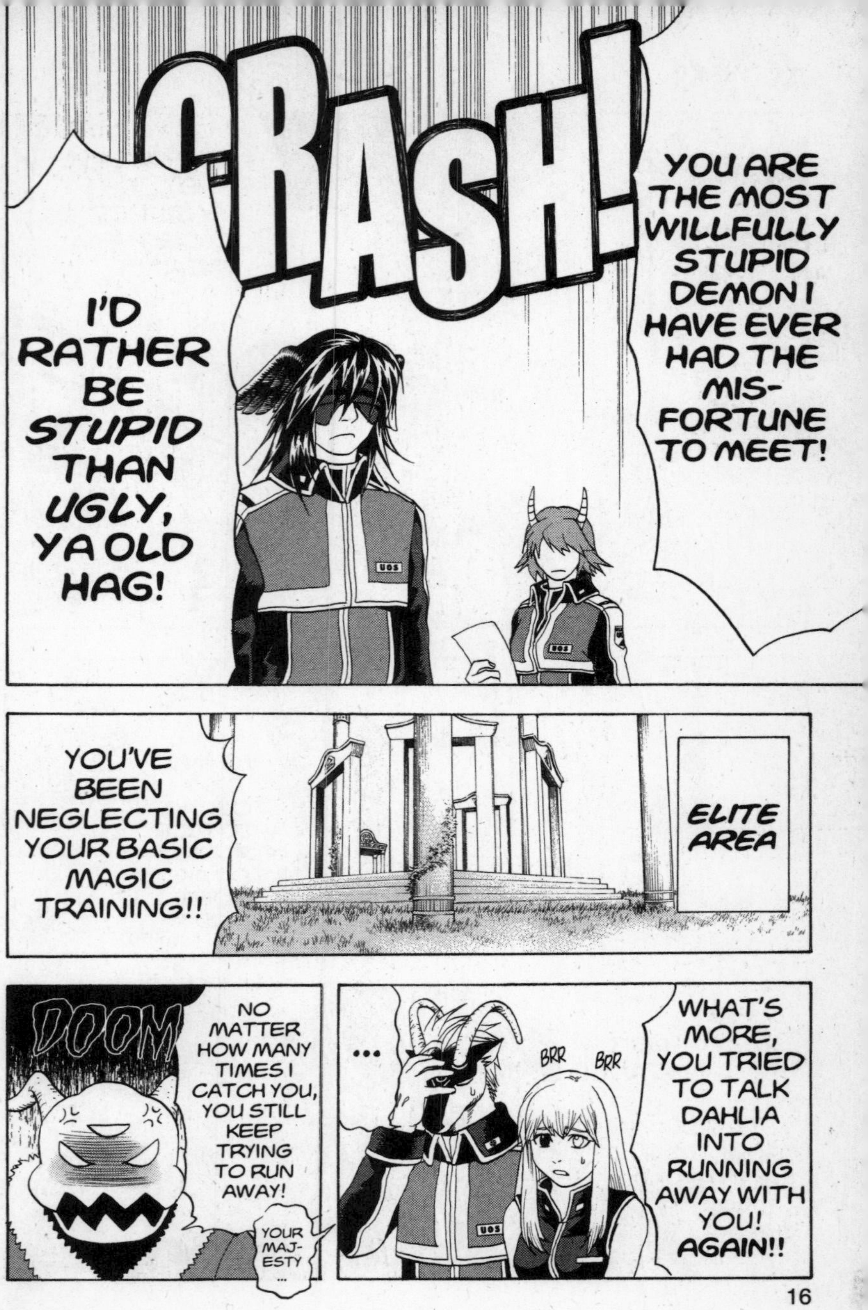
CRASH!
YOU ARE THE MOST WILLFULLY STUPID DEMON I HAVE EVER HAD THE MIS-FORTUNE TO MEET!
I'D RATHER BE STUPID THAN UGLY, YA OLD HAG!
ELITE AREA
YOU'VE BEEN NEGLECTING YOUR BASIC MAGIC TRAINING!!
WHAT'S MORE, YOU TRIED TO TALK DAHLIA INTO RUNNING AWAY WITH YOU! AGAIN!!
BRR BRR
...
NO MATTER HOW MANY TIMES I CATCH YOU, YOU STILL KEEP TRYING TO RUN AWAY!
YOUR MAJ-ESTY ...
DOOM

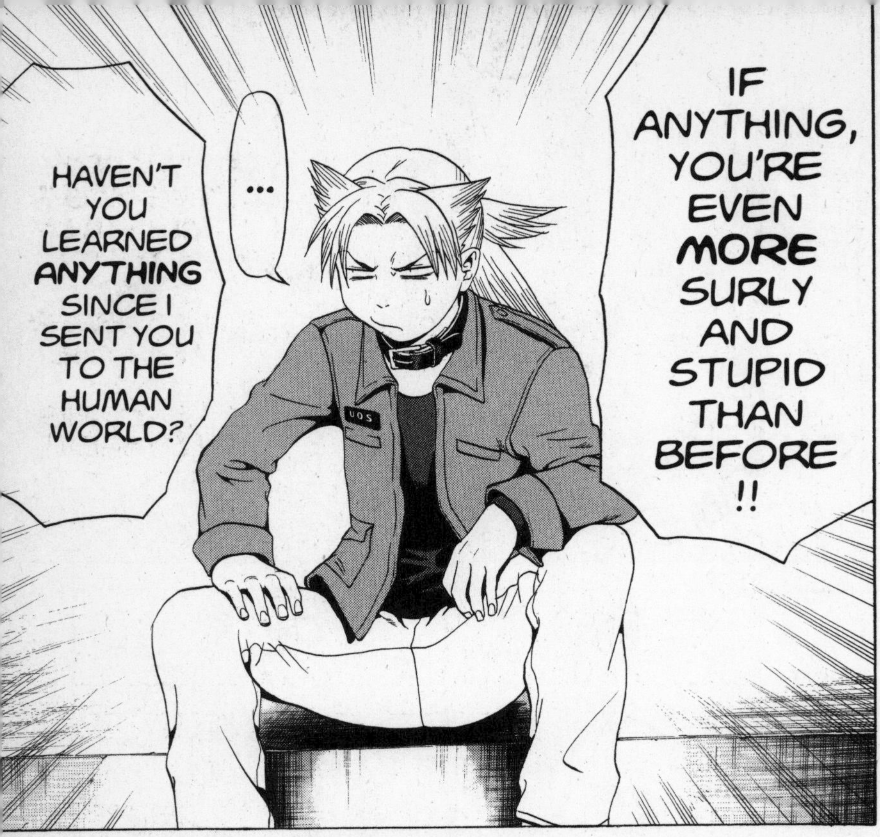
IF ANYTHING, YOU'RE EVEN MORE SURLY AND STUPID THAN BEFORE!!
...
HAVEN'T YOU LEARNED ANYTHING SINCE I SENT YOU TO THE HUMAN WORLD?

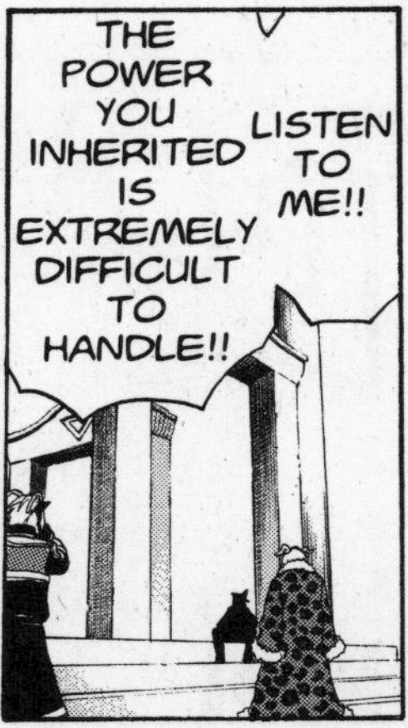
LISTEN TO ME!!
THE POWER YOU INHERITED IS EXTREMELY DIFFICULT TO HANDLE!!

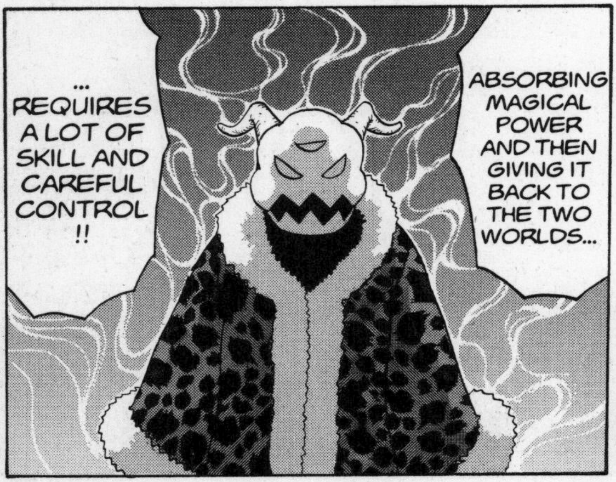
ABSORBING MAGICAL POWER AND THEN GIVING IT BACK TO THE TWO WORLDS...
...REQUIRES A LOT OF SKILL AND CAREFUL CONTROL!!

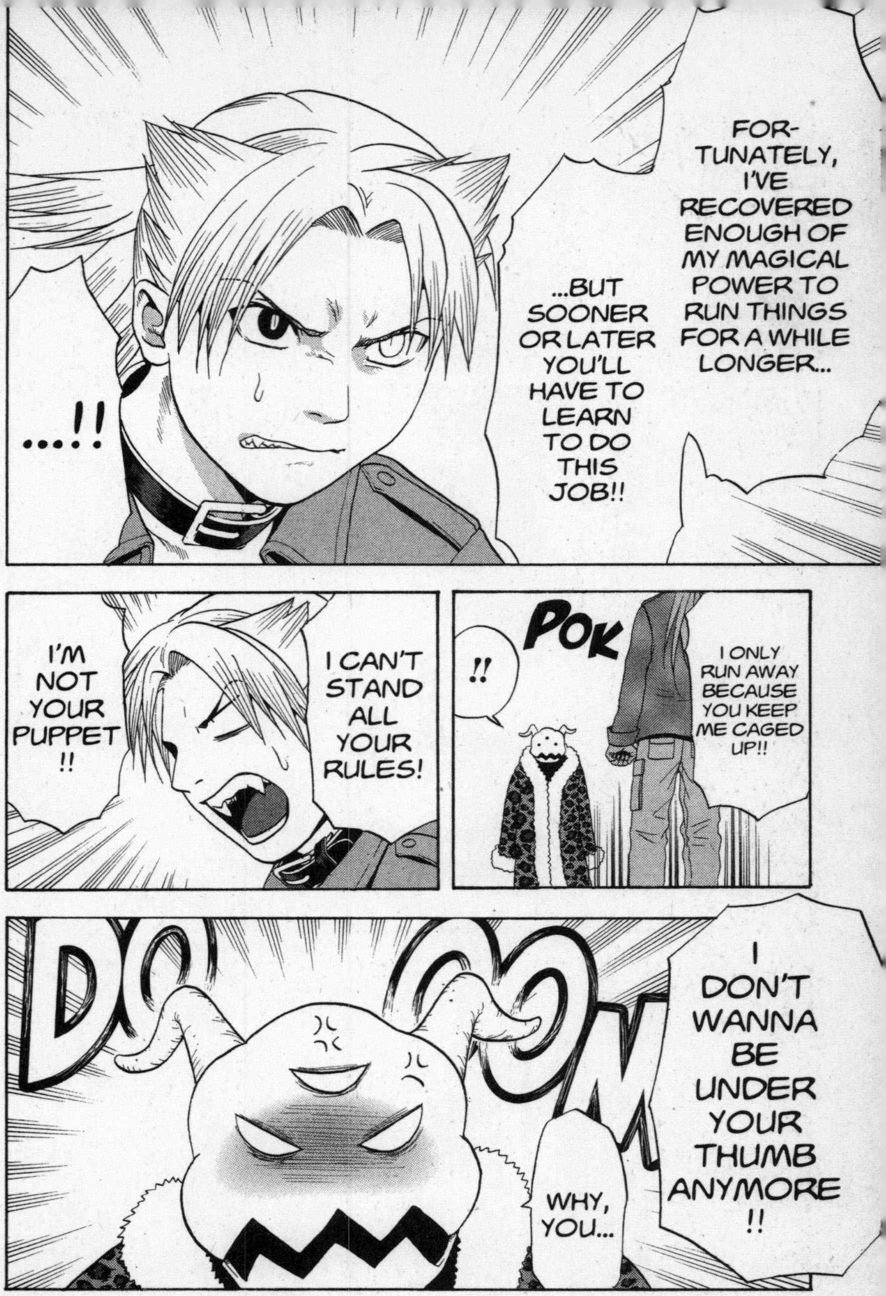
FOR-TUNATELY, I'VE RECOVERED ENOUGH OF MY MAGICAL POWER TO RUN THINGS FOR A WHILE LONGER...
...BUT SOONER OR LATER YOU'LL HAVE TO LEARN TO DO THIS JOB!!
...!!
I ONLY RUN AWAY BECAUSE YOU KEEP ME CAGED UP!!
POK
!!
I CAN'T STAND ALL YOUR RULES!
I'M NOT YOUR PUPPET!!
DOOOM
I DON'T WANNA BE UNDER YOUR THUMB ANYMORE!!
WHY, YOU...

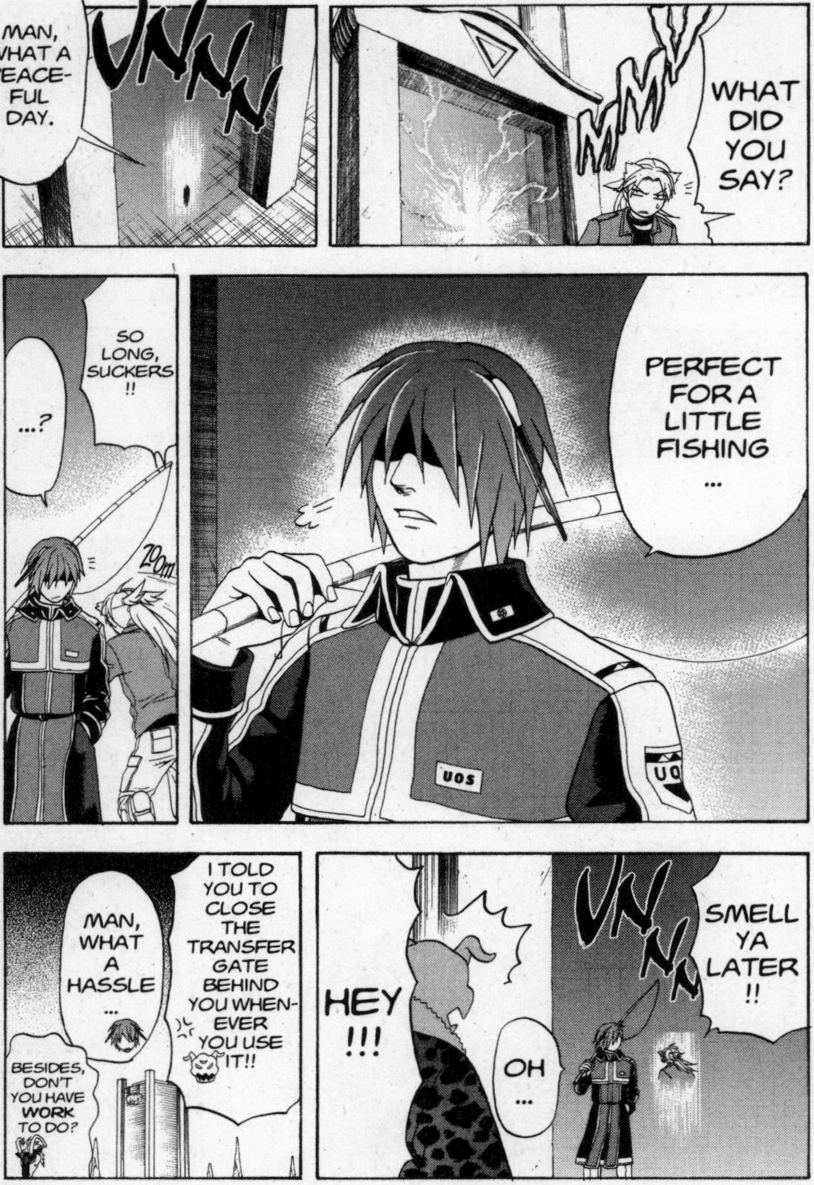
MMM
WHAT DID YOU SAY?
VNNN
MAN, WHAT A PEACE-FUL DAY.
PERFECT FOR A LITTLE FISHING ...
SO LONG, SUCKERS !!
...?
ZOOM
SMELL YA LATER !!
VNNN
HEY !!!
OH ...
I TOLD YOU TO CLOSE THE TRANSFER GATE BEHIND YOU WHEN-EVER YOU USE IT!!
MAN, WHAT A HASSLE ...
BESIDES, DON'T YOU HAVE **WORK** TO DO?

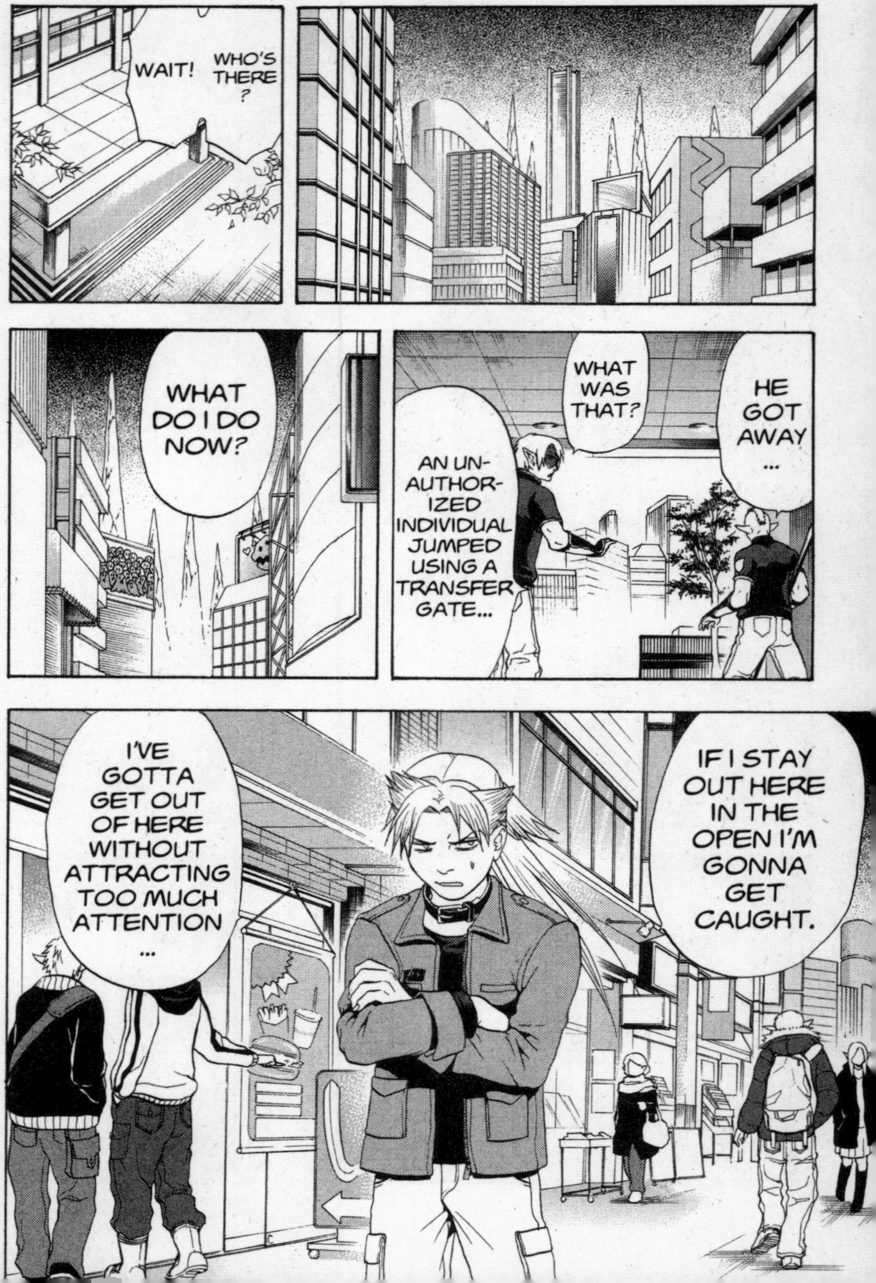
WHO'S THERE?
WAIT!
HE GOT AWAY...
WHAT WAS THAT?
AN UN-AUTHORIZED INDIVIDUAL JUMPED USING A TRANSFER GATE...
WHAT DO I DO NOW?
IF I STAY OUT HERE IN THE OPEN I'M GONNA GET CAUGHT.
I'VE GOTTA GET OUT OF HERE WITHOUT ATTRACTING TOO MUCH ATTENTION...

READ THIS WAY

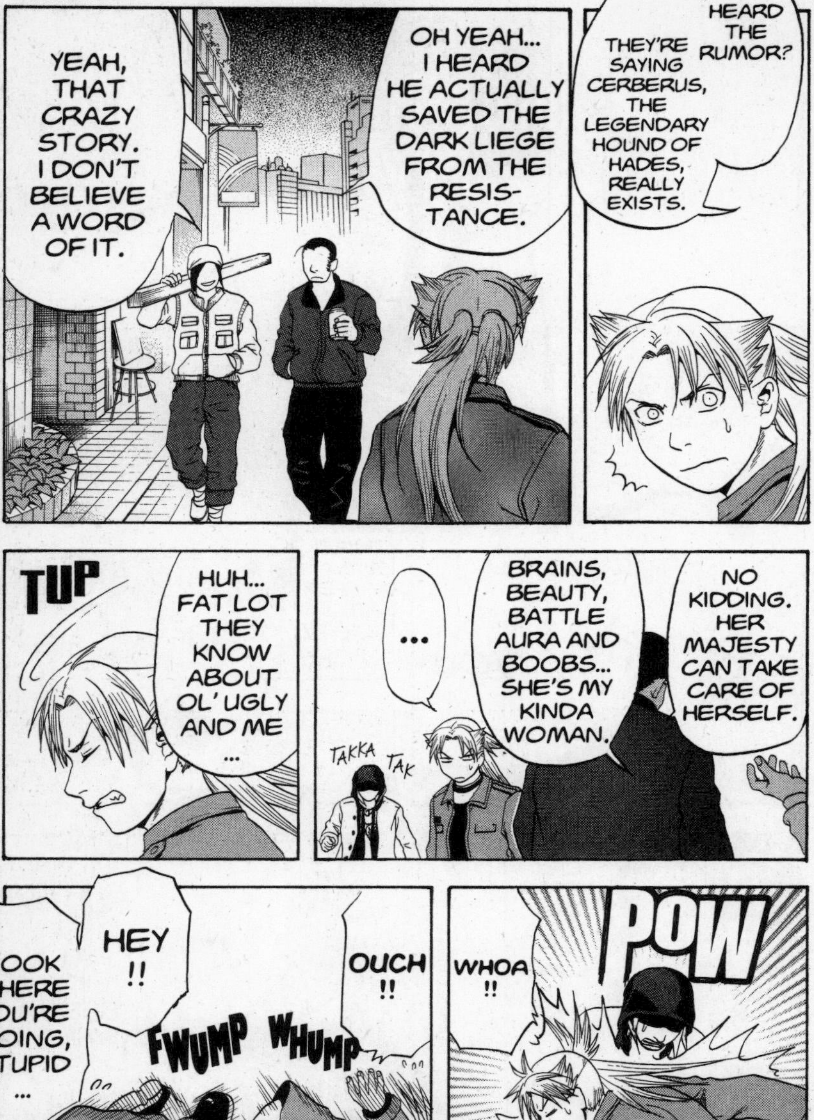

HEARD THE RUMOR?
THEY'RE SAYING CERBERUS, THE LEGENDARY HOUND OF HADES, REALLY EXISTS.
OH YEAH... I HEARD HE ACTUALLY SAVED THE DARK LIEGE FROM THE RESIS-TANCE.
YEAH, THAT CRAZY STORY. I DON'T BELIEVE A WORD OF IT.
NO KIDDING. HER MAJESTY CAN TAKE CARE OF HERSELF.
BRAINS, BEAUTY, BATTLE AURA AND BOOBS... SHE'S MY KINDA WOMAN.
...
TAKKA
TAK
HUH... FAT LOT THEY KNOW ABOUT OL' UGLY AND ME ...
TUP
POW
WHOA !!
OUCH !!
WHUMP
FWUMP
HEY !!
LOOK WHERE YOU'RE GOING, STUPID ...

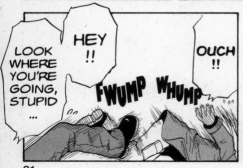

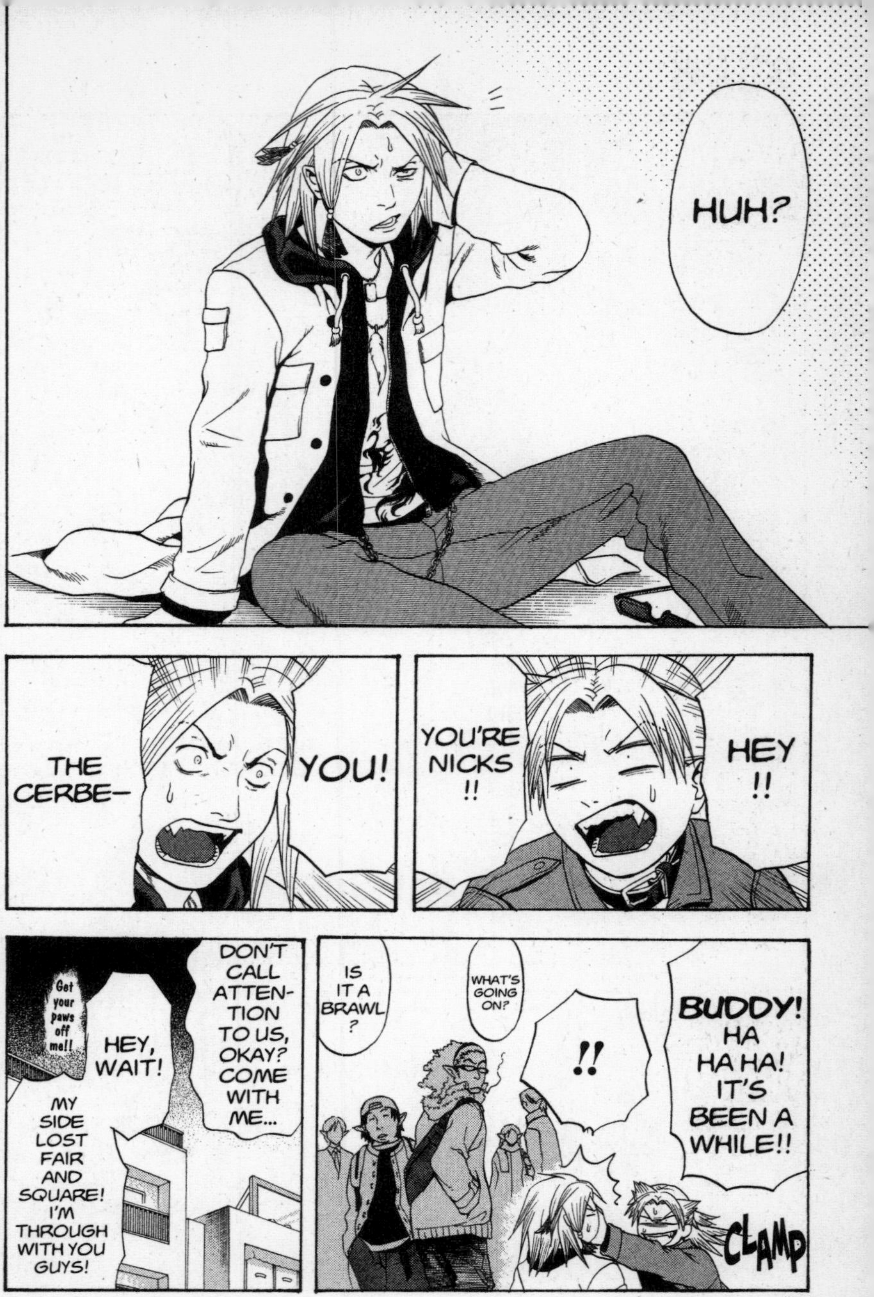
HUH?
HEY !!
YOU'RE NICKS !!
YOU!
THE CERBE—
BUDDY! HA HA HA! IT'S BEEN A WHILE!!
CLAMP
!!
WHAT'S GOING ON?
IS IT A BRAWL?
DON'T CALL ATTENTION TO US, OKAY? COME WITH ME...
HEY, WAIT!
Get your paws off me!!
MY SIDE LOST FAIR AND SQUARE! I'M THROUGH WITH YOU GUYS!

READ THIS WAY

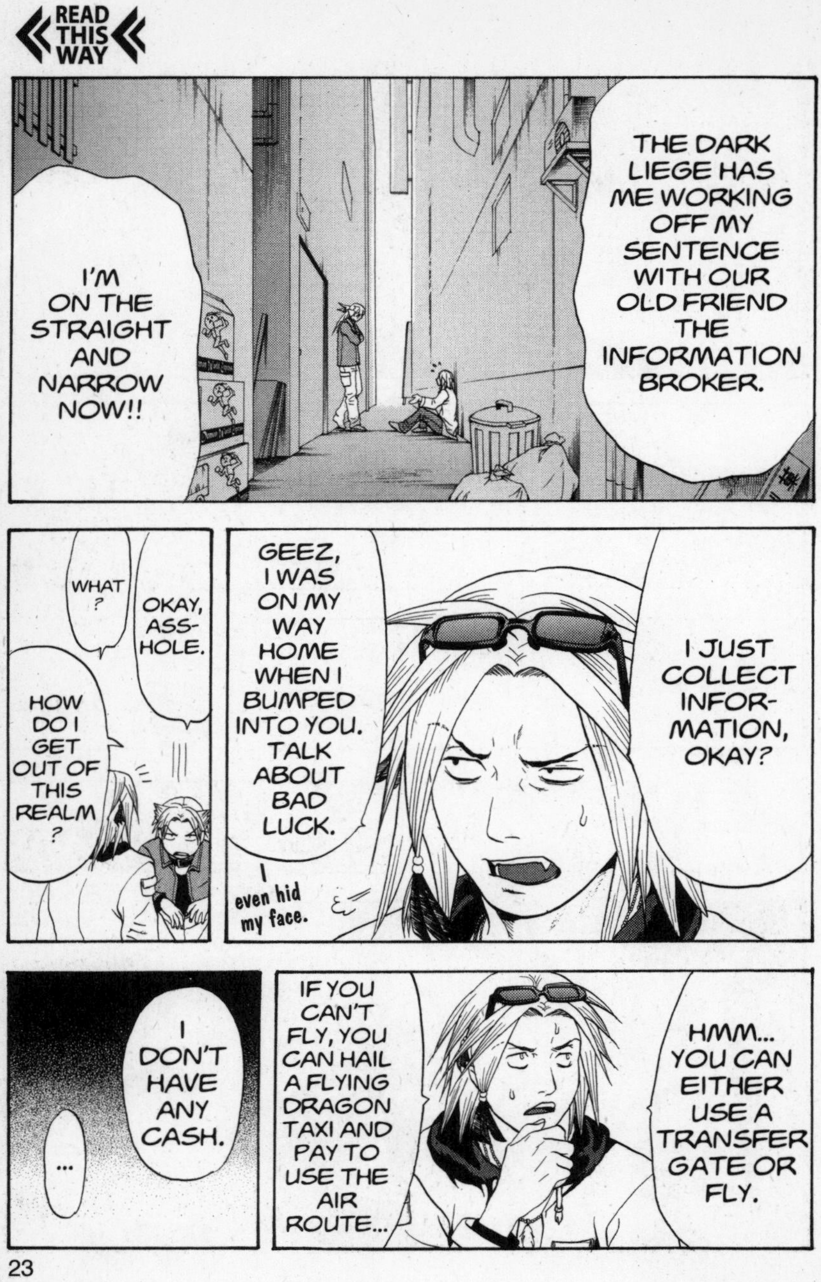
THE DARK LIEGE HAS ME WORKING OFF MY SENTENCE WITH OUR OLD FRIEND THE INFORMATION BROKER.
I'M ON THE STRAIGHT AND NARROW NOW!!
I JUST COLLECT INFOR-MATION, OKAY?
GEEZ, I WAS ON MY WAY HOME WHEN I BUMPED INTO YOU. TALK ABOUT BAD LUCK.
I even hid my face.
OKAY, ASS-HOLE.
WHAT?
HOW DO I GET OUT OF THIS REALM?
HMM... YOU CAN EITHER USE A TRANSFER GATE OR FLY.
IF YOU CAN'T FLY, YOU CAN HAIL A FLYING DRAGON TAXI AND PAY TO USE THE AIR ROUTE...
I DON'T HAVE ANY CASH.
...

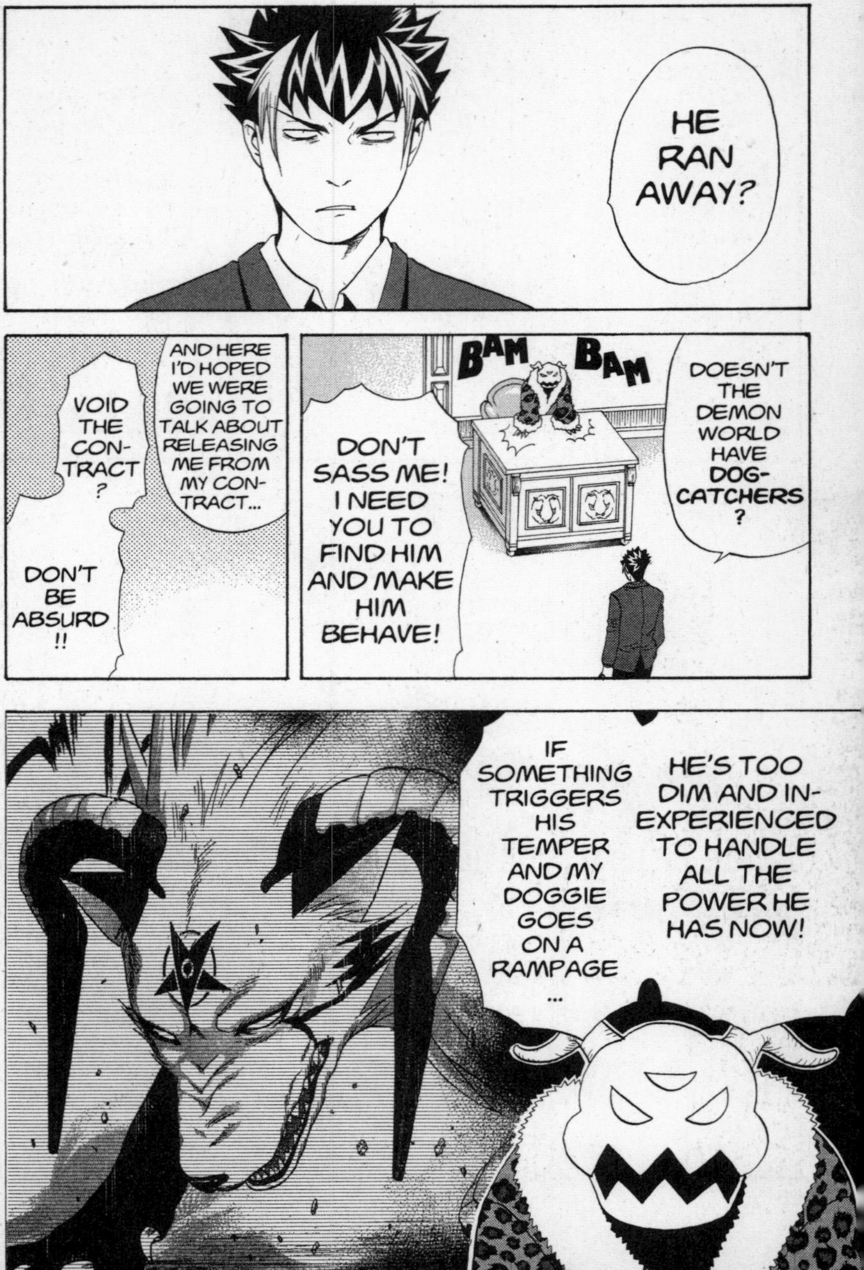
HE RAN AWAY?
DOESN'T THE DEMON WORLD HAVE DOG-CATCHERS?
BAM BAM
DON'T SASS ME! I NEED YOU TO FIND HIM AND MAKE HIM BEHAVE!
AND HERE I'D HOPED WE WERE GOING TO TALK ABOUT RELEASING ME FROM MY CONTRACT...
VOID THE CONTRACT?
DON'T BE ABSURD!!
HE'S TOO DIM AND INEXPERIENCED TO HANDLE ALL THE POWER HE HAS NOW!
IF SOMETHING TRIGGERS HIS TEMPER AND MY DOGGIE GOES ON A RAMPAGE...

READ THIS WAY

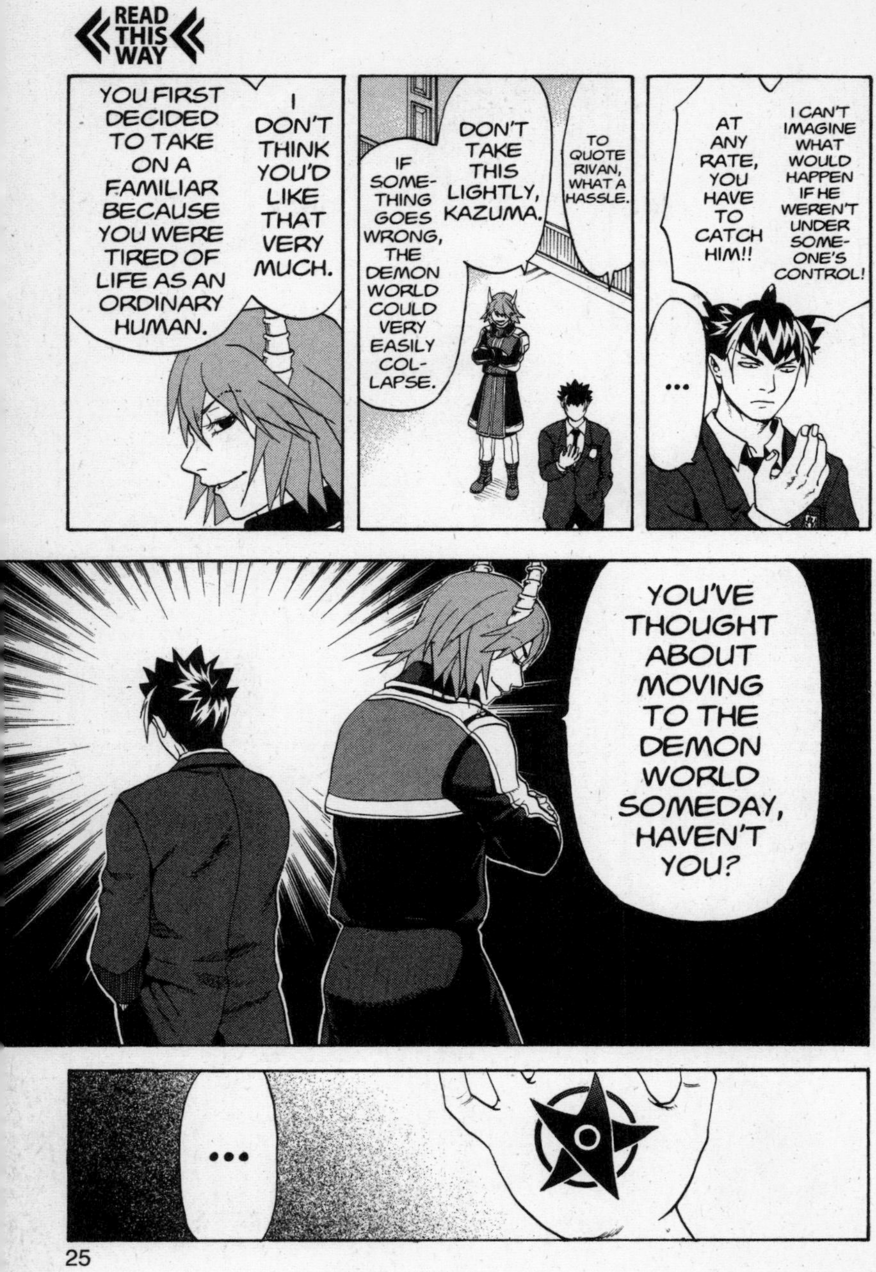

I CAN'T IMAGINE WHAT WOULD HAPPEN IF HE WEREN'T UNDER SOME-ONE'S CONTROL!
AT ANY RATE, YOU HAVE TO CATCH HIM!!
...
TO QUOTE RIVAN, WHAT A HASSLE.
DON'T TAKE THIS LIGHTLY, KAZUMA.
IF SOME-THING GOES WRONG, THE DEMON WORLD COULD VERY EASILY COL-LAPSE.
I DON'T THINK YOU'D LIKE THAT VERY MUCH.
YOU FIRST DECIDED TO TAKE ON A FAMILIAR BECAUSE YOU WERE TIRED OF LIFE AS AN ORDINARY HUMAN.
YOU'VE THOUGHT ABOUT MOVING TO THE DEMON WORLD SOMEDAY, HAVEN'T YOU?
...

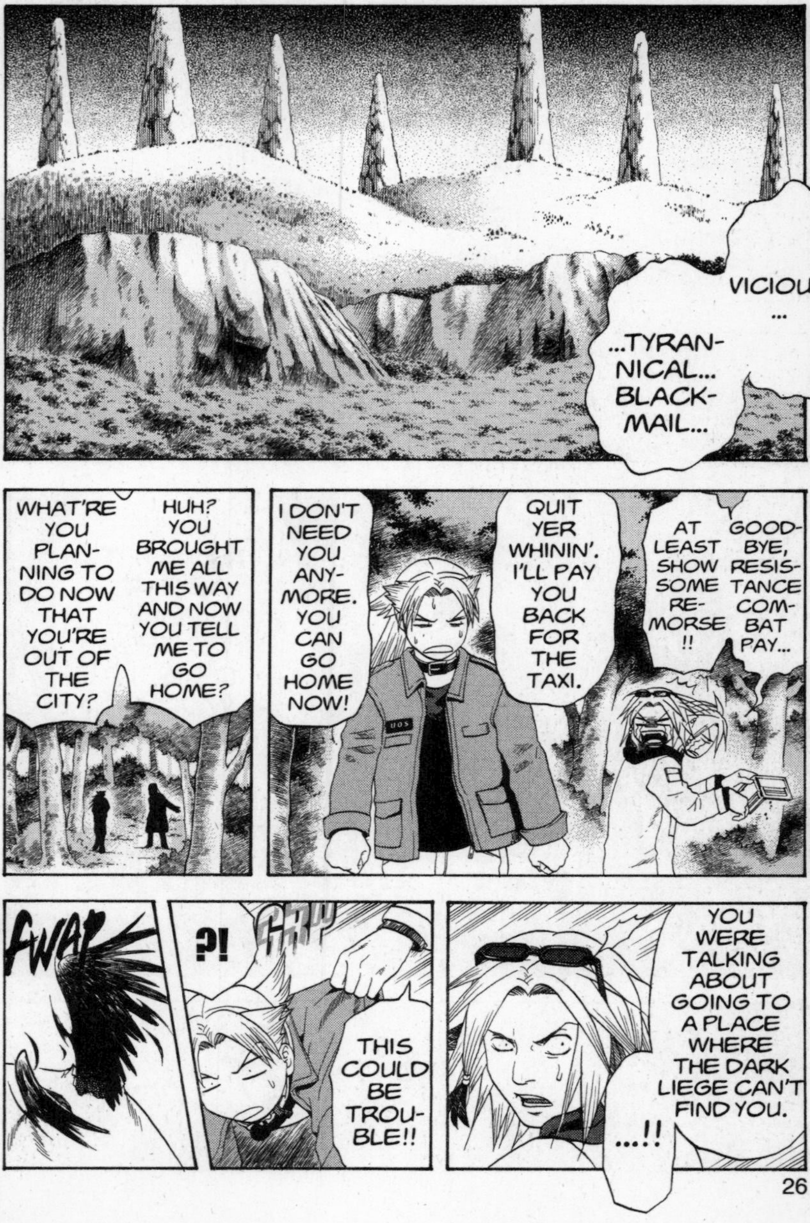
VICIOUS ... ...TYRANNICAL... BLACKMAIL...
GOOD-BYE, RESISTANCE COMBAT PAY...
AT LEAST SHOW SOME REMORSE!!
QUIT YER WHININ'. I'LL PAY YOU BACK FOR THE TAXI.
I DON'T NEED YOU ANYMORE. YOU CAN GO HOME NOW!
HUH? YOU BROUGHT ME ALL THIS WAY AND NOW YOU TELL ME TO GO HOME?
WHAT'RE YOU PLANNING TO DO NOW THAT YOU'RE OUT OF THE CITY?
YOU WERE TALKING ABOUT GOING TO A PLACE WHERE THE DARK LIEGE CAN'T FIND YOU.
...!!
?!
THIS COULD BE TROUBLE!!
FWAP

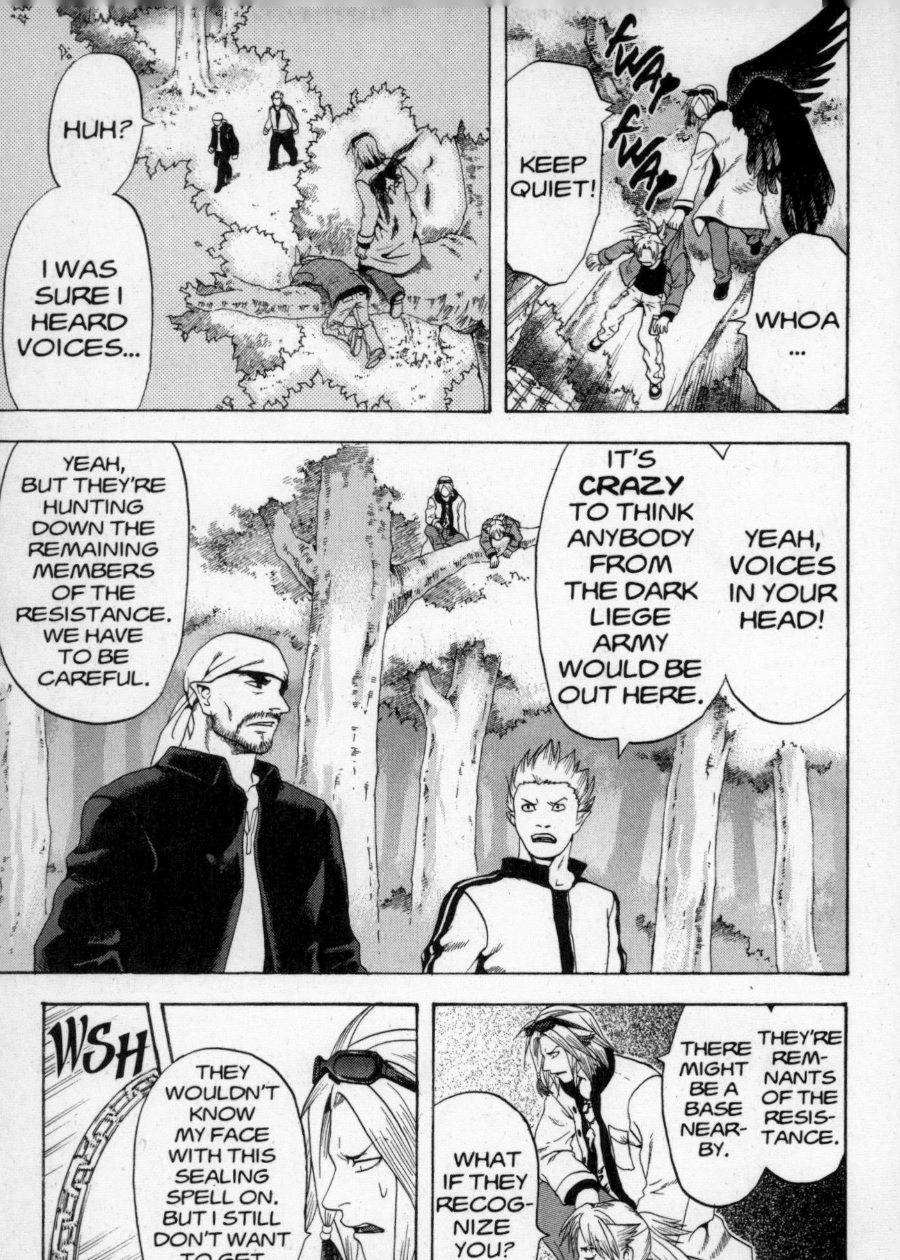
FWAP FWAP
KEEP QUIET!
WHOA ...
HUH?
I WAS SURE I HEARD VOICES...
IT'S **CRAZY** TO THINK ANYBODY FROM THE DARK LIEGE ARMY WOULD BE OUT HERE.
YEAH, VOICES IN YOUR HEAD!
YEAH, BUT THEY'RE HUNTING DOWN THE REMAINING MEMBERS OF THE RESISTANCE. WE HAVE TO BE CAREFUL.
THEY'RE REM-NANTS OF THE RESIS-TANCE.
THERE MIGHT BE A BASE NEAR-BY.
WHAT IF THEY RECOG-NIZE YOU?
WSH
THEY WOULDN'T KNOW MY FACE WITH THIS SEALING SPELL ON. BUT I STILL DON'T WANT TO GET INVOLVED ...

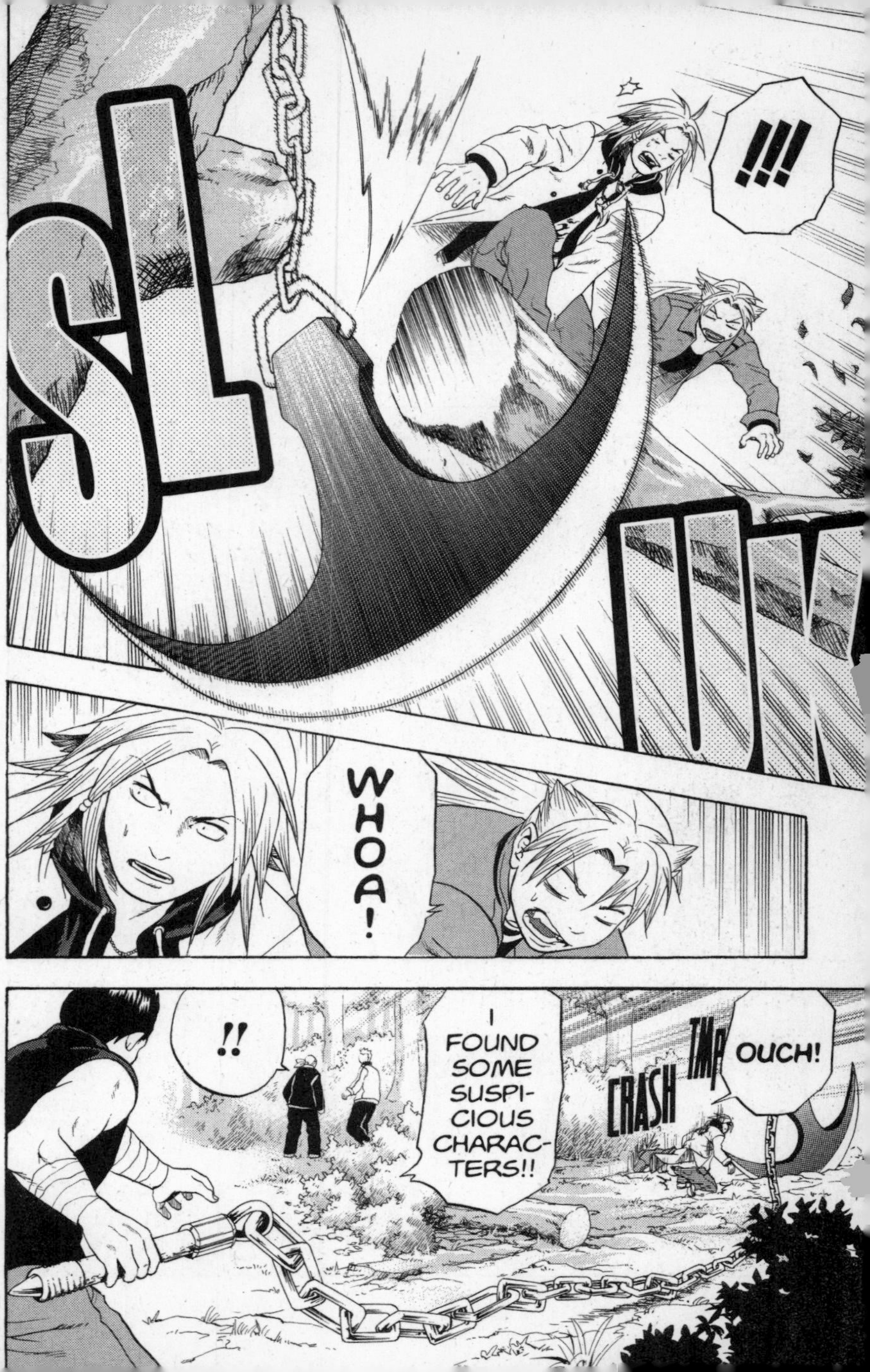
!!!
SL
UN
WHOA!
OUCH!
TMP
CRASH
I FOUND SOME SUSPICIOUS CHARACTERS!!
!!

READ THIS WAY

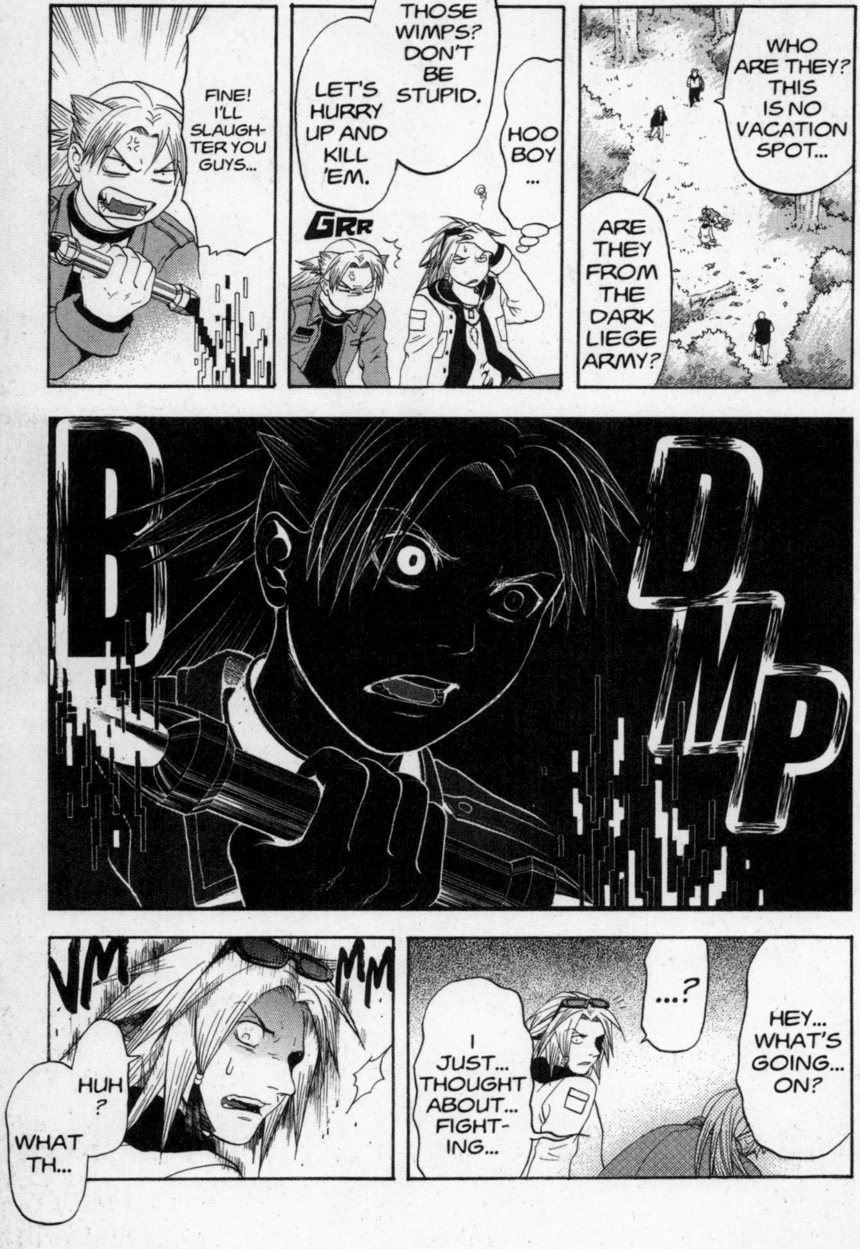
WHO ARE THEY? THIS IS NO VACATION SPOT...
ARE THEY FROM THE DARK LIEGE ARMY?
THOSE WIMPS? DON'T BE STUPID.
HOO BOY ...
LET'S HURRY UP AND KILL 'EM.
GRR
FINE! I'LL SLAUGHTER YOU GUYS...
B
DMP
HEY... WHAT'S GOING... ON?
...?
I JUST... THOUGHT ABOUT... FIGHT-ING...
VM
MM
HUH?
WHAT TH...

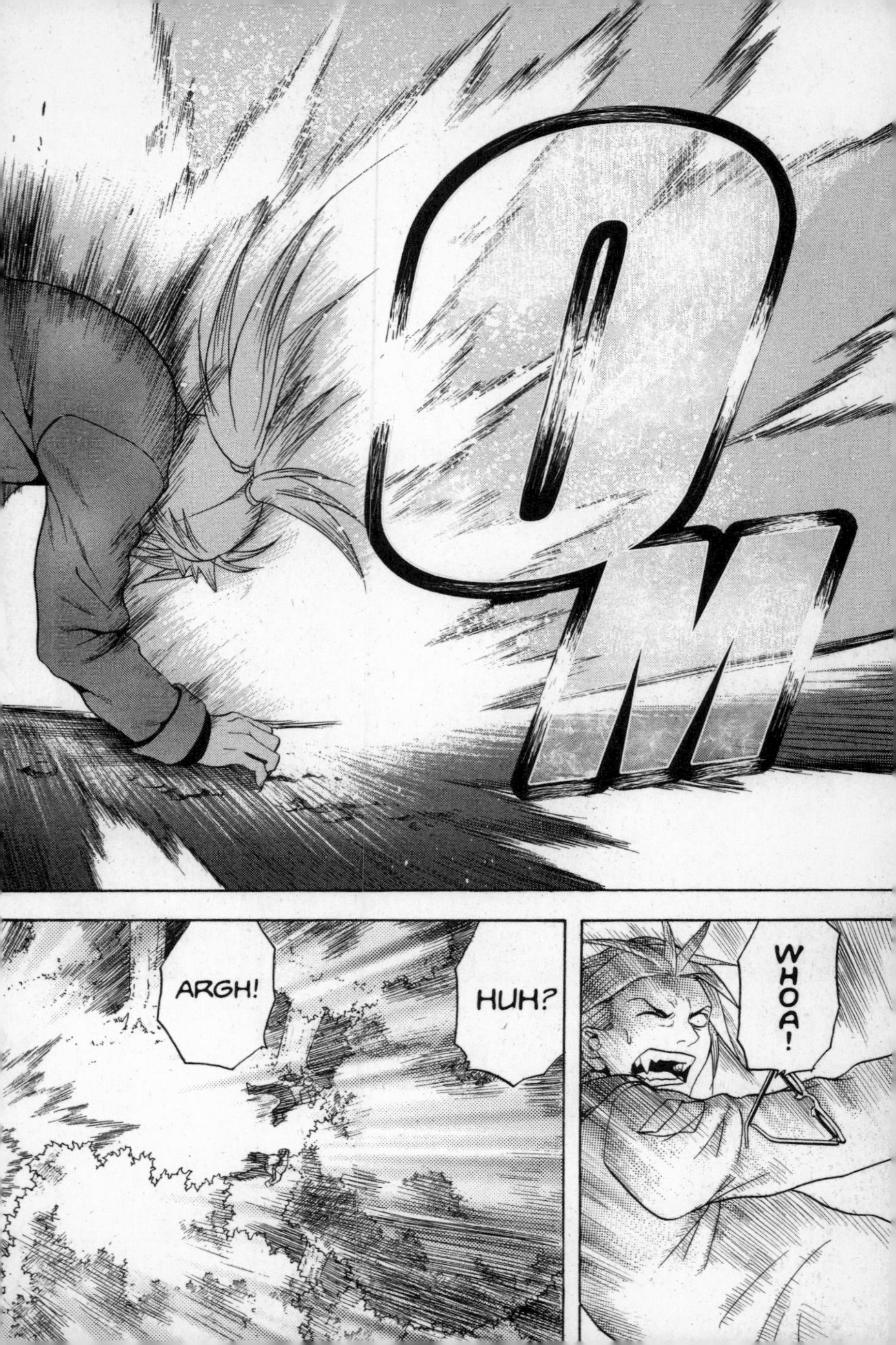
WHOA!
HUH?
ARGH!

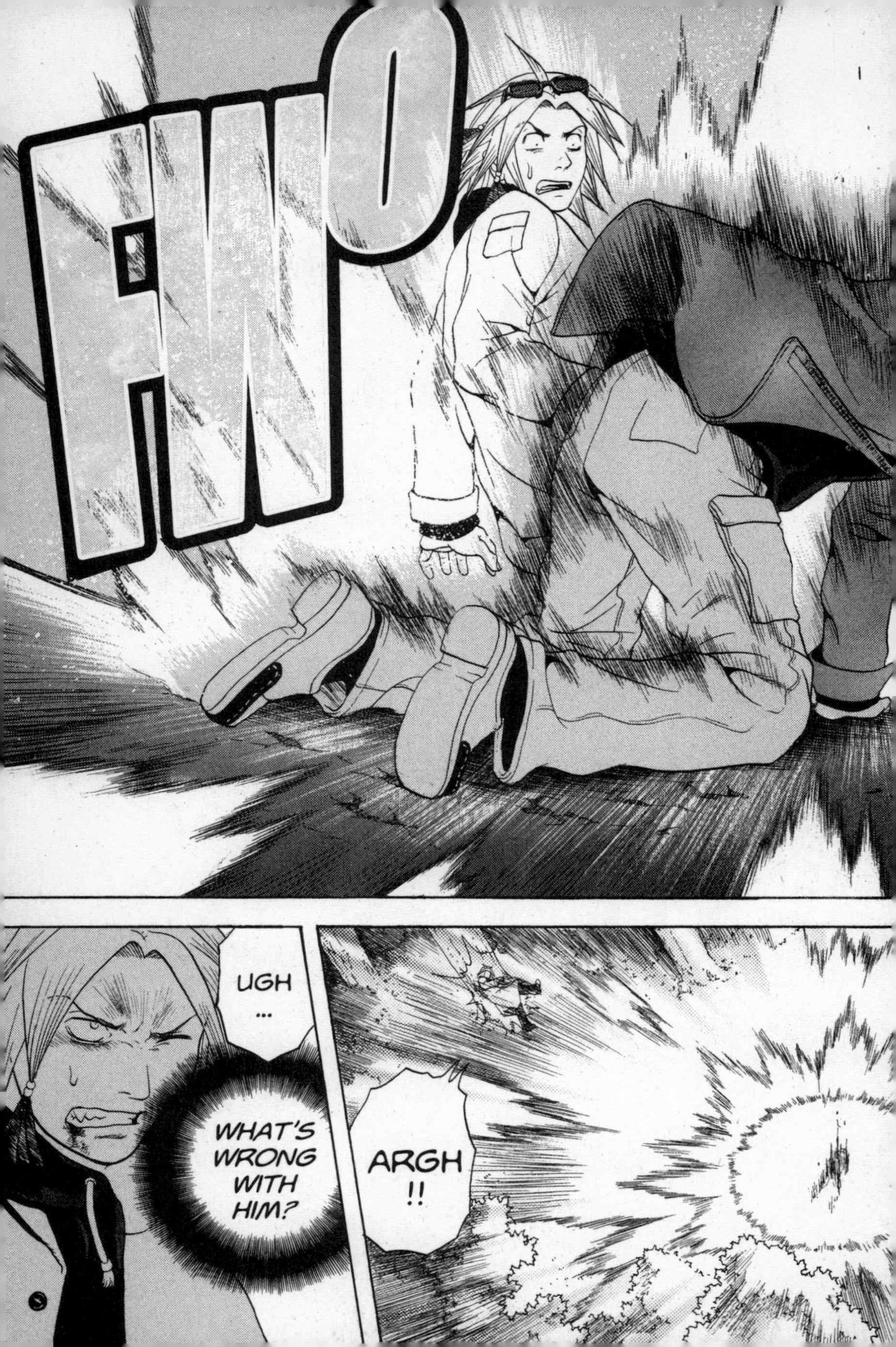
FWO
ARGH!!
UGH...
WHAT'S WRONG WITH HIM?

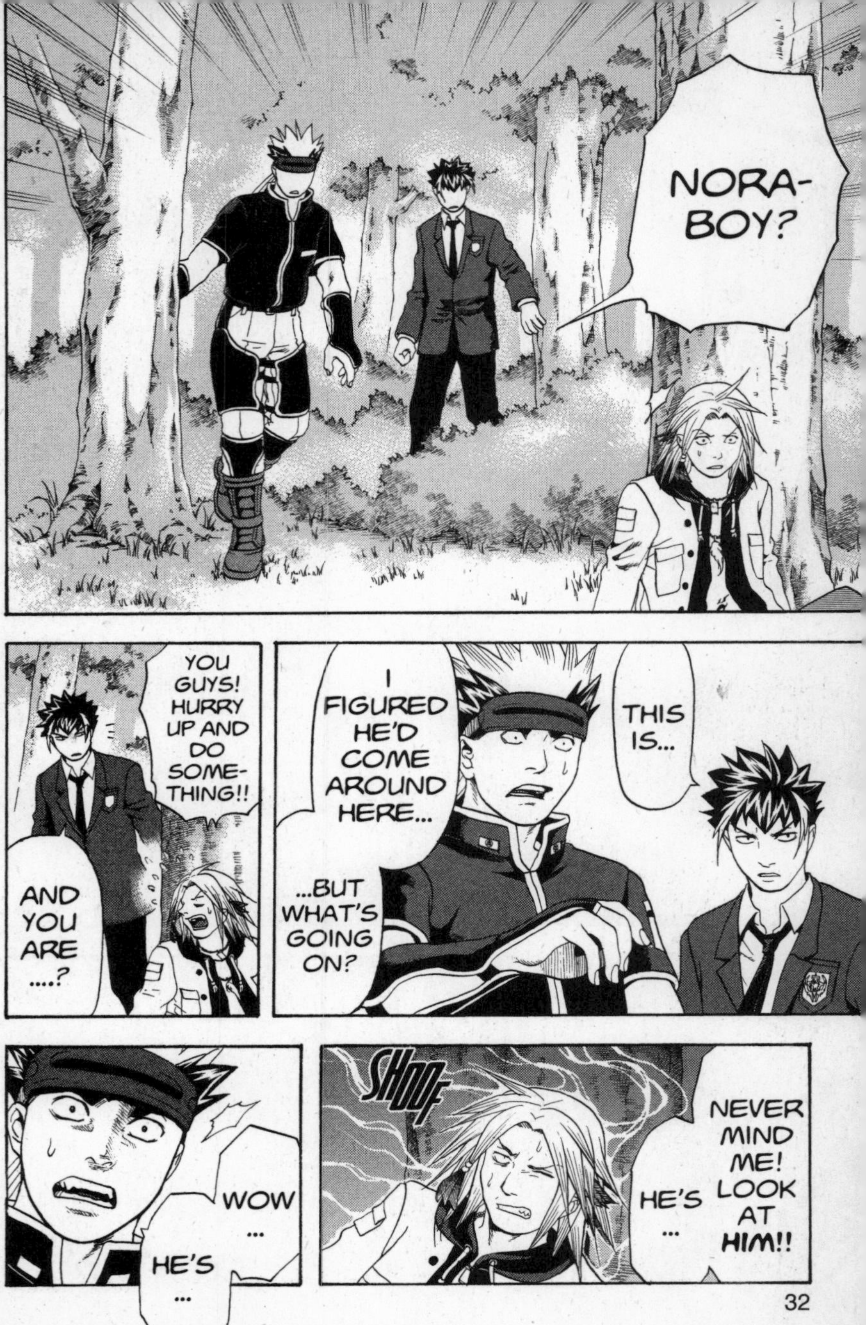
NORA-BOY?
THIS IS...
I FIGURED HE'D COME AROUND HERE...
...BUT WHAT'S GOING ON?
YOU GUYS! HURRY UP AND DO SOME-THING!!
AND YOU ARE ....?
SHOOF
NEVER MIND ME! LOOK AT HIM!!
HE'S ...
WOW ...
HE'S ...

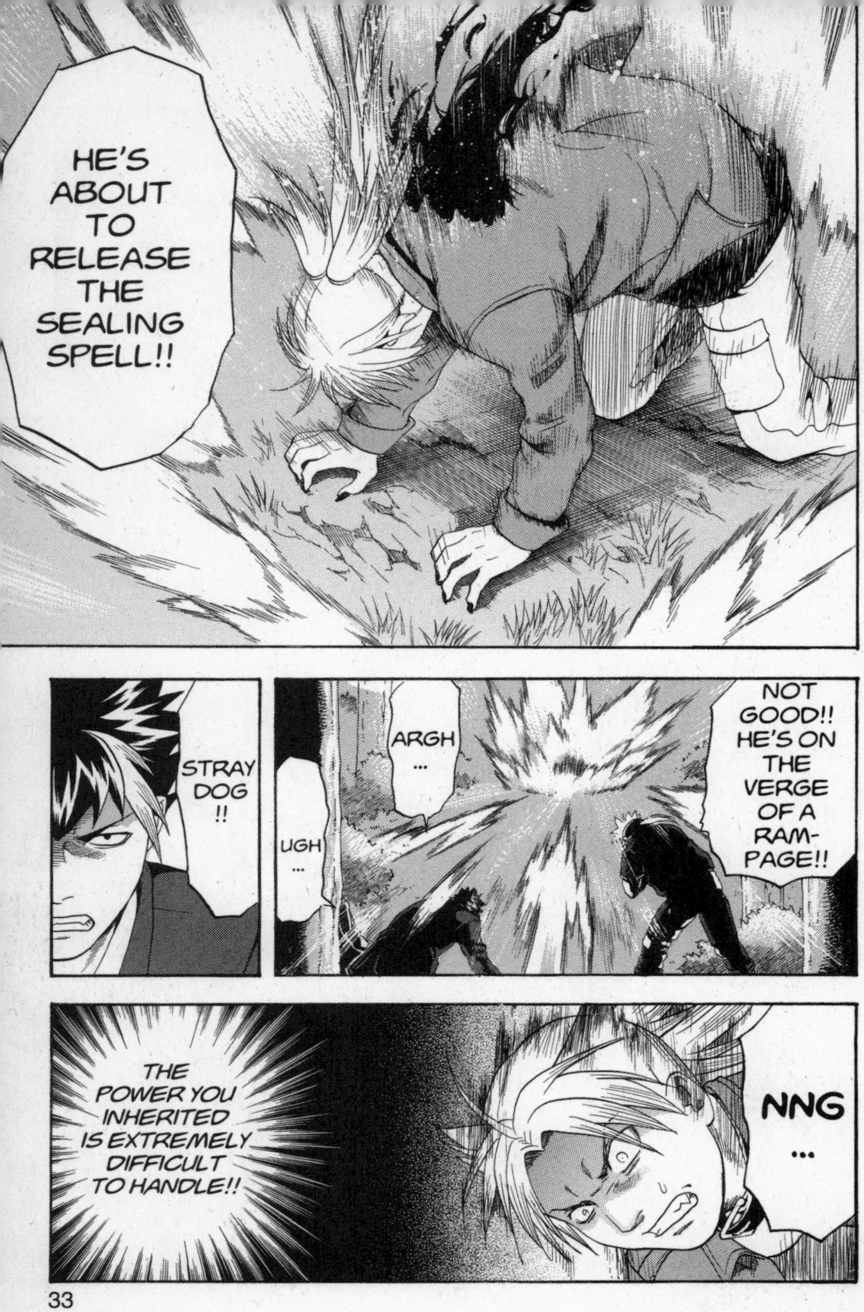
HE'S ABOUT TO RELEASE THE SEALING SPELL!!
NOT GOOD!! HE'S ON THE VERGE OF A RAM-PAGE!!
ARGH ...
UGH ...
STRAY DOG !!
NNG ...
THE POWER YOU INHERITED IS EXTREMELY DIFFICULT TO HANDLE!!

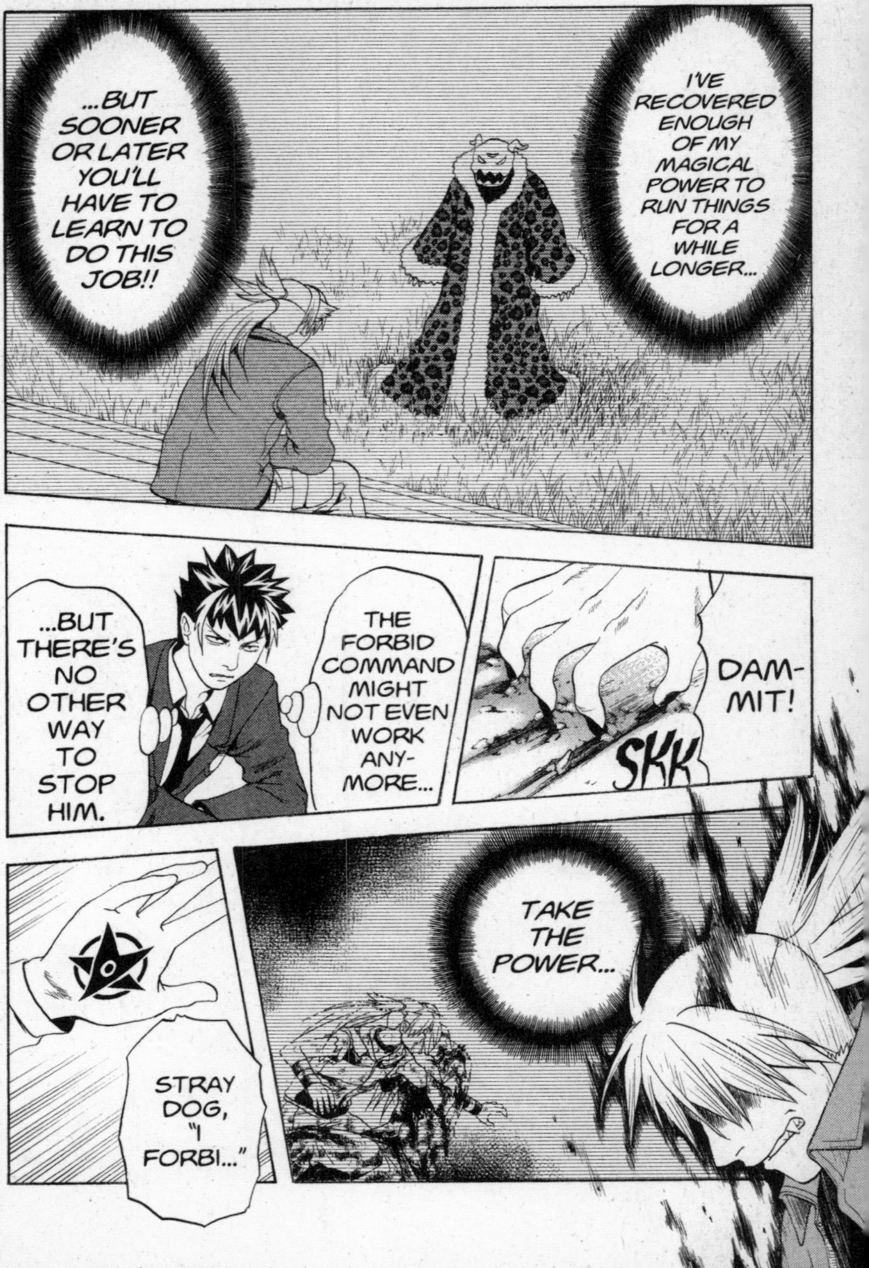
I'VE RECOVERED ENOUGH OF MY MAGICAL POWER TO RUN THINGS FOR A WHILE LONGER...
...BUT SOONER OR LATER YOU'LL HAVE TO LEARN TO DO THIS JOB!!
DAM-MIT!
SKK
THE FORBID COMMAND MIGHT NOT EVEN WORK ANY-MORE...
...BUT THERE'S NO OTHER WAY TO STOP HIM.
TAKE THE POWER...
STRAY DOG, "I FORBI..."

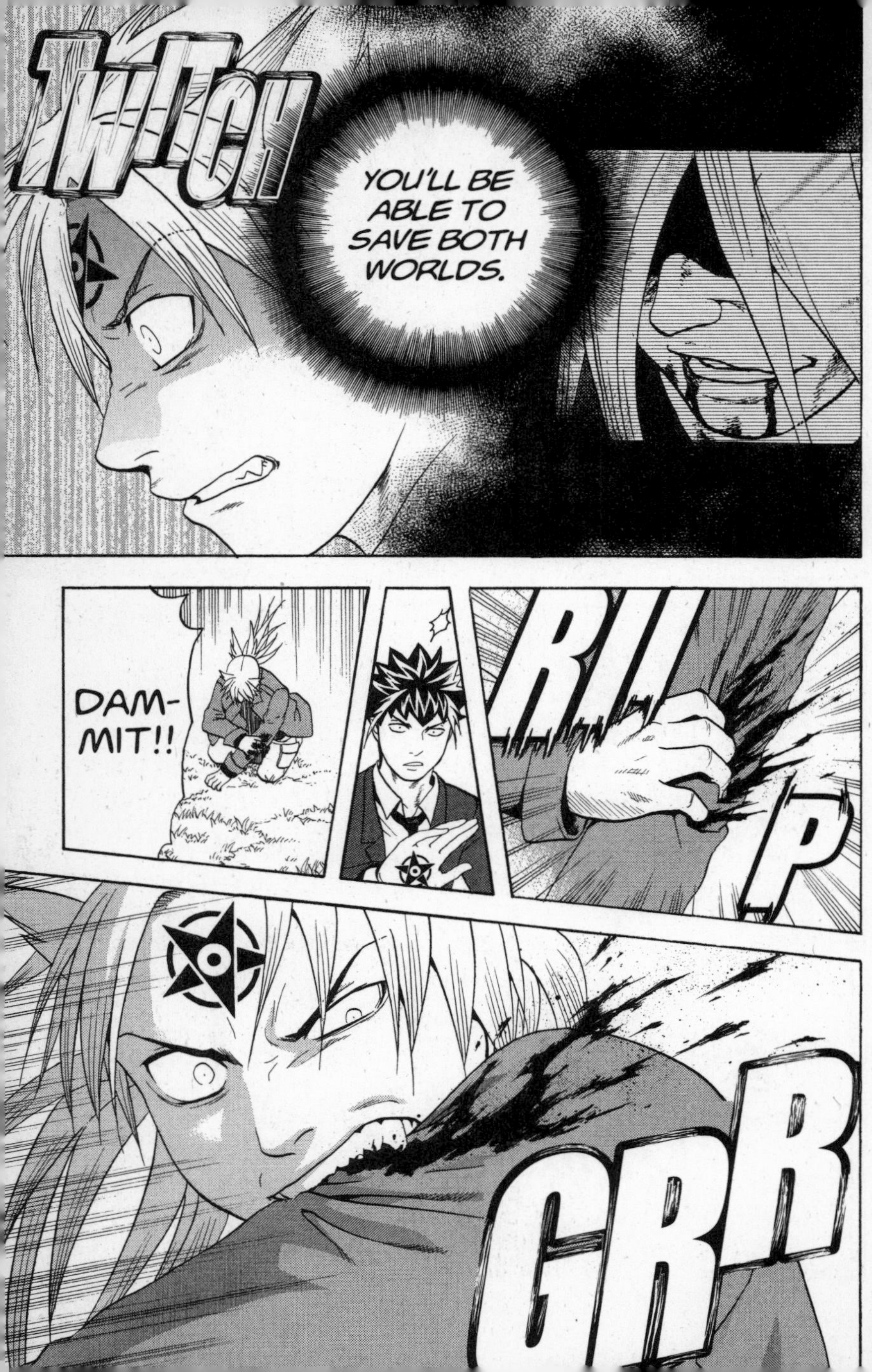
TWITCH
YOU'LL BE ABLE TO SAVE BOTH WORLDS.
RIP
DAM-MIT!!
GRR

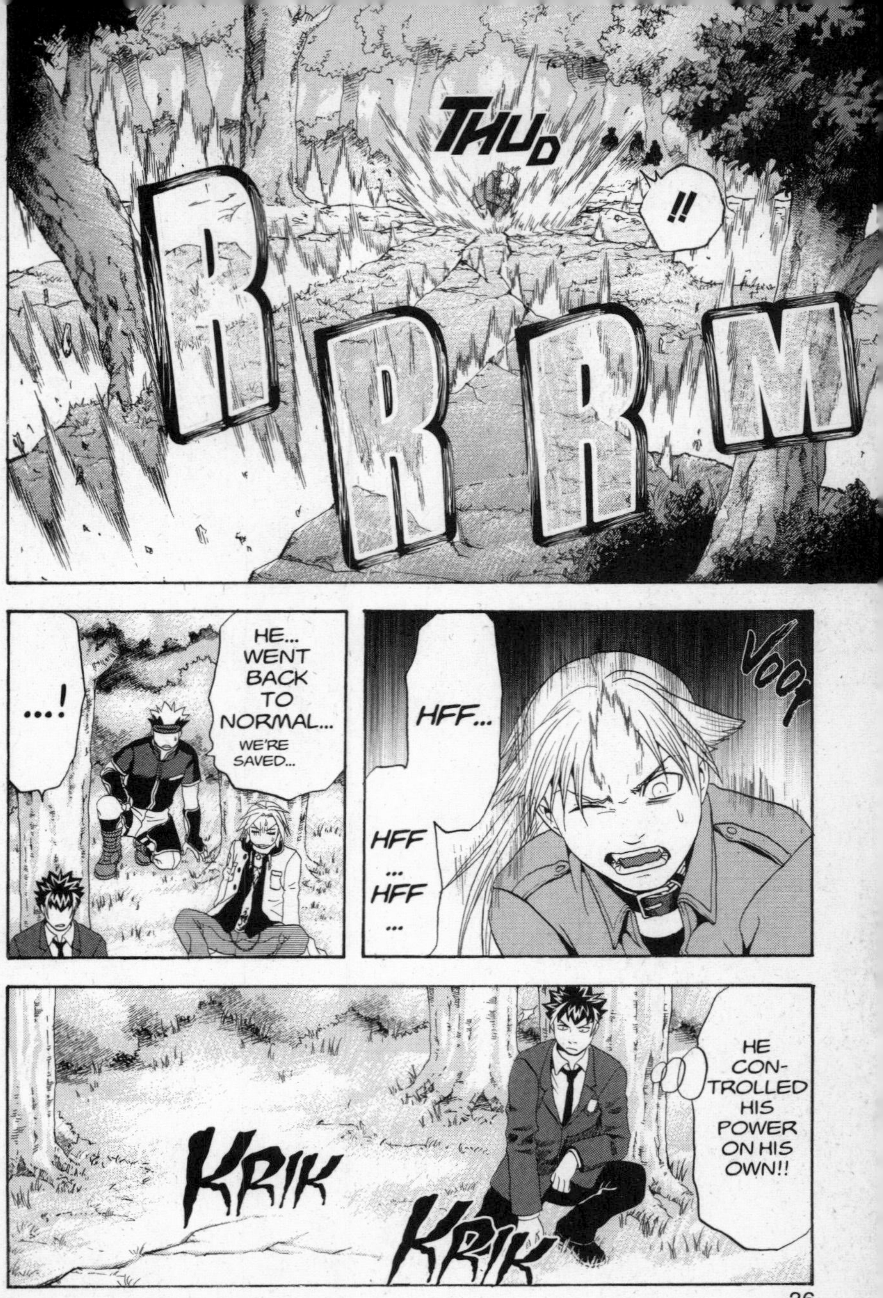
THUD
!!
RRRM
VOO
HFF...
HFF ... HFF ...
HE... WENT BACK TO NORMAL... WE'RE SAVED...
...!
HE CON-TROLLED HIS POWER ON HIS OWN!!
KRIK
KRIK

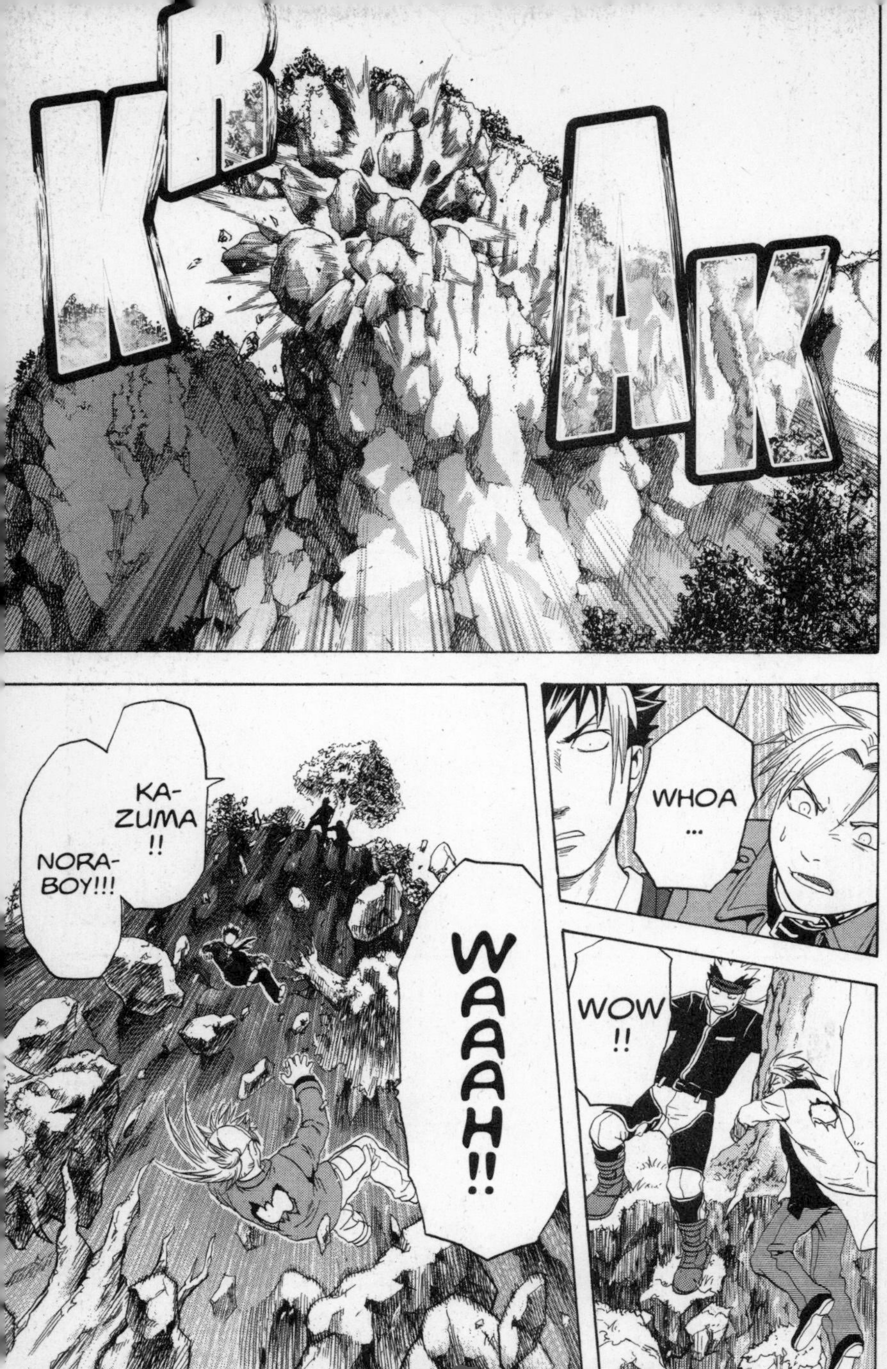
KRAK
WHOA ...
WOW !!
WAAAH!!
KA-ZUMA !!
NORA-BOY!!!

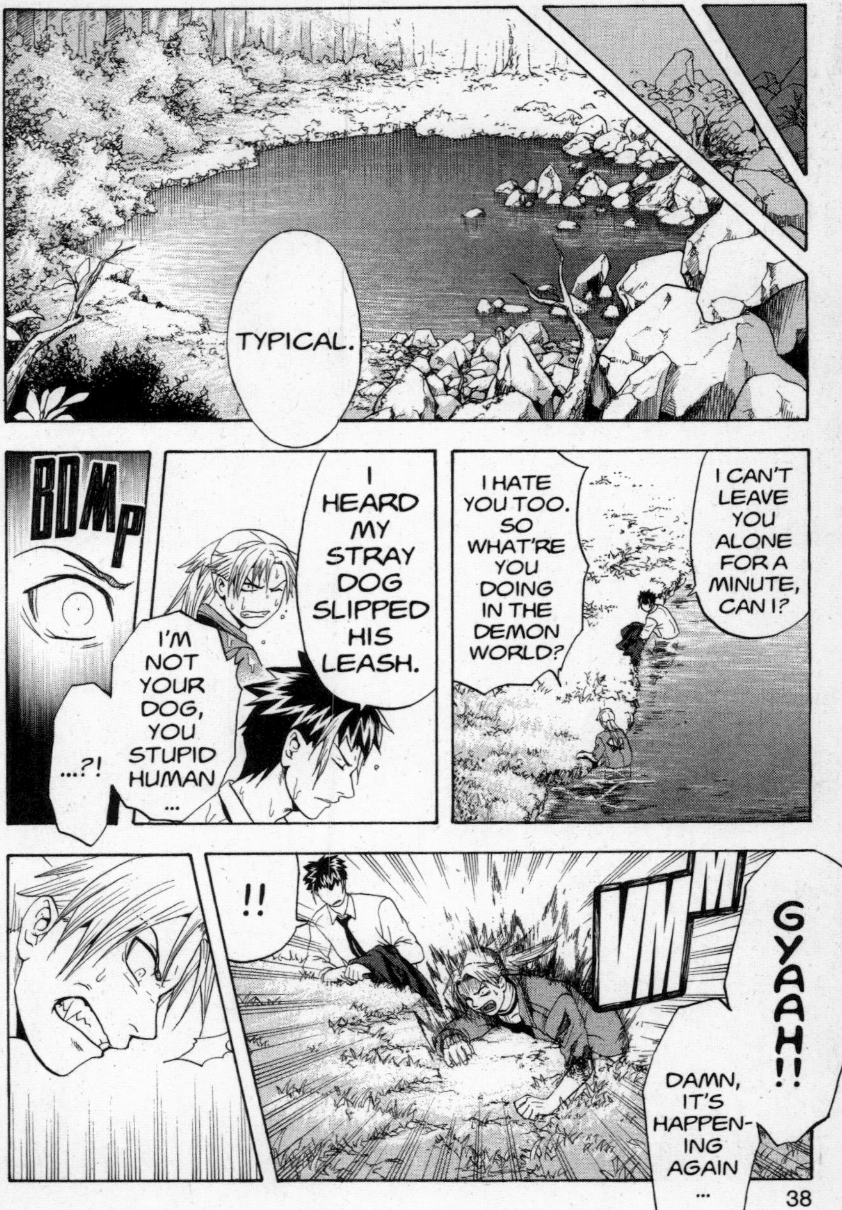
TYPICAL.
I CAN'T LEAVE YOU ALONE FOR A MINUTE, CAN I?
I HATE YOU TOO. SO WHAT'RE YOU DOING IN THE DEMON WORLD?
I HEARD MY STRAY DOG SLIPPED HIS LEASH.
I'M NOT YOUR DOG, YOU STUPID HUMAN ...
BDMP
...?!
GYAAH!!
DAMN, IT'S HAPPEN-ING AGAIN ...
VMM
!!

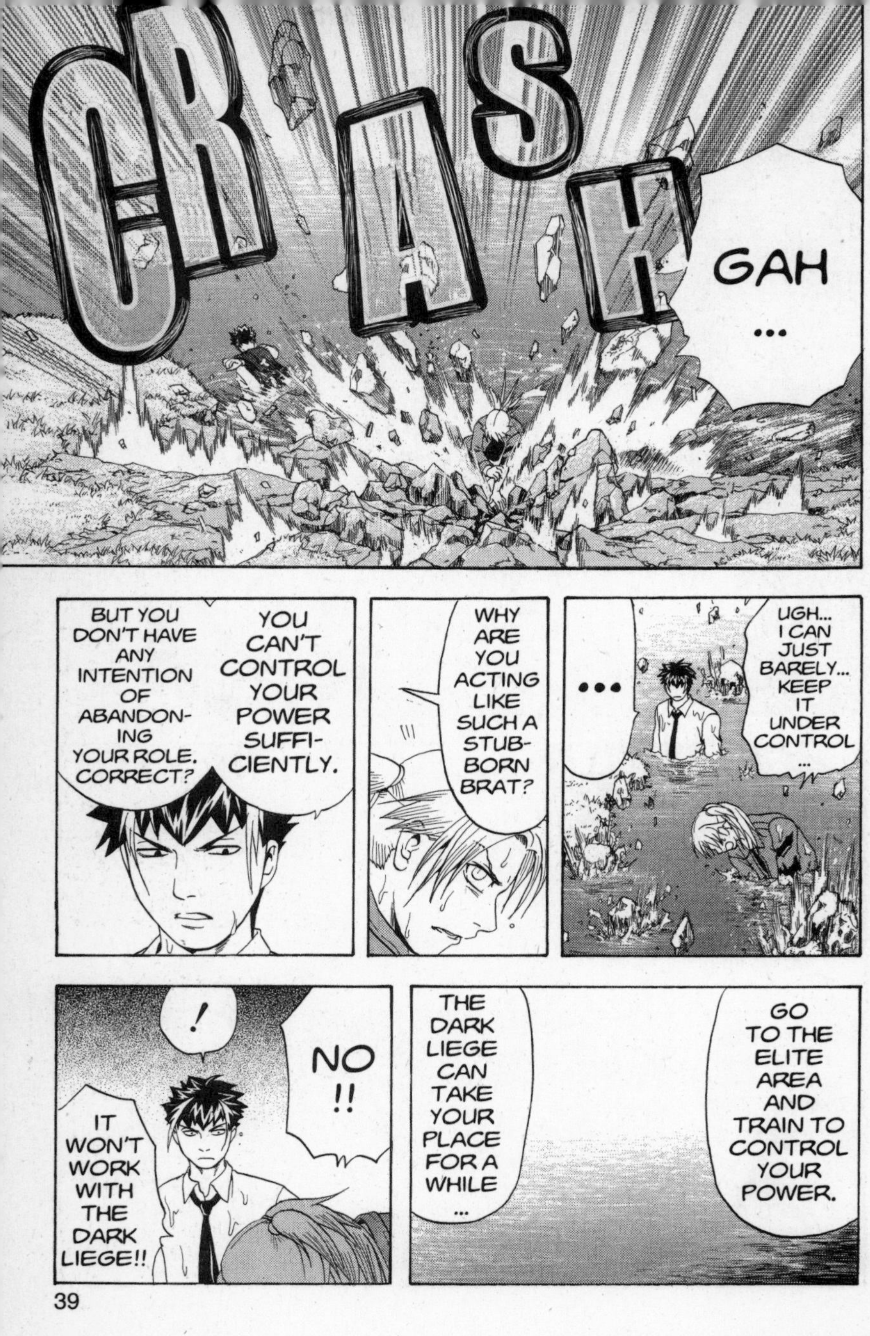
CRASH
GAH ...
UGH... I CAN JUST BARELY... KEEP IT UNDER CONTROL ...
...
WHY ARE YOU ACTING LIKE SUCH A STUBBORN BRAT?
YOU CAN'T CONTROL YOUR POWER SUFFICIENTLY.
BUT YOU DON'T HAVE ANY INTENTION OF ABANDONING YOUR ROLE. CORRECT?
GO TO THE ELITE AREA AND TRAIN TO CONTROL YOUR POWER.
THE DARK LIEGE CAN TAKE YOUR PLACE FOR A WHILE ...
NO !!
!
IT WON'T WORK WITH THE DARK LIEGE!!

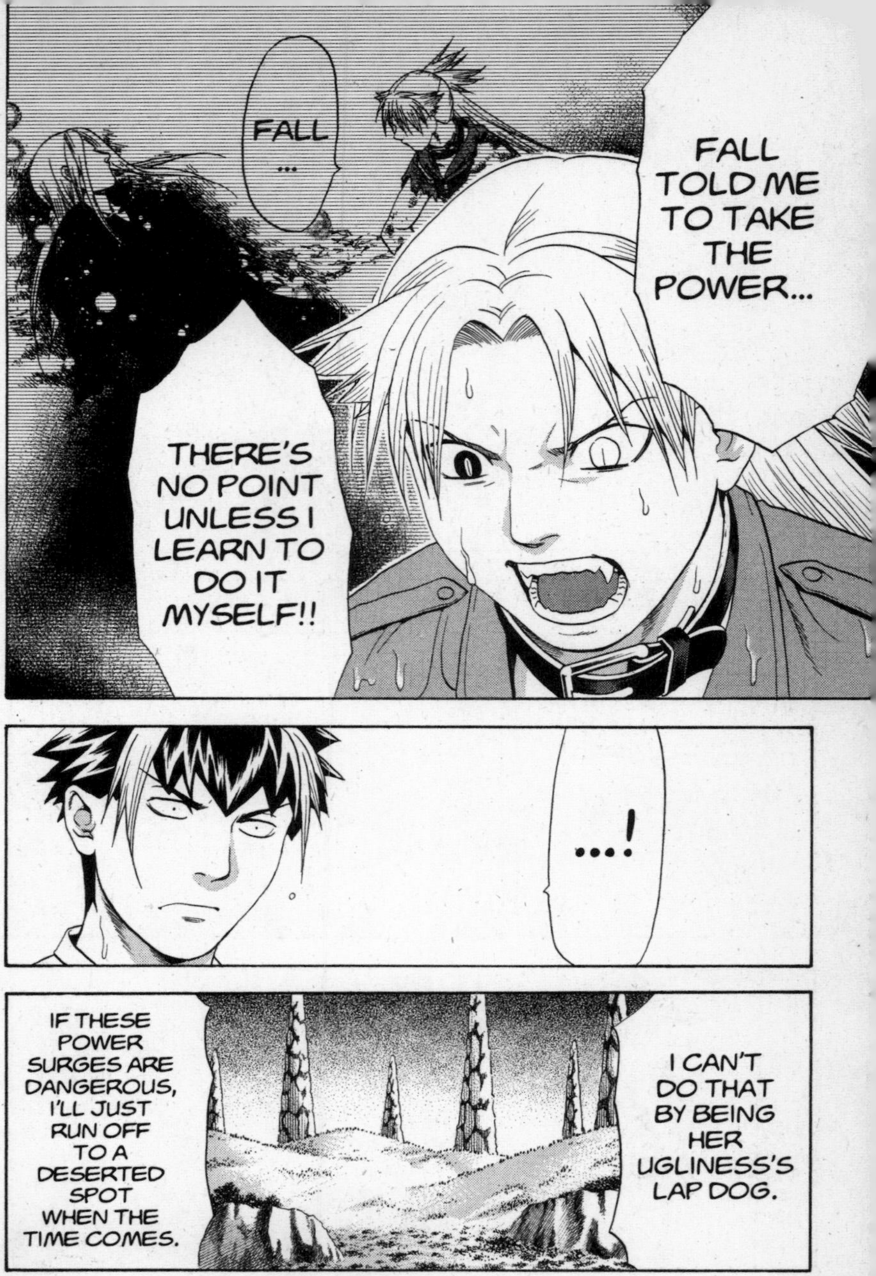
FALL TOLD ME TO TAKE THE POWER...
FALL ...
THERE'S NO POINT UNLESS I LEARN TO DO IT MYSELF!!
...!
I CAN'T DO THAT BY BEING HER UGLINESS'S LAP DOG.
IF THESE POWER SURGES ARE DANGEROUS, I'LL JUST RUN OFF TO A DESERTED SPOT WHEN THE TIME COMES.

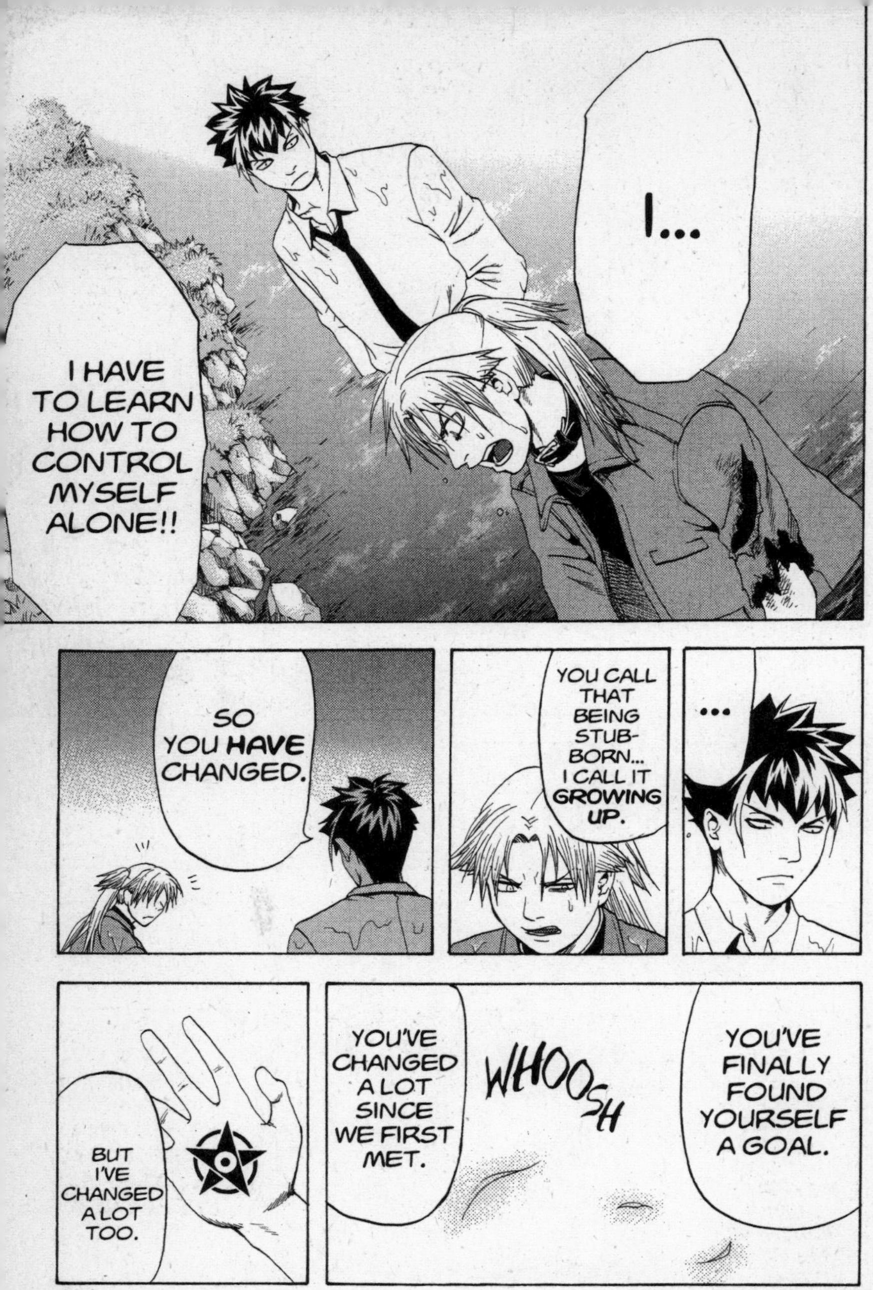
I...
I HAVE TO LEARN HOW TO CONTROL MYSELF ALONE!!
...
YOU CALL THAT BEING STUBBORN... I CALL IT **GROWING UP**.
SO YOU **HAVE** CHANGED.
YOU'VE FINALLY FOUND YOURSELF A GOAL.
WHOOSH
YOU'VE CHANGED A LOT SINCE WE FIRST MET.
BUT I'VE CHANGED A LOT TOO.

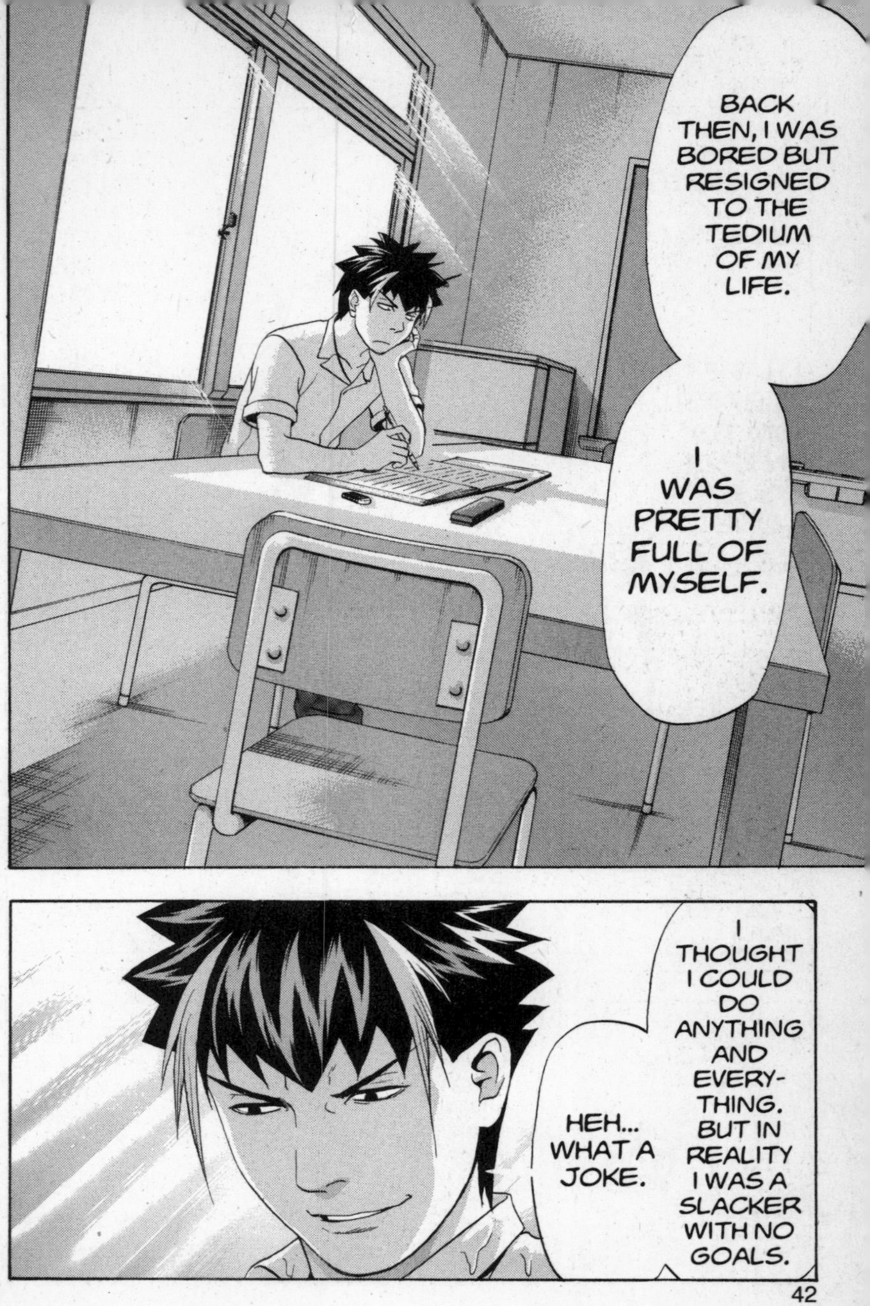
BACK THEN, I WAS BORED BUT RESIGNED TO THE TEDIUM OF MY LIFE.
I WAS PRETTY FULL OF MYSELF.
I THOUGHT I COULD DO ANYTHING AND EVERY-THING. BUT IN REALITY I WAS A SLACKER WITH NO GOALS.
HEH... WHAT A JOKE.

READ THIS WAY

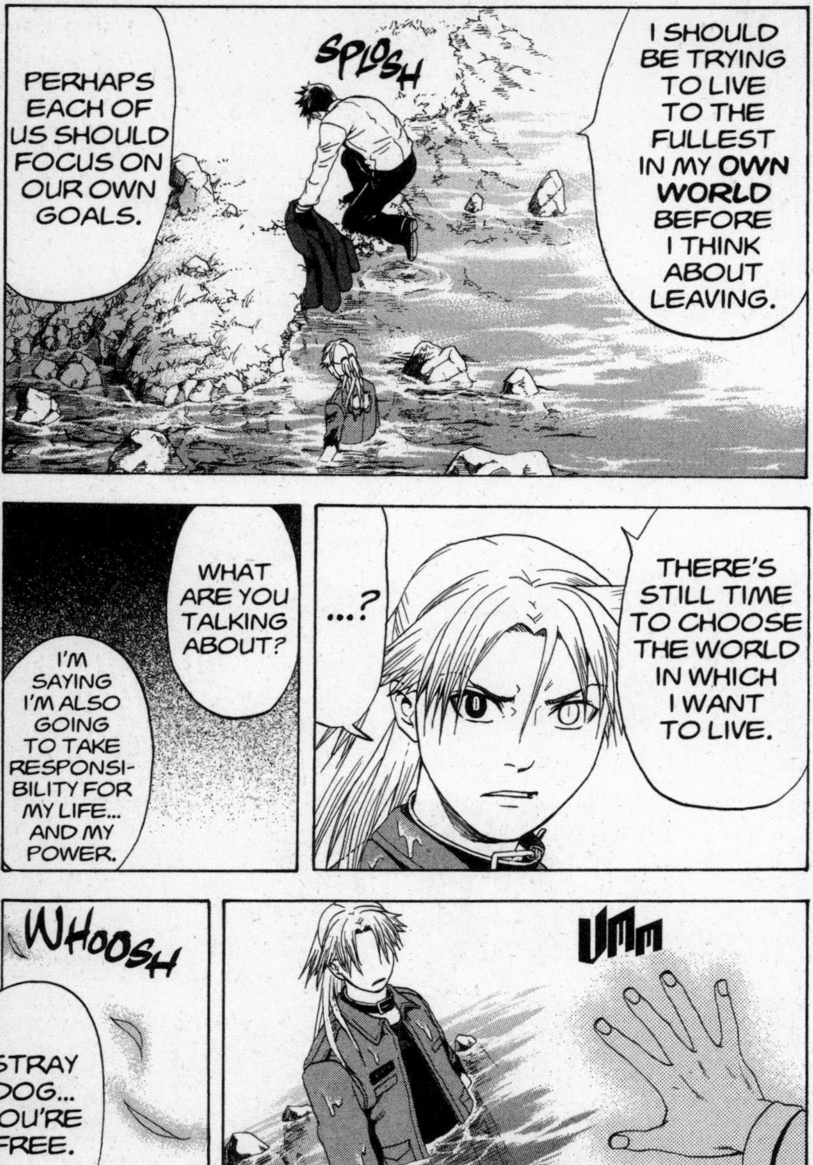
I SHOULD BE TRYING TO LIVE TO THE FULLEST IN MY **OWN WORLD** BEFORE I THINK ABOUT LEAVING.
SPLOSH
PERHAPS EACH OF US SHOULD FOCUS ON OUR OWN GOALS.
THERE'S STILL TIME TO CHOOSE THE WORLD IN WHICH I WANT TO LIVE.
...?
WHAT ARE YOU TALKING ABOUT?
I'M SAYING I'M ALSO GOING TO TAKE RESPONSI-BILITY FOR MY LIFE... AND MY POWER.
UMM
WHOOSH
STRAY DOG... YOU'RE FREE.

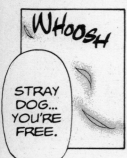

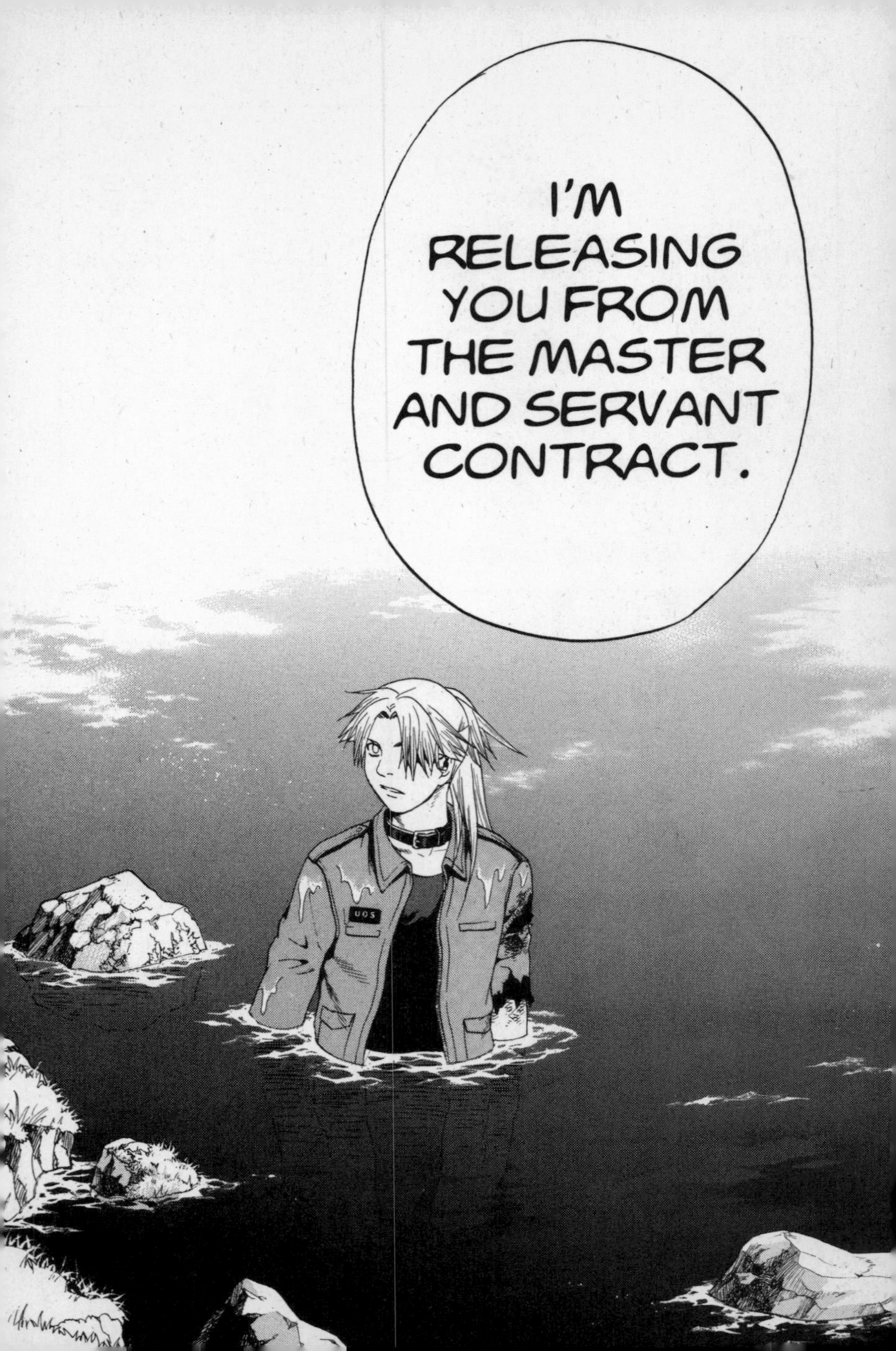
I'M RELEASING YOU FROM THE MASTER AND SERVANT CONTRACT.

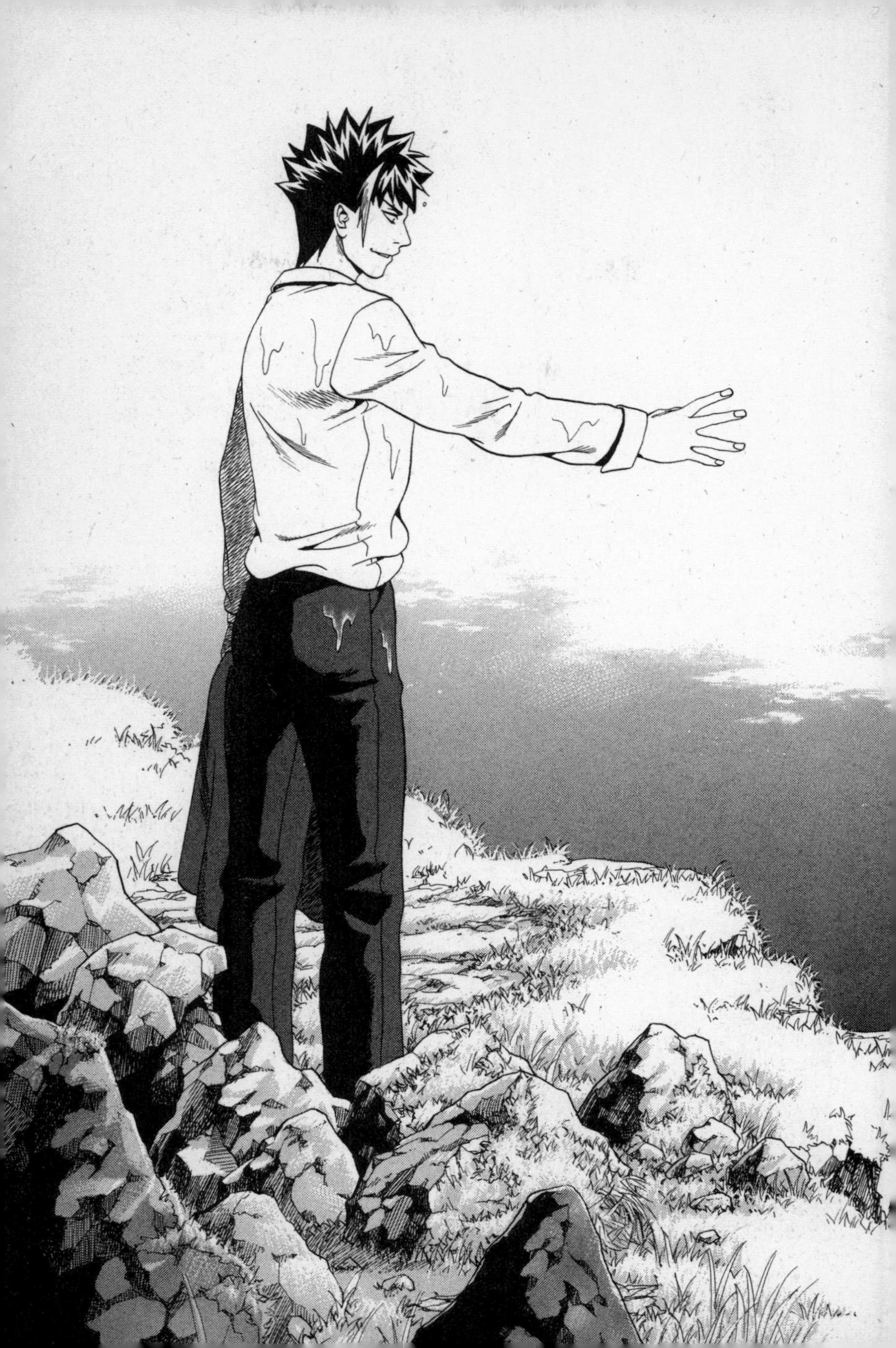

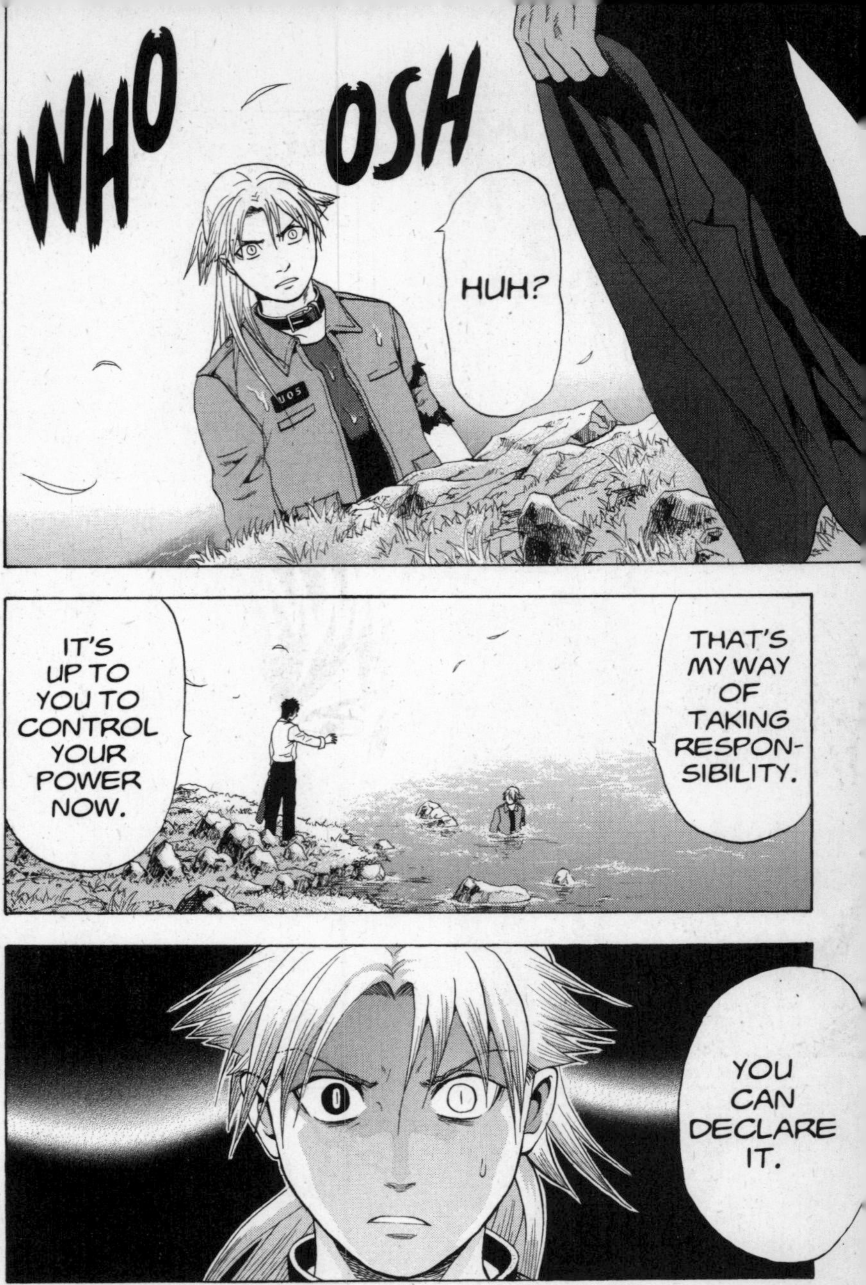
WHOOSH
HUH?
THAT'S MY WAY OF TAKING RESPON-SIBILITY.
IT'S UP TO YOU TO CONTROL YOUR POWER NOW.
YOU CAN DECLARE IT.

READ THIS WAY

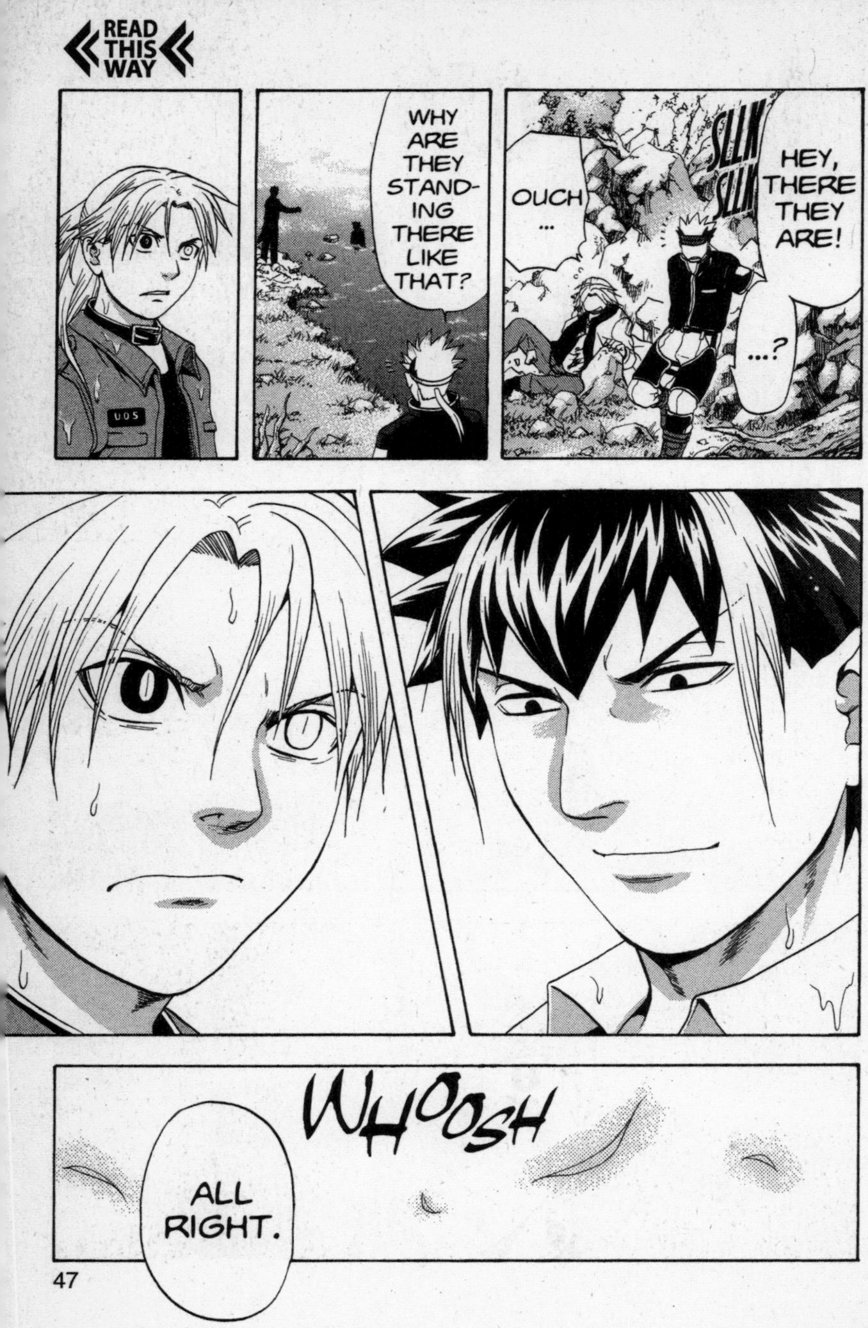
HEY, THERE THEY ARE!
SLINK SLINK
OUCH ...
...?
WHY ARE THEY STAND-ING THERE LIKE THAT?
WHOOSH
ALL RIGHT.

"I DECLARE" THE MASTER AND SERVANT CONTRACT **NULL AND VOID!!**

HEY, NORA-BOY!

WHAT ARE YOU SAYING ...?

WHA...?

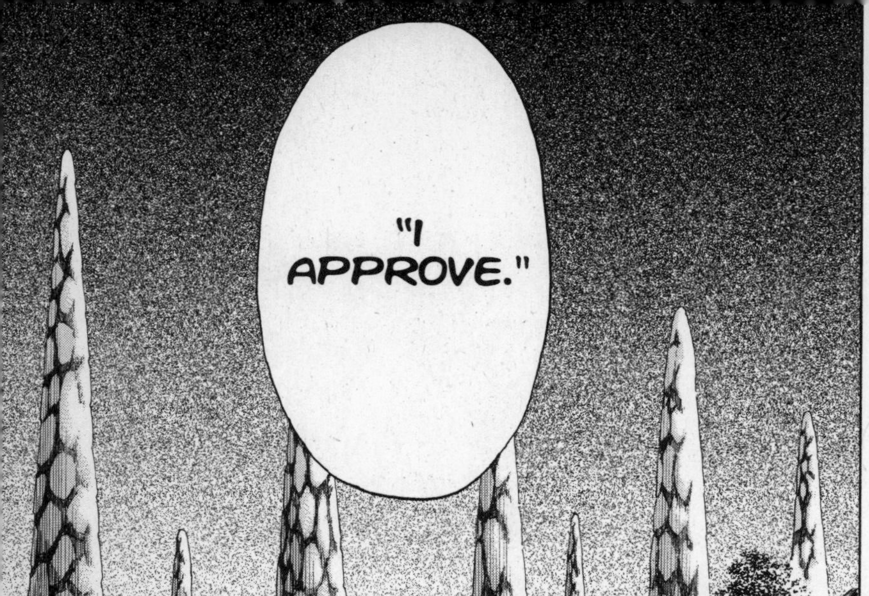
"I APPROVE."

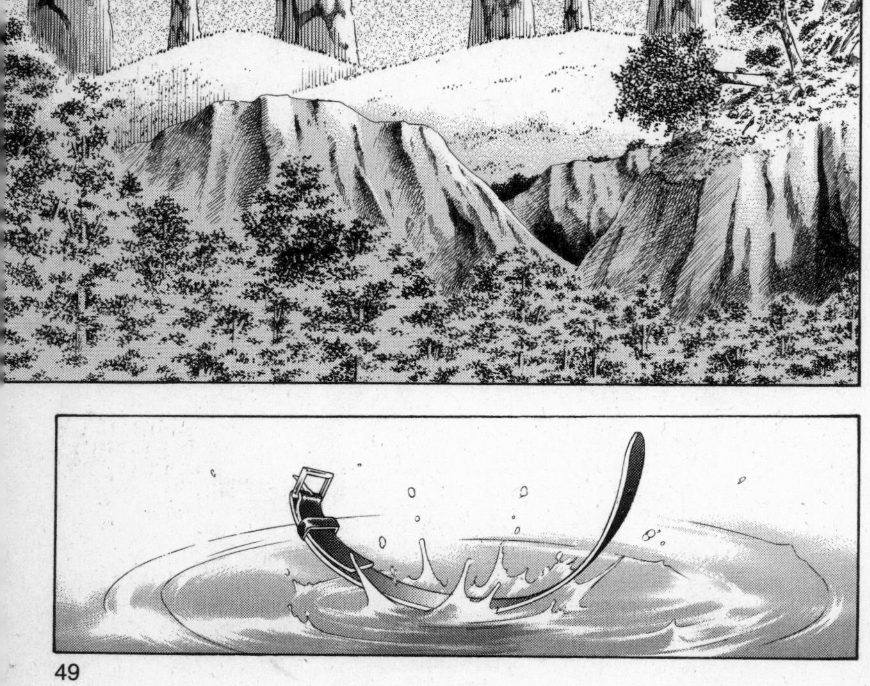

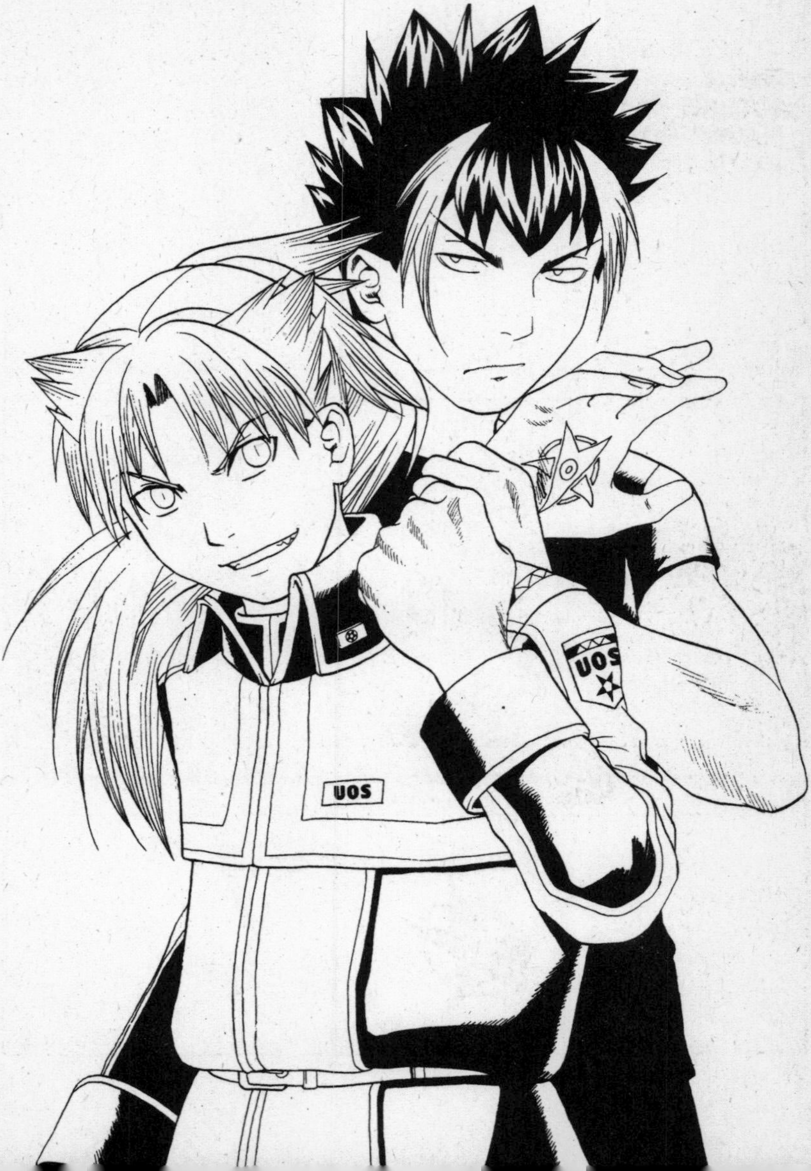
UOS
UOS

Story 34: Null and Void

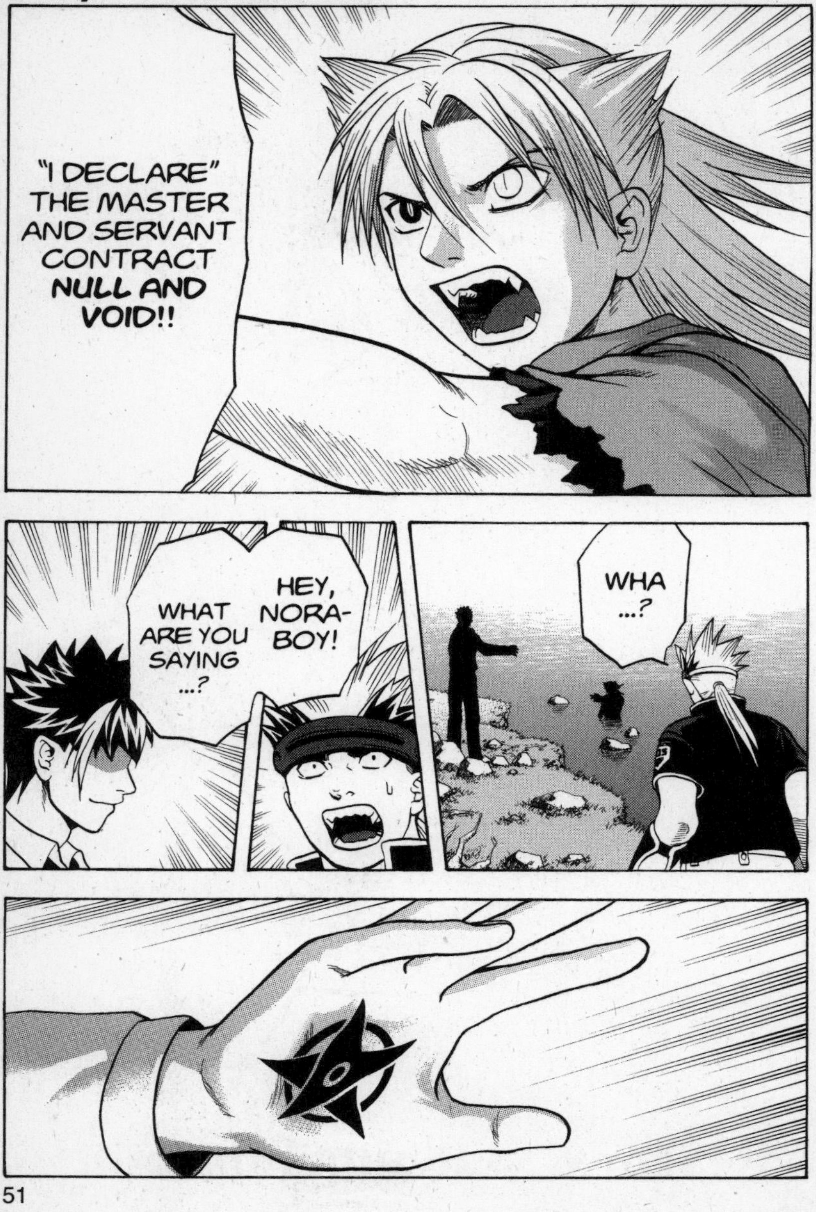
"I DECLARE" THE MASTER AND SERVANT CONTRACT NULL AND VOID!!
WHA ...?
HEY, NORA-BOY!
WHAT ARE YOU SAYING ...?

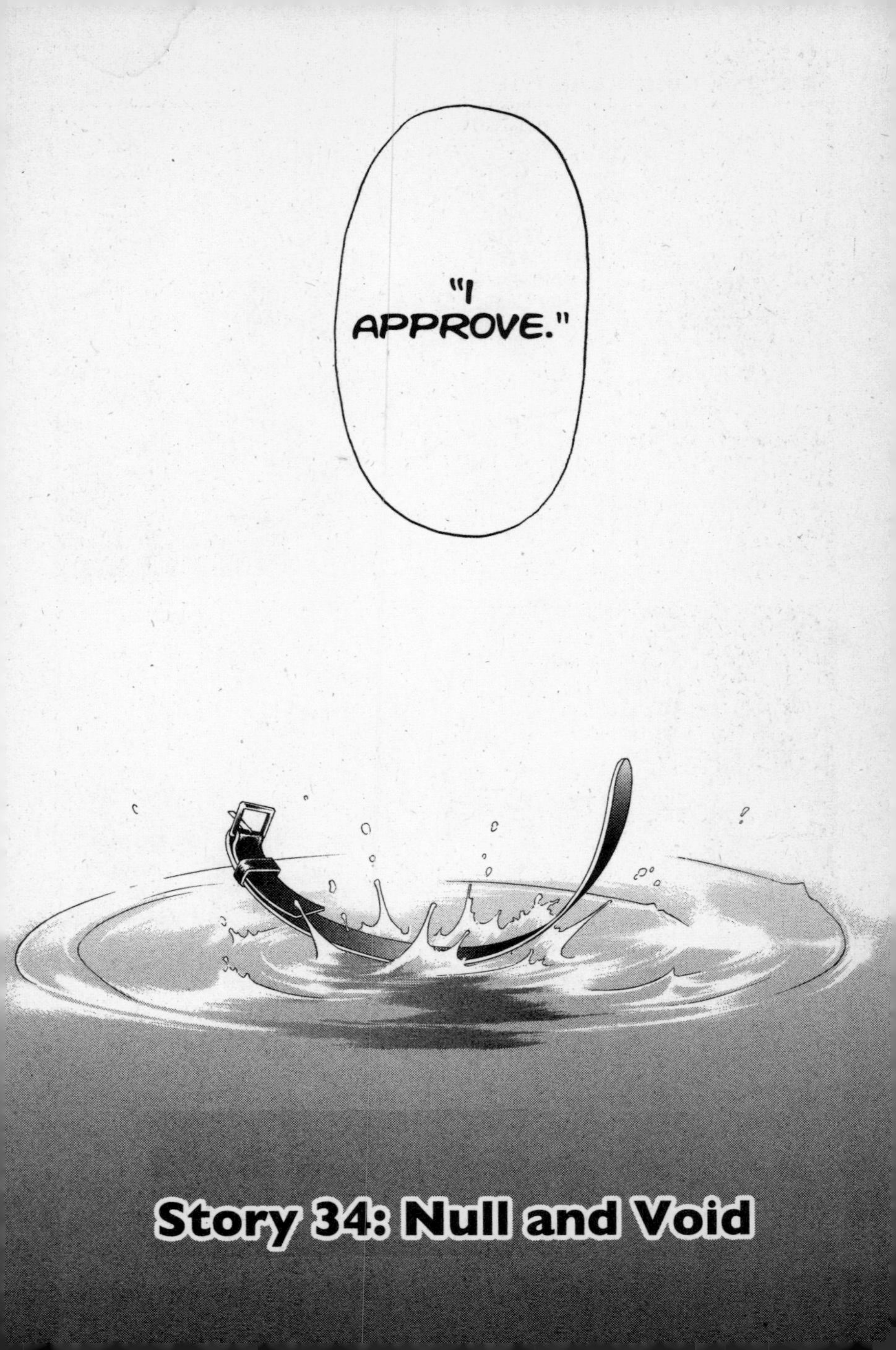
"I APPROVE."

Story 34: Null and Void

READ THIS WAY

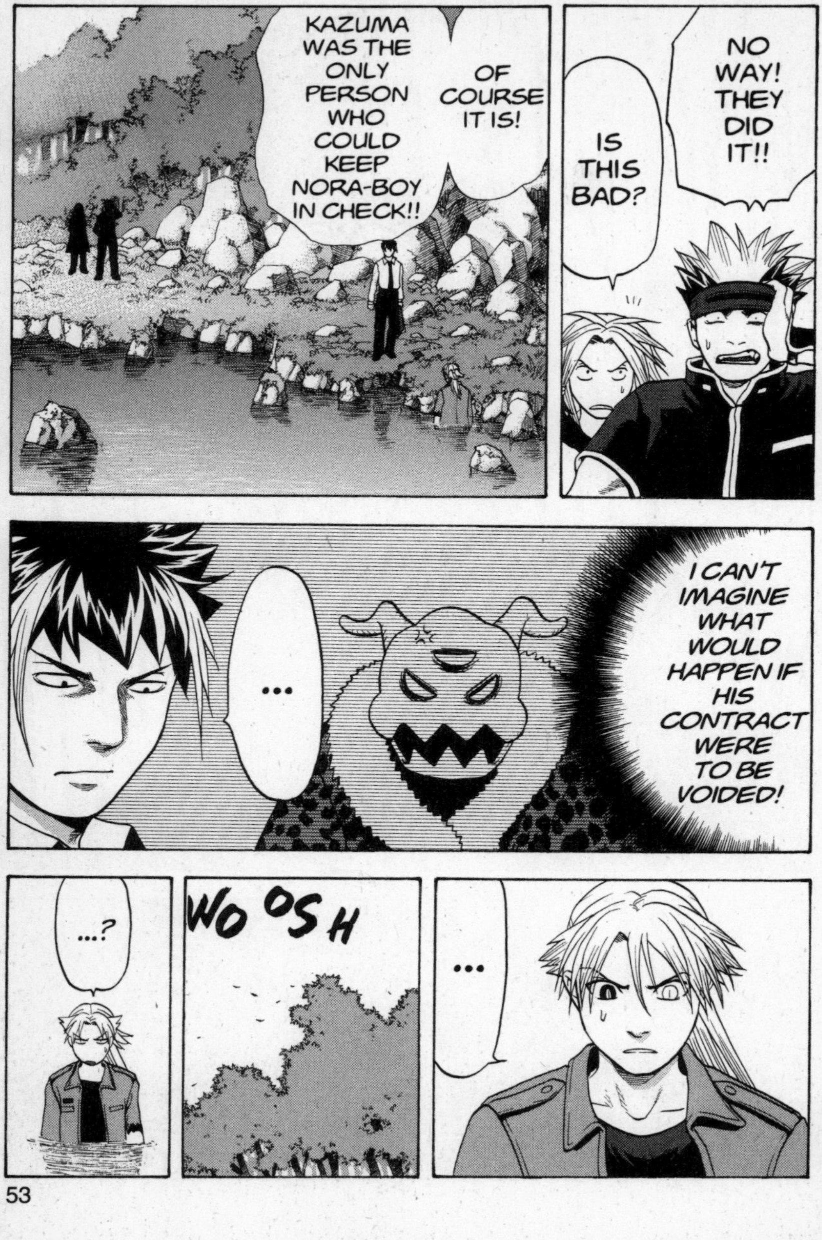

NO WAY! THEY DID IT!!
IS THIS BAD?
OF COURSE IT IS!
KAZUMA WAS THE ONLY PERSON WHO COULD KEEP NORA-BOY IN CHECK!!
I CAN'T IMAGINE WHAT WOULD HAPPEN IF HIS CONTRACT WERE TO BE VOIDED!
...
...
WOOSH
...?

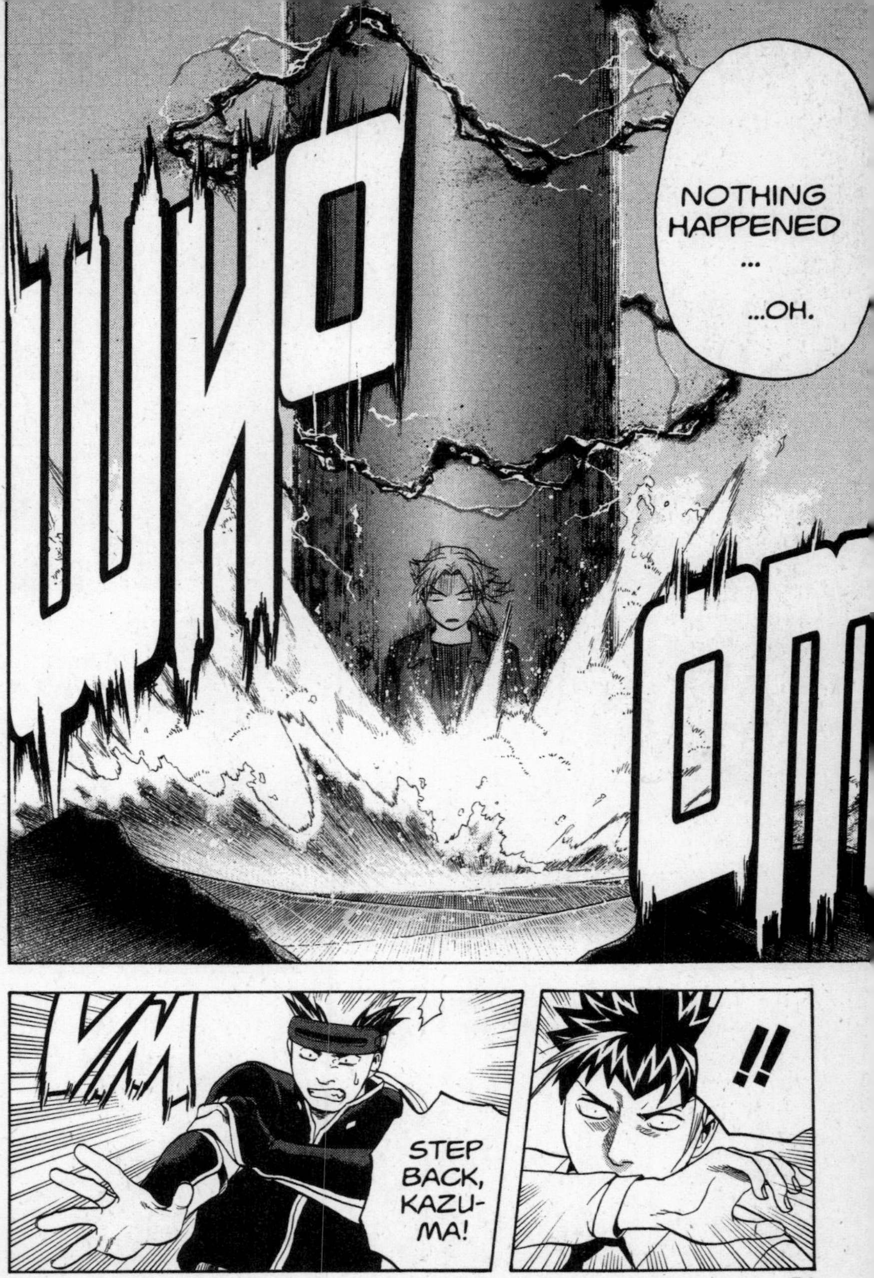
NOTHING HAPPENED ... ...OH.
!!
STEP BACK, KAZUMA!

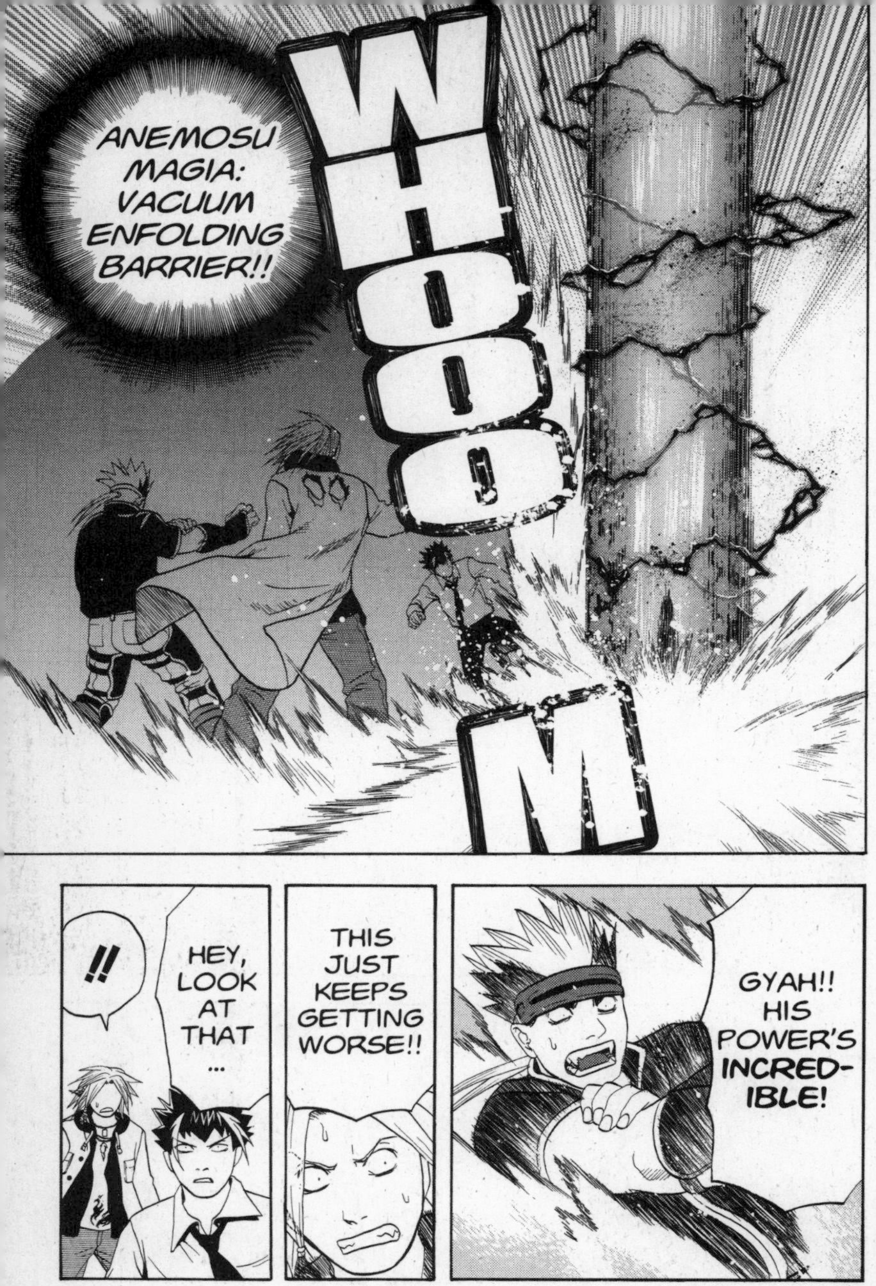
ANEMOSU MAGIA: VACUUM ENFOLDING BARRIER!!
WHOOOM
GYAH!! HIS POWER'S INCREDIBLE!
THIS JUST KEEPS GETTING WORSE!!
HEY, LOOK AT THAT ...
!!

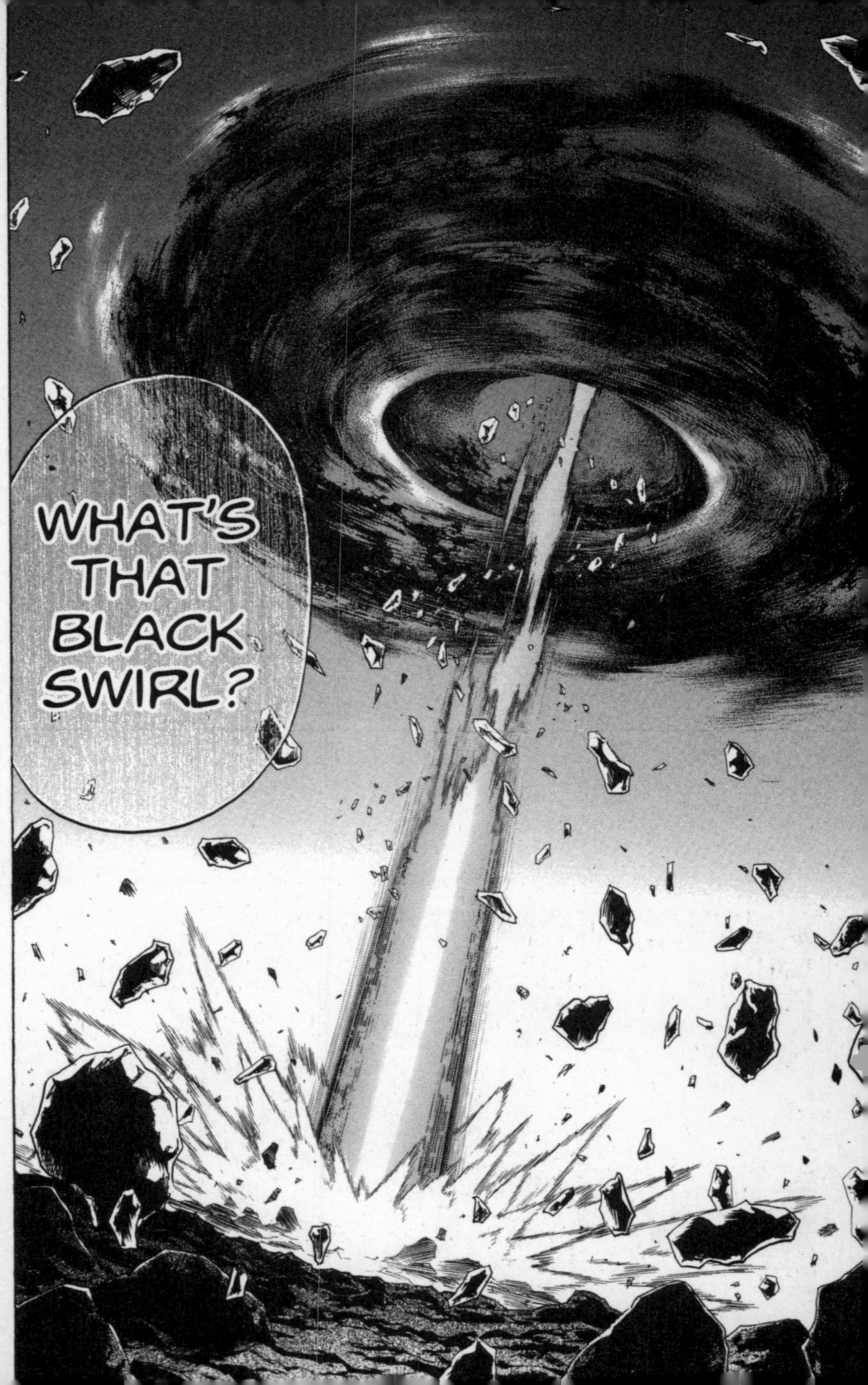
WHAT'S THAT BLACK SWIRL?

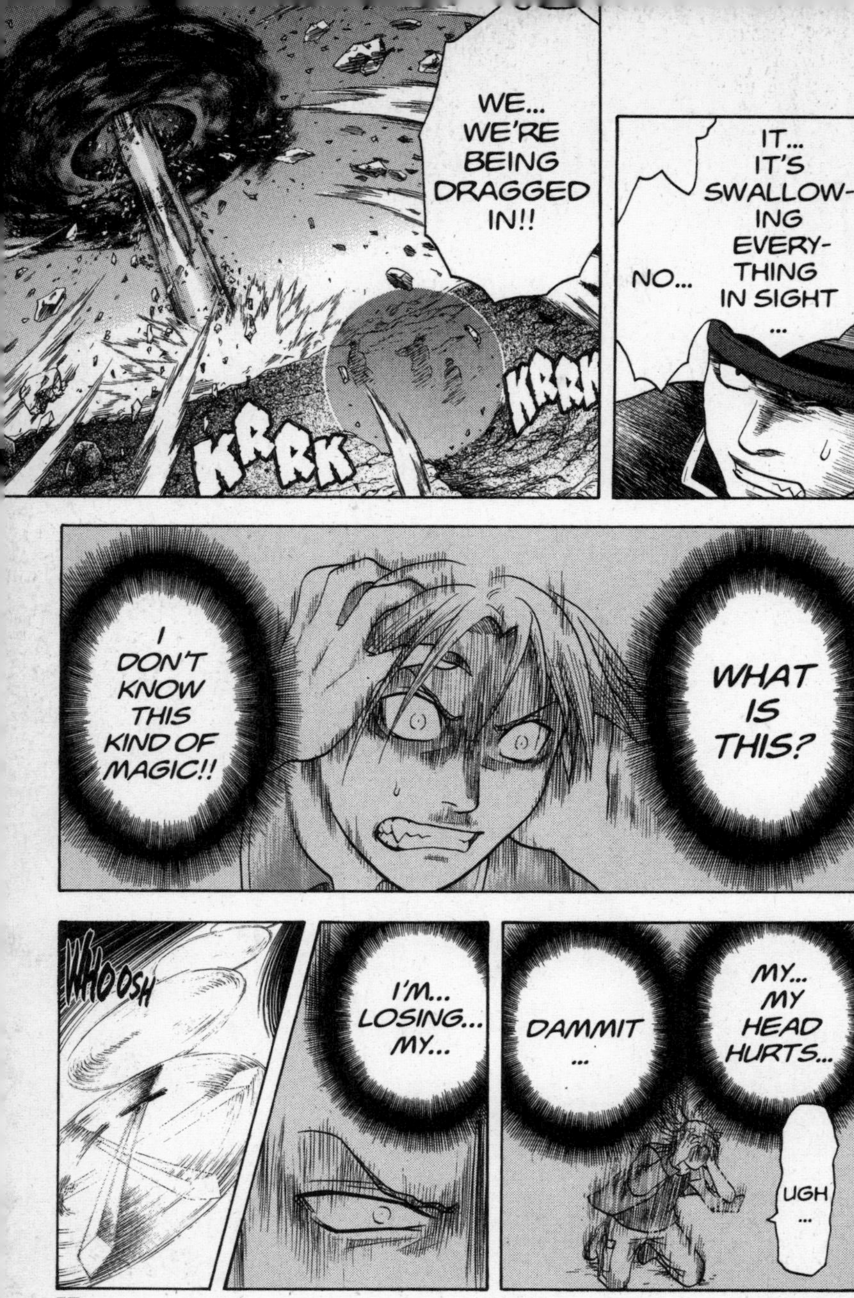
IT... IT'S SWALLOWING-ING EVERY-THING IN SIGHT ...
NO...
WE... WE'RE BEING DRAGGED IN!!
KRRK
KRRK
WHAT IS THIS?
I DON'T KNOW THIS KIND OF MAGIC!!
MY... MY HEAD HURTS...
DAMMIT ...
UGH ...
I'M... LOSING... MY...
WHOOSH

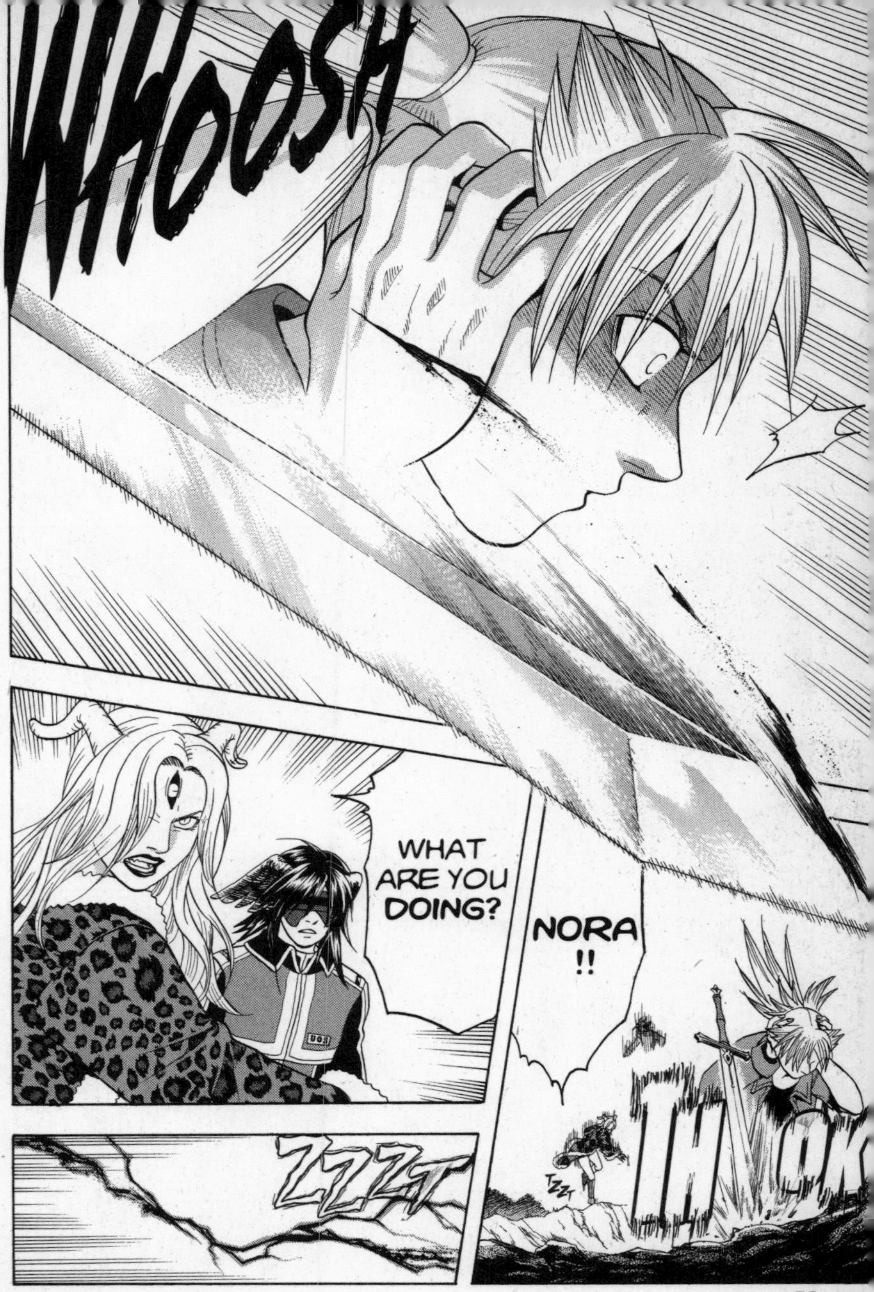
WHOOSH
NORA !!
WHAT ARE YOU DOING?
ZZZT

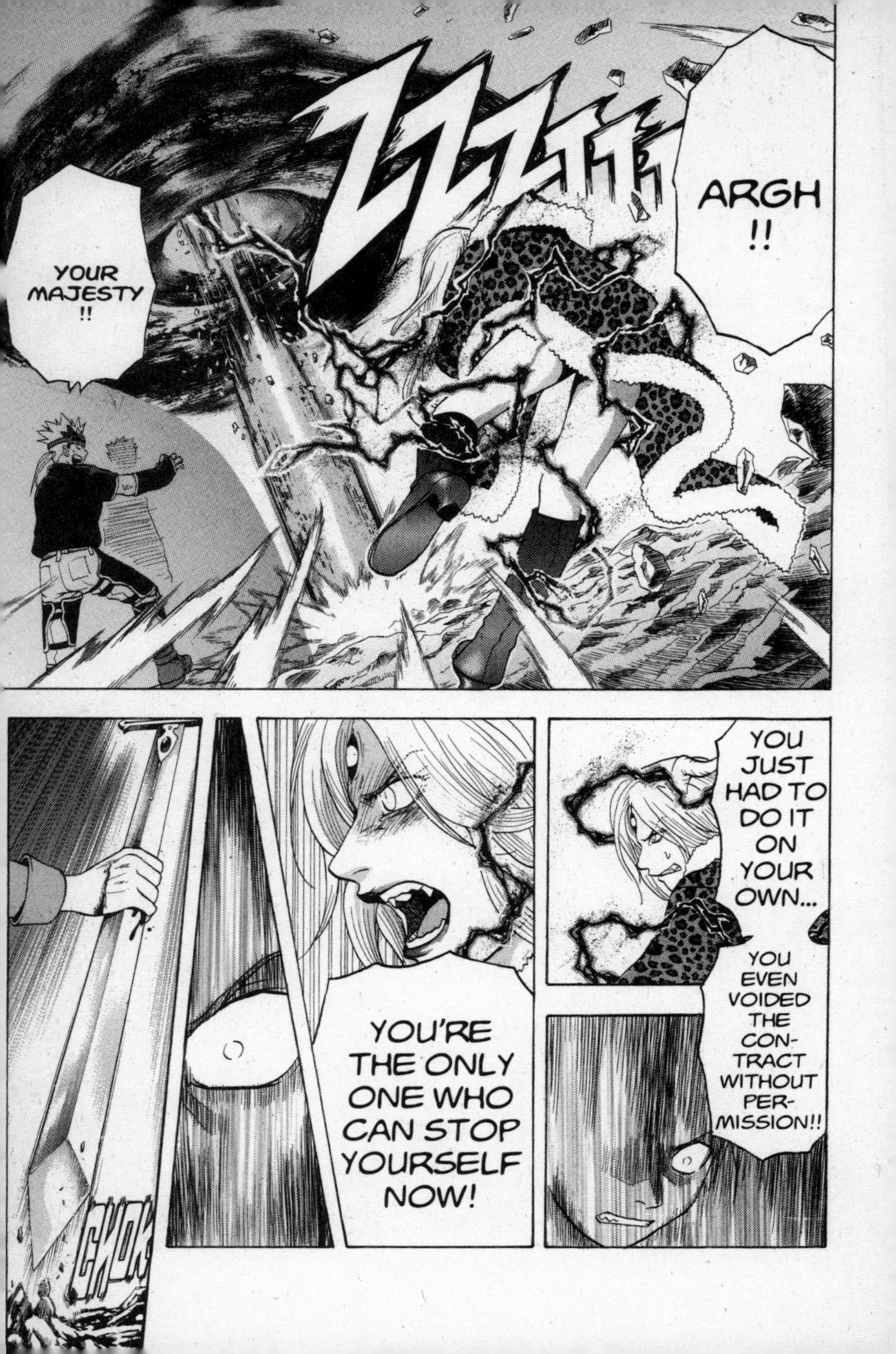
ARGH !!
YOUR MAJESTY !!
YOU JUST HAD TO DO IT ON YOUR OWN...
YOU EVEN VOIDED THE CON-TRACT WITHOUT PER-MISSION!!
YOU'RE THE ONLY ONE WHO CAN STOP YOURSELF NOW!

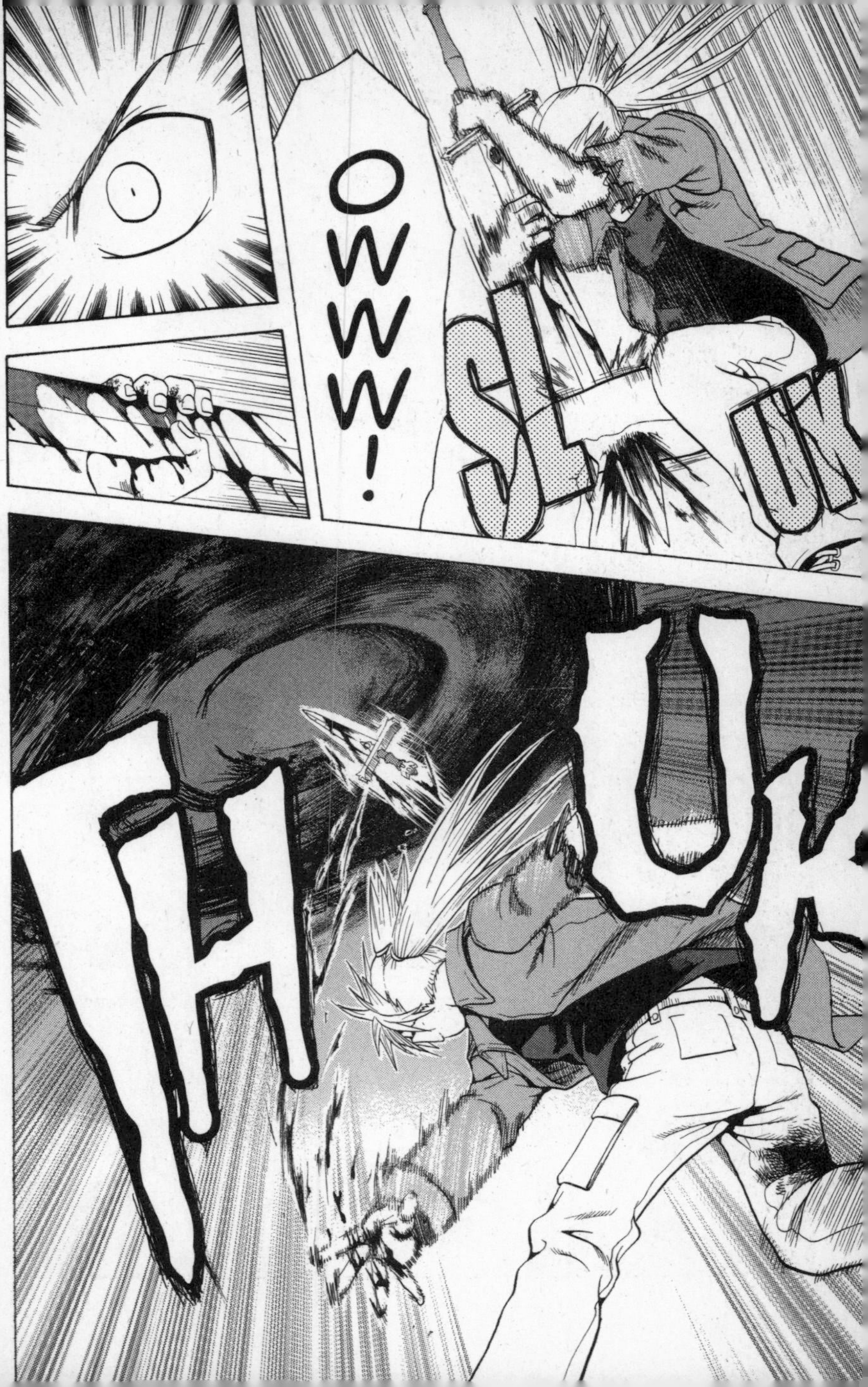
OWWW!

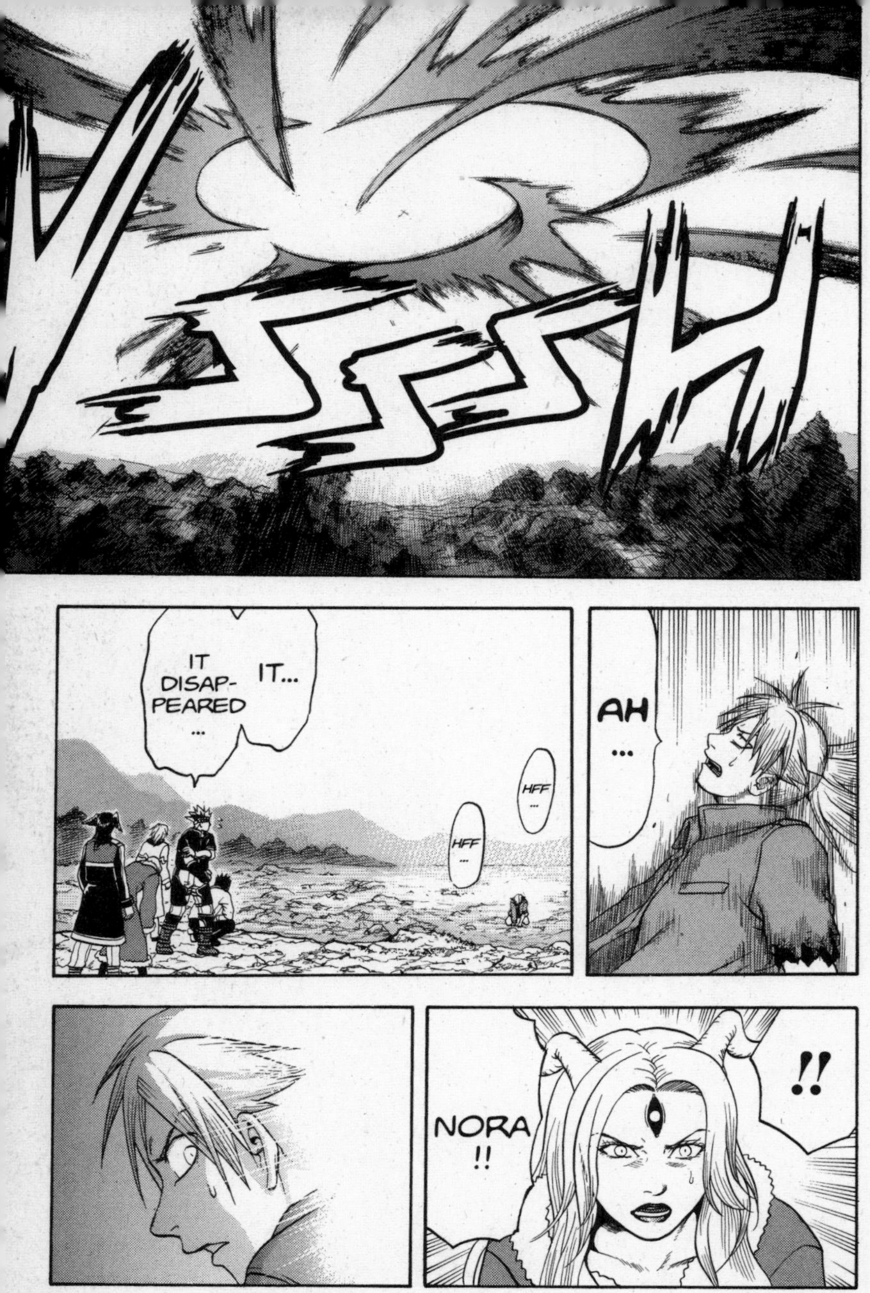
AH ...
IT...
IT DISAP-PEARED ...
HFF ...
HFF ...
!!
NORA !!

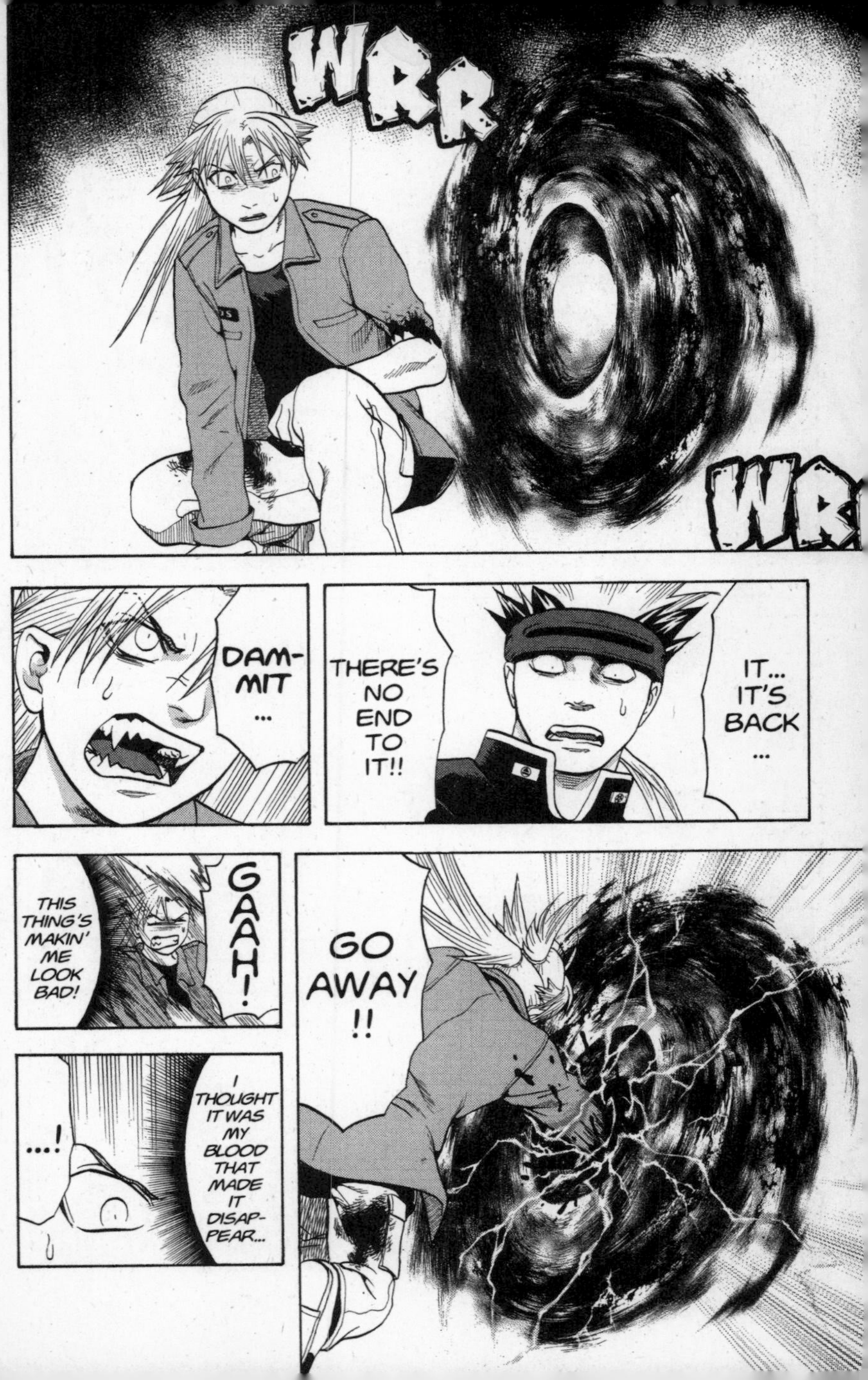
WRR
WRR
IT... IT'S BACK...
THERE'S NO END TO IT!!
DAM-MIT...
GO AWAY!!
GAAAH!
THIS THING'S MAKIN' ME LOOK BAD!
I THOUGHT IT WAS MY BLOOD THAT MADE IT DISAP-PEAR...
...!

READ THIS WAY

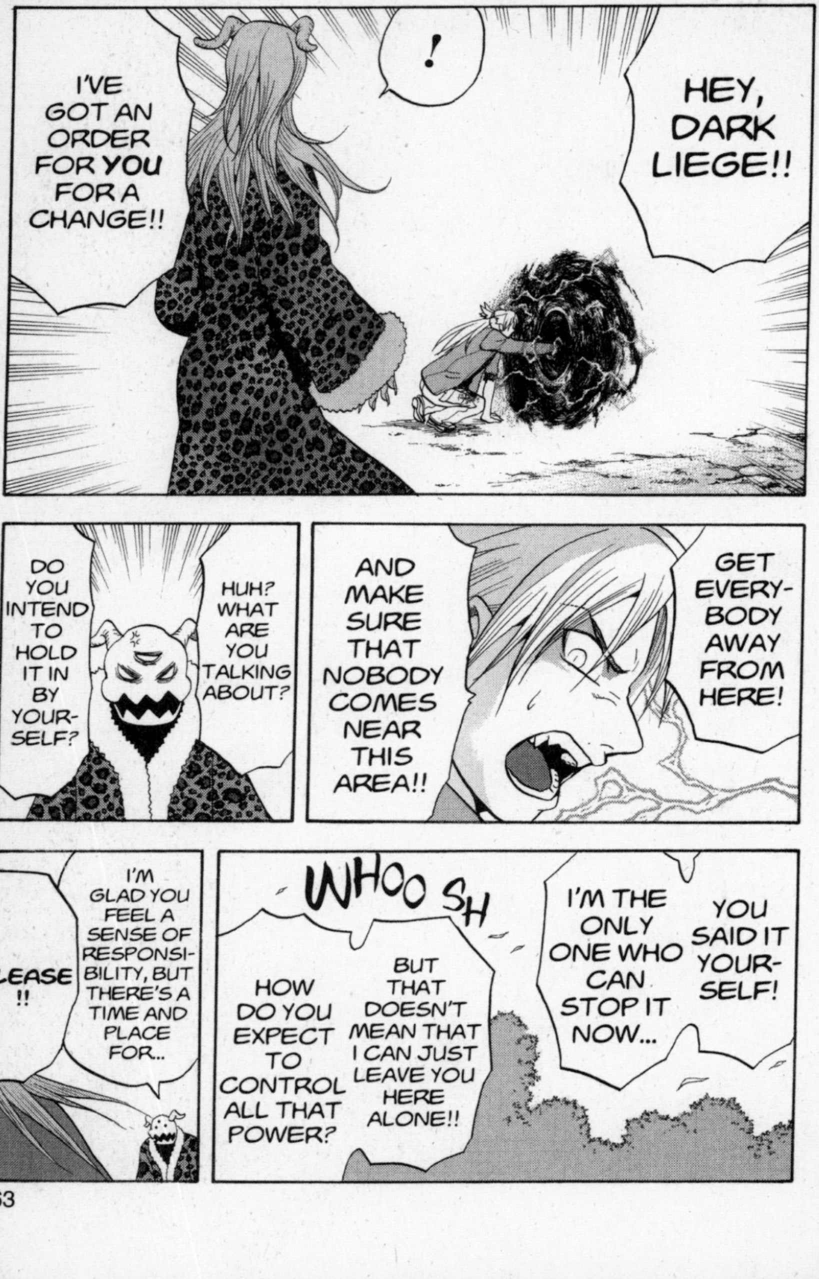
HEY, DARK LIEGE!!
!
I'VE GOT AN ORDER FOR YOU FOR A CHANGE!!
GET EVERY-BODY AWAY FROM HERE!
AND MAKE SURE THAT NOBODY COMES NEAR THIS AREA!!
HUH? WHAT ARE YOU TALKING ABOUT?
DO YOU INTEND TO HOLD IT IN BY YOUR-SELF?
WHOOSH
YOU SAID IT YOUR-SELF!
I'M THE ONLY ONE WHO CAN STOP IT NOW...
BUT THAT DOESN'T MEAN THAT I CAN JUST LEAVE YOU HERE ALONE!!
HOW DO YOU EXPECT TO CONTROL ALL THAT POWER?
I'M GLAD YOU FEEL A SENSE OF RESPONSI-BILITY, BUT THERE'S A TIME AND PLACE FOR...
PLEASE!!

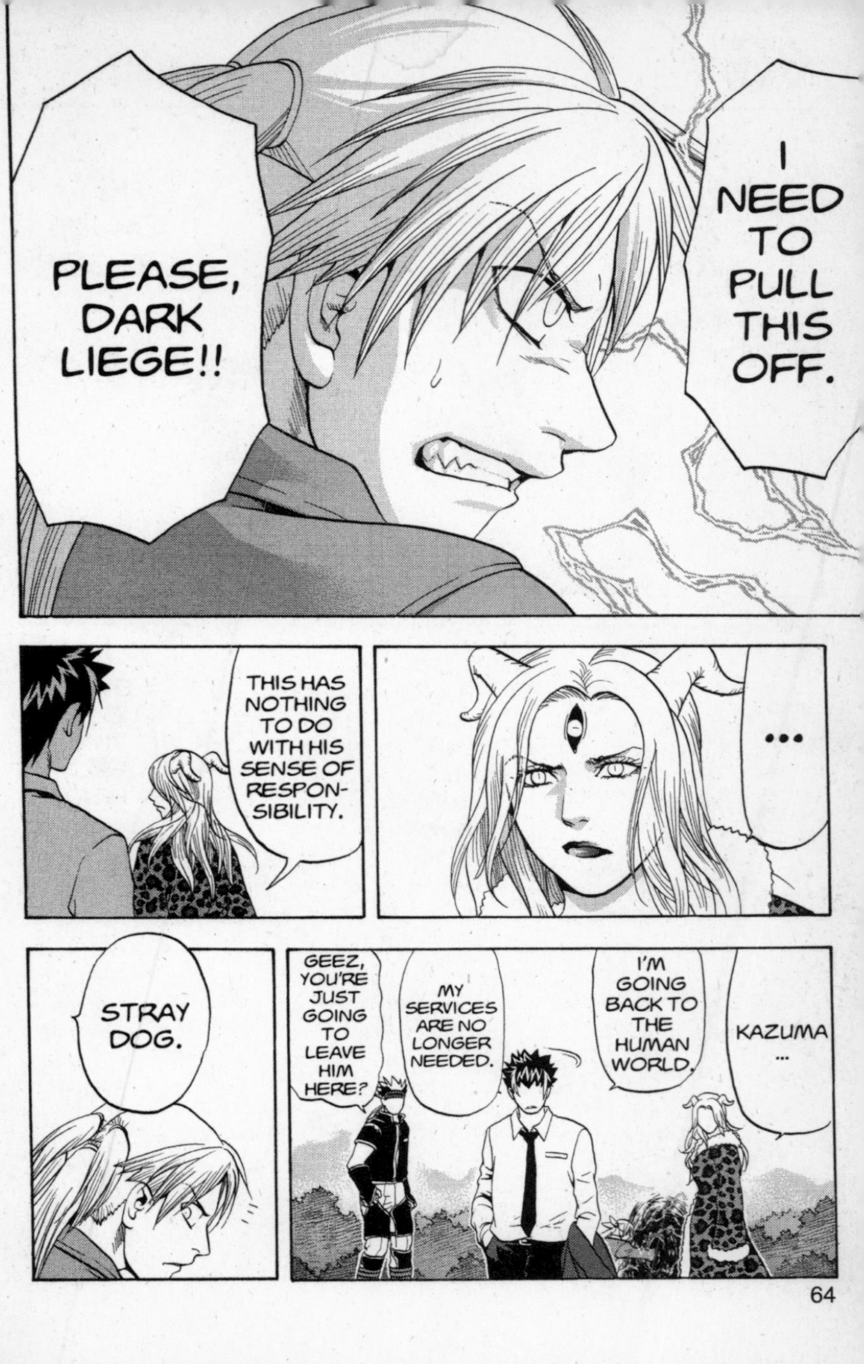
I NEED TO PULL THIS OFF.
PLEASE, DARK LIEGE!!
...
THIS HAS NOTHING TO DO WITH HIS SENSE OF RESPONSIBILITY.
KAZUMA...
I'M GOING BACK TO THE HUMAN WORLD.
MY SERVICES ARE NO LONGER NEEDED.
GEEZ, YOU'RE JUST GOING TO LEAVE HIM HERE?
STRAY DOG.

READ THIS WAY

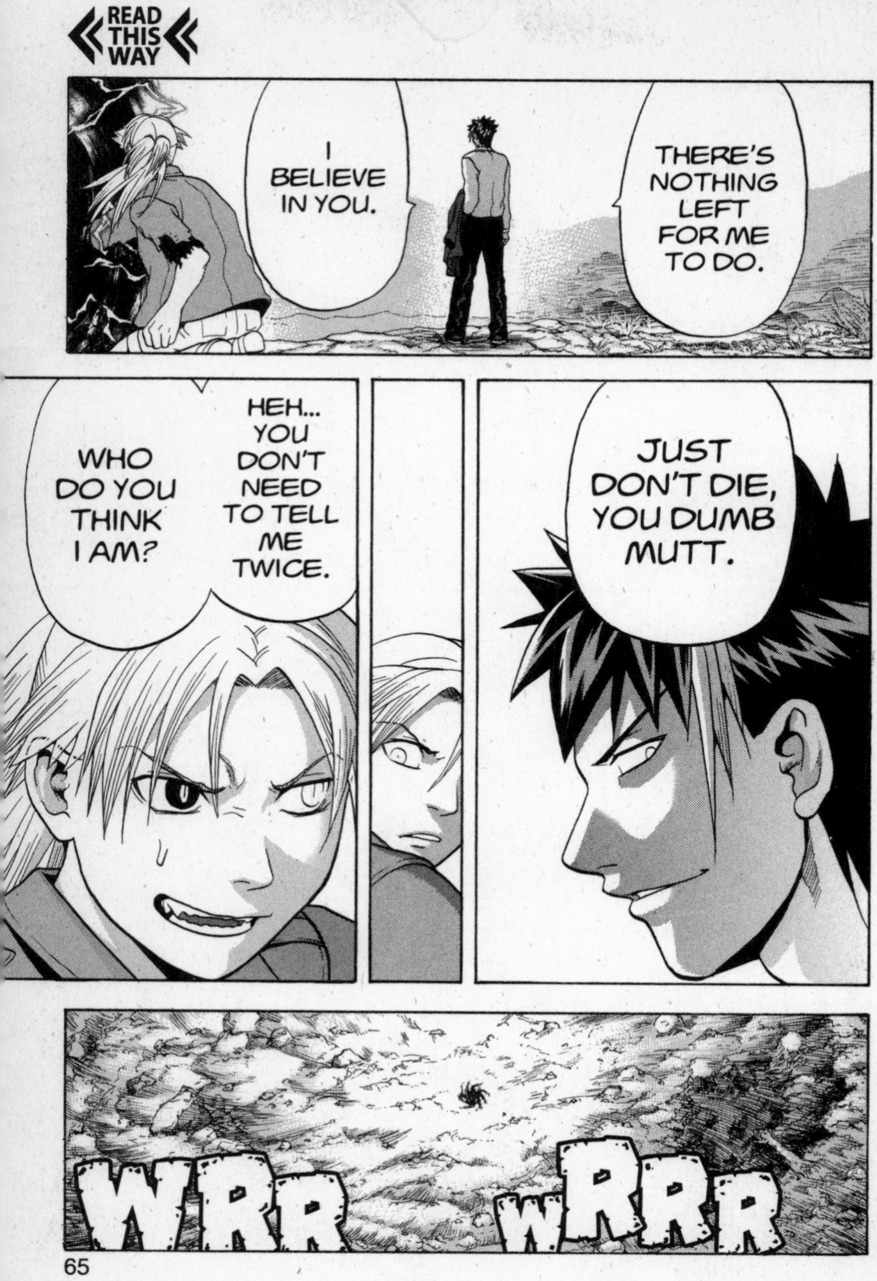
THERE'S NOTHING LEFT FOR ME TO DO.
I BELIEVE IN YOU.
JUST DON'T DIE, YOU DUMB MUTT.
HEH... YOU DON'T NEED TO TELL ME TWICE.
WHO DO YOU THINK I AM?
wRRR
WRR

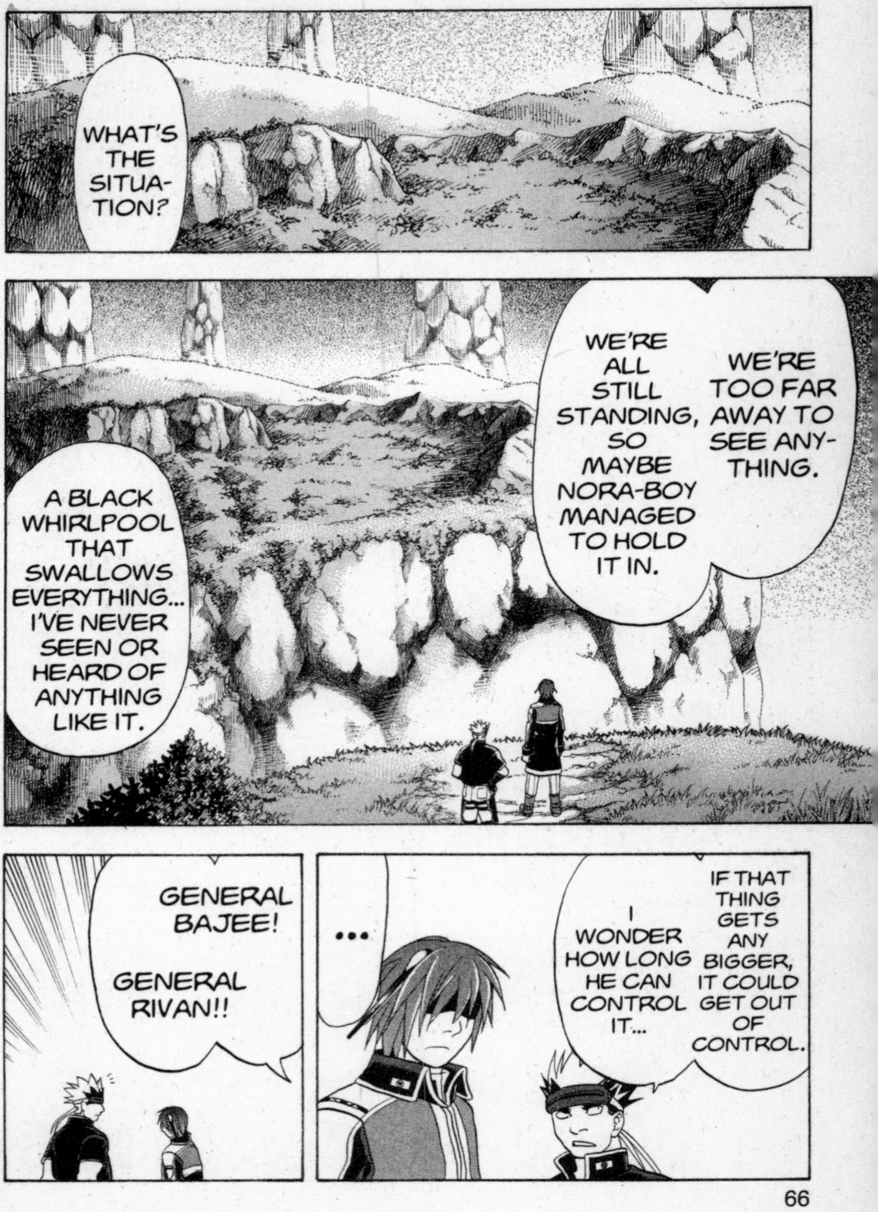
WHAT'S THE SITUATION?
WE'RE TOO FAR AWAY TO SEE ANYTHING.
WE'RE ALL STILL STANDING, SO MAYBE NORA-BOY MANAGED TO HOLD IT IN.
A BLACK WHIRLPOOL THAT SWALLOWS EVERYTHING... I'VE NEVER SEEN OR HEARD OF ANYTHING LIKE IT.
IF THAT THING GETS ANY BIGGER, IT COULD GET OUT OF CONTROL.
I WONDER HOW LONG HE CAN CONTROL IT...
...
GENERAL BAJEE!
GENERAL RIVAN!!

READ THIS WAY

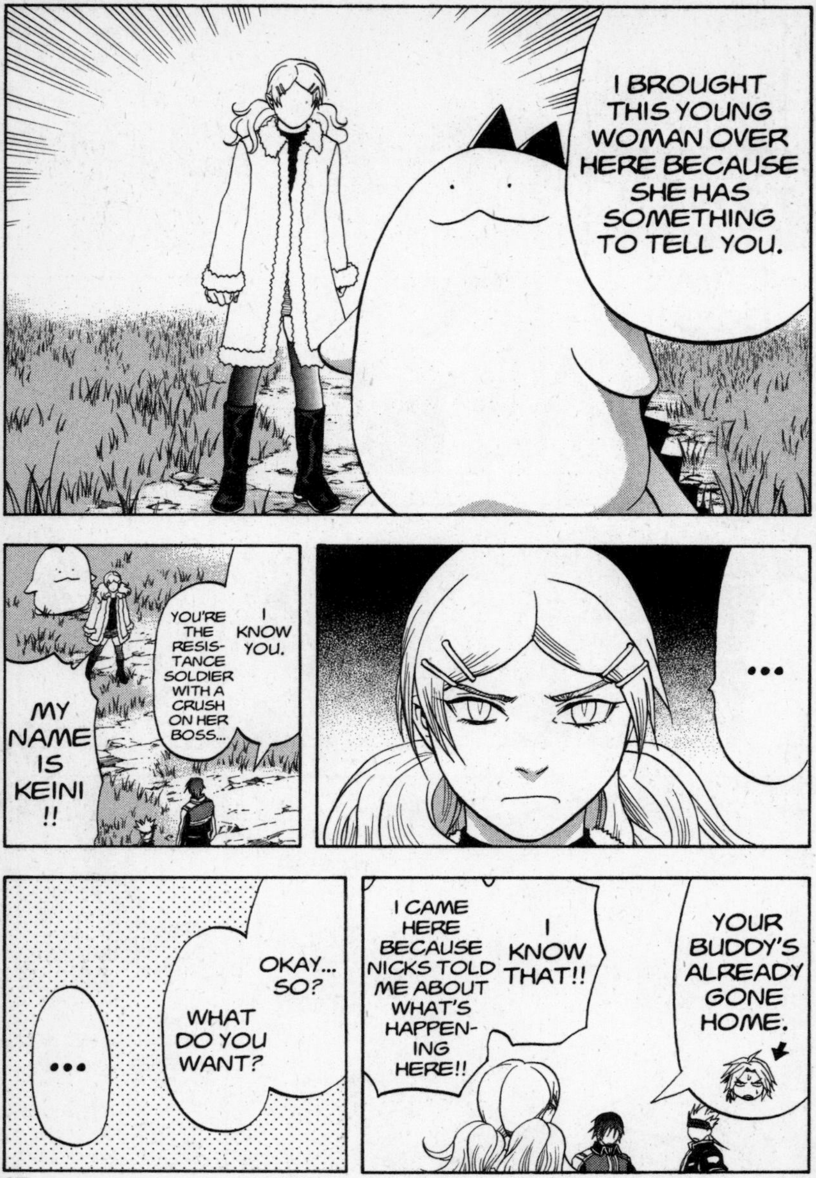

I BROUGHT THIS YOUNG WOMAN OVER HERE BECAUSE SHE HAS SOMETHING TO TELL YOU.
...
I KNOW YOU.
YOU'RE THE RESIS-TANCE SOLDIER WITH A CRUSH ON HER BOSS...
MY NAME IS KEINI !!
YOUR BUDDY'S ALREADY GONE HOME.
I KNOW THAT!!
I CAME HERE BECAUSE NICKS TOLD ME ABOUT WHAT'S HAPPEN-ING HERE!!
OKAY... SO?
WHAT DO YOU WANT?
...

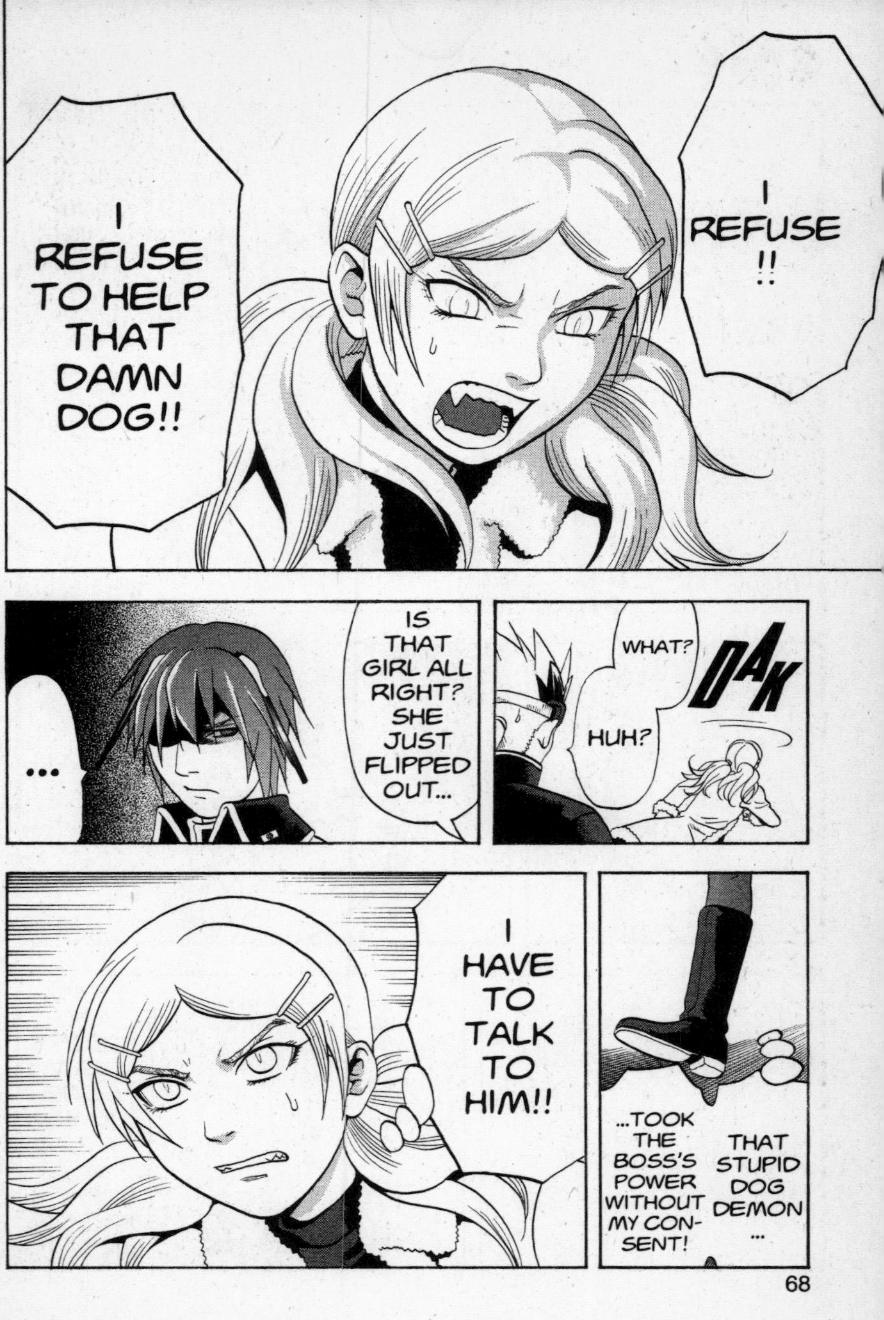
I REFUSE!!
I REFUSE TO HELP THAT DAMN DOG!!
DAK
WHAT?
HUH?
IS THAT GIRL ALL RIGHT? SHE JUST FLIPPED OUT...
...
THAT STUPID DOG DEMON...
...TOOK THE BOSS'S POWER WITHOUT MY CON-SENT!
I HAVE TO TALK TO HIM!!

READ THIS WAY

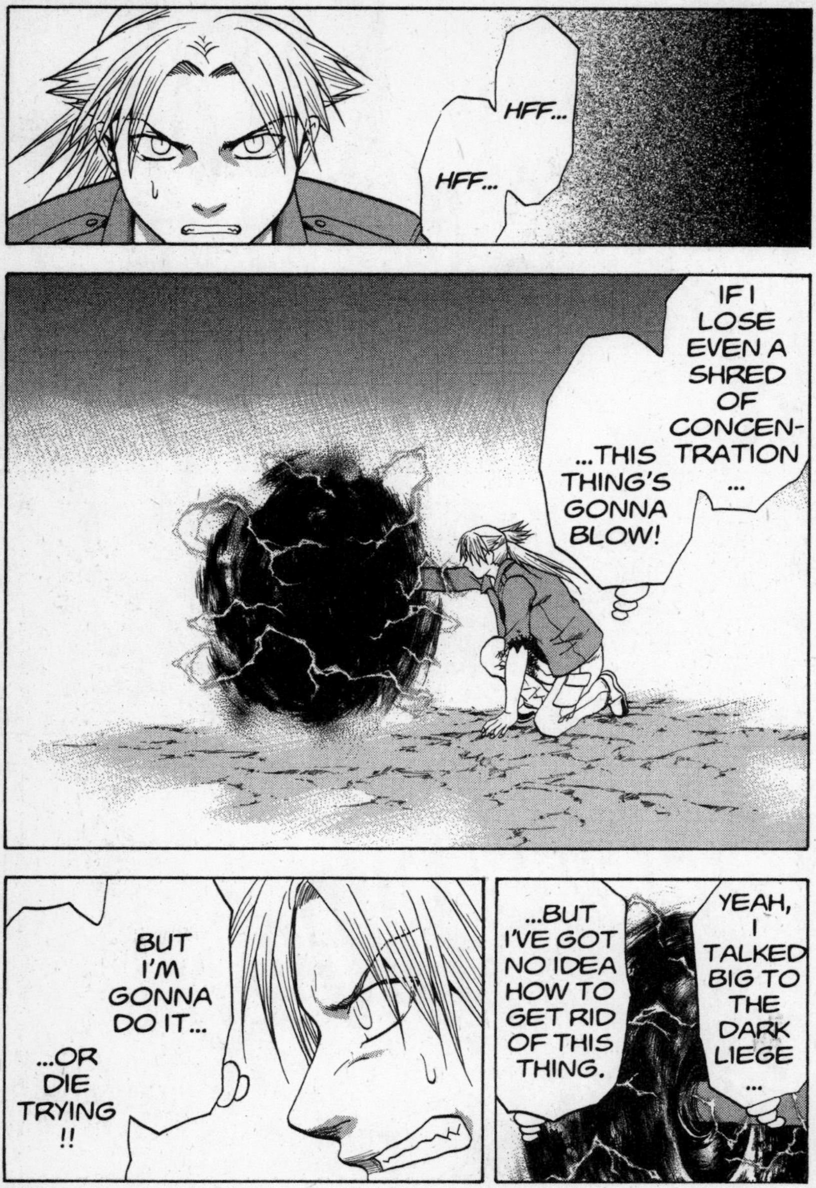
HFF...
HFF...
IF I LOSE EVEN A SHRED OF CONCENTRATION...
...THIS THING'S GONNA BLOW!
YEAH, I TALKED BIG TO THE DARK LIEGE...
...BUT I'VE GOT NO IDEA HOW TO GET RID OF THIS THING.
BUT I'M GONNA DO IT...
...OR DIE TRYING!!

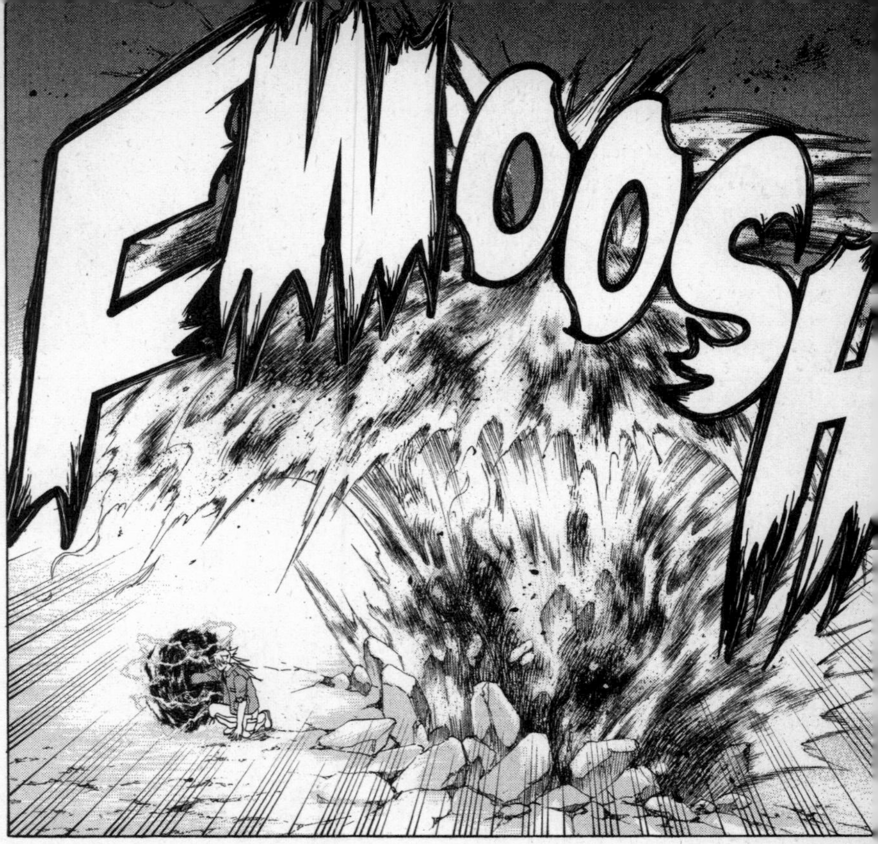
FWOOSH

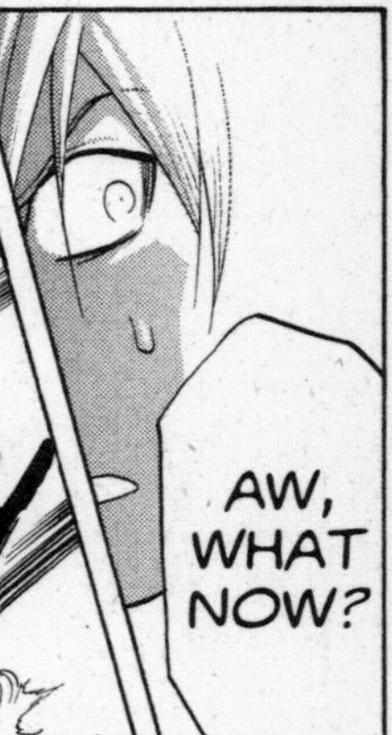
AW, WHAT NOW?

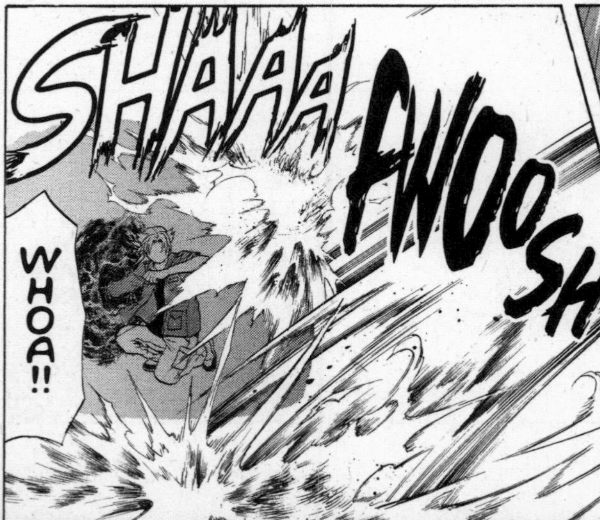
SHAAA
FWOOSH
WHOA!!

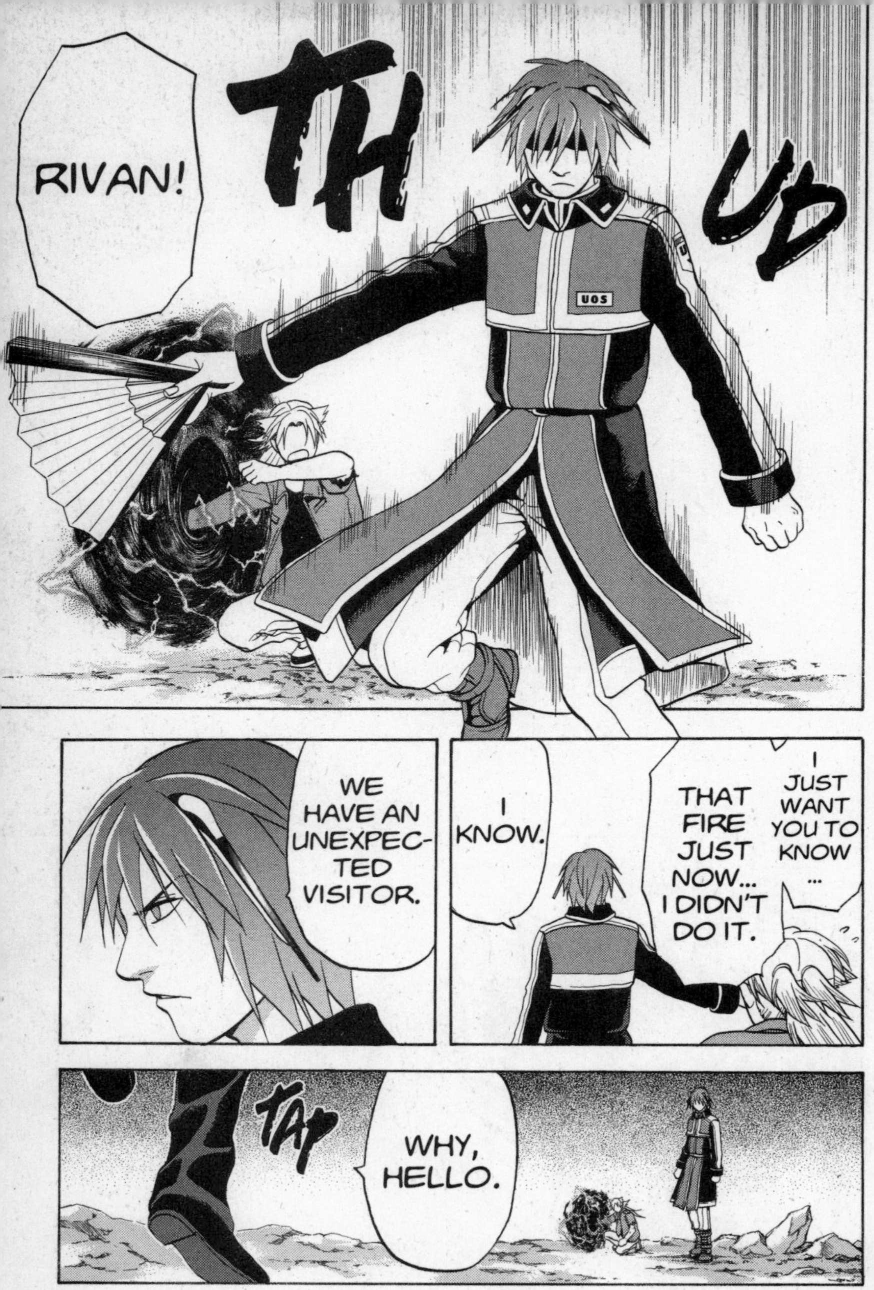
THUD
RIVAN!
I JUST WANT YOU TO KNOW ...
THAT FIRE JUST NOW... I DIDN'T DO IT.
I KNOW.
WE HAVE AN UNEXPECTED VISITOR.
WHY, HELLO.
TAP

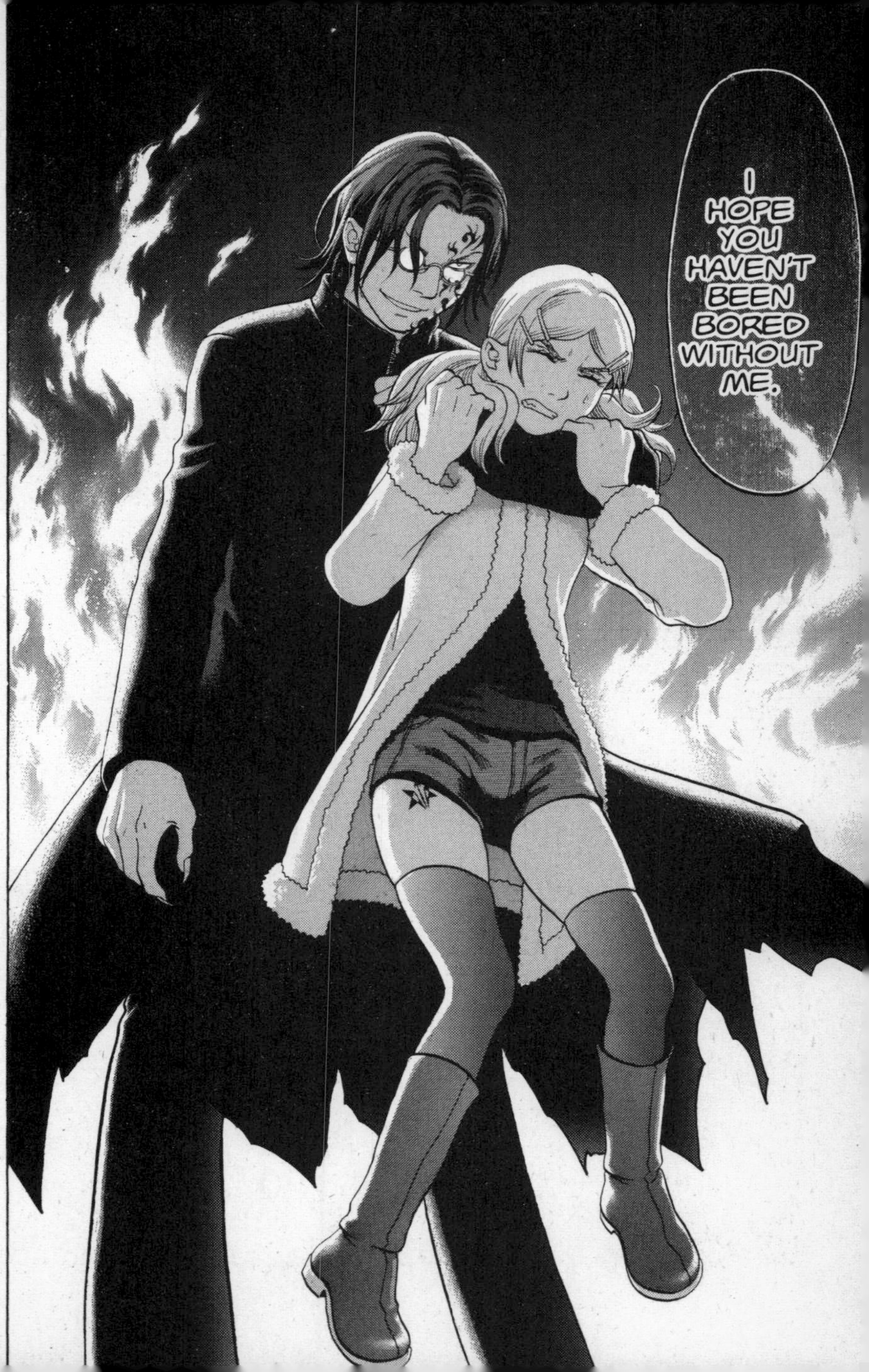
I HOPE YOU HAVEN'T BEEN BORED WITHOUT ME.

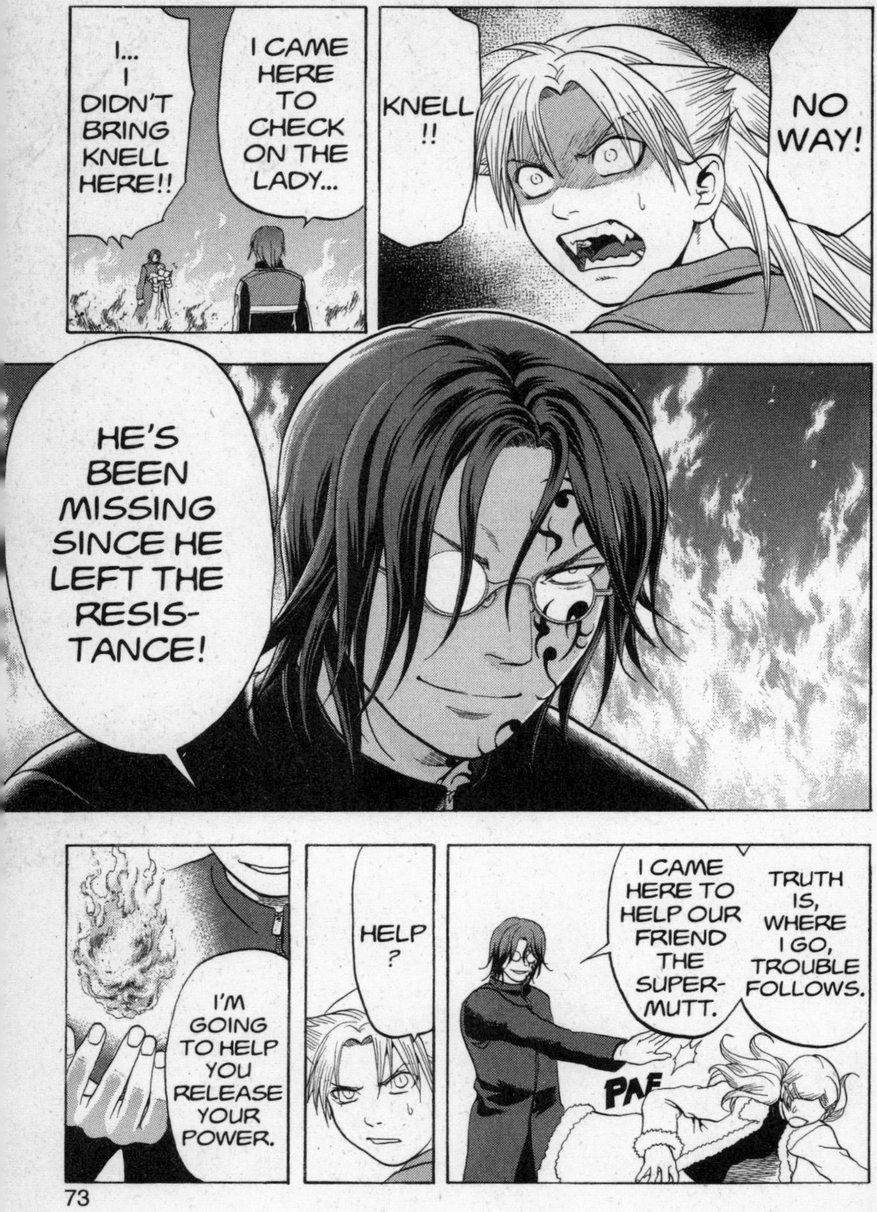
NO WAY!
KNELL!!
I CAME HERE TO CHECK ON THE LADY...
I... I DIDN'T BRING KNELL HERE!!
HE'S BEEN MISSING SINCE HE LEFT THE RESISTANCE!
TRUTH IS, WHERE I GO, TROUBLE FOLLOWS.
I CAME HERE TO HELP OUR FRIEND THE SUPER-MUTT.
PAF
HELP?
I'M GOING TO HELP YOU RELEASE YOUR POWER.

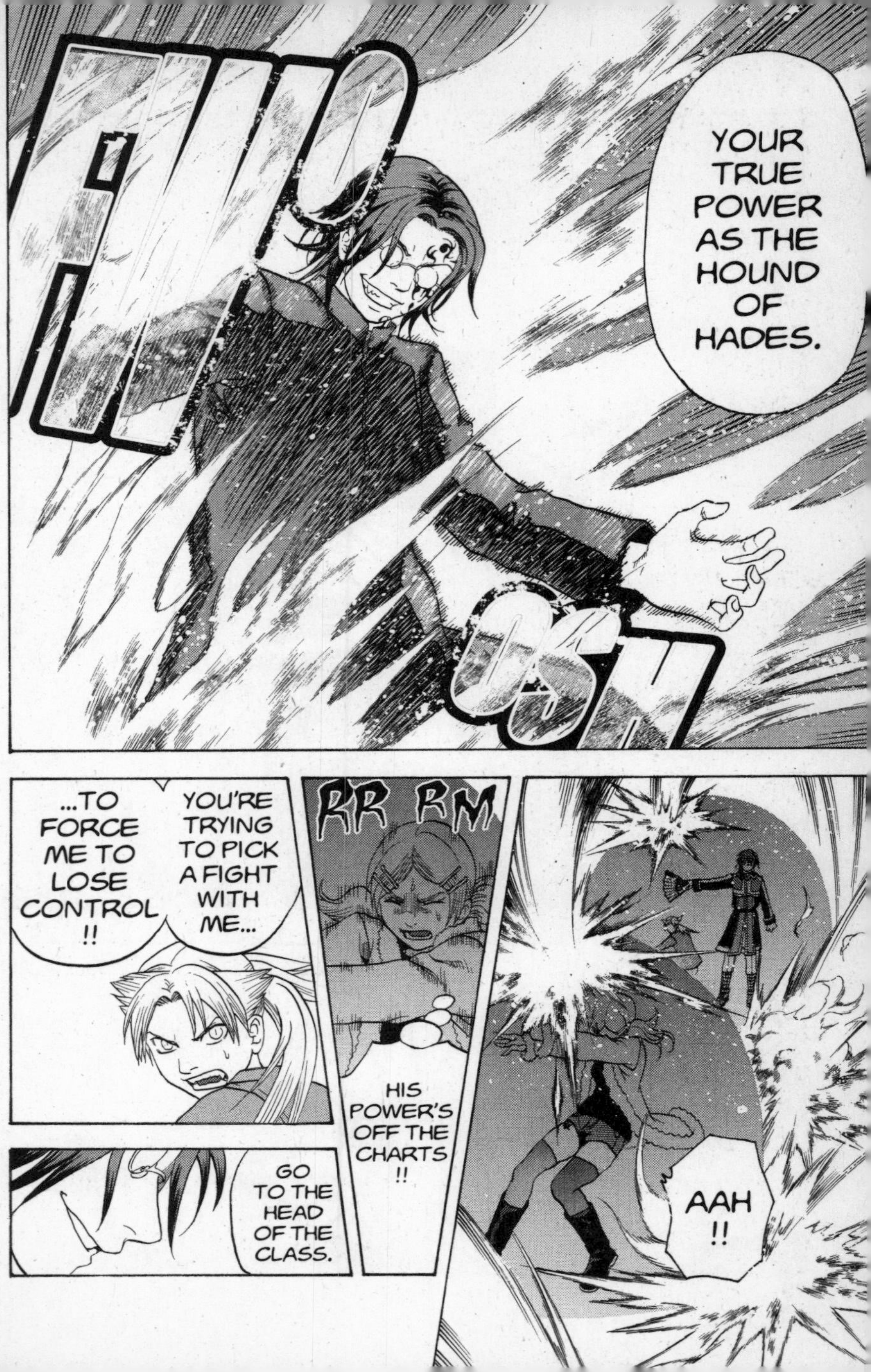
YOUR TRUE POWER AS THE HOUND OF HADES.
AAH !!
RR RM
HIS POWER'S OFF THE CHARTS !!
YOU'RE TRYING TO PICK A FIGHT WITH ME...
...TO FORCE ME TO LOSE CONTROL !!
GO TO THE HEAD OF THE CLASS.

READ THIS WAY

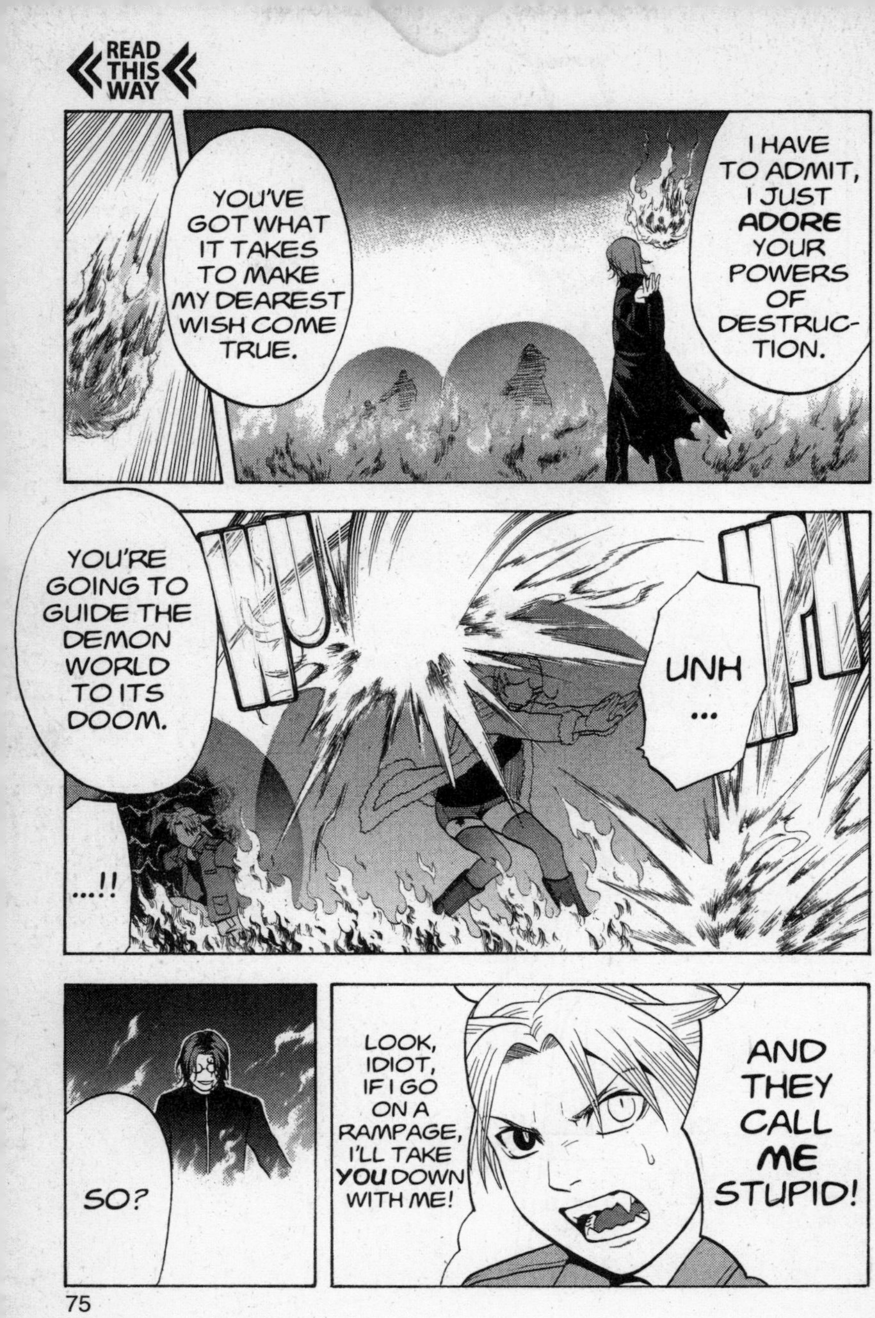
I HAVE TO ADMIT, I JUST **ADORE** YOUR POWERS OF DESTRUCTION.
YOU'VE GOT WHAT IT TAKES TO MAKE MY DEAREST WISH COME TRUE.
UNH ...
YOU'RE GOING TO GUIDE THE DEMON WORLD TO ITS DOOM.
...!!
AND THEY CALL **ME** STUPID!
LOOK, IDIOT, IF I GO ON A RAMPAGE, I'LL TAKE **YOU** DOWN WITH ME!
SO?

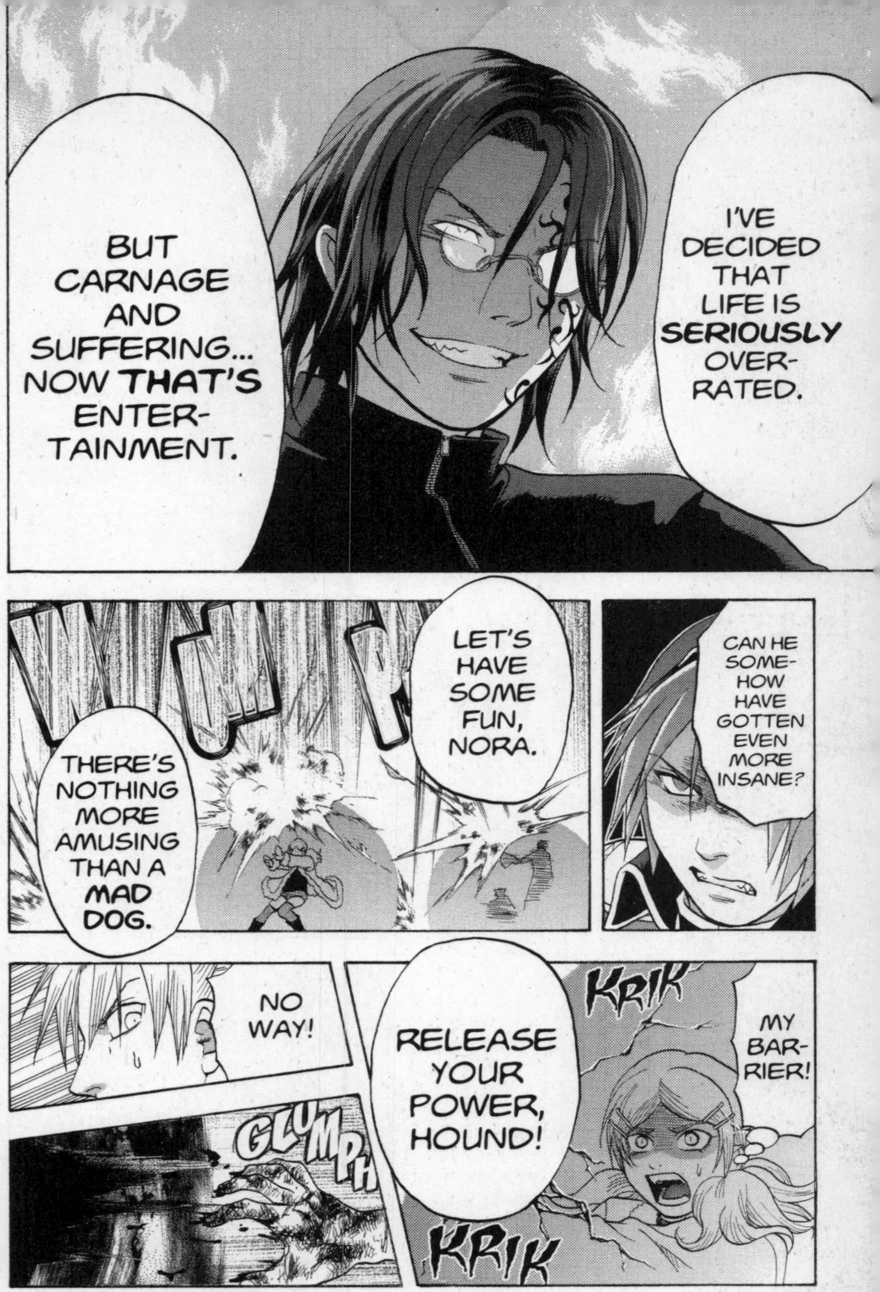
I'VE DECIDED THAT LIFE IS SERIOUSLY OVER-RATED.
BUT CARNAGE AND SUFFERING... NOW THAT'S ENTER-TAINMENT.
CAN HE SOME-HOW HAVE GOTTEN EVEN MORE INSANE?
LET'S HAVE SOME FUN, NORA.
THERE'S NOTHING MORE AMUSING THAN A MAD DOG.
KRIK
MY BAR-RIER!
RELEASE YOUR POWER, HOUND!
KRIK
NO WAY!
GLUMPH

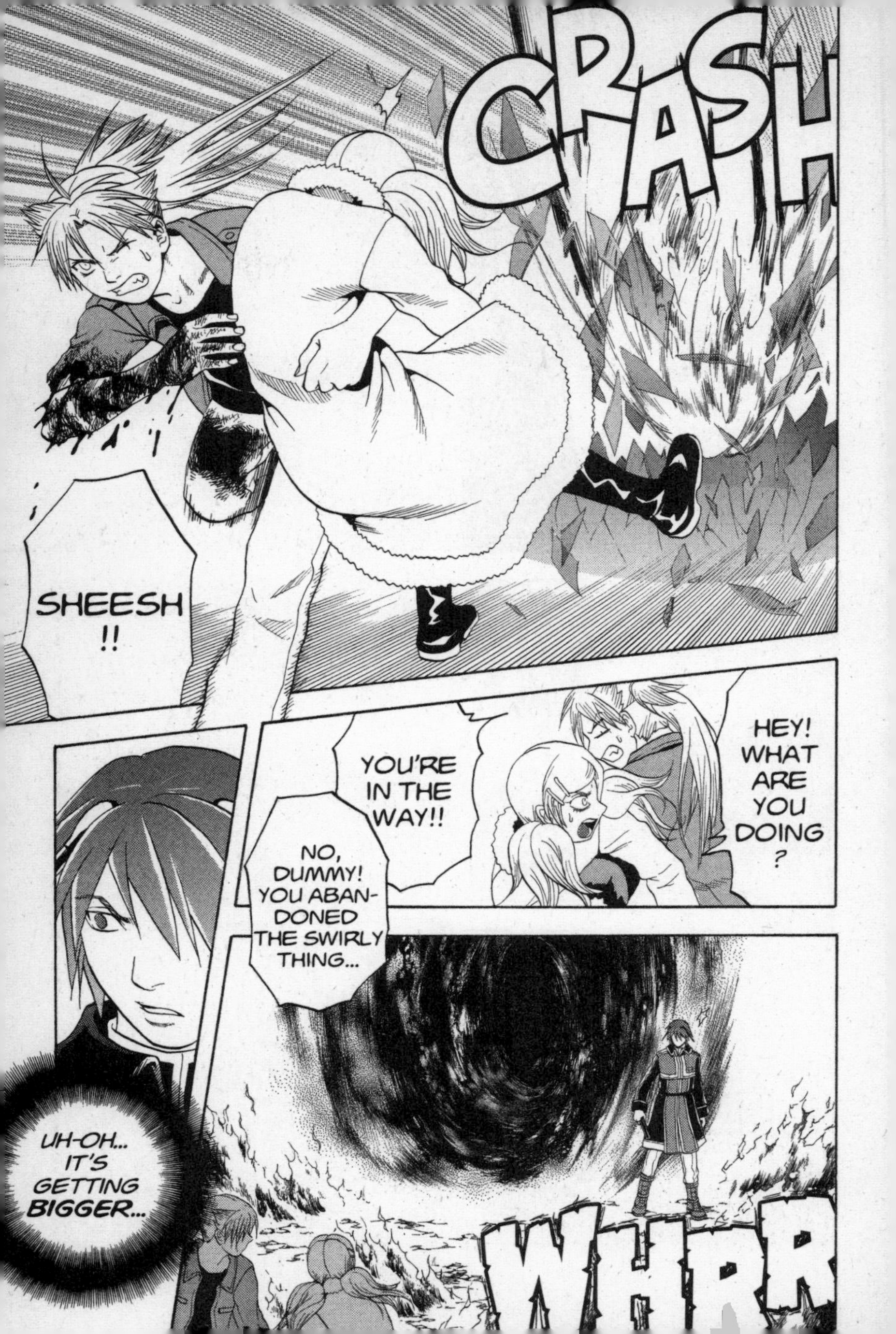
CRASH
SHEESH!!
HEY! WHAT ARE YOU DOING?
YOU'RE IN THE WAY!!
NO, DUMMY! YOU ABANDONED THE SWIRLY THING...
WHRR
UH-OH... IT'S GETTING BIGGER...

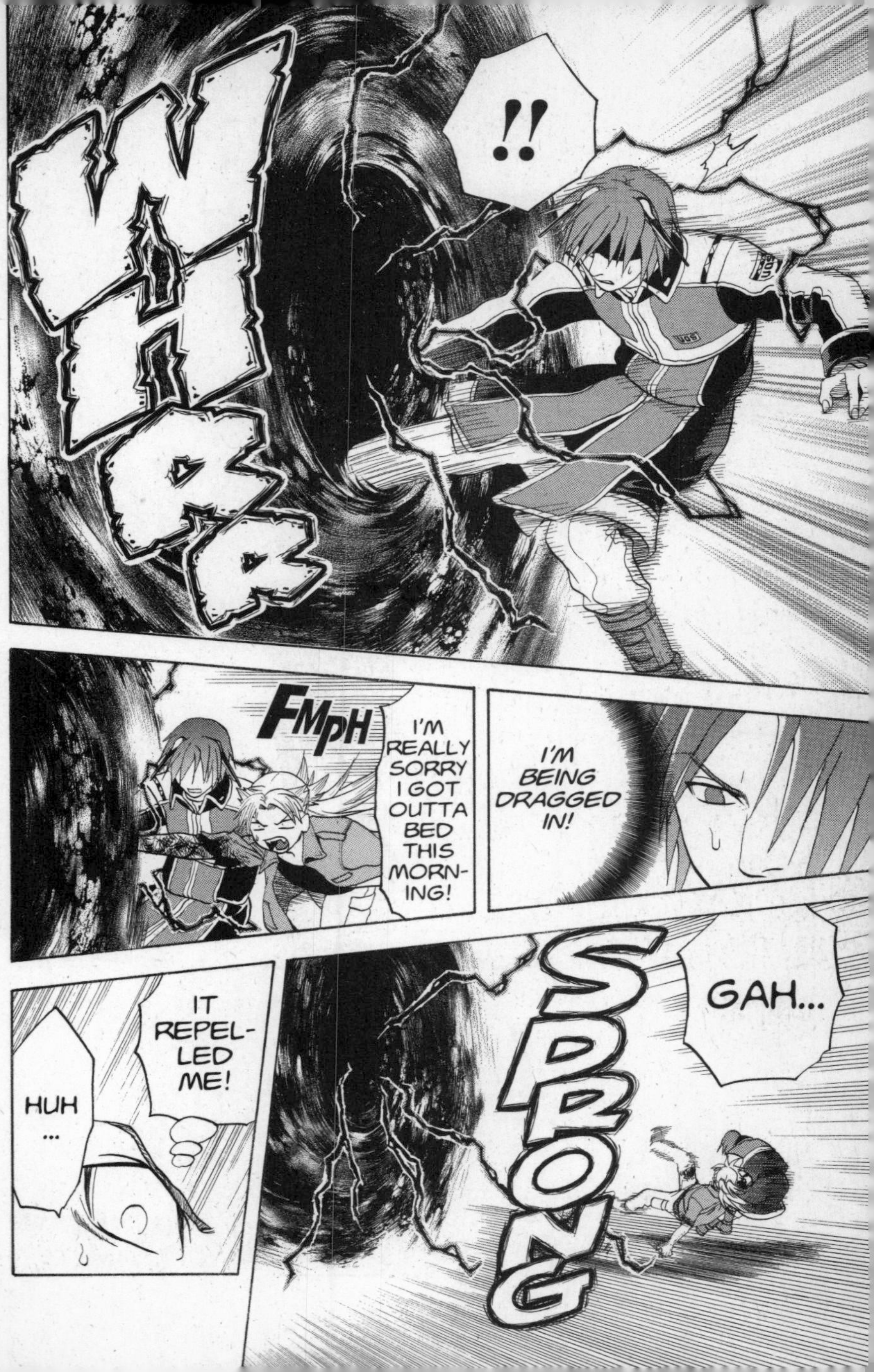
!!
I'M BEING DRAGGED IN!
FMPH
I'M REALLY SORRY I GOT OUTTA BED THIS MORNING!
GAH...
SPRONG
IT REPEL-LED ME!
HUH ...

READ THIS WAY

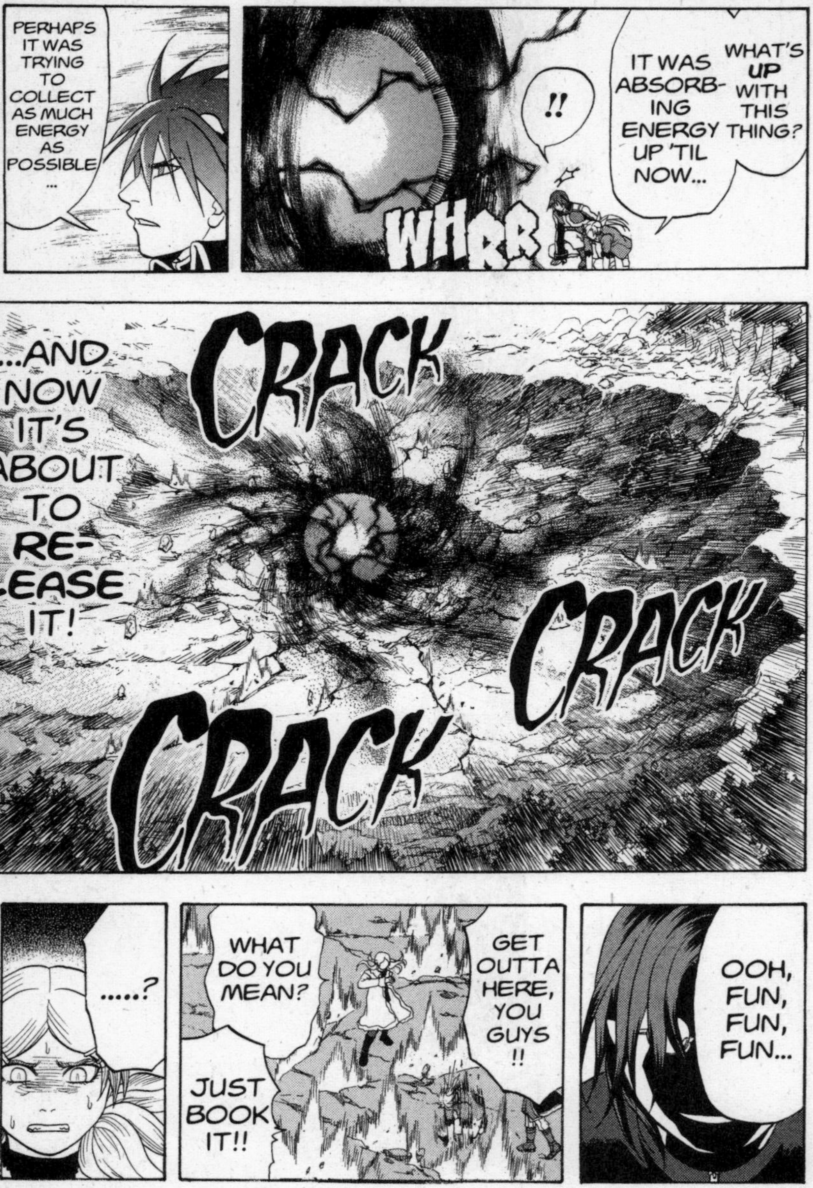
WHAT'S UP WITH THIS THING?
IT WAS ABSORBING ENERGY UP 'TIL NOW...
!!
WHRR
PERHAPS IT WAS TRYING TO COLLECT AS MUCH ENERGY AS POSSIBLE...
CRACK
...AND NOW IT'S ABOUT TO RELEASE IT!
CRACK
CRACK
OOH, FUN, FUN, FUN...
GET OUTTA HERE, YOU GUYS!!
WHAT DO YOU MEAN?
JUST BOOK IT!!
.....?

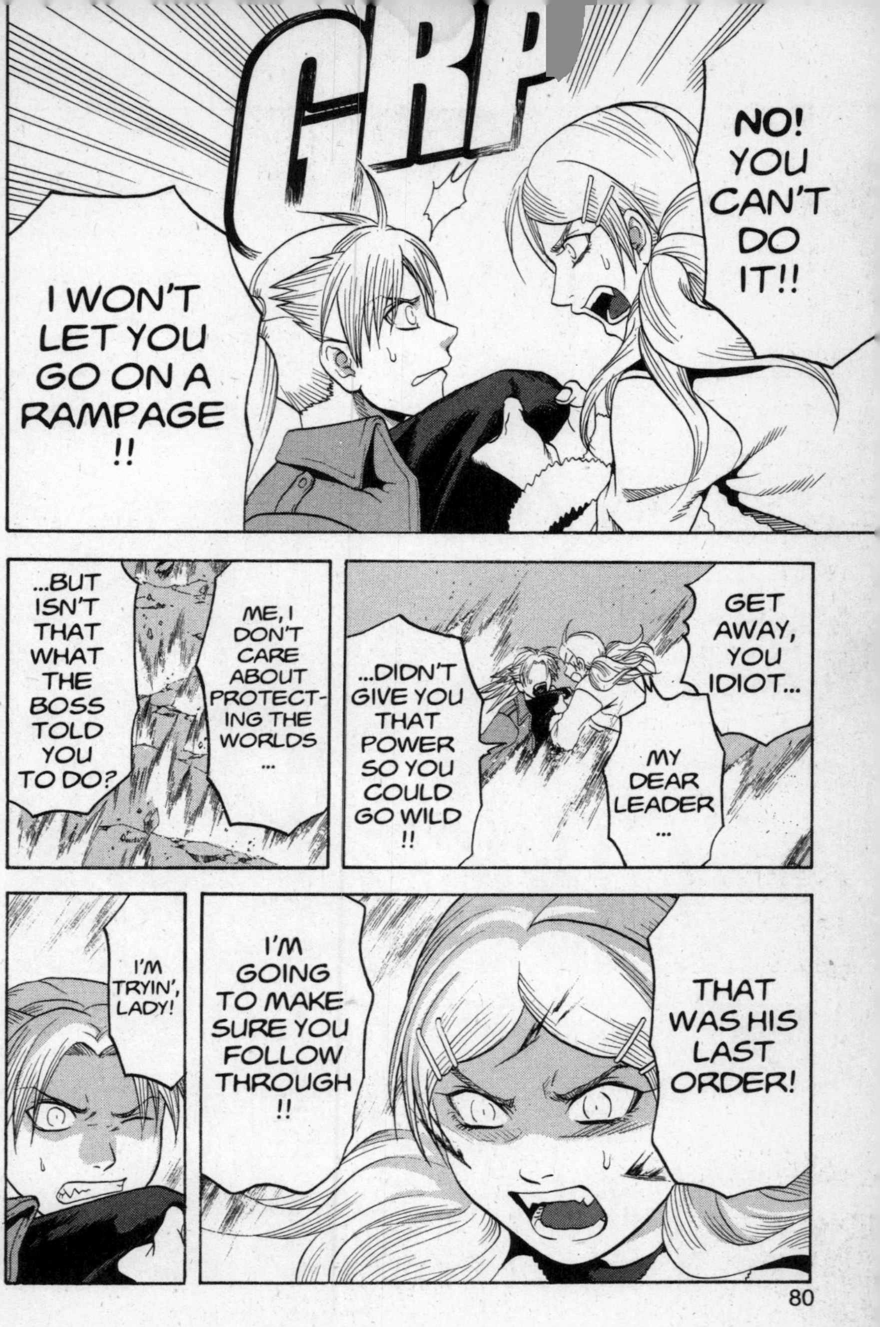
CRP
NO! YOU CAN'T DO IT!!
I WON'T LET YOU GO ON A RAMPAGE!!
GET AWAY, YOU IDIOT...
MY DEAR LEADER...
...DIDN'T GIVE YOU THAT POWER SO YOU COULD GO WILD!!
ME, I DON'T CARE ABOUT PROTECTING THE WORLDS...
...BUT ISN'T THAT WHAT THE BOSS TOLD YOU TO DO?
THAT WAS HIS LAST ORDER!
I'M GOING TO MAKE SURE YOU FOLLOW THROUGH!!
I'M TRYIN', LADY!

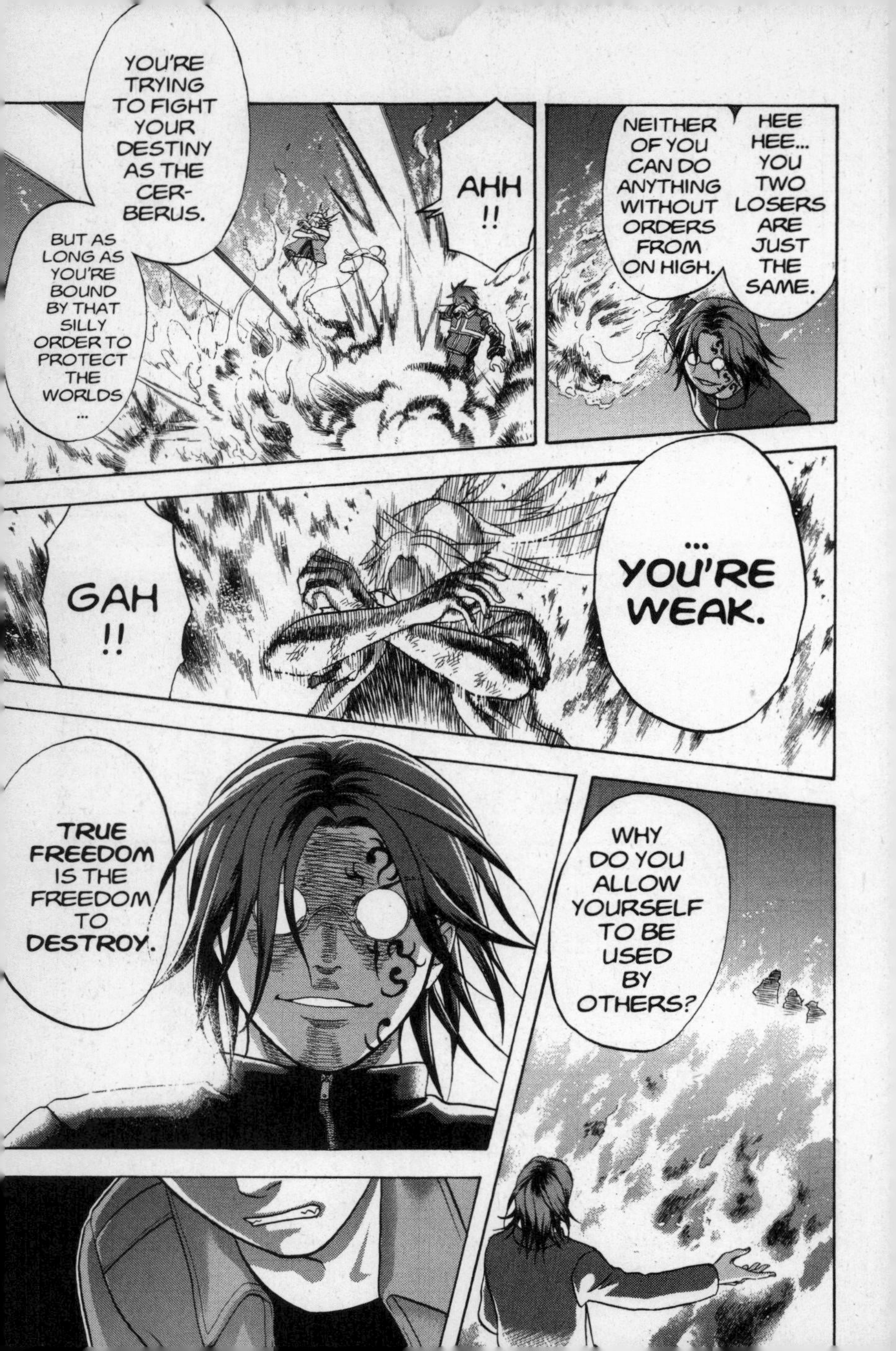
HEE HEE... YOU TWO LOSERS ARE JUST THE SAME.
NEITHER OF YOU CAN DO ANYTHING WITHOUT ORDERS FROM ON HIGH.
YOU'RE TRYING TO FIGHT YOUR DESTINY AS THE CER-BERUS.
AHH!!
BUT AS LONG AS YOU'RE BOUND BY THAT SILLY ORDER TO PROTECT THE WORLDS...
...YOU'RE WEAK.
GAH!!
WHY DO YOU ALLOW YOURSELF TO BE USED BY OTHERS?
TRUE FREEDOM IS THE FREEDOM TO DESTROY.

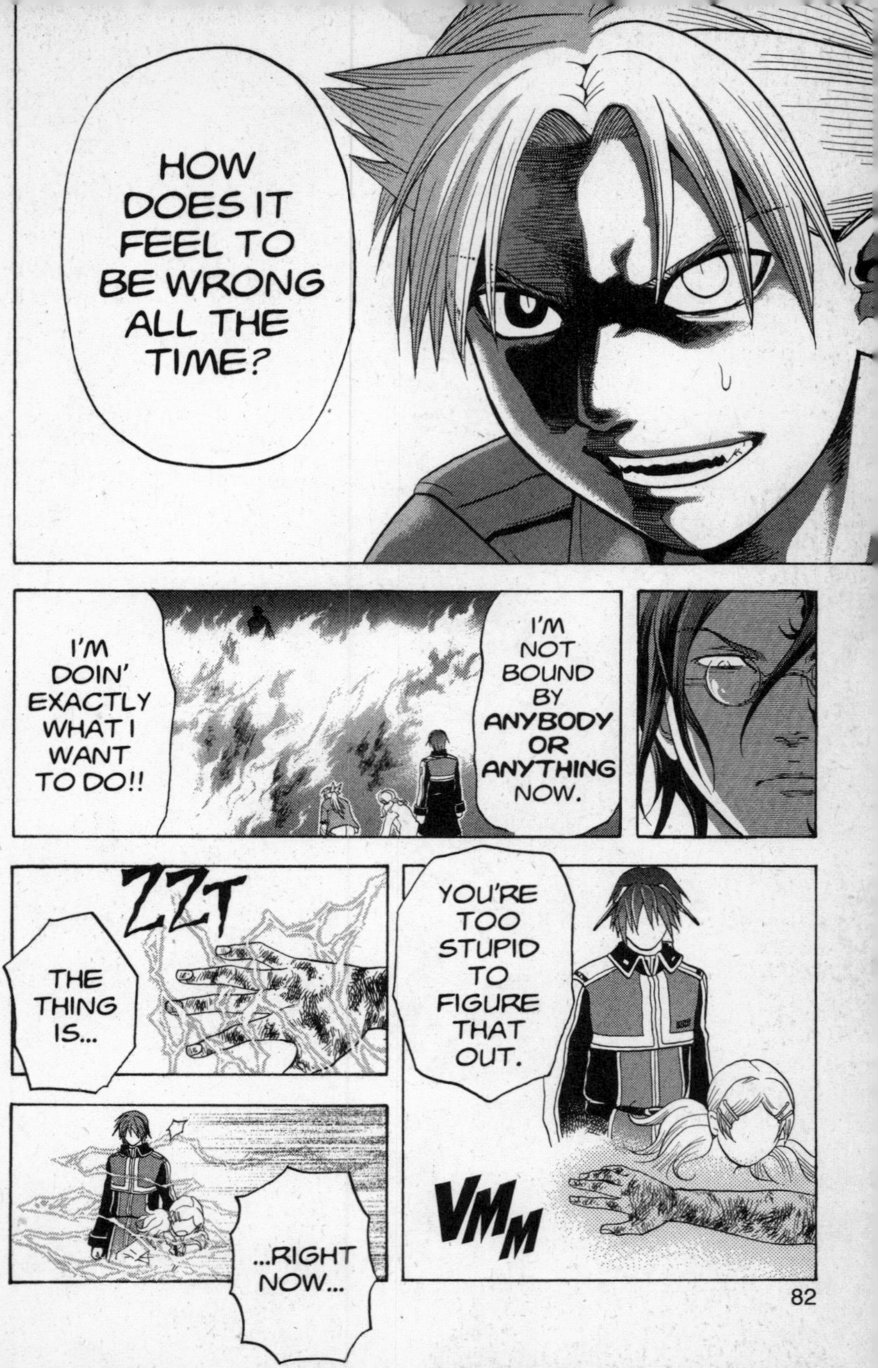
HOW DOES IT FEEL TO BE WRONG ALL THE TIME?
I'M NOT BOUND BY ANYBODY OR ANYTHING NOW.
I'M DOIN' EXACTLY WHAT I WANT TO DO!!
YOU'RE TOO STUPID TO FIGURE THAT OUT.
VMM
ZZT
THE THING IS...
...RIGHT NOW...

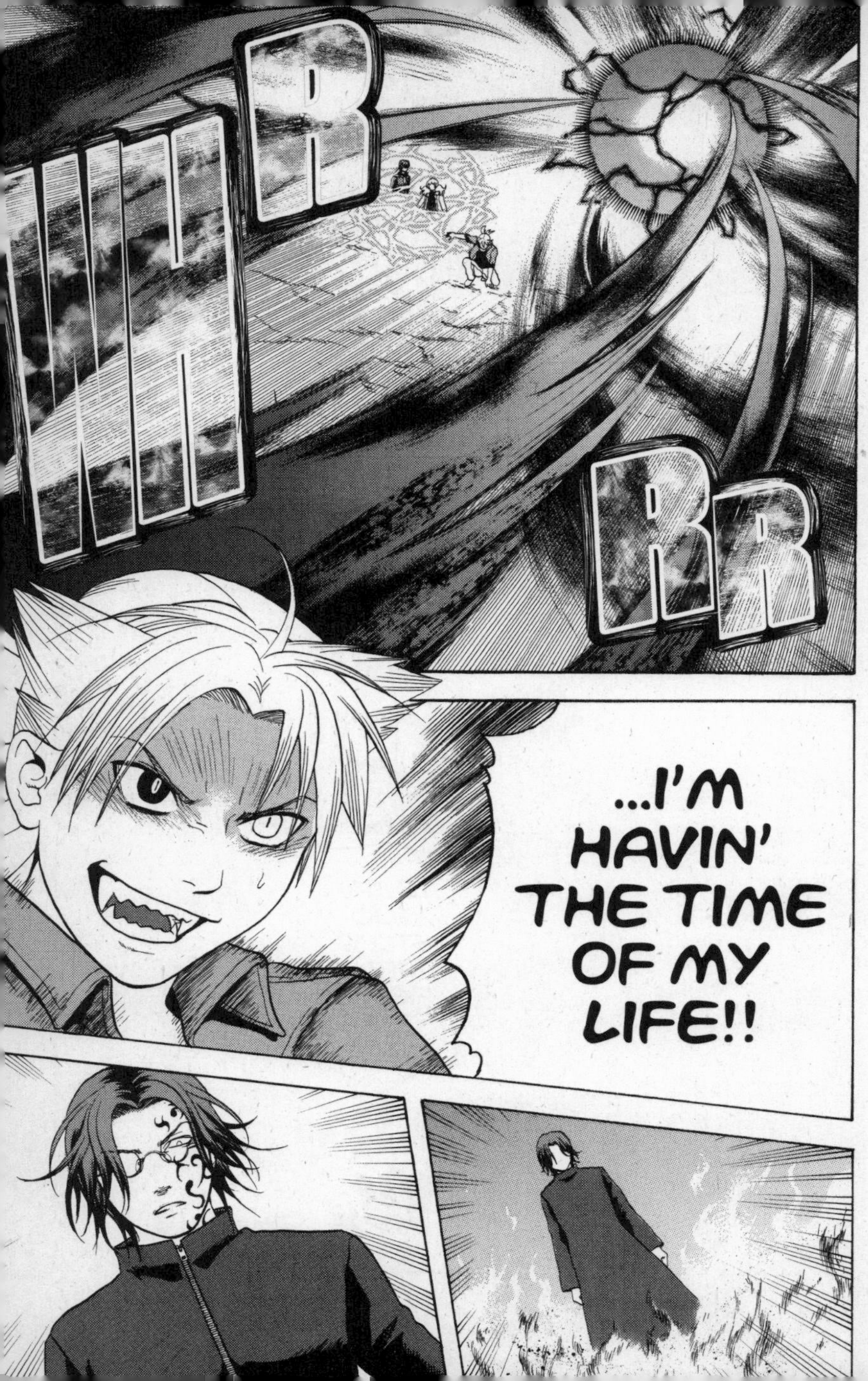
WHRRR
...I'M HAVIN' THE TIME OF MY LIFE!!

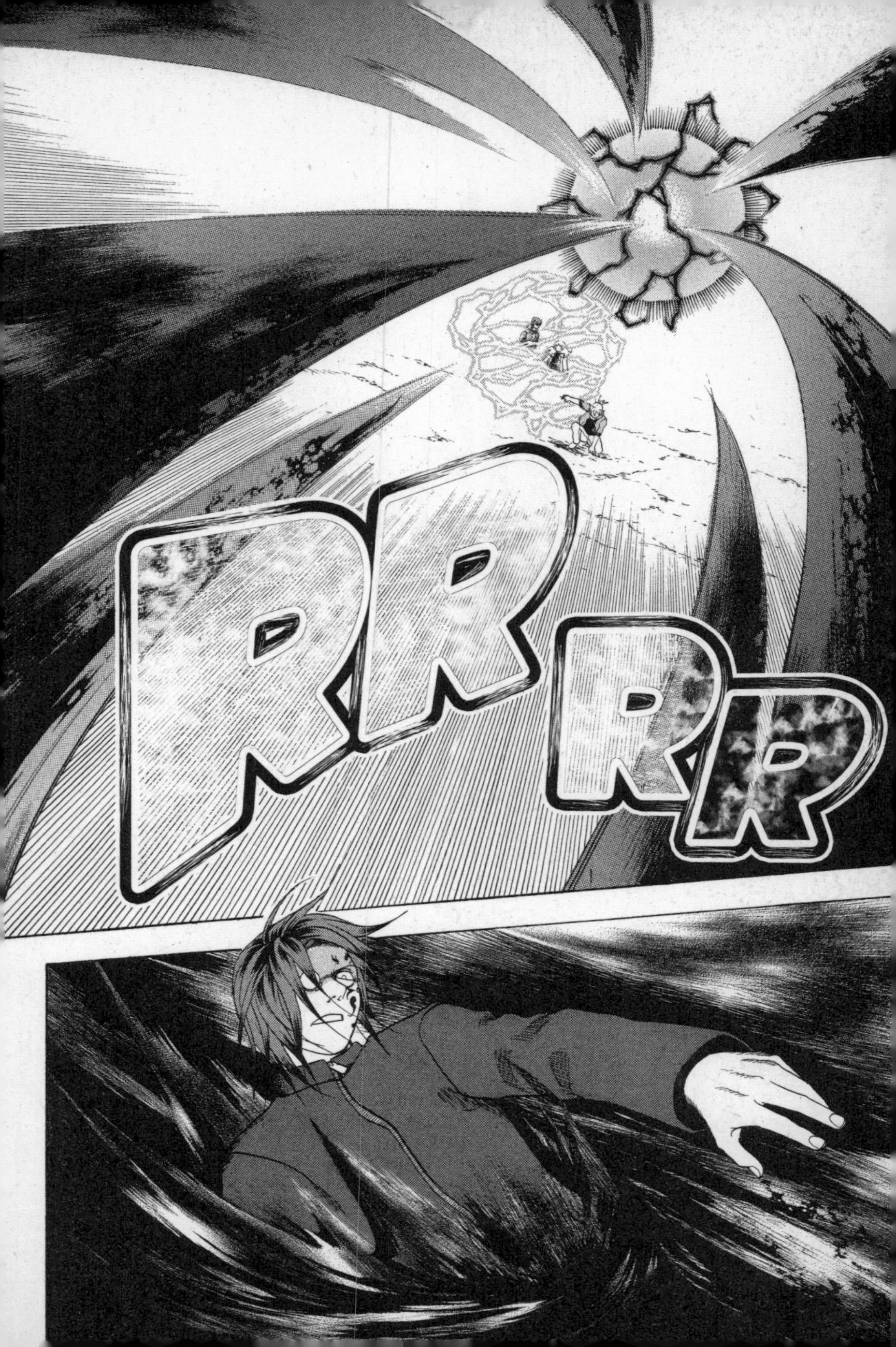
RRRR

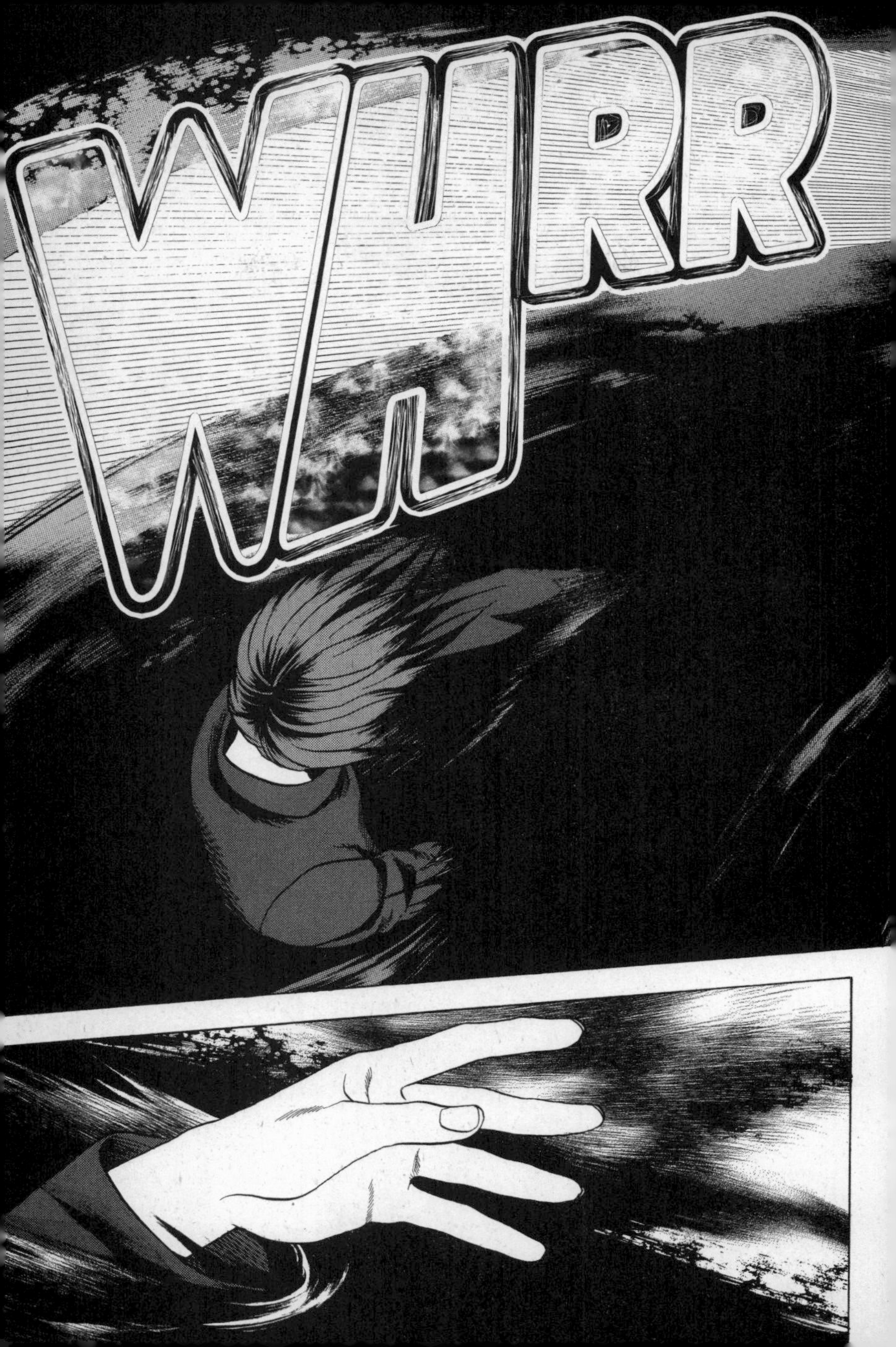
WHRR

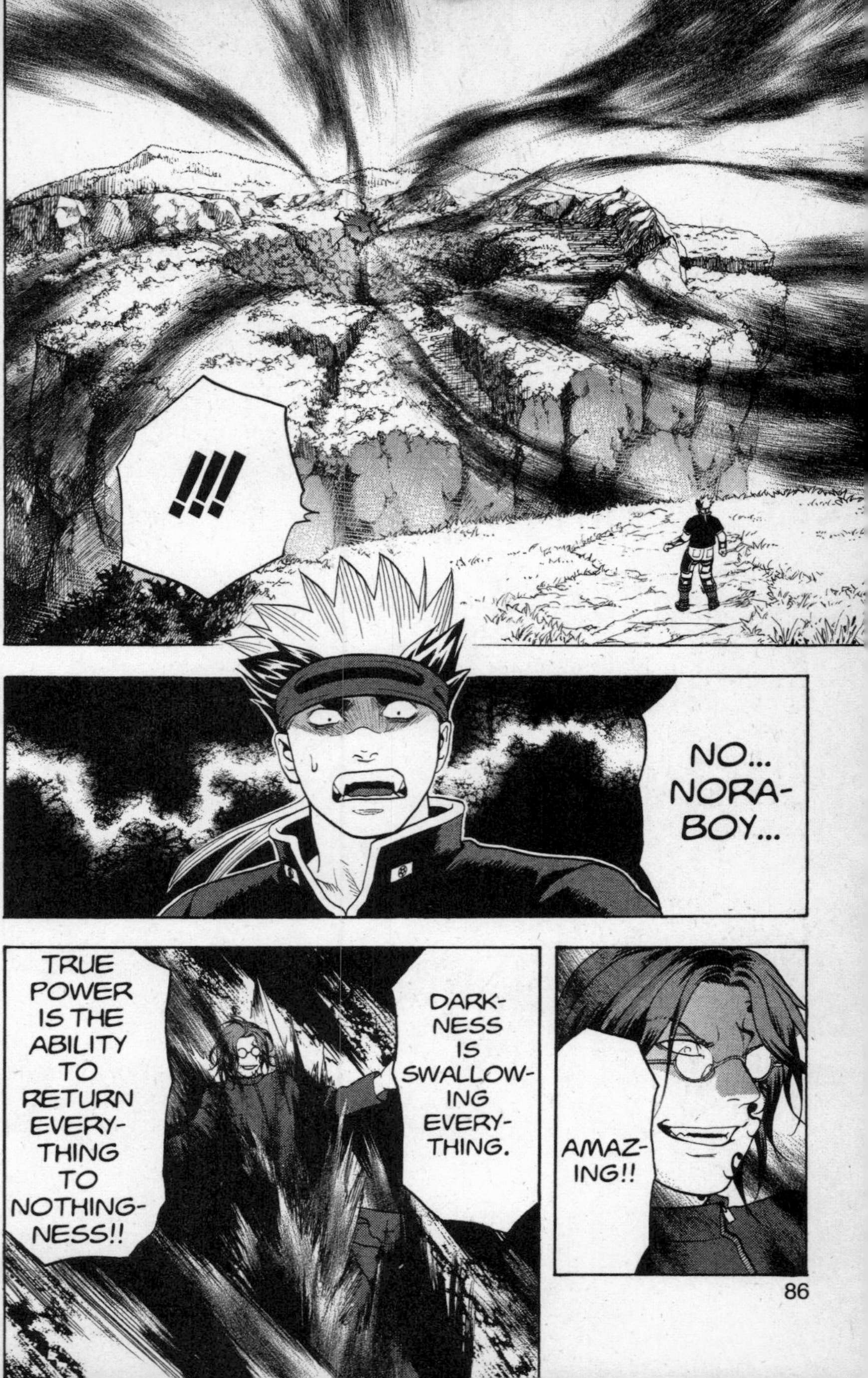
!!!
NO... NORA-BOY...
AMAZ-ING!!
DARK-NESS IS SWALLOW-ING EVERY-THING.
TRUE POWER IS THE ABILITY TO RETURN EVERY-THING TO NOTHING-NESS!!

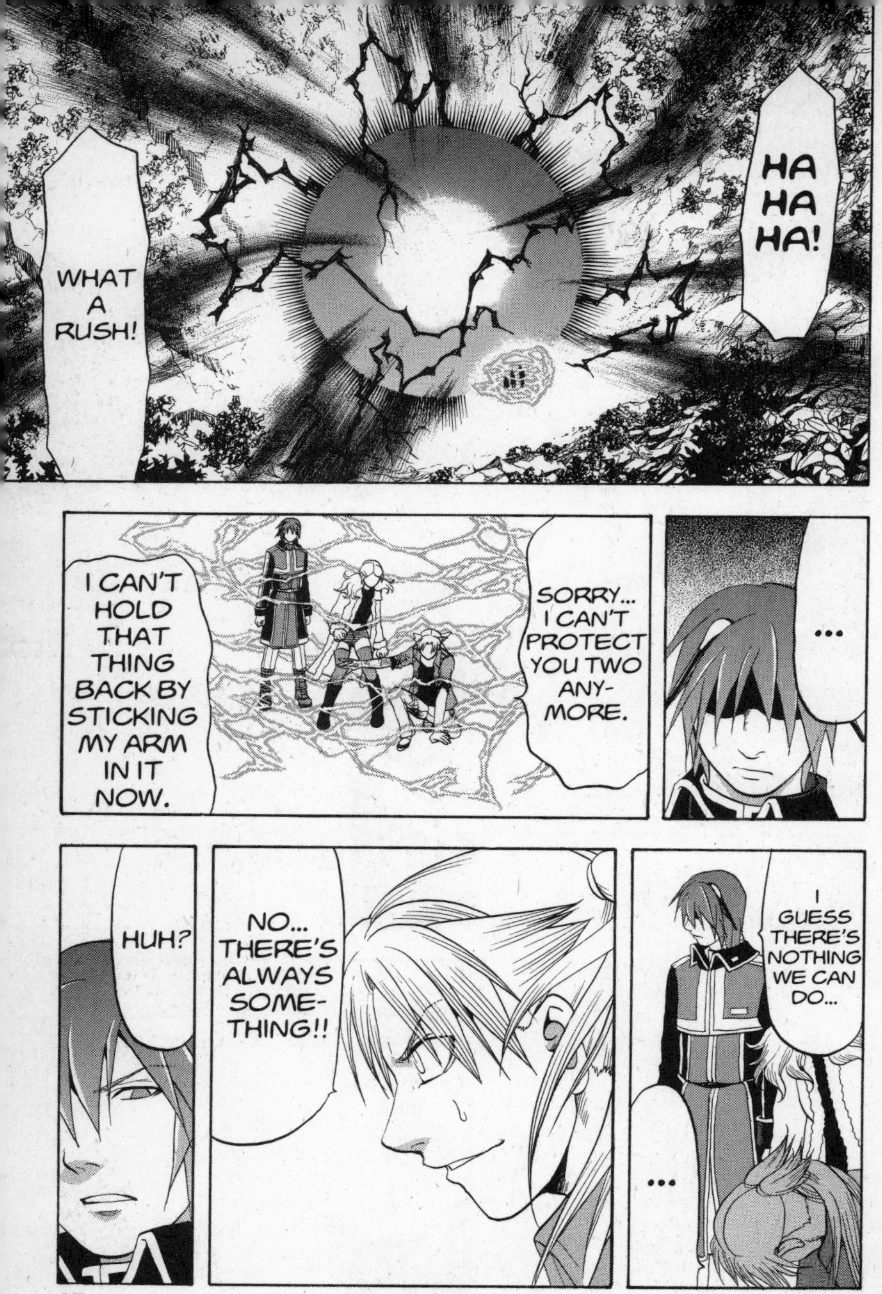
HA HA HA!
WHAT A RUSH!
...
SORRY... I CAN'T PROTECT YOU TWO ANY-MORE.
I CAN'T HOLD THAT THING BACK BY STICKING MY ARM IN IT NOW.
I GUESS THERE'S NOTHING WE CAN DO...
...
NO... THERE'S ALWAYS SOME-THING!!
HUH?

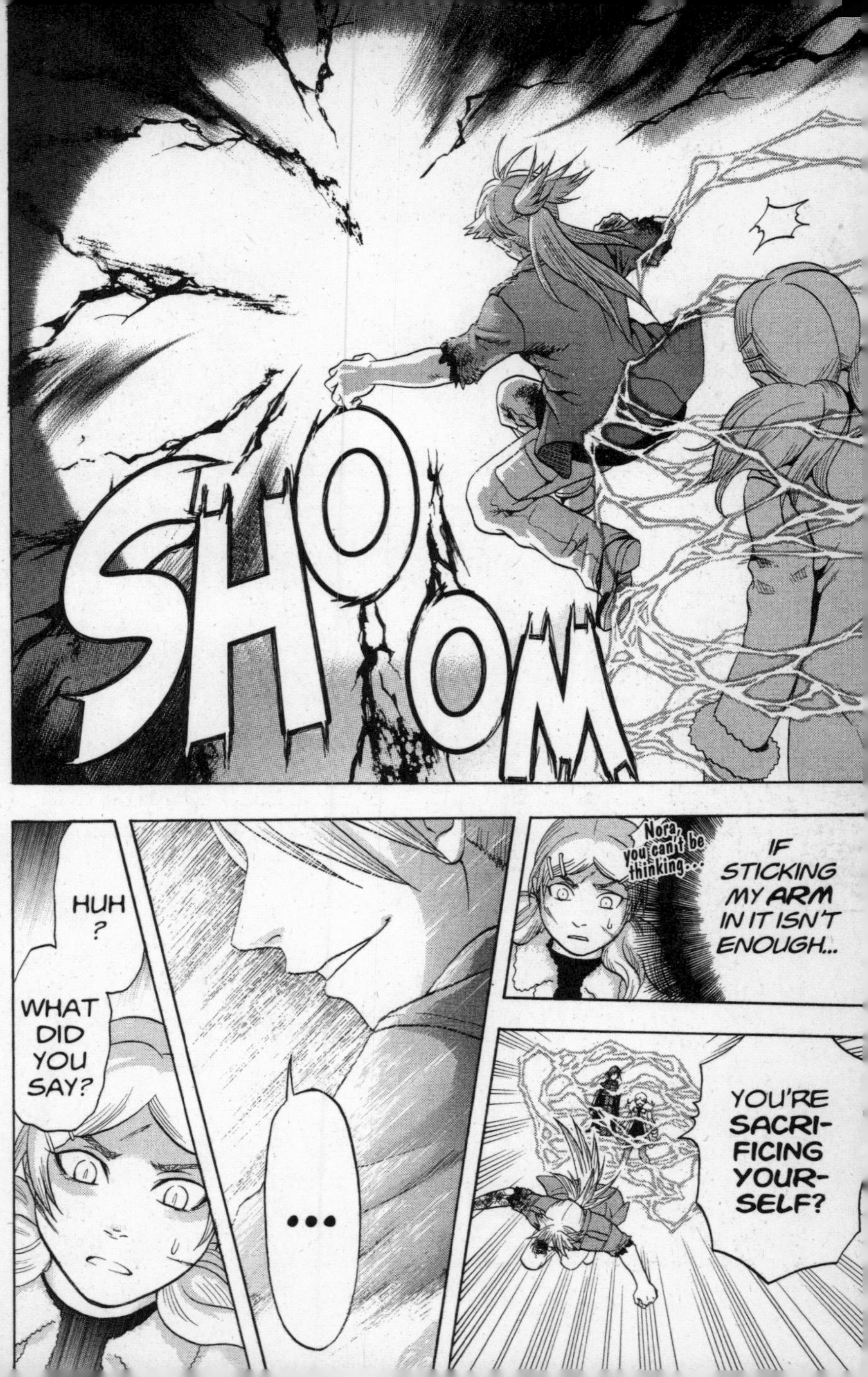
SHOOM
IF STICKING MY ARM IN IT ISN'T ENOUGH...
Nora, you can't be thinking...
YOU'RE SACRIFICING YOURSELF?
...
HUH?
WHAT DID YOU SAY?

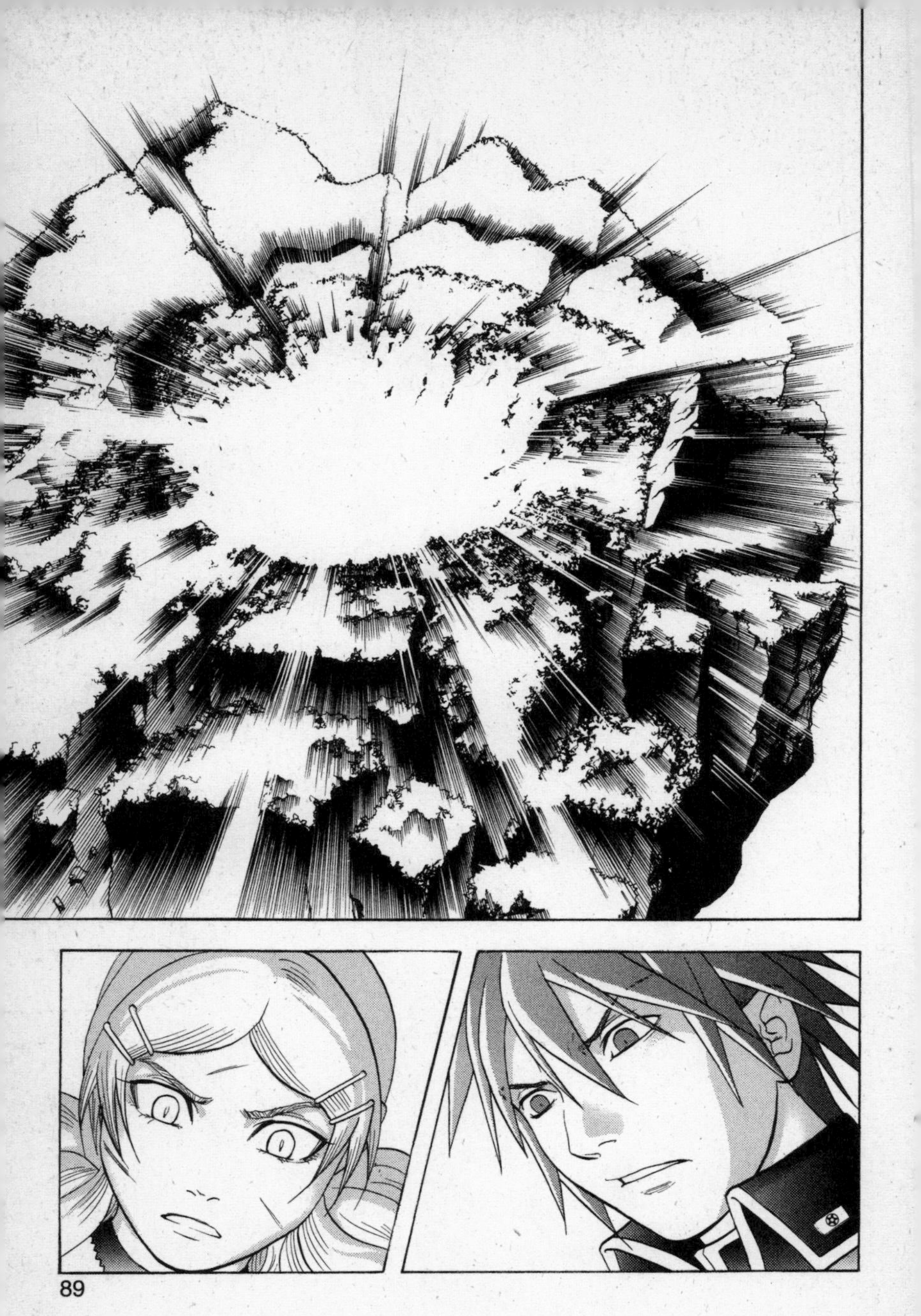

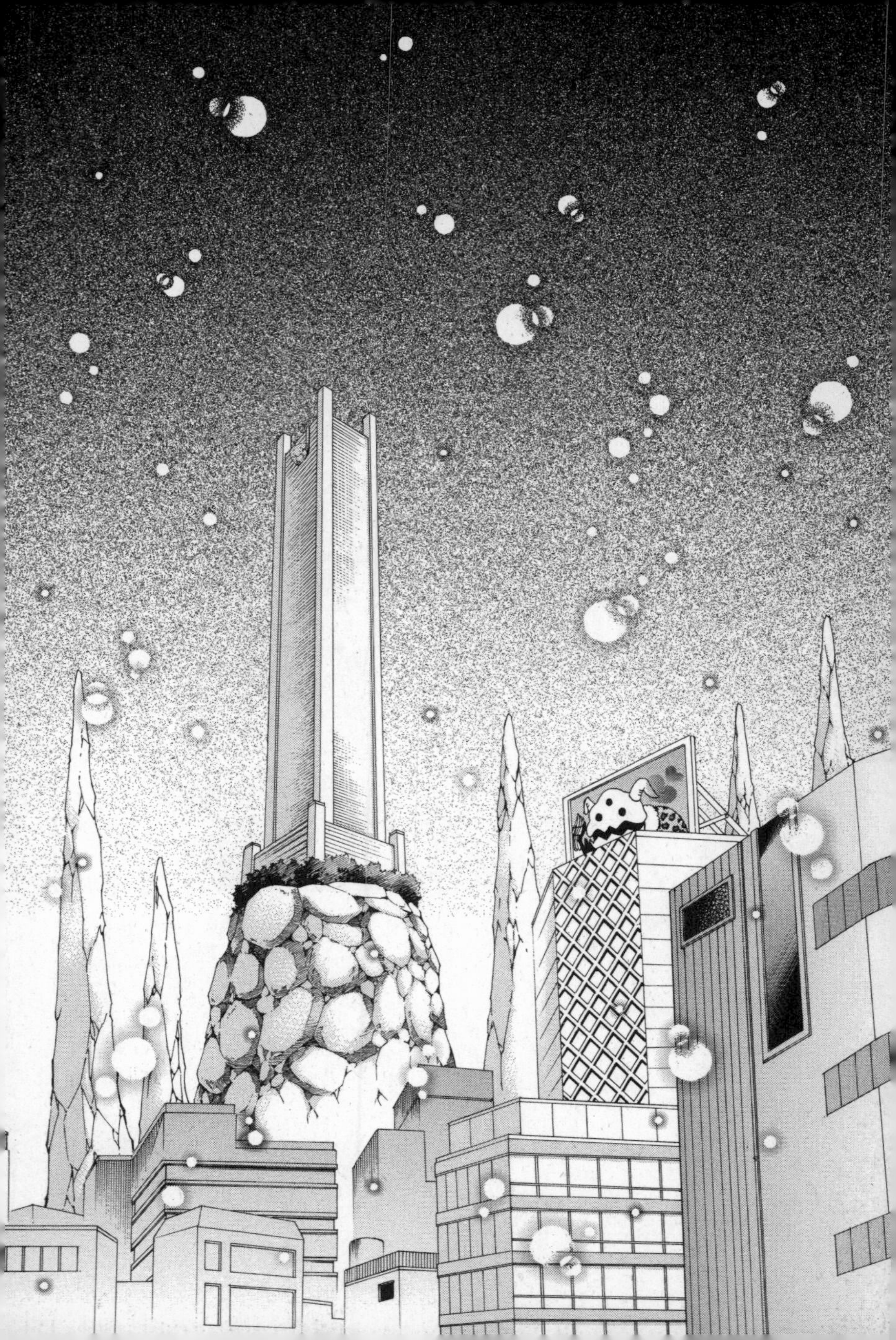

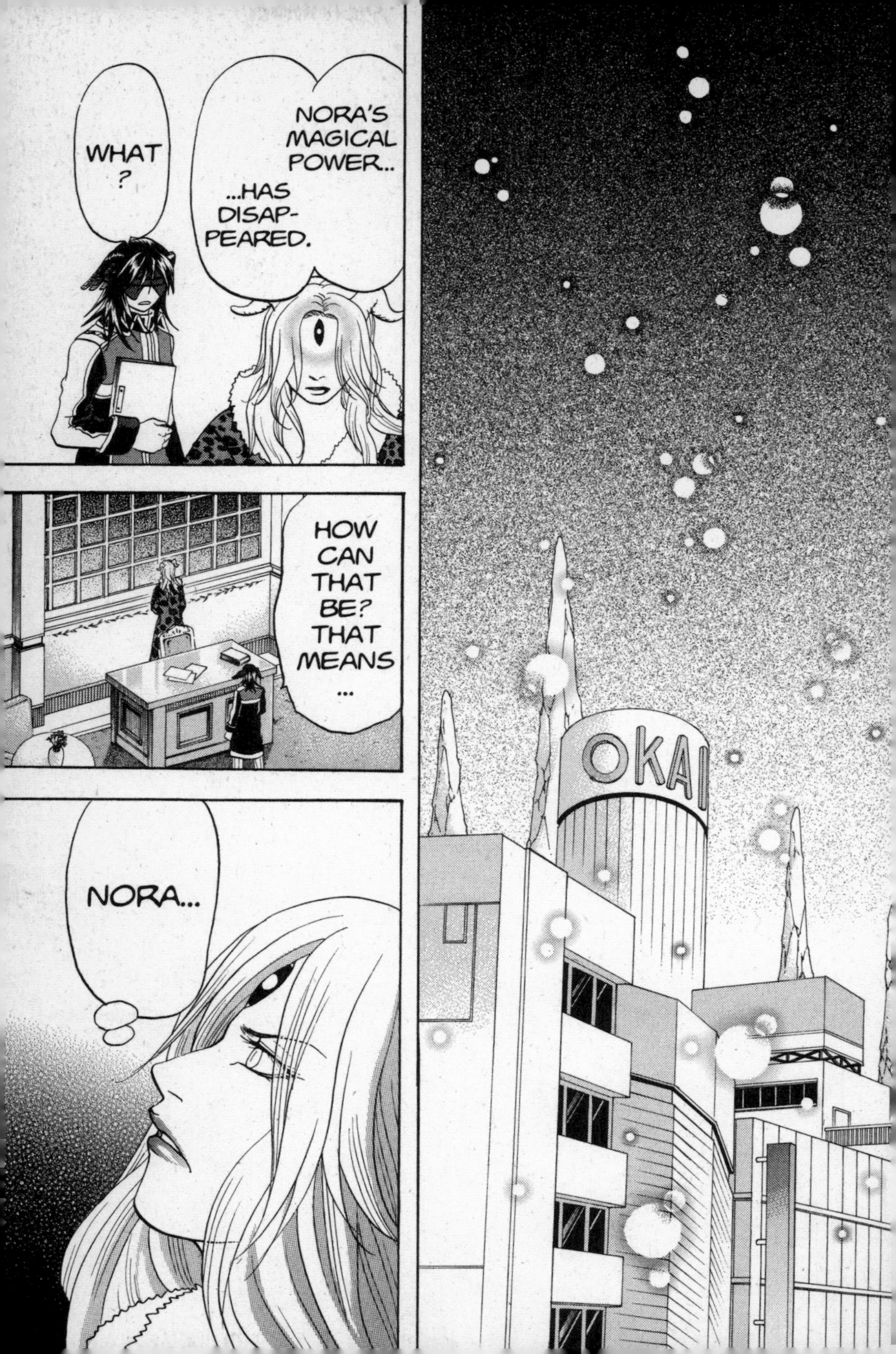
OKAI
NORA'S MAGICAL POWER...
...HAS DISAPPEARED.
WHAT?
HOW CAN THAT BE? THAT MEANS...
NORA...

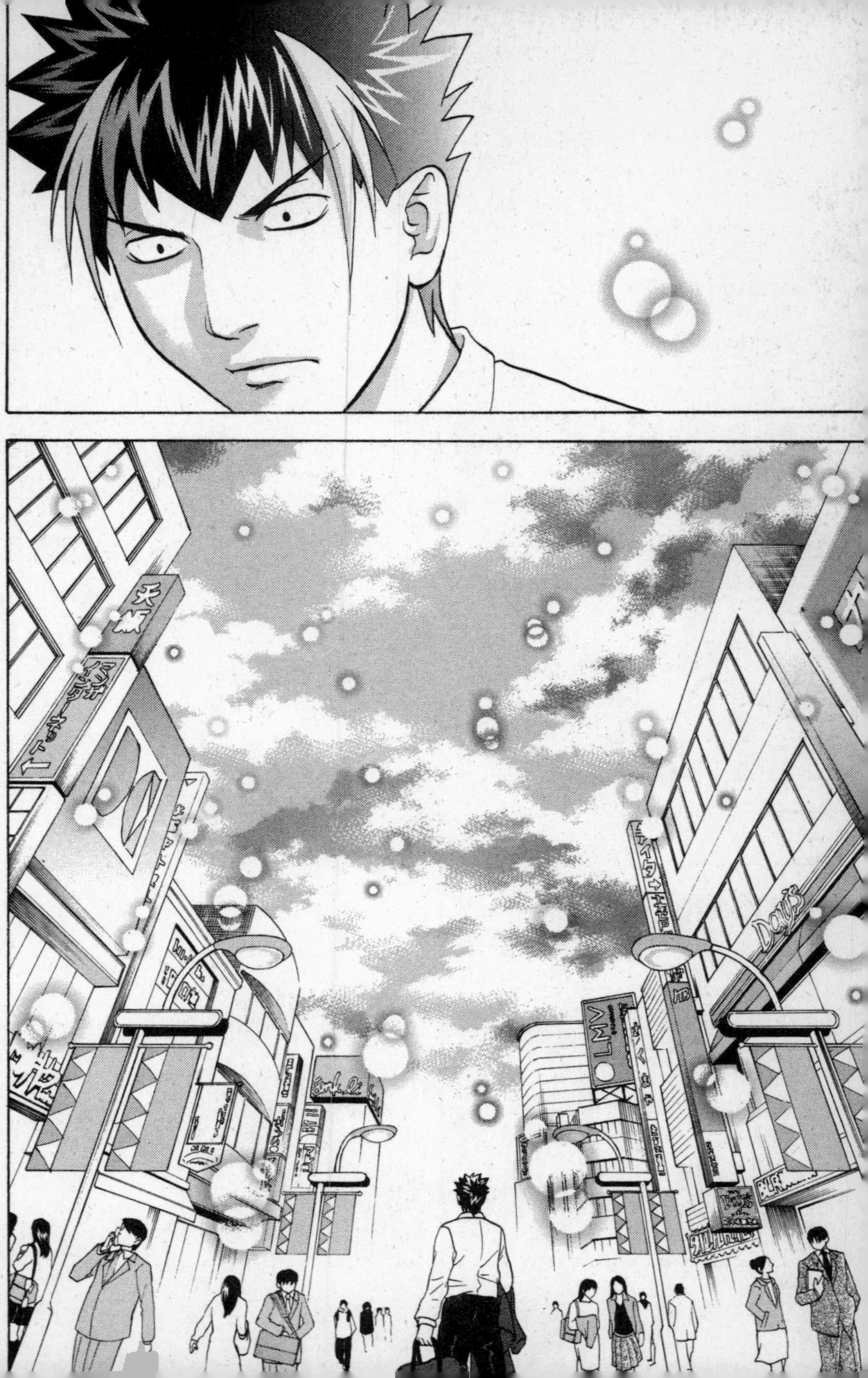
LMV
Days

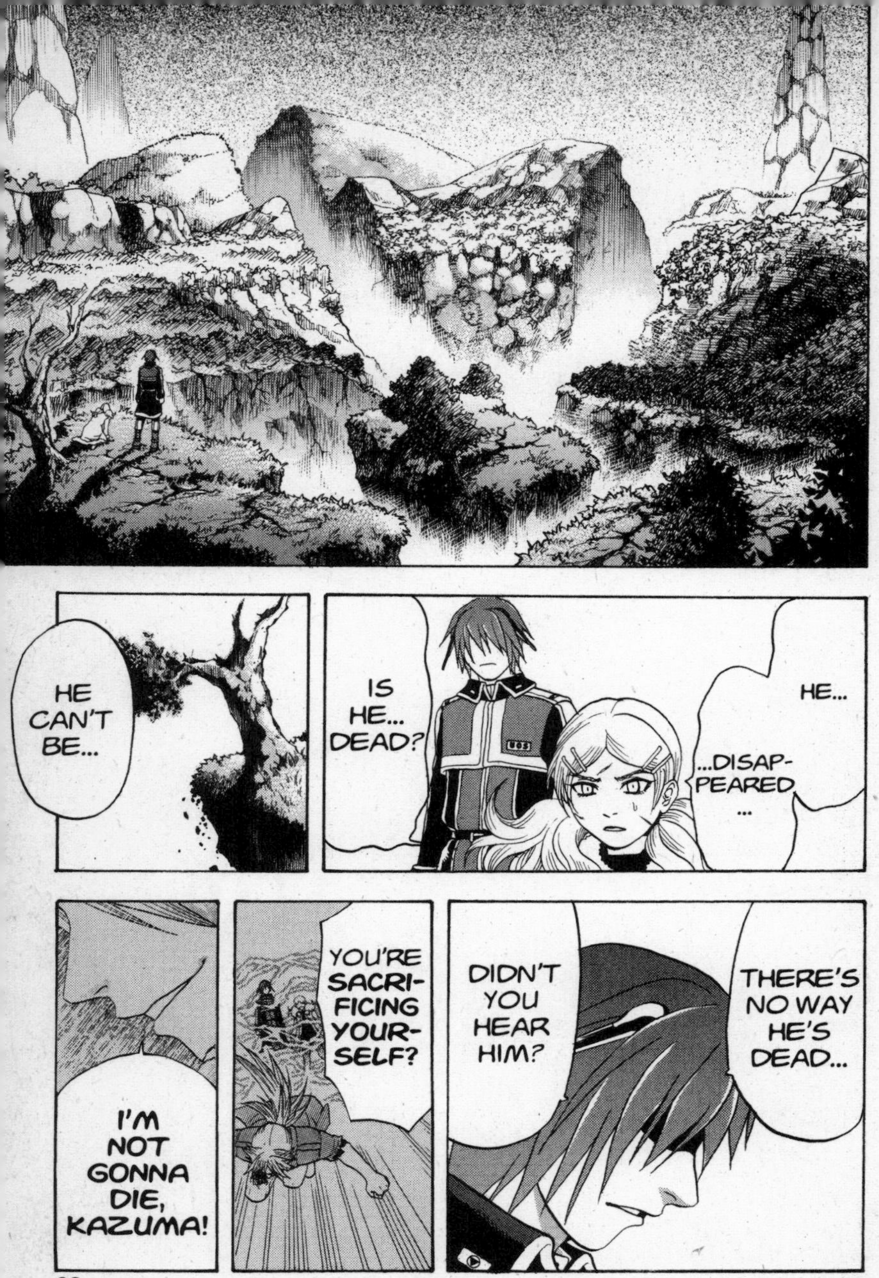
HE...
...DISAPPEARED...
IS HE... DEAD?
HE CAN'T BE...
THERE'S NO WAY HE'S DEAD...
DIDN'T YOU HEAR HIM?
YOU'RE SACRIFICING YOURSELF?
I'M NOT GONNA DIE, KAZUMA!

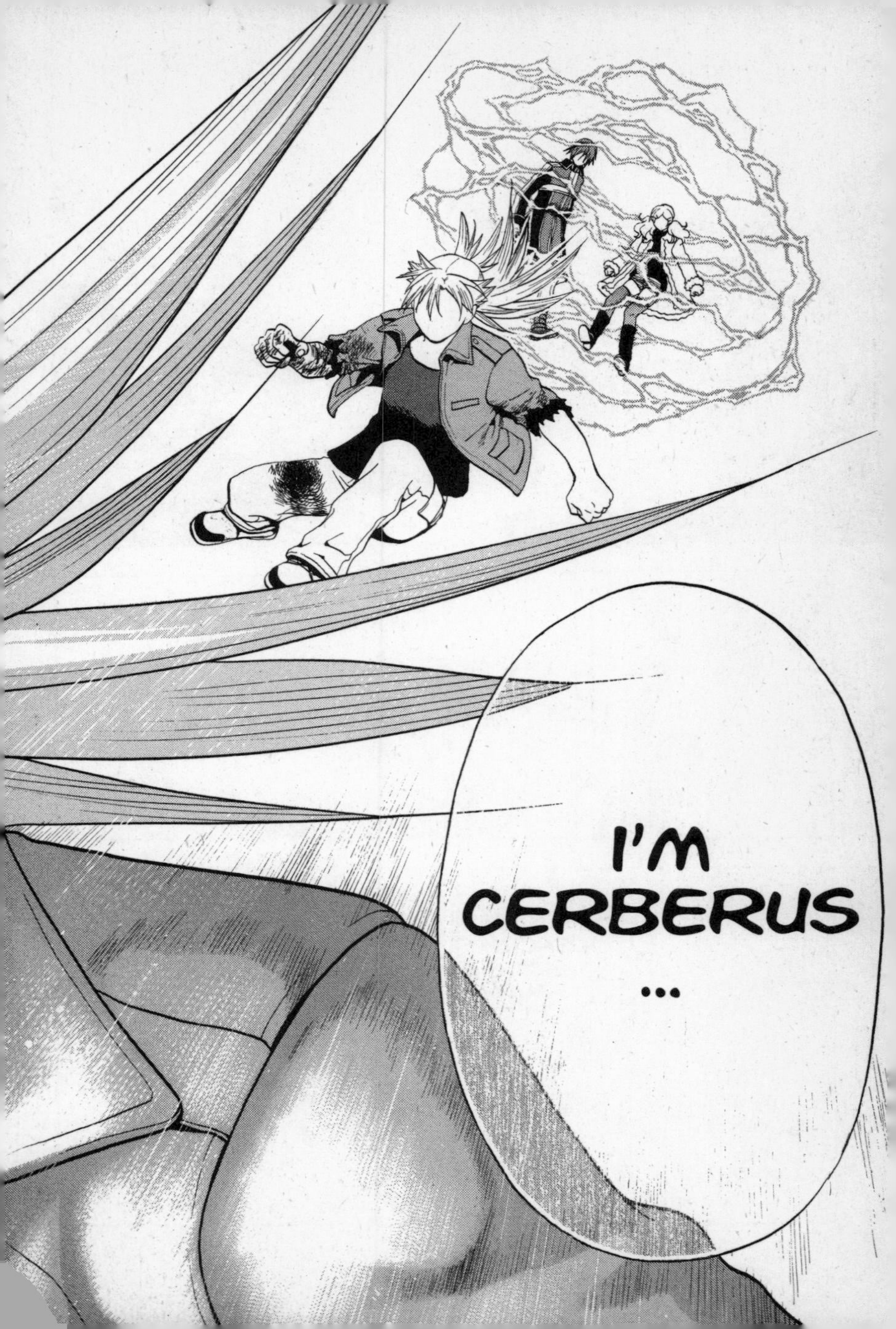
I'M CERBERUS ...

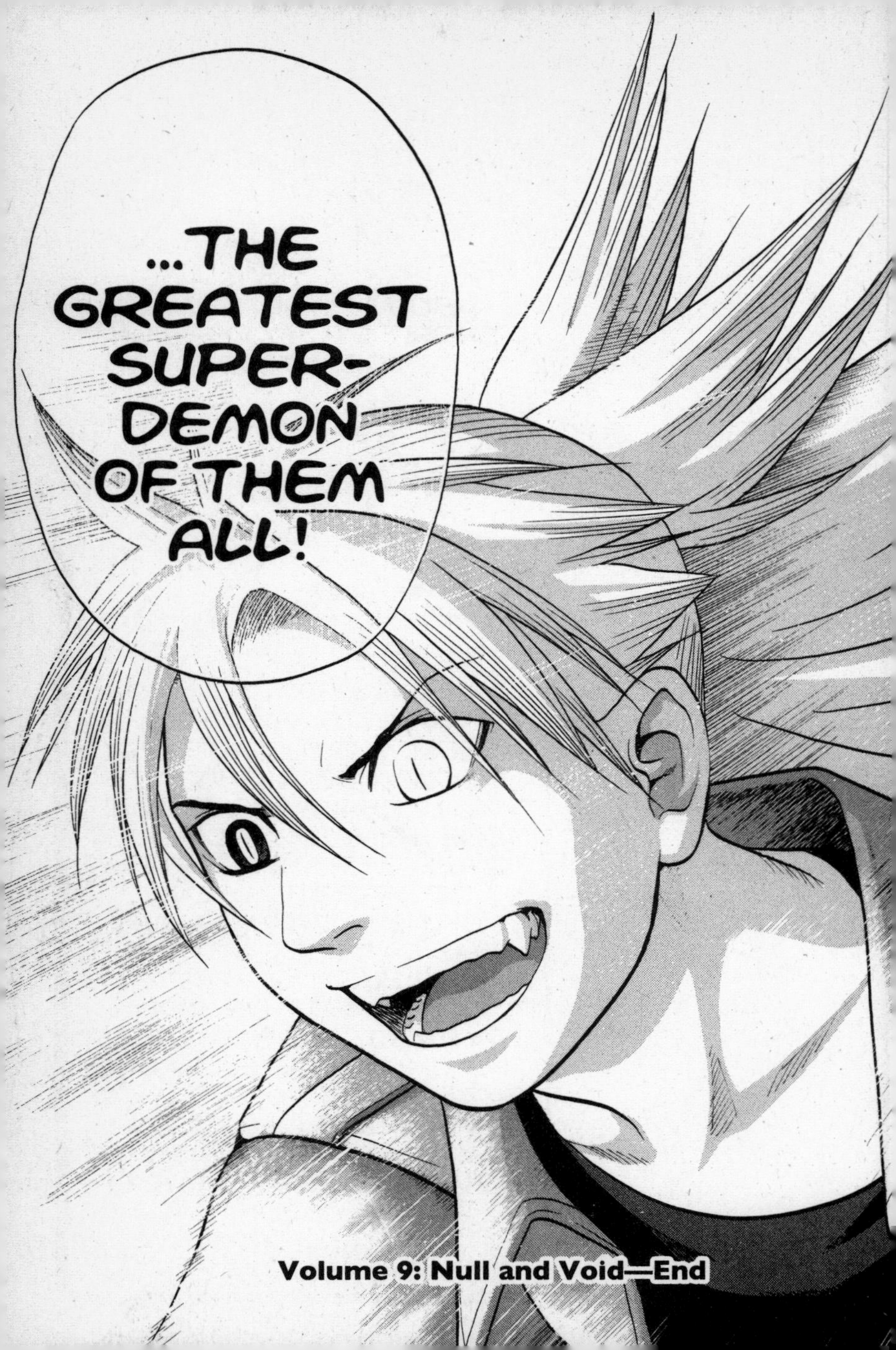
...THE GREATEST SUPER-DEMON OF THEM ALL!

Volume 9: Null and Void—End

ABOUT THE ORIGINAL SHORT STORY VERSION OF *NORA*...

I'M SURE A LOT OF MANGA ARTISTS HAVE THIS PROBLEM, BUT I CAN'T READ MY OWN DEBUT PIECE. IT'S TOO EMBARRASSING. BUT NONETHELESS, I'VE DECIDED TO REPRINT IT HERE WITH NO CORRECTIONS OR REVISIONS. AT THE TIME, I WAS SATISFIED WITH THE RESULT BECAUSE I FELT LIKE I WAS ABLE TO DO WHAT I WANTED TO DO WITH THESE TWO CHARACTERS AS A DUO. BUT I ALSO REMEMBER HOW DIFFICULT IT WAS TO FIND NEW THINGS TO DO WITH THE CHARACTERS WHEN *NORA* WAS PICKED UP AS AN ONGOING SERIES.

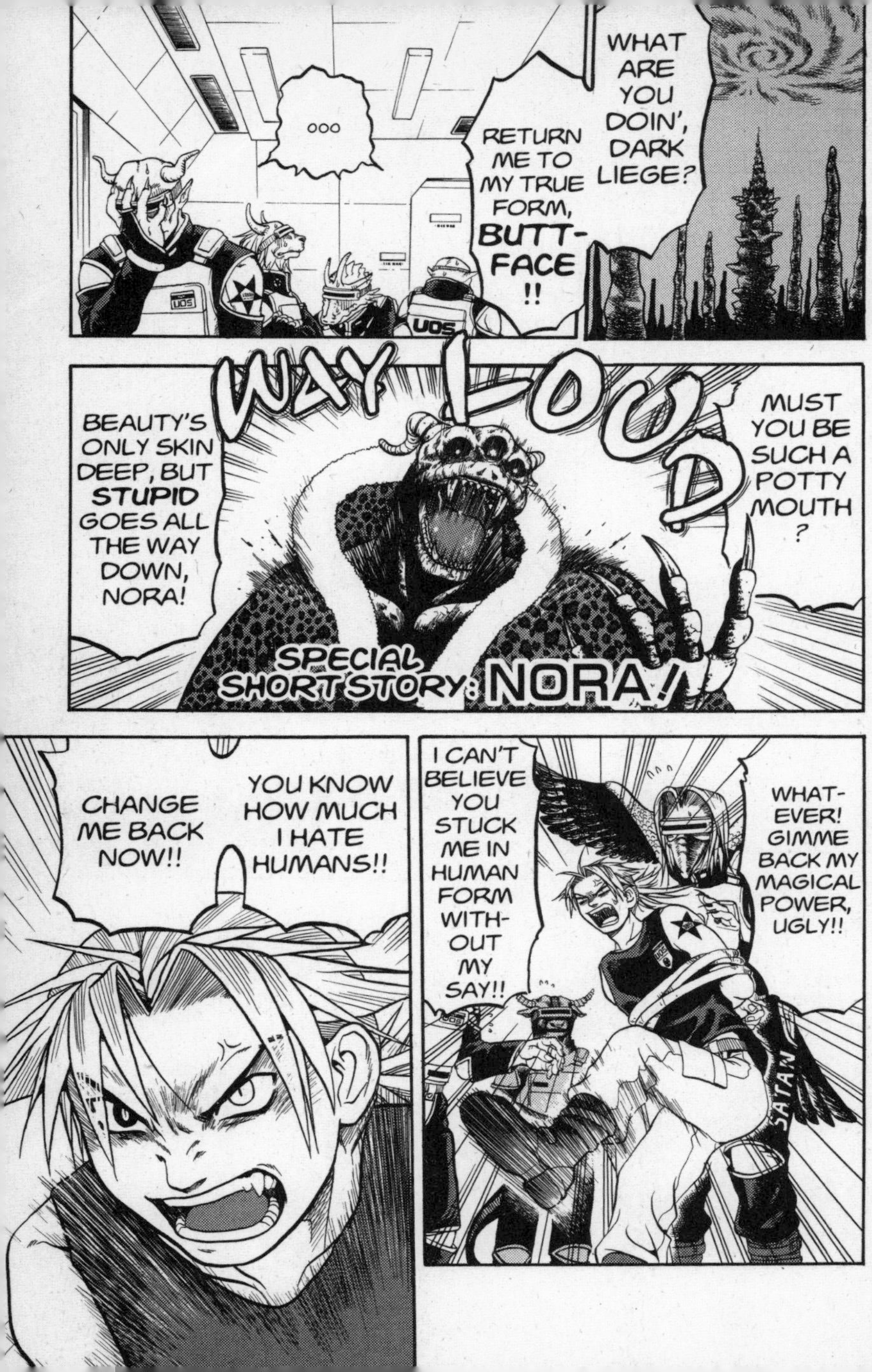
WHAT ARE YOU DOIN', DARK LIEGE?
RETURN ME TO MY TRUE FORM, BUTT-FACE!!
ooo
WAY LOUD
MUST YOU BE SUCH A POTTY MOUTH?
BEAUTY'S ONLY SKIN DEEP, BUT STUPID GOES ALL THE WAY DOWN, NORA!
SPECIAL SHORT STORY: NORA!
WHAT-EVER! GIMME BACK MY MAGICAL POWER, UGLY!!
I CAN'T BELIEVE YOU STUCK ME IN HUMAN FORM WITH-OUT MY SAY!!
SATAN
YOU KNOW HOW MUCH I HATE HUMANS!!
CHANGE ME BACK NOW!!

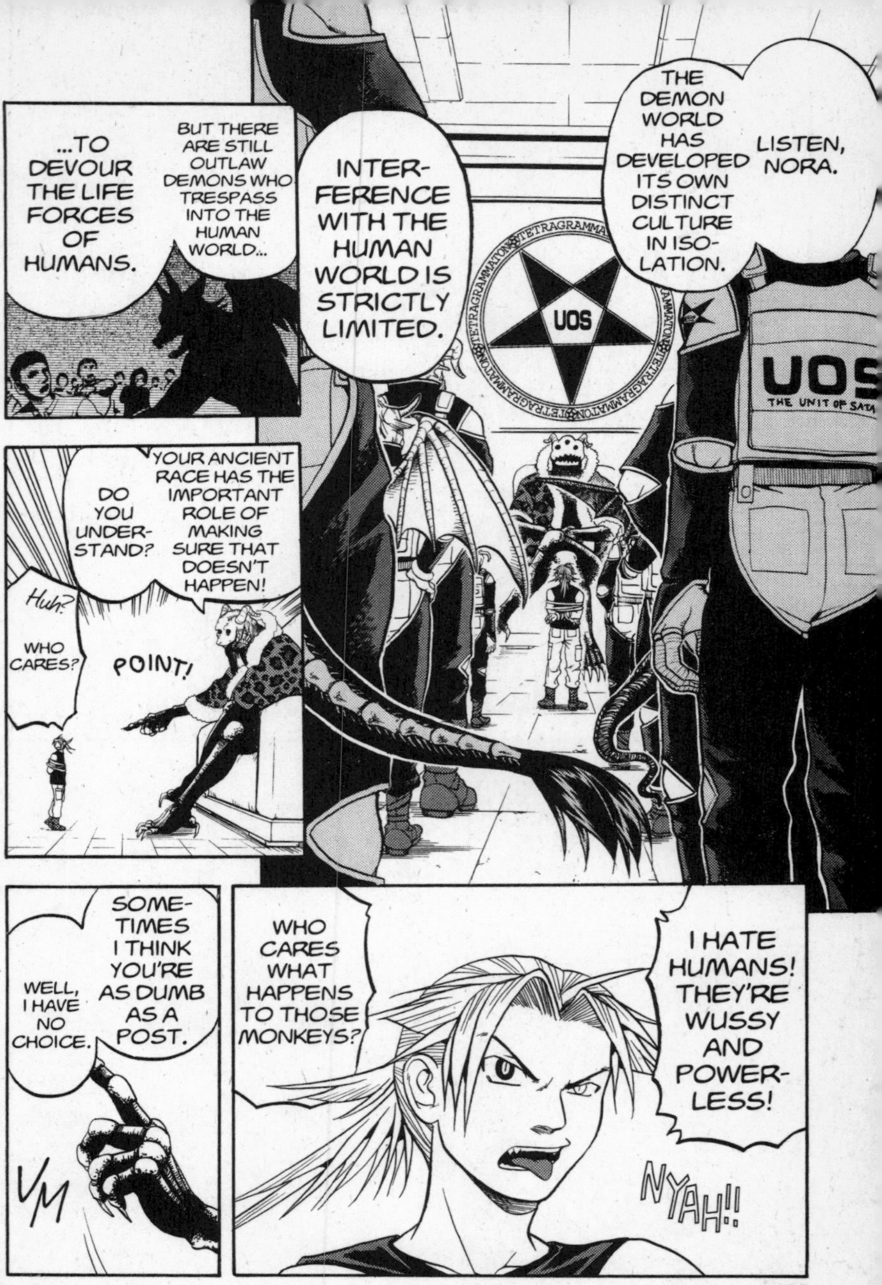
LISTEN, NORA.
THE DEMON WORLD HAS DEVELOPED ITS OWN DISTINCT CULTURE IN ISOLATION.
INTERFERENCE WITH THE HUMAN WORLD IS STRICTLY LIMITED.
TETRAGRAMMATON
UOS
UOS
THE UNIT OF SATA
BUT THERE ARE STILL OUTLAW DEMONS WHO TRESPASS INTO THE HUMAN WORLD...
...TO DEVOUR THE LIFE FORCES OF HUMANS.
YOUR ANCIENT RACE HAS THE IMPORTANT ROLE OF MAKING SURE THAT DOESN'T HAPPEN!
DO YOU UNDERSTAND?
Huh?
WHO CARES?
POINT!
I HATE HUMANS! THEY'RE WUSSY AND POWERLESS!
WHO CARES WHAT HAPPENS TO THOSE MONKEYS?
NYAH!!
SOMETIMES I THINK YOU'RE AS DUMB AS A POST.
WELL, I HAVE NO CHOICE.
VM

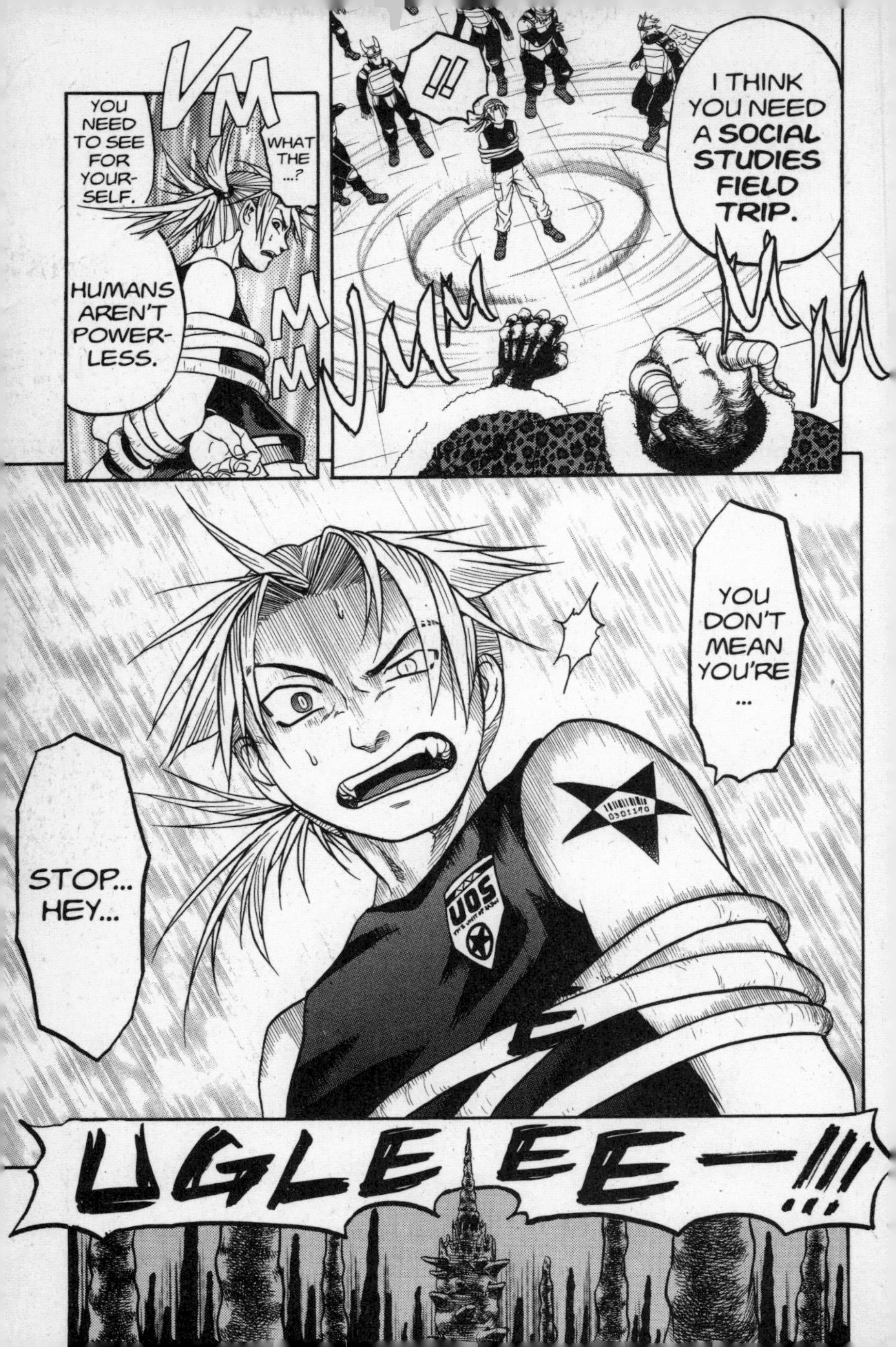

I THINK YOU NEED A **SOCIAL STUDIES FIELD TRIP.**
!!
VMMM
VM
YOU NEED TO SEE FOR YOUR-SELF.
WHAT THE ...?
HUMANS AREN'T POWER-LESS.
MMM
YOU DON'T MEAN YOU'RE ...
STOP... HEY...
UGLEEE—!!!

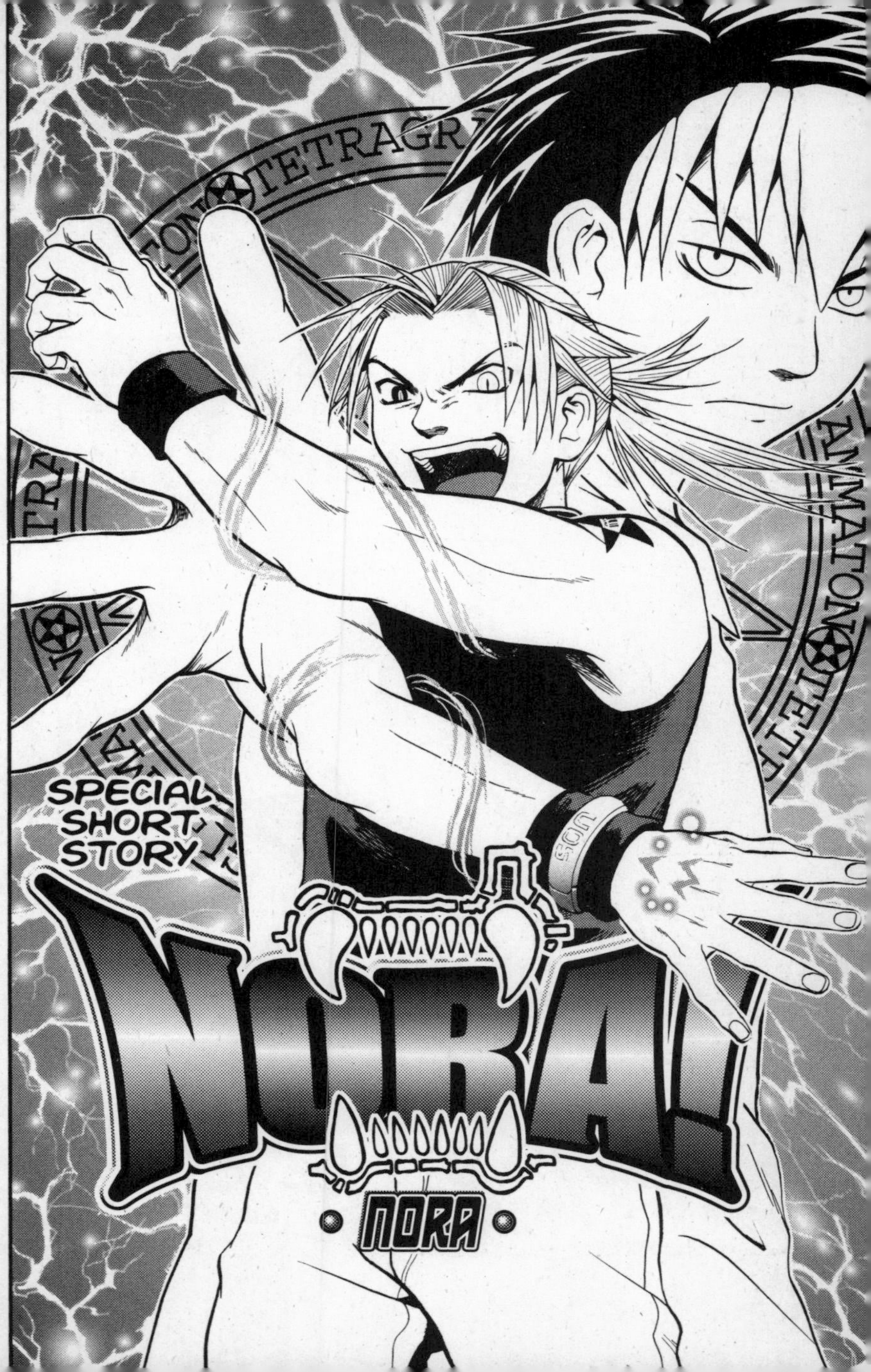
TETRAGRAMMATON
SPECIAL SHORT STORY
NORA!
NORA

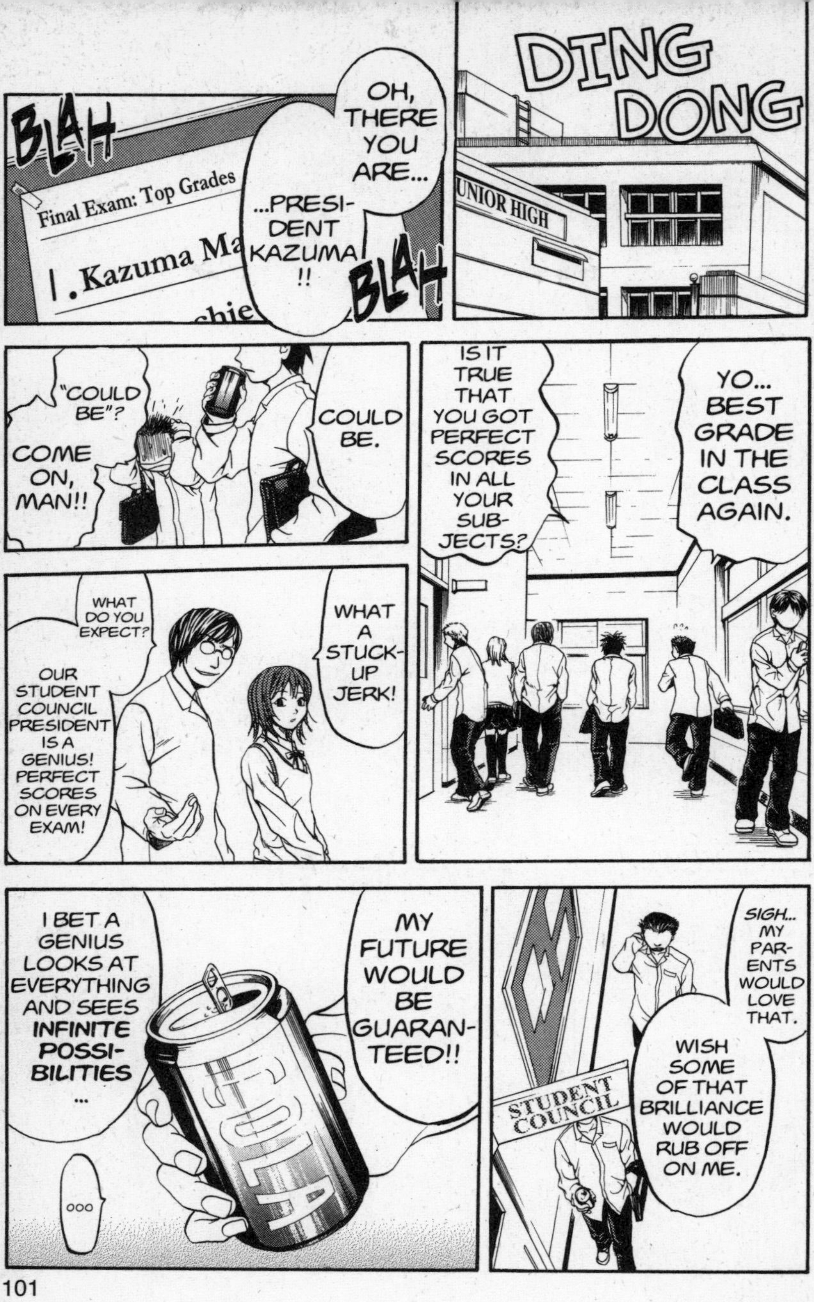
DING DONG
UNIOR HIGH
BLAH
Final Exam: Top Grades
1. Kazuma Ma
OH, THERE YOU ARE...
...PRESIDENT KAZUMA!!
BLAH
YO... BEST GRADE IN THE CLASS AGAIN.
IS IT TRUE THAT YOU GOT PERFECT SCORES IN ALL YOUR SUBJECTS?
COULD BE.
"COULD BE"?
COME ON, MAN!!
WHAT A STUCK-UP JERK!
WHAT DO YOU EXPECT?
OUR STUDENT COUNCIL PRESIDENT IS A GENIUS! PERFECT SCORES ON EVERY EXAM!
SIGH... MY PARENTS WOULD LOVE THAT.
WISH SOME OF THAT BRILLIANCE WOULD RUB OFF ON ME.
STUDENT COUNCIL
MY FUTURE WOULD BE GUARANTEED!!
I BET A GENIUS LOOKS AT EVERYTHING AND SEES INFINITE POSSIBILITIES...
...

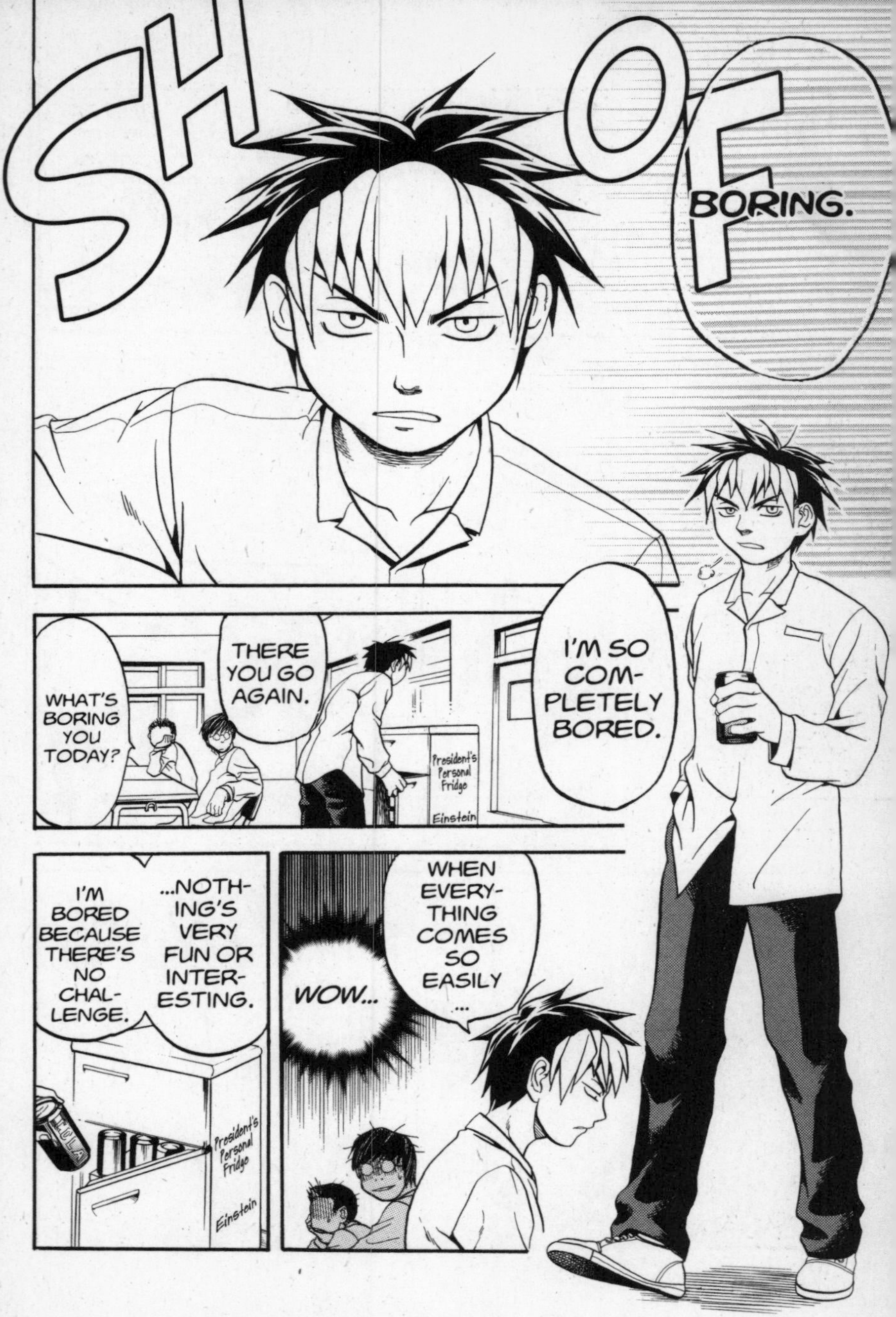
SHOOF
BORING.
I'M SO COMPLETELY BORED.
THERE YOU GO AGAIN.
WHAT'S BORING YOU TODAY?
President's Personal Fridge
Einstein
WHEN EVERYTHING COMES SO EASILY...
WOW...
...NOTHING'S VERY FUN OR INTERESTING.
I'M BORED BECAUSE THERE'S NO CHALLENGE.
President's Personal Fridge
Einstein

READ THIS WAY

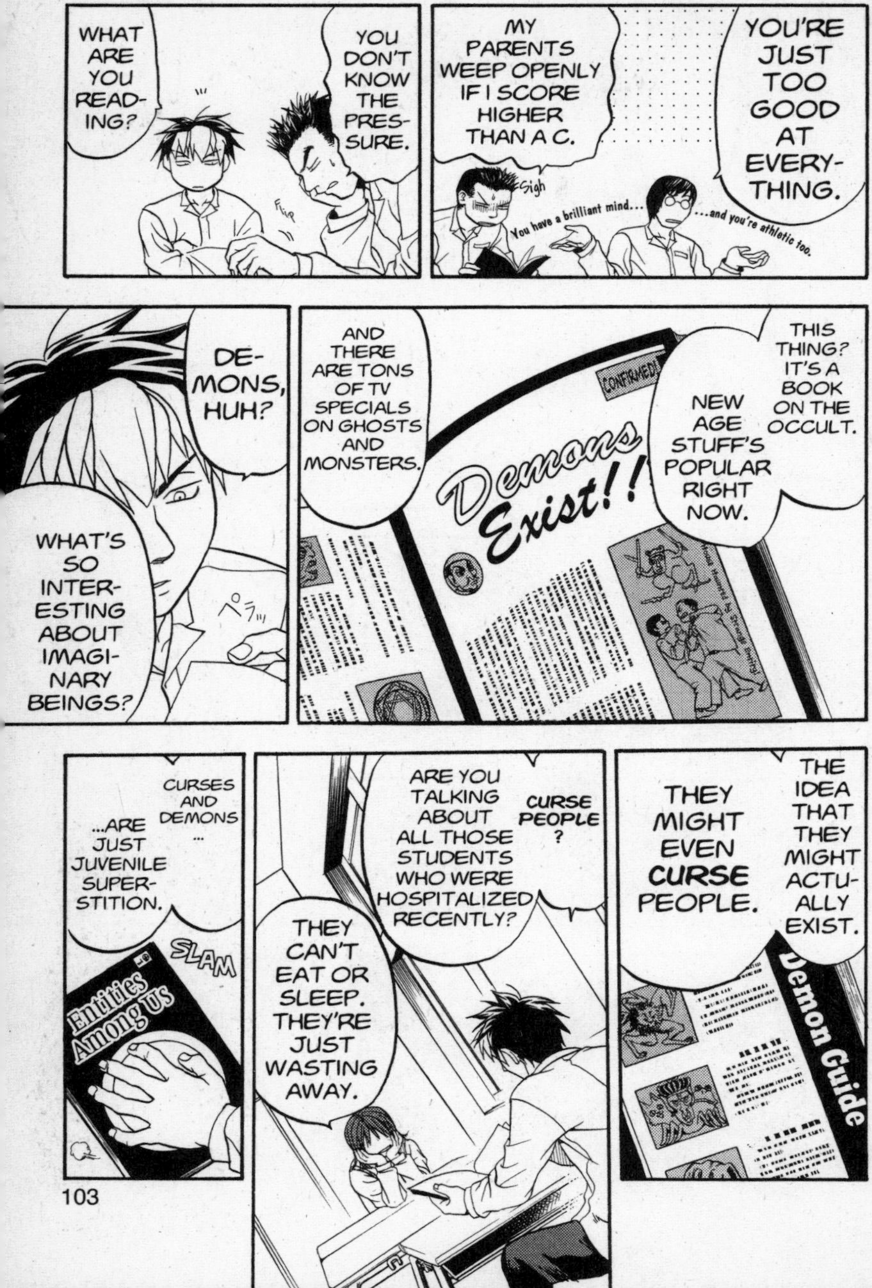

YOU'RE JUST TOO GOOD AT EVERY-THING.
MY PARENTS WEEP OPENLY IF I SCORE HIGHER THAN A C.
Sigh
You have a brilliant mind...
...and you're athletic too.
YOU DON'T KNOW THE PRES-SURE.
WHAT ARE YOU READ-ING?
Flip
THIS THING? IT'S A BOOK ON THE OCCULT.
NEW AGE STUFF'S POPULAR RIGHT NOW.
AND THERE ARE TONS OF TV SPECIALS ON GHOSTS AND MONSTERS.
CONFIRMED!
Demons Exist!!
DE-MONS, HUH?
WHAT'S SO INTER-ESTING ABOUT IMAGI-NARY BEINGS?
ペラッ
THE IDEA THAT THEY MIGHT ACTU-ALLY EXIST.
THEY MIGHT EVEN CURSE PEOPLE.
Demon Guide
CURSE PEOPLE?
ARE YOU TALKING ABOUT ALL THOSE STUDENTS WHO WERE HOSPITALIZED RECENTLY?
THEY CAN'T EAT OR SLEEP. THEY'RE JUST WASTING AWAY.
CURSES AND DEMONS...
...ARE JUST JUVENILE SUPER-STITION.
SLAM
Entities Among Us

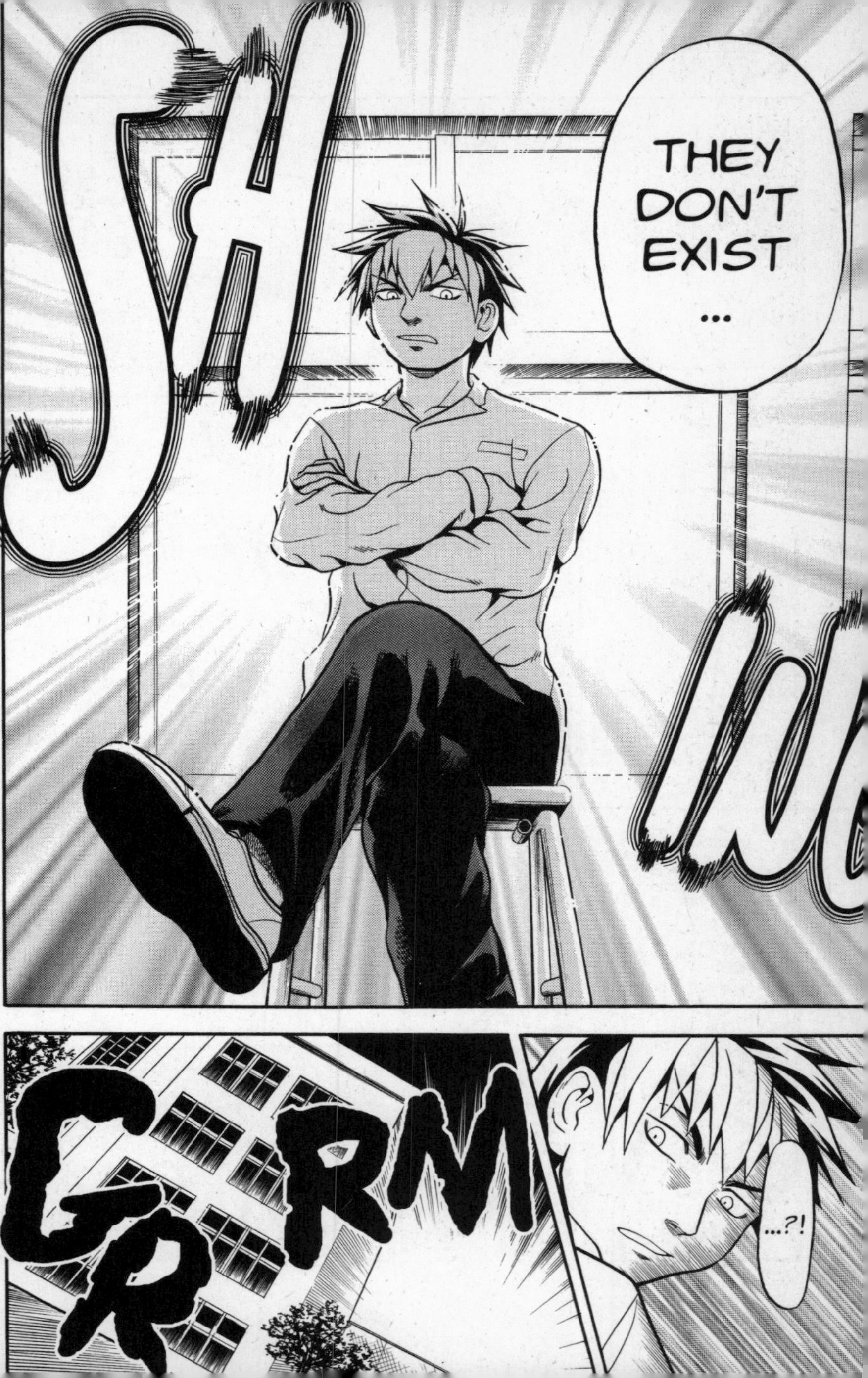
SH
THEY DON'T EXIST ...
...?!
GRRM
GR

READ THIS WAY

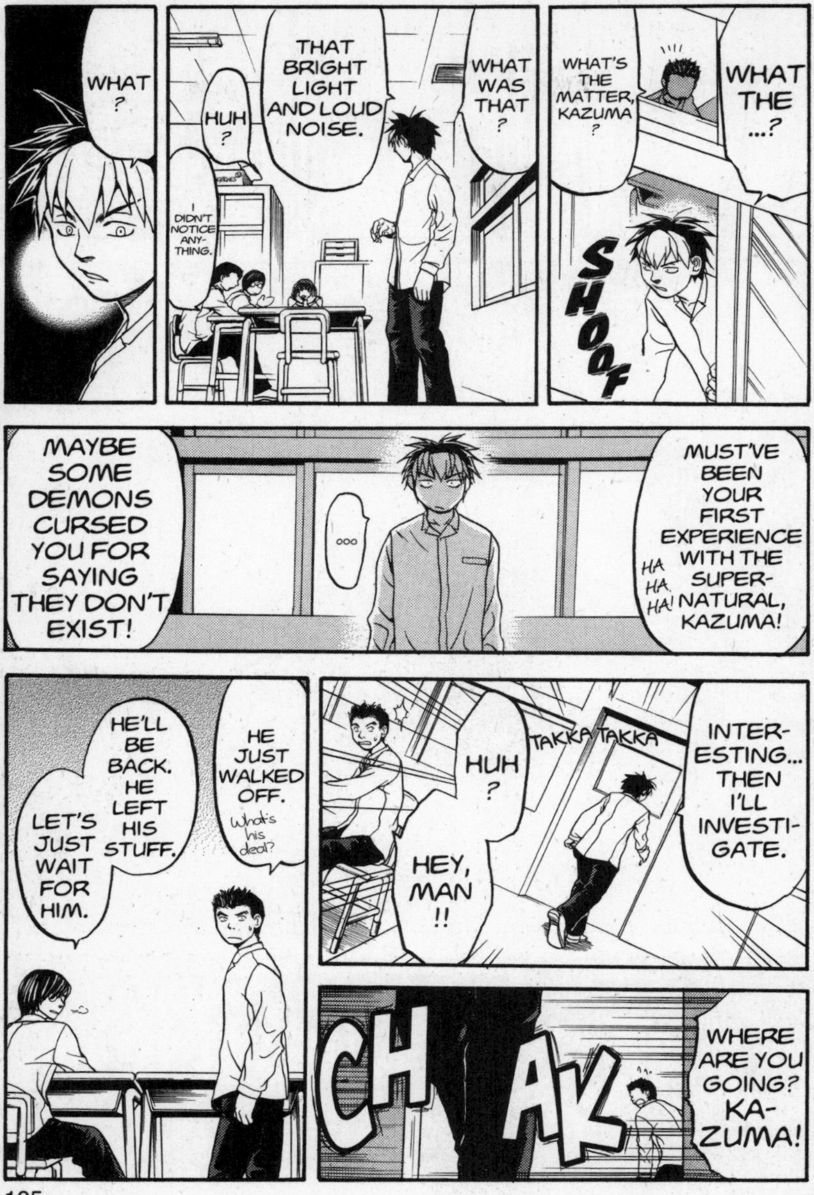
WHAT THE ...?
WHAT'S THE MATTER, KAZUMA?
SHOOF
WHAT WAS THAT?
THAT BRIGHT LIGHT AND LOUD NOISE.
HUH?
I DIDN'T NOTICE ANYTHING.
WHAT?
MUST'VE BEEN YOUR FIRST EXPERIENCE WITH THE SUPERNATURAL, KAZUMA!
HA HA HA!
...
MAYBE SOME DEMONS CURSED YOU FOR SAYING THEY DON'T EXIST!
INTERESTING... THEN I'LL INVESTIGATE.
TAKKA TAKKA
HUH?
HEY, MAN!!
WHERE ARE YOU GOING? KAZUMA!
CHAK
HE JUST WALKED OFF.
What's his deal?
HE'LL BE BACK. HE LEFT HIS STUFF.
LET'S JUST WAIT FOR HIM.

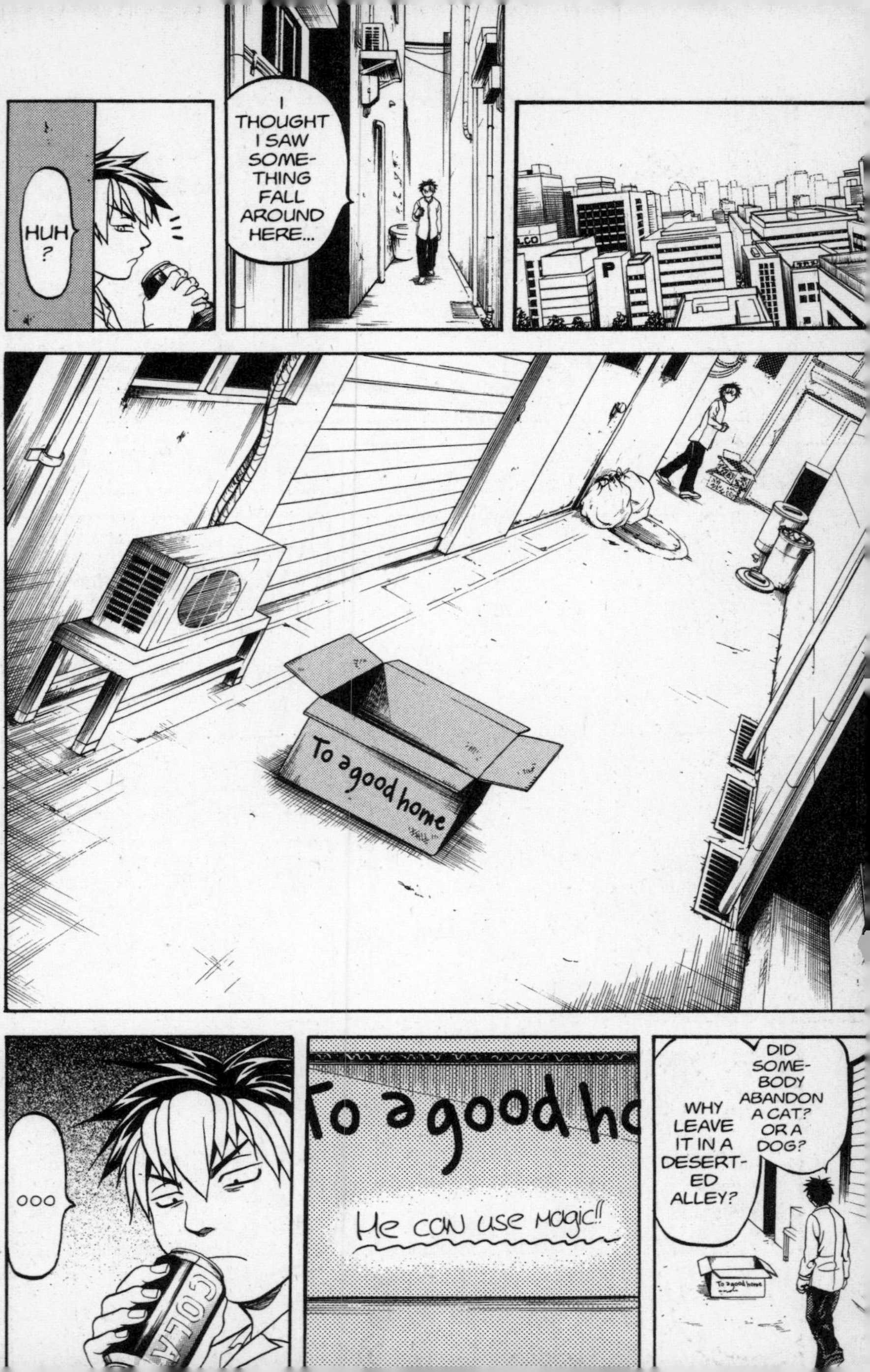
I THOUGHT I SAW SOME-THING FALL AROUND HERE...
HUH?
To a good home
DID SOME-BODY ABANDON A CAT? OR A DOG?
WHY LEAVE IT IN A DESERT-ED ALLEY?
To a good home
To a good ho
He can use magic!!
...
COLA

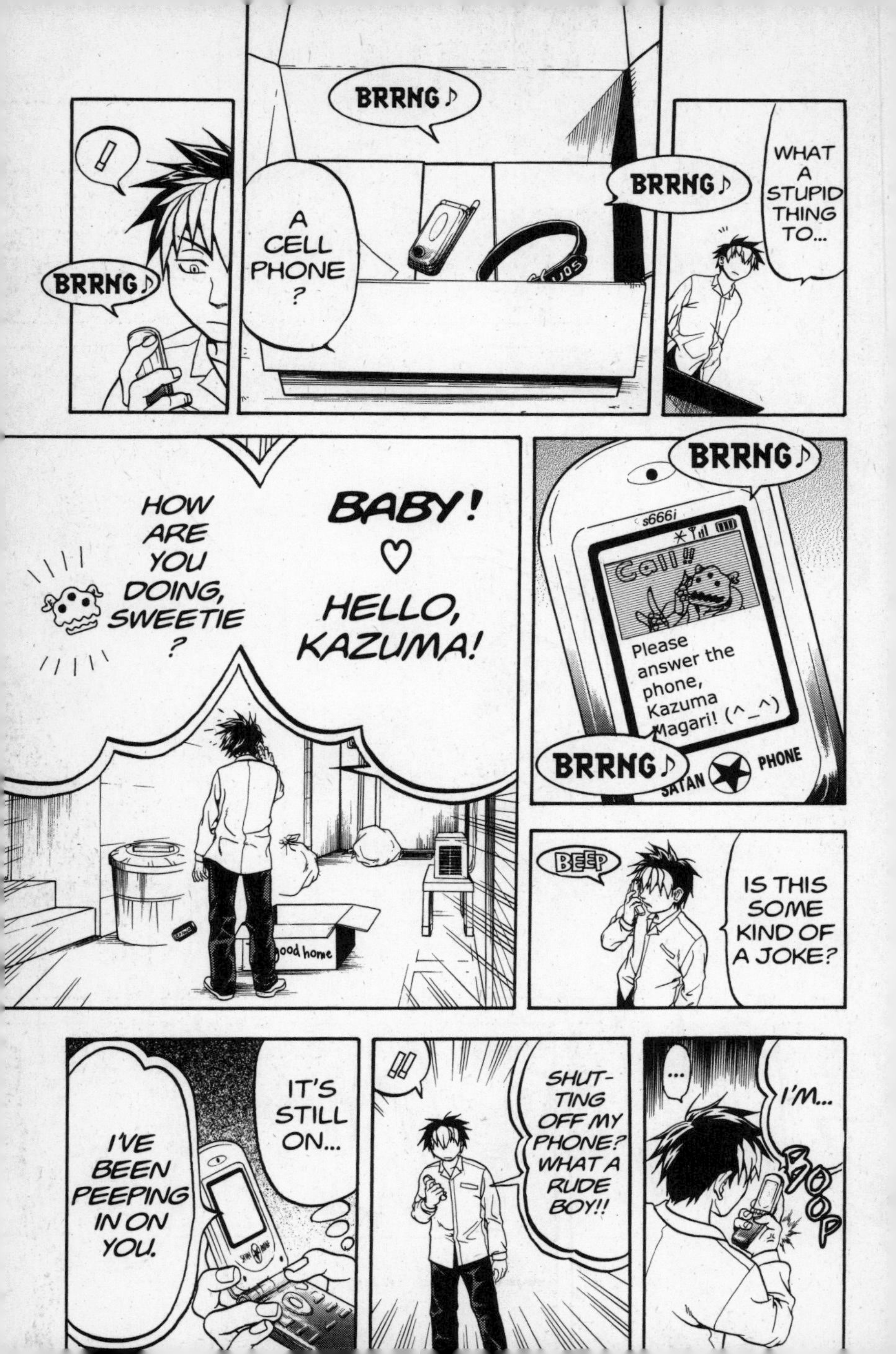
WHAT A STUPID THING TO...
BRRNG♪
BRRNG♪
A CELL PHONE?
!
BRRNG♪
BRRNG♪
s666i
Call!!
Please answer the phone, Kazuma Magari! (^_^)
BRRNG♪
SATAN PHONE
IS THIS SOME KIND OF A JOKE?
BEEP
BABY! ♡
HELLO, KAZUMA!
HOW ARE YOU DOING, SWEETIE?
good home
I'M...
...
BOOP
SHUT-TING OFF MY PHONE? WHAT A RUDE BOY!!
!!
IT'S STILL ON...
I'VE BEEN PEEPING IN ON YOU.

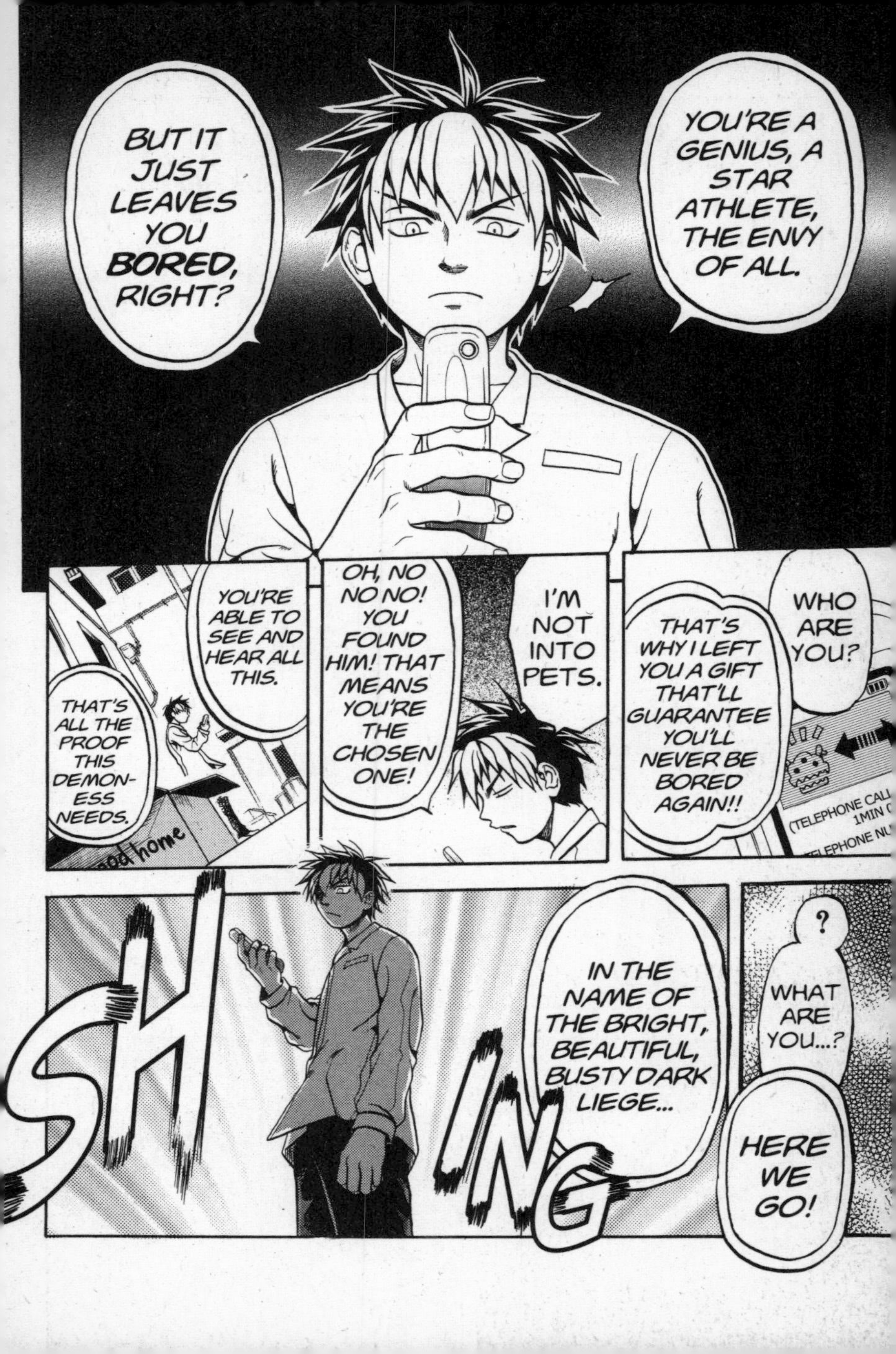
YOU'RE A GENIUS, A STAR ATHLETE, THE ENVY OF ALL.
BUT IT JUST LEAVES YOU BORED, RIGHT?
WHO ARE YOU?
THAT'S WHY I LEFT YOU A GIFT THAT'LL GUARANTEE YOU'LL NEVER BE BORED AGAIN!!
I'M NOT INTO PETS.
OH, NO NO NO! YOU FOUND HIM! THAT MEANS YOU'RE THE CHOSEN ONE!
YOU'RE ABLE TO SEE AND HEAR ALL THIS.
THAT'S ALL THE PROOF THIS DEMONESS NEEDS.
?
WHAT ARE YOU...?
HERE WE GO!
IN THE NAME OF THE BRIGHT, BEAUTIFUL, BUSTY DARK LIEGE...
SHING

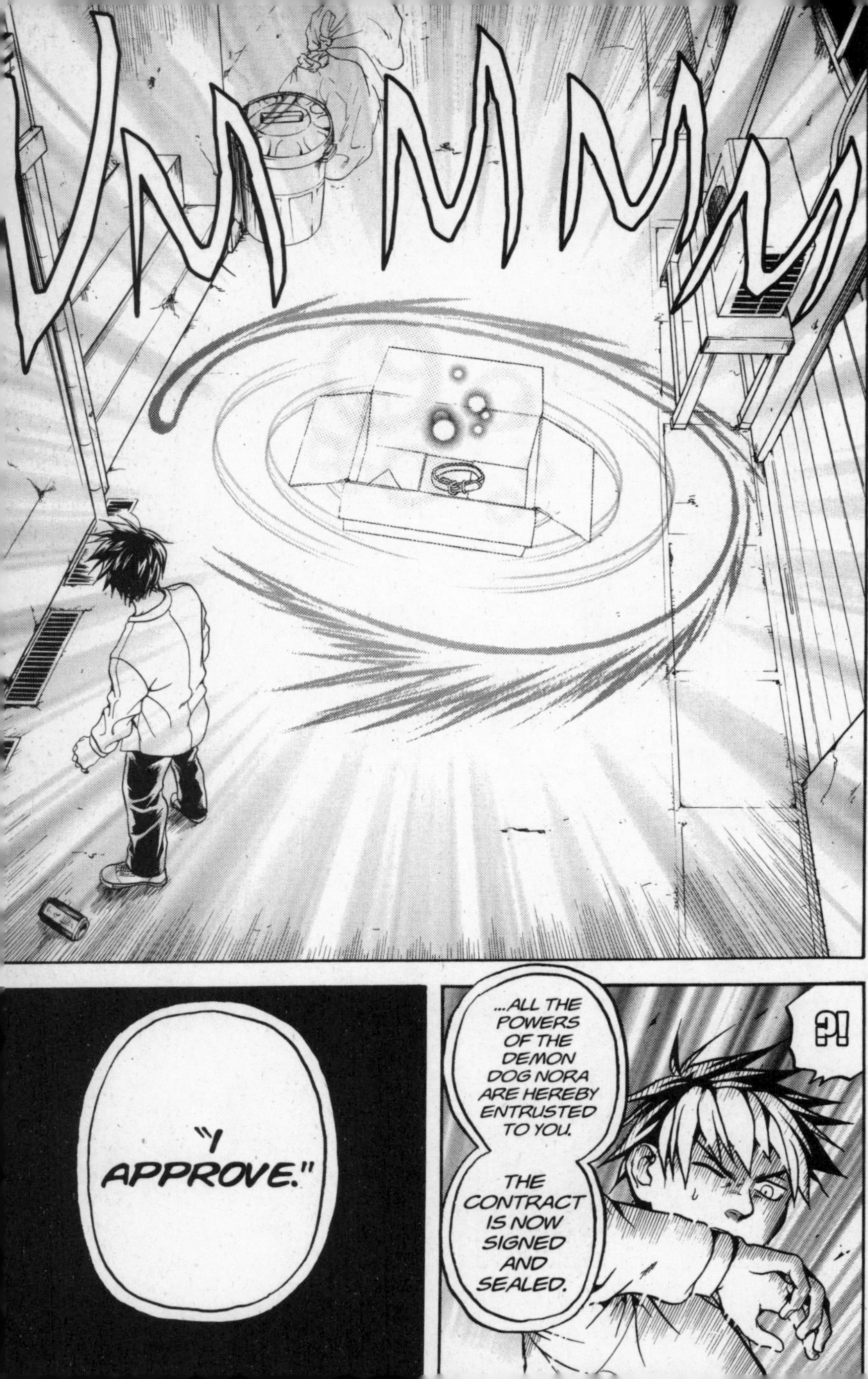
VMMMM
?!
...ALL THE POWERS OF THE DEMON DOG NORA ARE HEREBY ENTRUSTED TO YOU.
THE CONTRACT IS NOW SIGNED AND SEALED.
"I APPROVE."

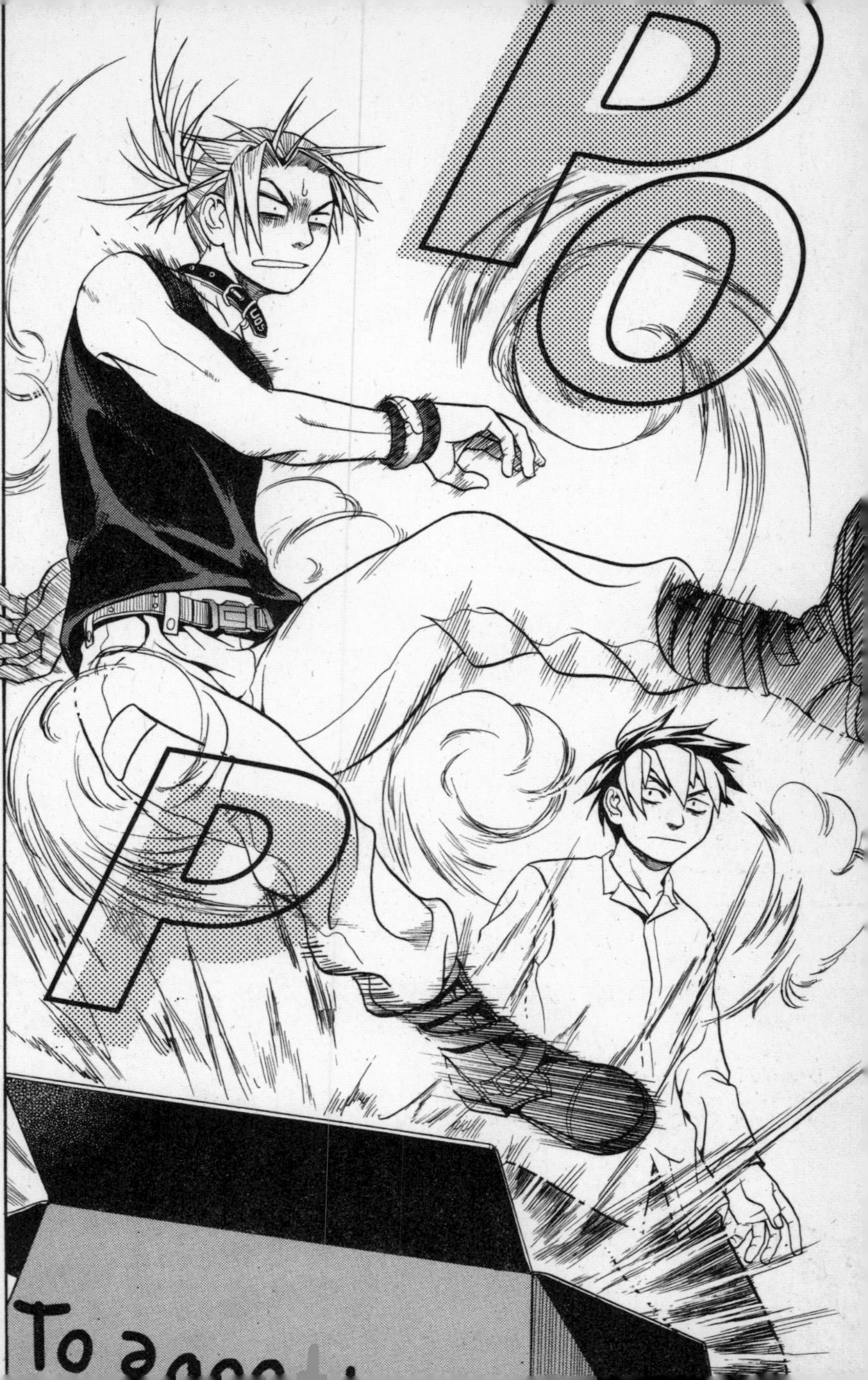
POP
To

READ THIS WAY

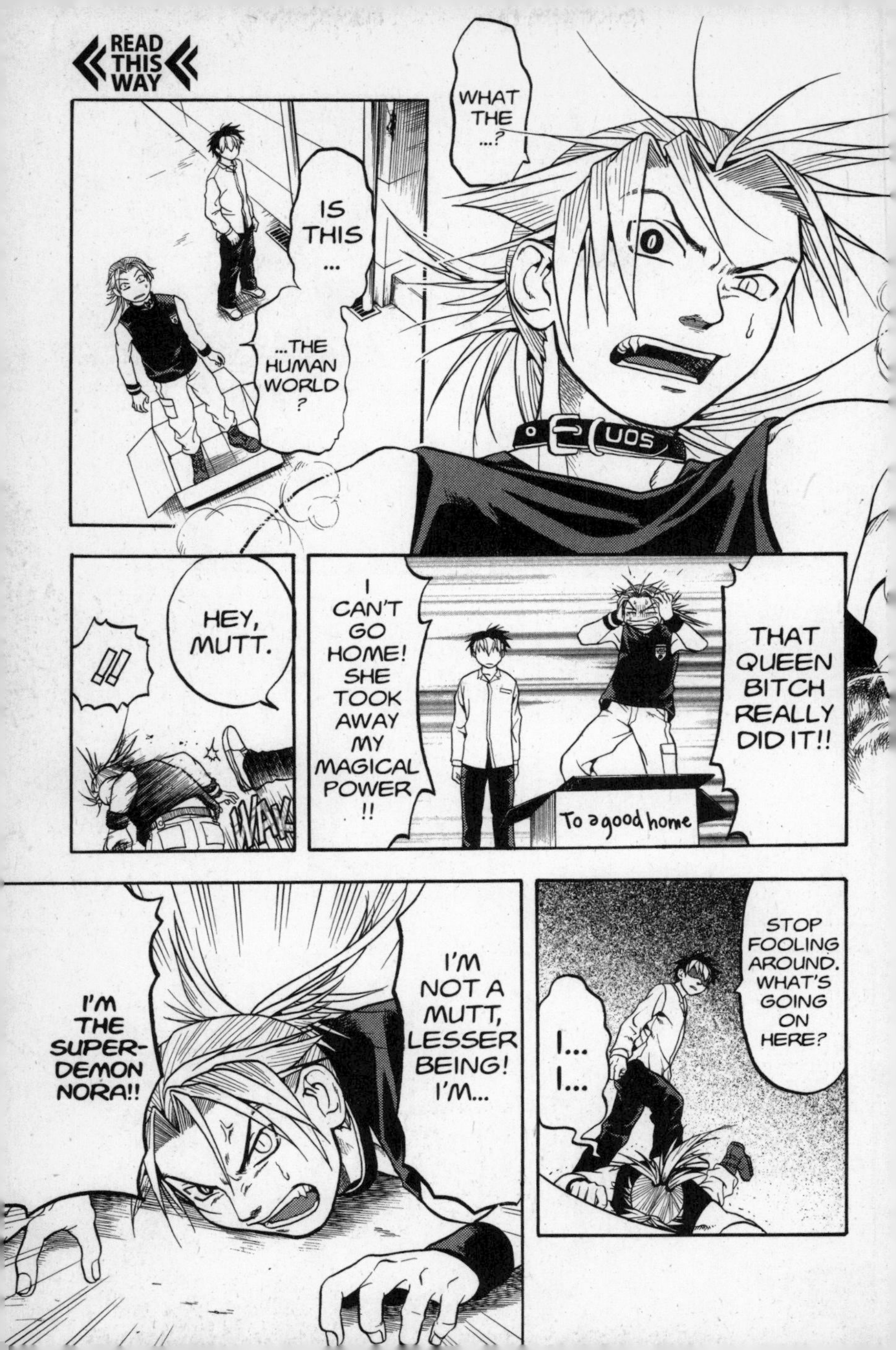
WHAT THE ...?
IS THIS ...
...THE HUMAN WORLD?
THAT QUEEN BITCH REALLY DID IT!!
I CAN'T GO HOME! SHE TOOK AWAY MY MAGICAL POWER!!
To a good home
HEY, MUTT.
!!
WAK
STOP FOOLING AROUND. WHAT'S GOING ON HERE?
I... I...
I'M NOT A MUTT, LESSER BEING! I'M...
I'M THE SUPER-DEMON NORA!!

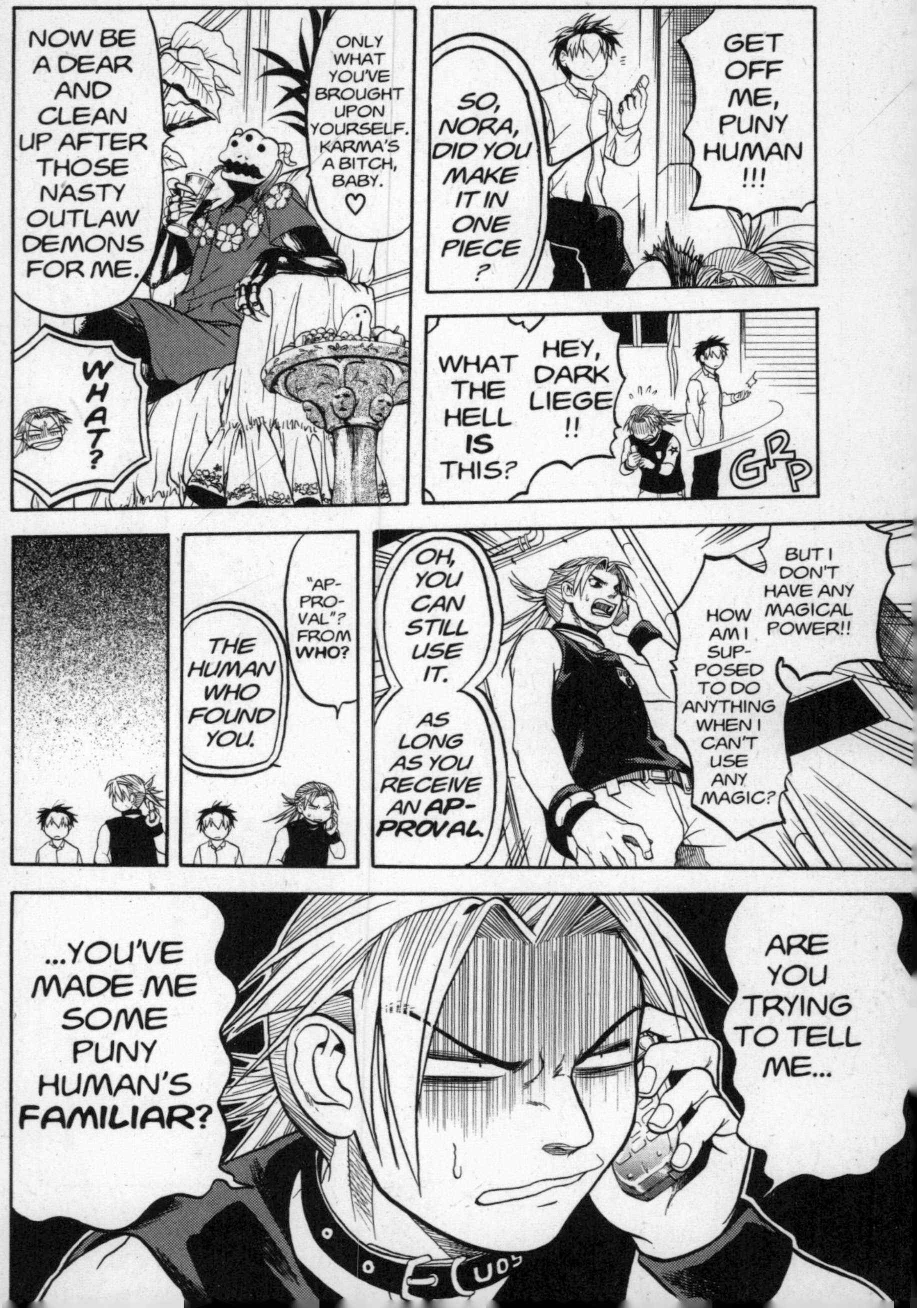
GET OFF ME, PUNY HUMAN!!!
SO, NORA, DID YOU MAKE IT IN ONE PIECE?
HEY, DARK LIEGE!!
WHAT THE HELL IS THIS?
GRP
ONLY WHAT YOU'VE BROUGHT UPON YOURSELF. KARMA'S A BITCH, BABY. ♡
NOW BE A DEAR AND CLEAN UP AFTER THOSE NASTY OUTLAW DEMONS FOR ME.
WHAT?
BUT I DON'T HAVE ANY MAGICAL POWER!!
HOW AM I SUP-POSED TO DO ANYTHING WHEN I CAN'T USE ANY MAGIC?
OH, YOU CAN STILL USE IT.
AS LONG AS YOU RECEIVE AN AP-PROVAL.
"AP-PRO-VAL"? FROM WHO?
THE HUMAN WHO FOUND YOU.
ARE YOU TRYING TO TELL ME...
...YOU'VE MADE ME SOME PUNY HUMAN'S FAMILIAR?

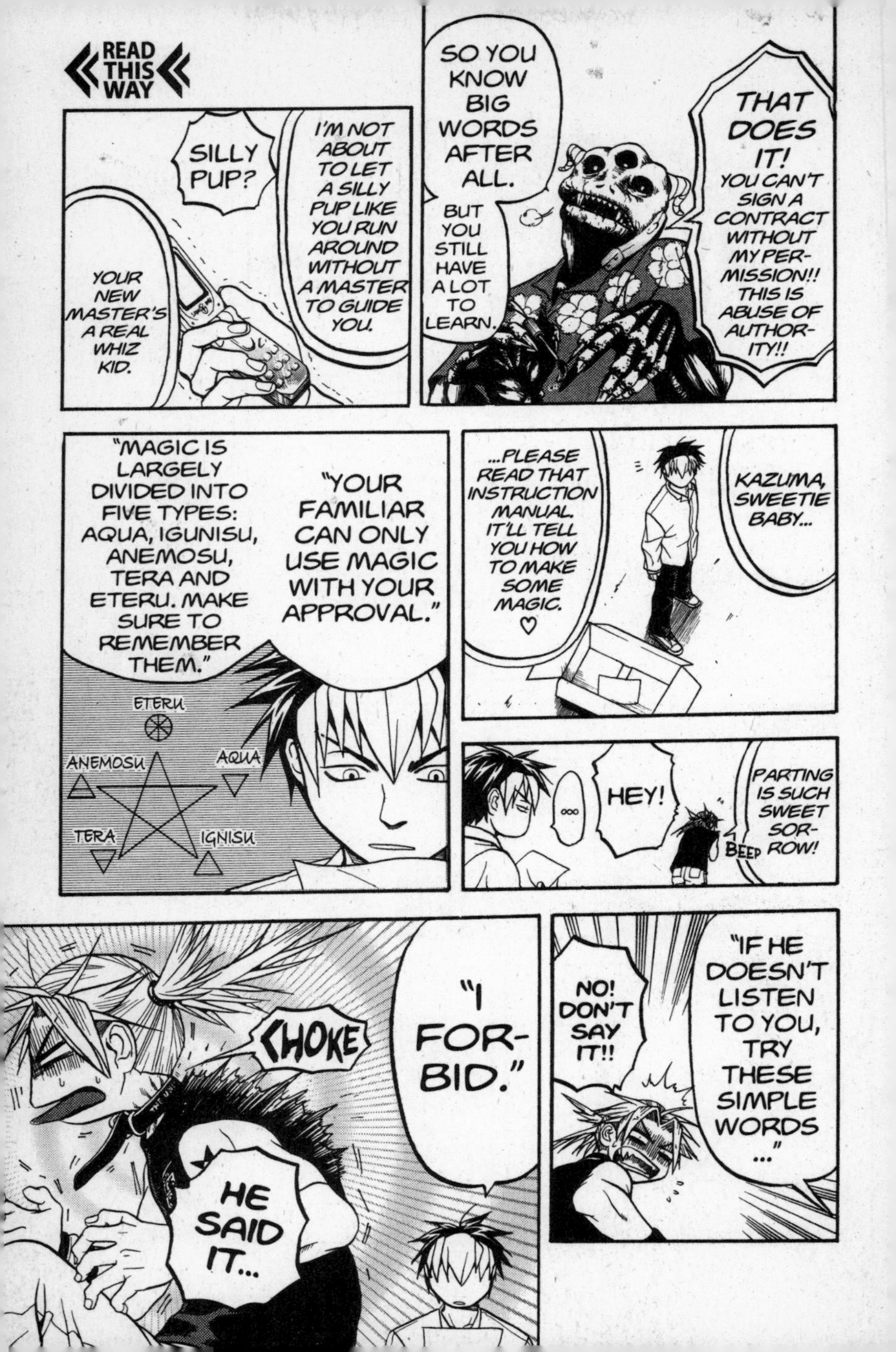
READ THIS WAY
THAT DOES IT! YOU CAN'T SIGN A CONTRACT WITHOUT MY PER-MISSION!! THIS IS ABUSE OF AUTHOR-ITY!!
SO YOU KNOW BIG WORDS AFTER ALL.
BUT YOU STILL HAVE A LOT TO LEARN.
I'M NOT ABOUT TO LET A SILLY PUP LIKE YOU RUN AROUND WITHOUT A MASTER TO GUIDE YOU.
SILLY PUP?
YOUR NEW MASTER'S A REAL WHIZ KID.
KAZUMA, SWEETIE BABY...
...PLEASE READ THAT INSTRUCTION MANUAL. IT'LL TELL YOU HOW TO MAKE SOME MAGIC. ♡
PARTING IS SUCH SWEET SOR-ROW!
BEEP
HEY!
...
"YOUR FAMILIAR CAN ONLY USE MAGIC WITH YOUR APPROVAL."
"MAGIC IS LARGELY DIVIDED INTO FIVE TYPES: AQUA, IGUNISU, ANEMOSU, TERA AND ETERU. MAKE SURE TO REMEMBER THEM."
ETERU
ANEMOSU
AQUA
TERA
IGNISU
"IF HE DOESN'T LISTEN TO YOU, TRY THESE SIMPLE WORDS..."
NO! DON'T SAY IT!!
"I FOR-BID."
CHOKE
HE SAID IT...

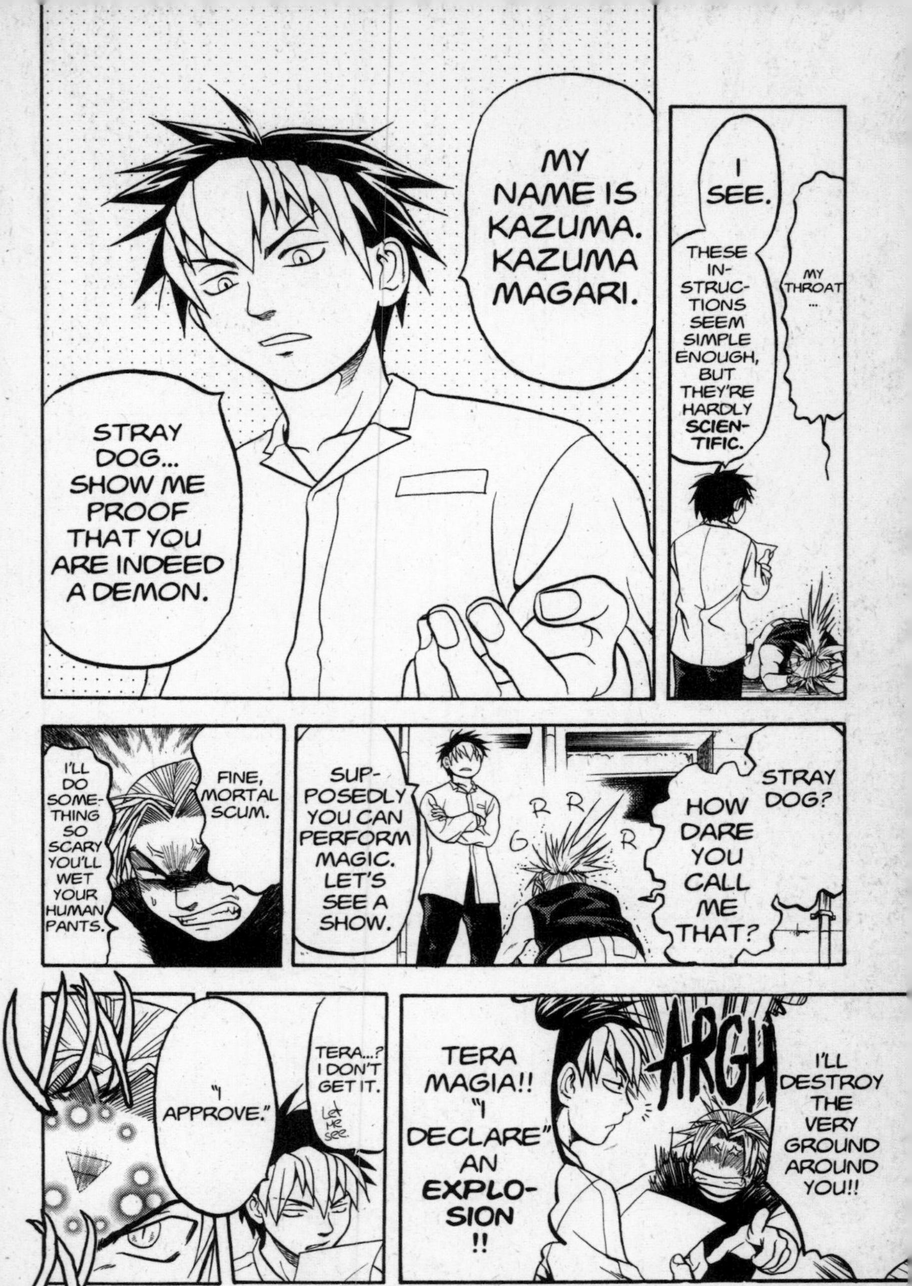
I SEE.
THESE IN-STRUC-TIONS SEEM SIMPLE ENOUGH, BUT THEY'RE HARDLY SCIEN-TIFIC.
MY THROAT...
MY NAME IS KAZUMA. KAZUMA MAGARI.
STRAY DOG... SHOW ME PROOF THAT YOU ARE INDEED A DEMON.
STRAY DOG?
HOW DARE YOU CALL ME THAT?
G R R R
SUP-POSEDLY YOU CAN PERFORM MAGIC. LET'S SEE A SHOW.
FINE, MORTAL SCUM.
I'LL DO SOME-THING SO SCARY YOU'LL WET YOUR HUMAN PANTS.
I'LL DESTROY THE VERY GROUND AROUND YOU!!
ARGH
TERA MAGIA!! "I DECLARE" AN EXPLO-SION!!
TERA...? I DON'T GET IT.
Let me see.
"I APPROVE."

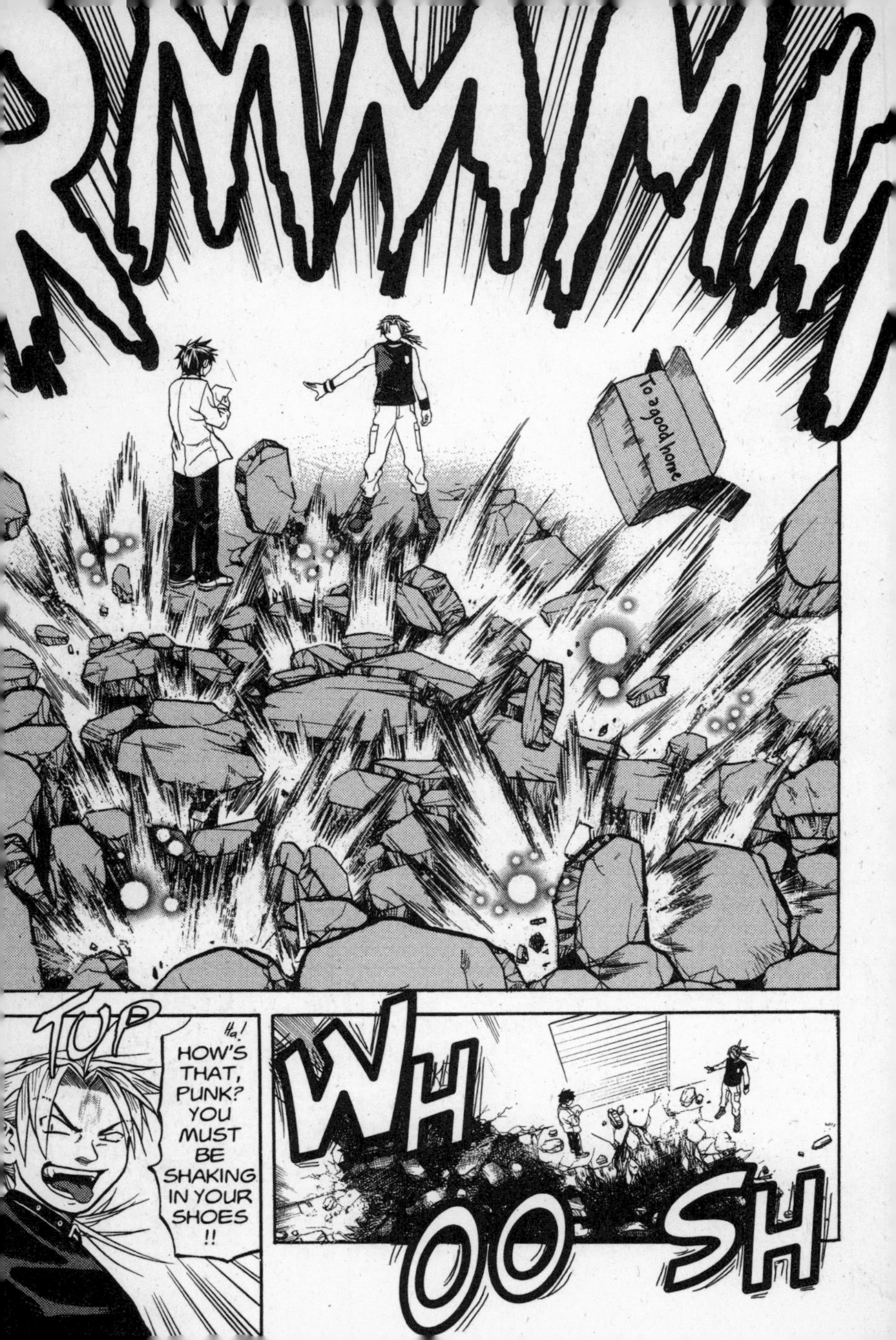
To good home
WHOOSH
TUP
Ha!
HOW'S THAT, PUNK? YOU MUST BE SHAKING IN YOUR SHOES!!

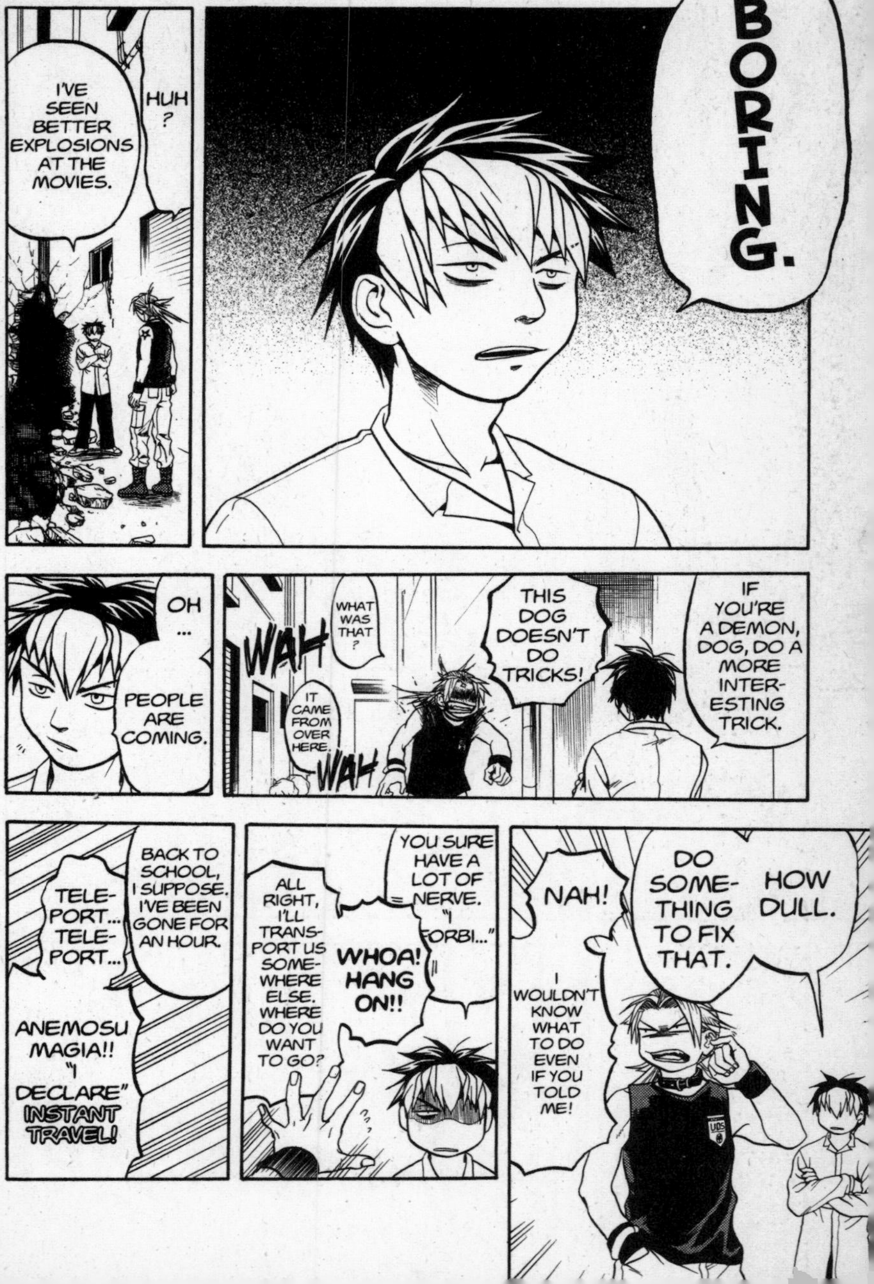
BORING.
HUH?
I'VE SEEN BETTER EXPLOSIONS AT THE MOVIES.
IF YOU'RE A DEMON, DOG, DO A MORE INTER-ESTING TRICK.
THIS DOG DOESN'T DO TRICKS!
WHAT WAS THAT?
WAH
IT CAME FROM OVER HERE.
WAH
OH...
PEOPLE ARE COMING.
HOW DULL.
DO SOME-THING TO FIX THAT.
NAH!
I WOULDN'T KNOW WHAT TO DO EVEN IF YOU TOLD ME!
YOU SURE HAVE A LOT OF NERVE. "I FORBI..."
WHOA! HANG ON!!
ALL RIGHT, I'LL TRANS-PORT US SOME-WHERE ELSE. WHERE DO YOU WANT TO GO?
BACK TO SCHOOL, I SUPPOSE. I'VE BEEN GONE FOR AN HOUR.
TELE-PORT... TELE-PORT...
ANEMOSU MAGIA!! "I DECLARE" INSTANT TRAVEL!

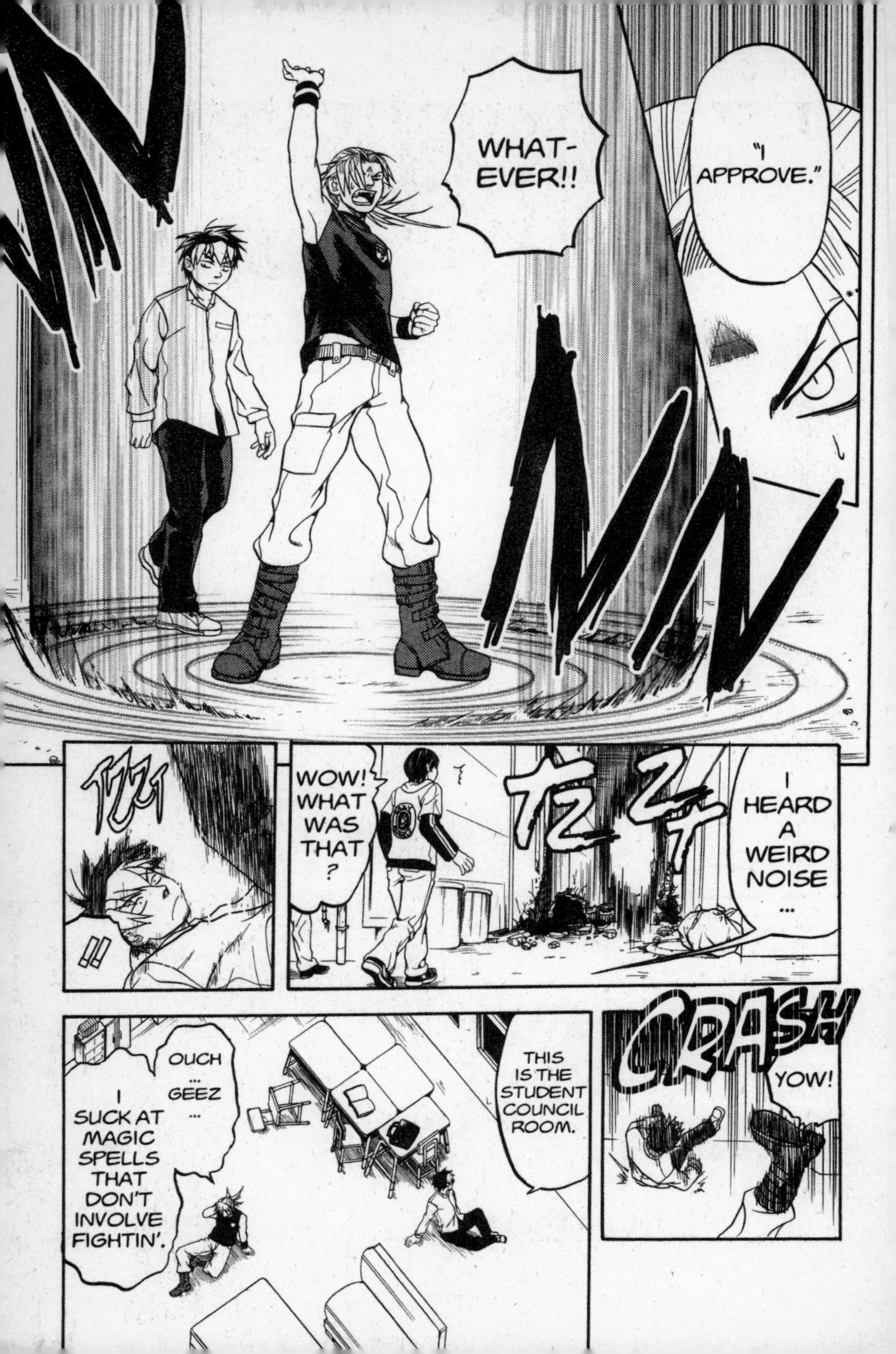
"I APPROVE."
WHAT-EVER!!
I HEARD A WEIRD NOISE ...
WOW! WHAT WAS THAT?
!!
CRASH
YOW!
THIS IS THE STUDENT COUNCIL ROOM.
OUCH ... GEEZ ...
I SUCK AT MAGIC SPELLS THAT DON'T INVOLVE FIGHTIN'.

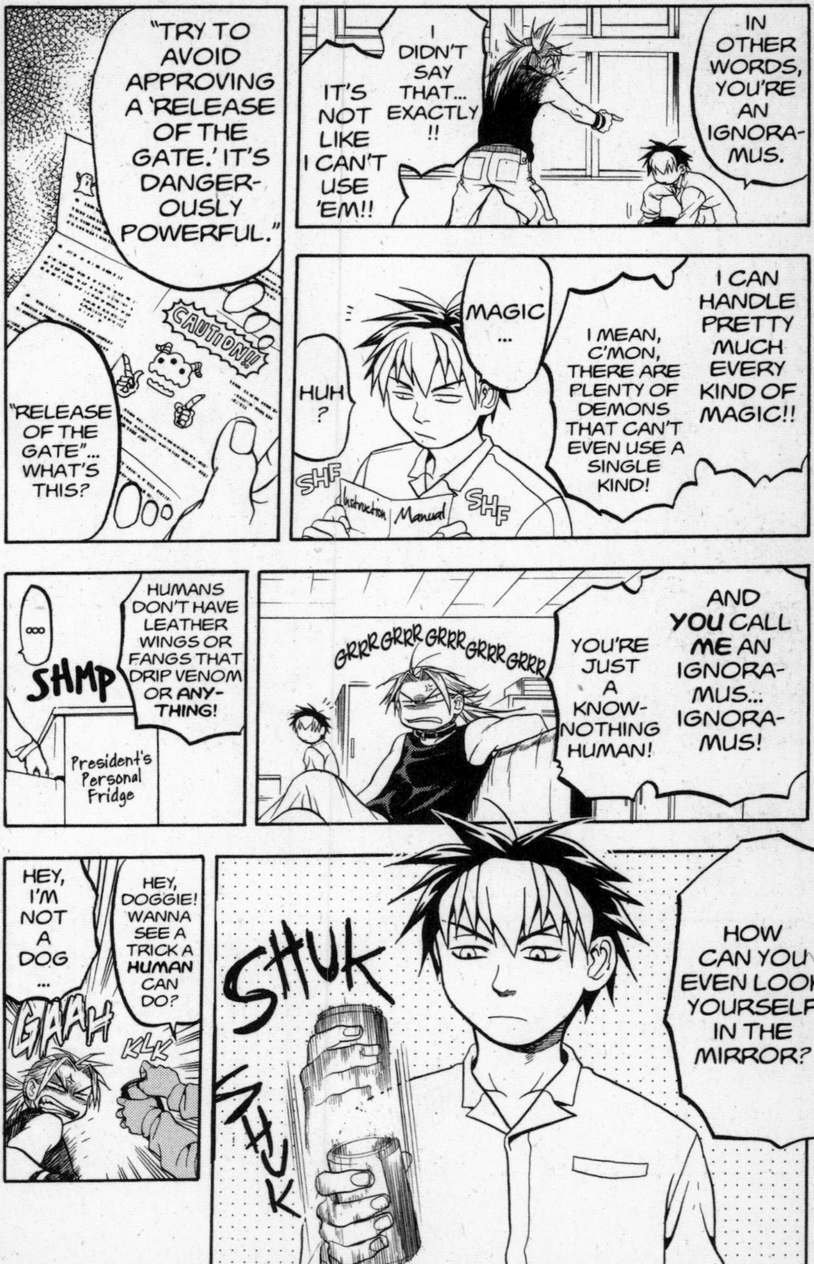
IN OTHER WORDS, YOU'RE AN IGNORAMUS.
I DIDN'T SAY THAT... EXACTLY!!
IT'S NOT LIKE I CAN'T USE 'EM!!
I CAN HANDLE PRETTY MUCH EVERY KIND OF MAGIC!!
I MEAN, C'MON, THERE ARE PLENTY OF DEMONS THAT CAN'T EVEN USE A SINGLE KIND!
MAGIC...
HUH?
SHF
Instruction Manual
SHF
"TRY TO AVOID APPROVING A 'RELEASE OF THE GATE.' IT'S DANGEROUSLY POWERFUL."
CAUTION!!
"RELEASE OF THE GATE"... WHAT'S THIS?
AND YOU CALL ME AN IGNORAMUS... IGNORAMUS!
YOU'RE JUST A KNOW-NOTHING HUMAN!
GRRR GRRR GRRR GRRR GRRR
HUMANS DON'T HAVE LEATHER WINGS OR FANGS THAT DRIP VENOM OR ANYTHING!
...
SHMP
President's Personal Fridge
HOW CAN YOU EVEN LOOK YOURSELF IN THE MIRROR?
SHUK
SHUK
SHUK
HEY, DOGGIE! WANNA SEE A TRICK A HUMAN CAN DO?
HEY, I'M NOT A DOG...
GAAH
KLK

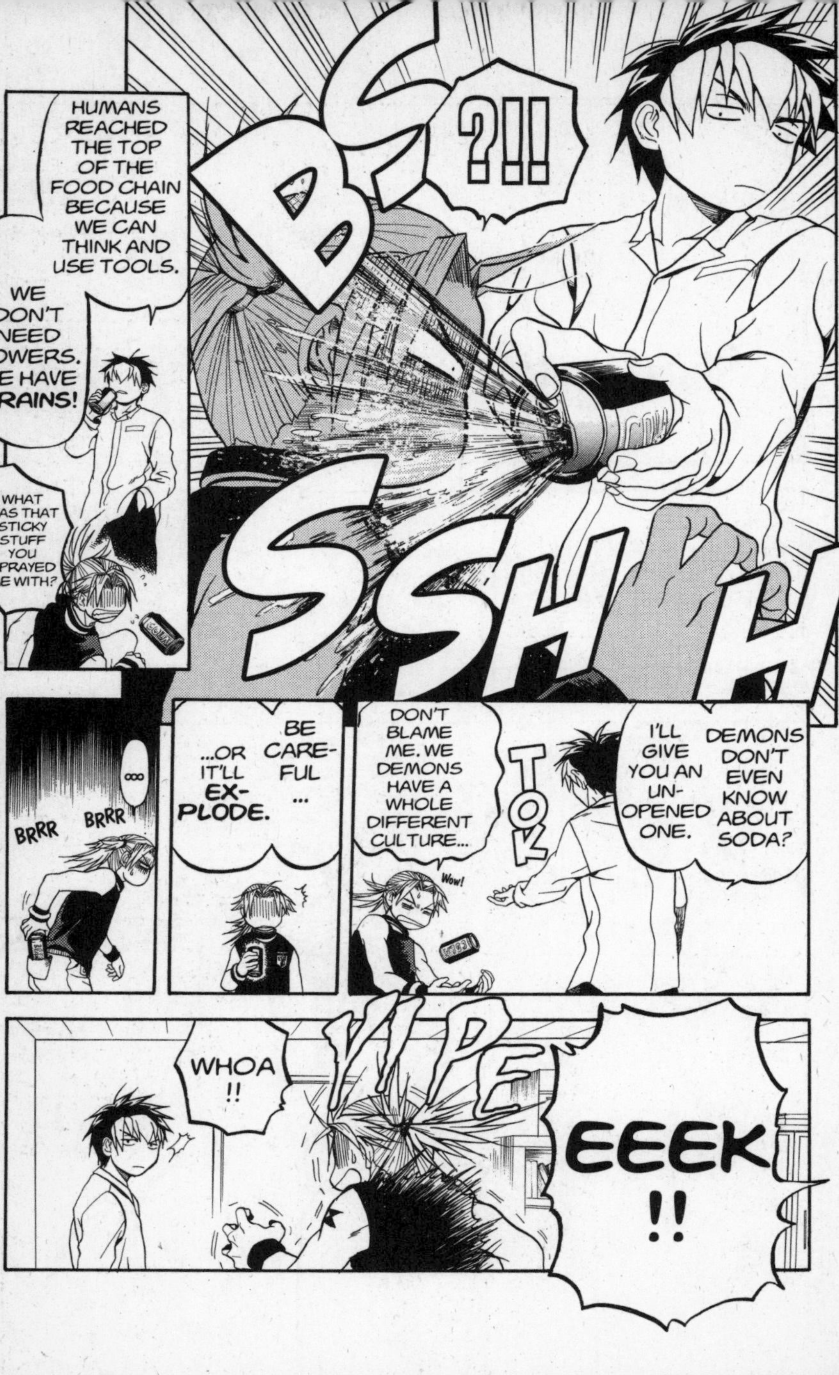
BS
?!!
SSHH
HUMANS REACHED THE TOP OF THE FOOD CHAIN BECAUSE WE CAN THINK AND USE TOOLS.
WE DON'T NEED POWERS. WE HAVE **BRAINS**!
WHAT WAS THAT STICKY STUFF YOU SPRAYED ME WITH?
DEMONS DON'T EVEN KNOW ABOUT SODA?
I'LL GIVE YOU AN UN-OPENED ONE.
TOK
DON'T BLAME ME. WE DEMONS HAVE A WHOLE DIFFERENT CULTURE...
Wow!
BE CARE-FUL ...
...OR IT'LL **EX-PLODE.**
...
BRRR
BRRR
YIPE
EEEK !!
WHOA !!

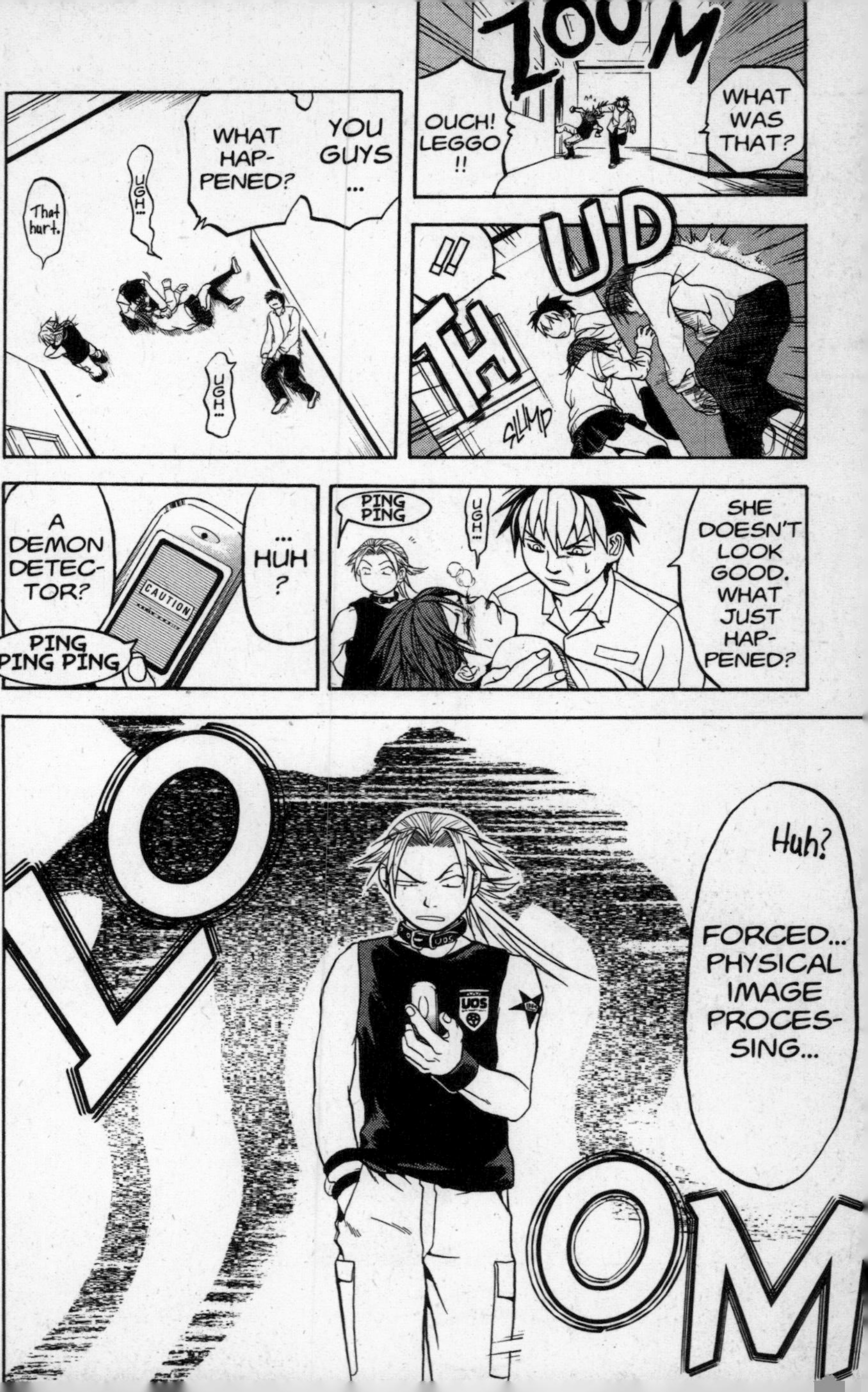
WHAT WAS THAT?
ZOOM
OUCH! LEGGO!!
!!
THUD
SLUMP
YOU GUYS...
WHAT HAPPENED?
UGH...
That hurt.
UGH...
SHE DOESN'T LOOK GOOD. WHAT JUST HAPPENED?
UGH...
PING PING
...HUH?
A DEMON DETECTOR?
CAUTION
PING PING PING
Huh?
FORCED... PHYSICAL IMAGE PROCESSING...

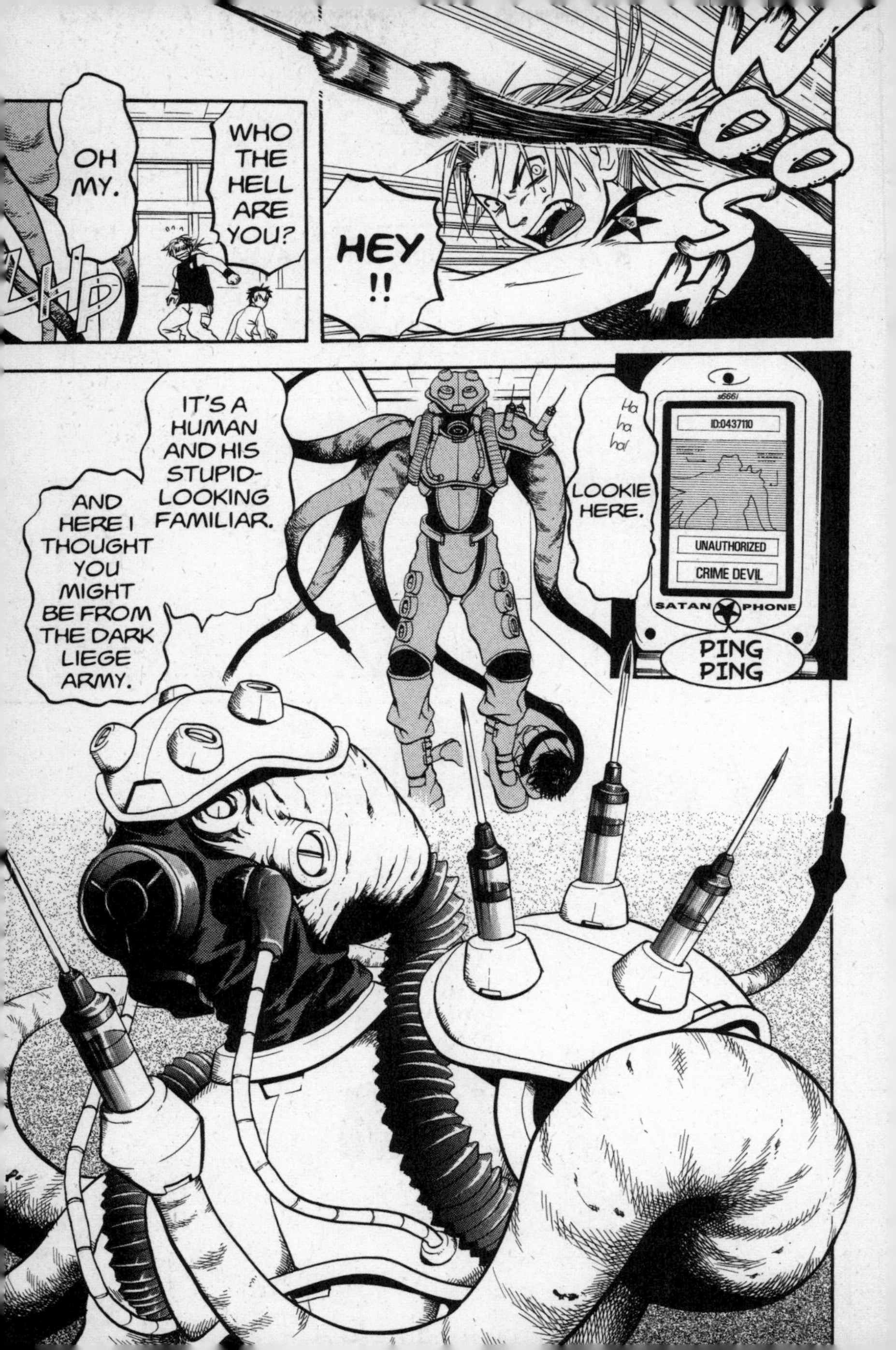
WHOOSH
HEY!!
WHO THE HELL ARE YOU?
OH MY.
Ha ha ha!
LOOKIE HERE.
s666i
ID:0437110
UNAUTHORIZED
CRIME DEVIL
SATAN PHONE
PING PING
IT'S A HUMAN AND HIS STUPID-LOOKING FAMILIAR.
AND HERE I THOUGHT YOU MIGHT BE FROM THE DARK LIEGE ARMY.

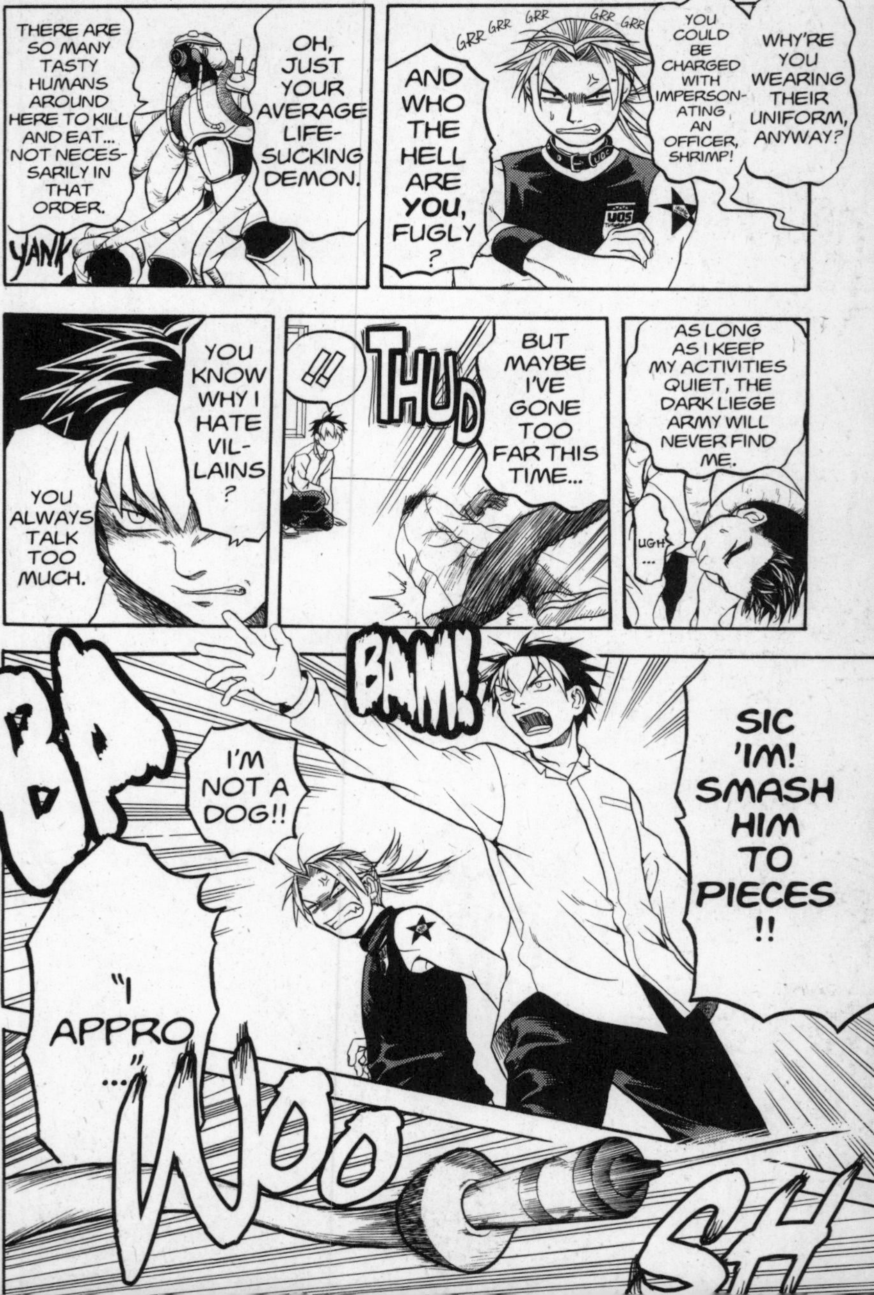
WHY'RE YOU WEARING THEIR UNIFORM, ANYWAY?
YOU COULD BE CHARGED WITH IMPERSONATING AN OFFICER, SHRIMP!
GRR GRR GRR GRR GRR
AND WHO THE HELL ARE YOU, FUGLY?
OH, JUST YOUR AVERAGE LIFE-SUCKING DEMON.
THERE ARE SO MANY TASTY HUMANS AROUND HERE TO KILL AND EAT... NOT NECESSARILY IN THAT ORDER.
YANK
AS LONG AS I KEEP MY ACTIVITIES QUIET, THE DARK LIEGE ARMY WILL NEVER FIND ME.
UGH...
BUT MAYBE I'VE GONE TOO FAR THIS TIME...
THUD
!!
YOU KNOW WHY I HATE VILLAINS?
YOU ALWAYS TALK TOO MUCH.
SIC 'IM! SMASH HIM TO PIECES!!
BAM!
I'M NOT A DOG!!
BA
"I APPRO..."
WOOSH

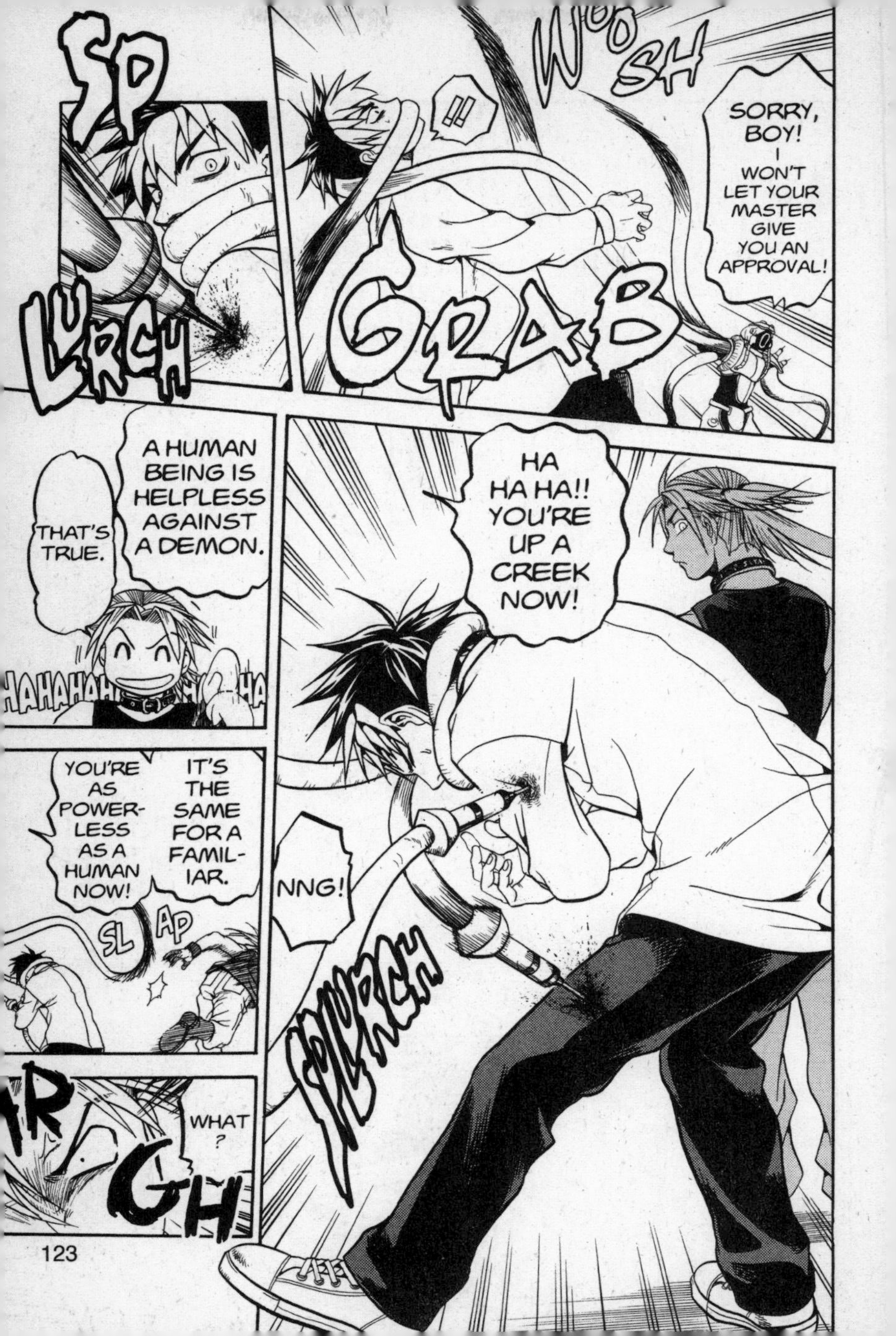
WOOSH
!!
SORRY, BOY! I WON'T LET YOUR MASTER GIVE YOU AN APPROVAL!
GRAB
SP
LURCH
HA HA HA!! YOU'RE UP A CREEK NOW!
NNG!
SPLURCH
A HUMAN BEING IS HELPLESS AGAINST A DEMON.
THAT'S TRUE.
HAHAHAH
HA
IT'S THE SAME FOR A FAMIL-IAR.
YOU'RE AS POWER-LESS AS A HUMAN NOW!
SLAP
WHAT?
ARGH

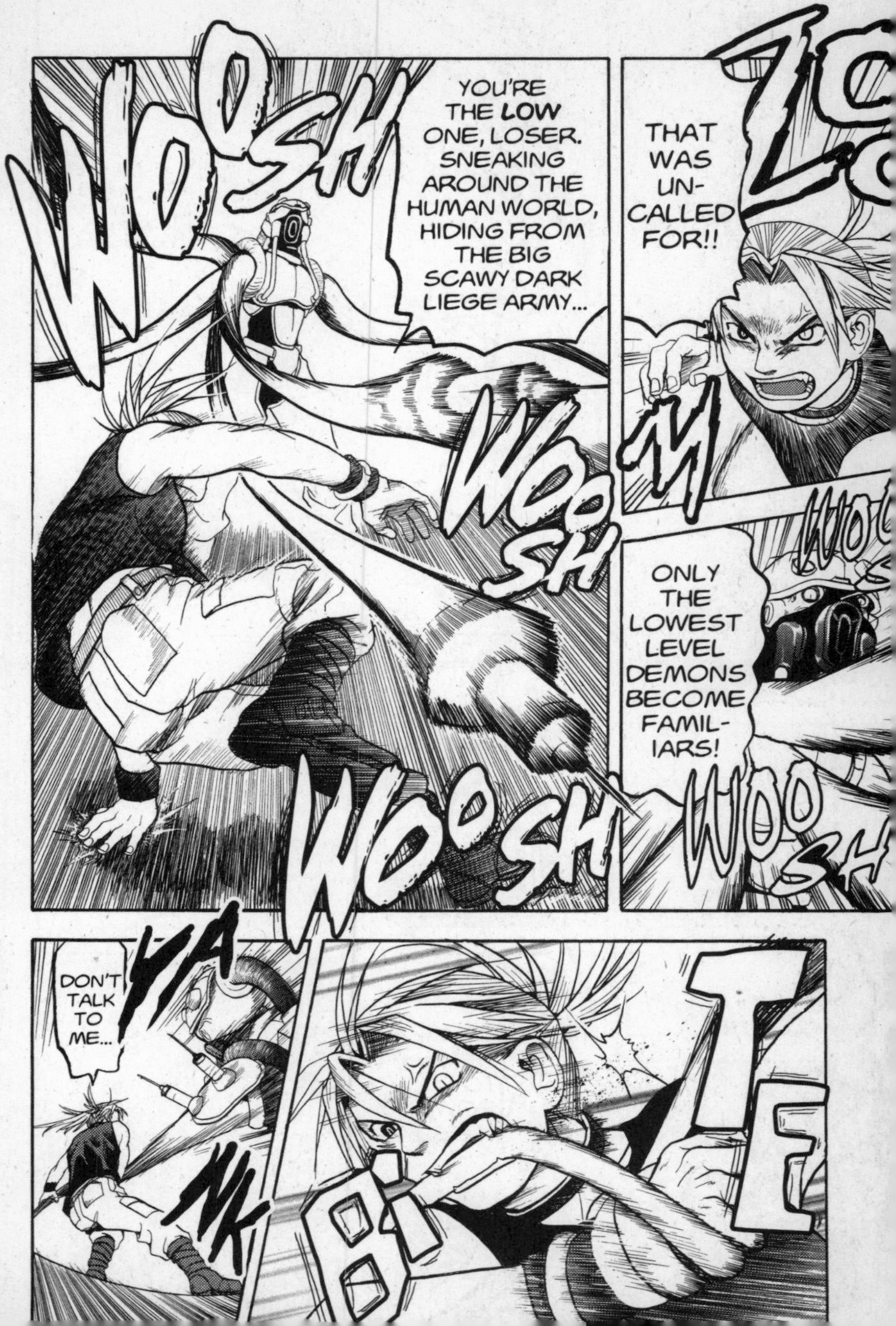

THAT WAS UN-CALLED FOR!!
ONLY THE LOWEST LEVEL DEMONS BECOME FAMIL-IARS!
WOOSH
WOOSH
YOU'RE THE **LOW** ONE, LOSER. SNEAKING AROUND THE HUMAN WORLD, HIDING FROM THE BIG SCAWY DARK LIEGE ARMY...
WOOSH
WOOSH
TE
DON'T TALK TO ME...
YANK

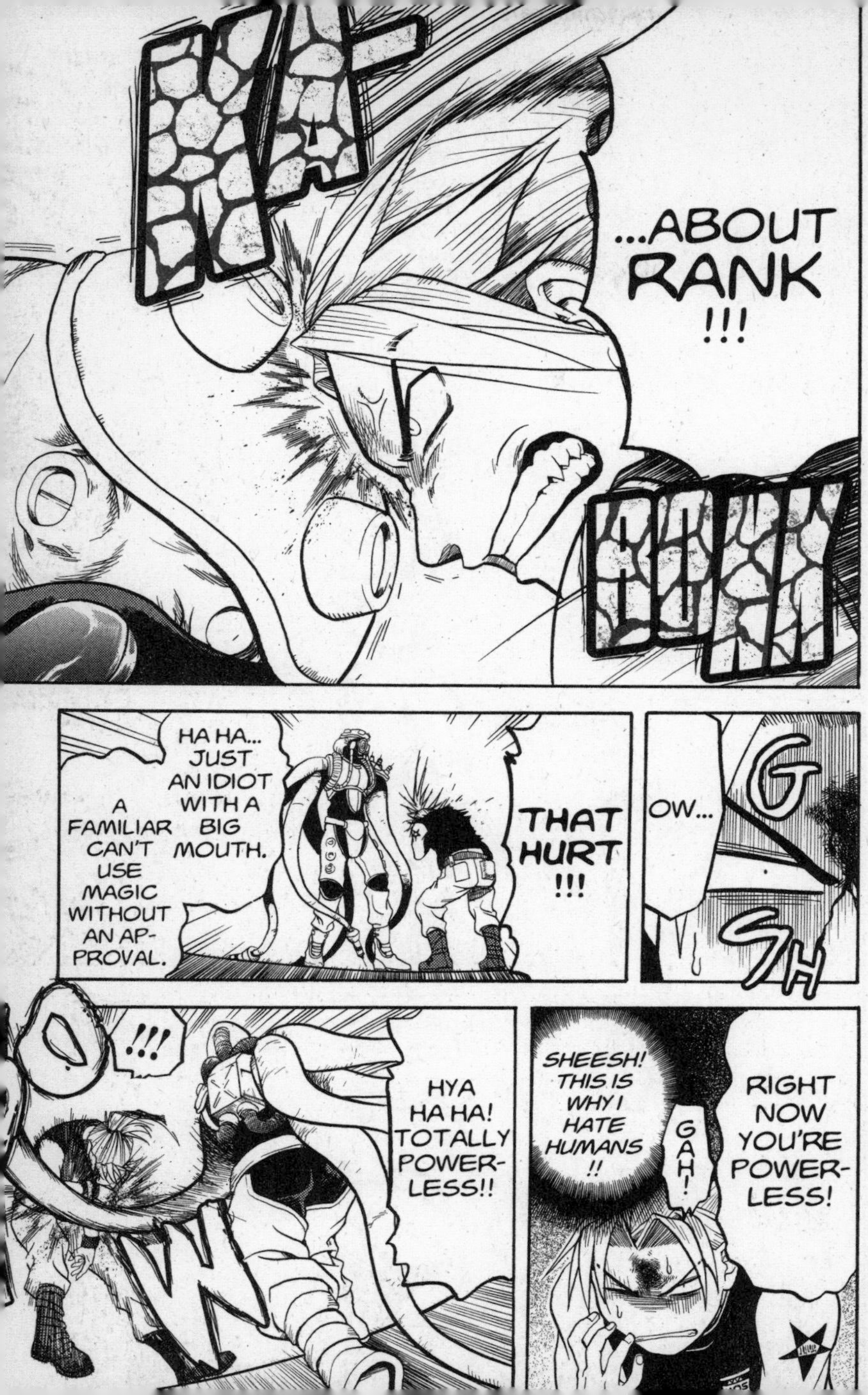

...ABOUT RANK !!!
OW...
THAT HURT !!!
HA HA... JUST AN IDIOT WITH A BIG MOUTH.
A FAMILIAR CAN'T USE MAGIC WITHOUT AN AP- PROVAL.
RIGHT NOW YOU'RE POWER- LESS!
GAH!
SHEESH! THIS IS WHY I HATE HUMANS !!
HYA HA HA! TOTALLY POWER- LESS!!
!!!

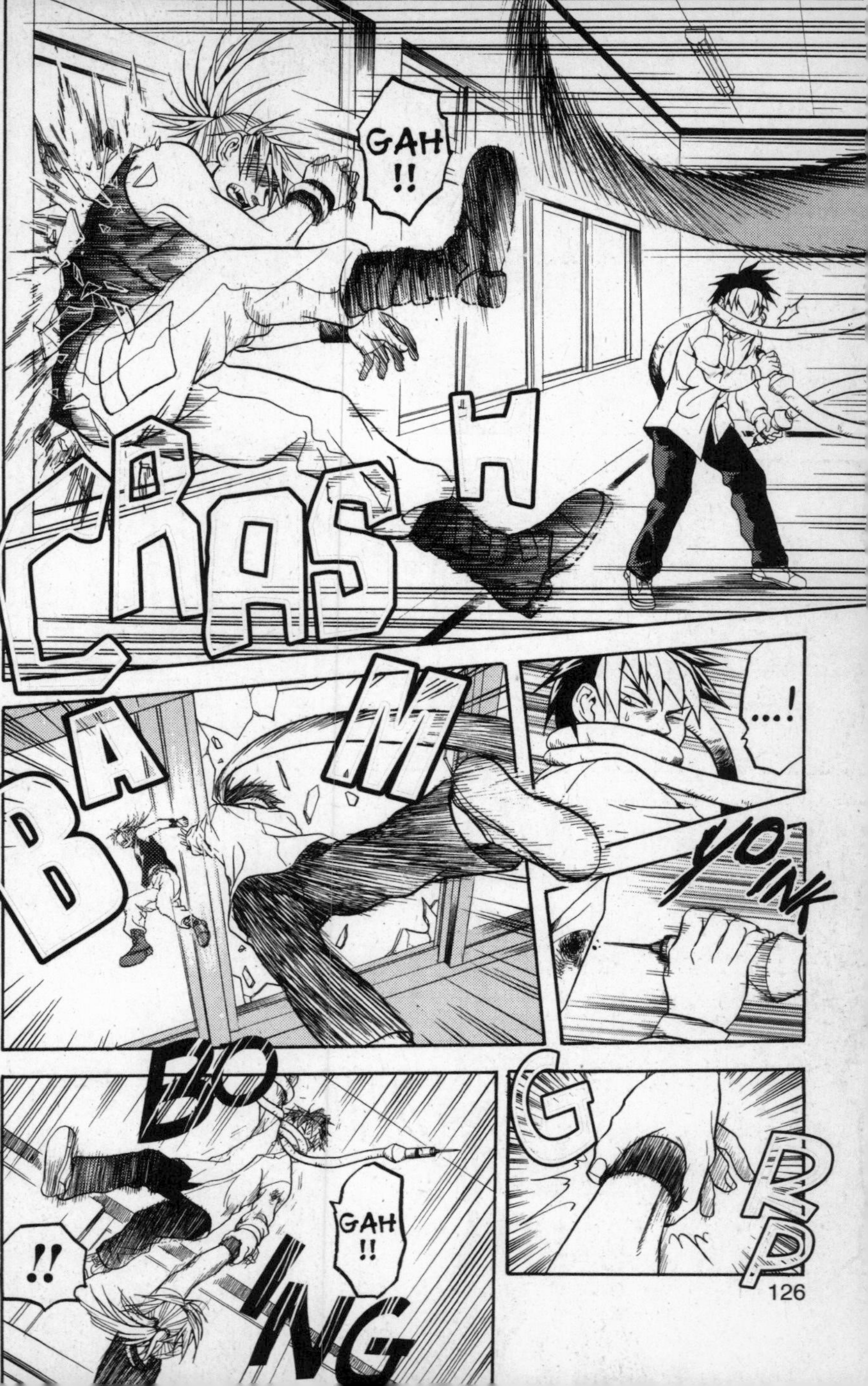
GAH !!
CRASH
...!
YOINK
BAM
GRRP
BOING
GAH !!
!!

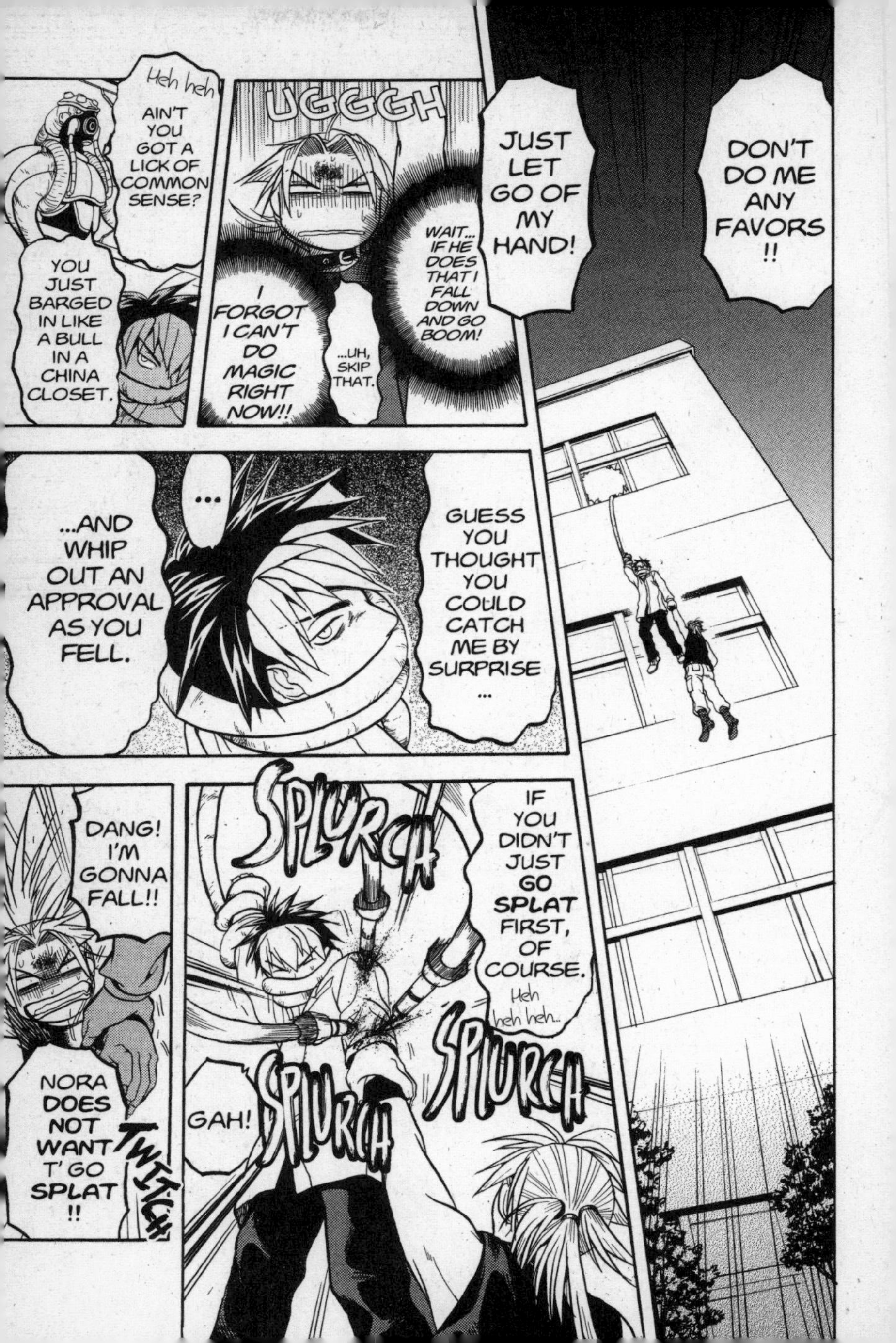
DON'T DO ME ANY FAVORS!!
JUST LET GO OF MY HAND!
UGGGH
WAIT... IF HE DOES THAT I FALL DOWN AND GO BOOM!
...UH, SKIP THAT.
I FORGOT I CAN'T DO MAGIC RIGHT NOW!!
Heh heh
AIN'T YOU GOT A LICK OF COMMON SENSE?
YOU JUST BARGED IN LIKE A BULL IN A CHINA CLOSET.
GUESS YOU THOUGHT YOU COULD CATCH ME BY SURPRISE...
...
...AND WHIP OUT AN APPROVAL AS YOU FELL.
SPLURCH
IF YOU DIDN'T JUST GO SPLAT FIRST, OF COURSE.
Heh heh heh...
SPLURCH
SPLURCH
GAH!
DANG! I'M GONNA FALL!!
TWITCH
NORA DOES NOT WANT T' GO SPLAT!!

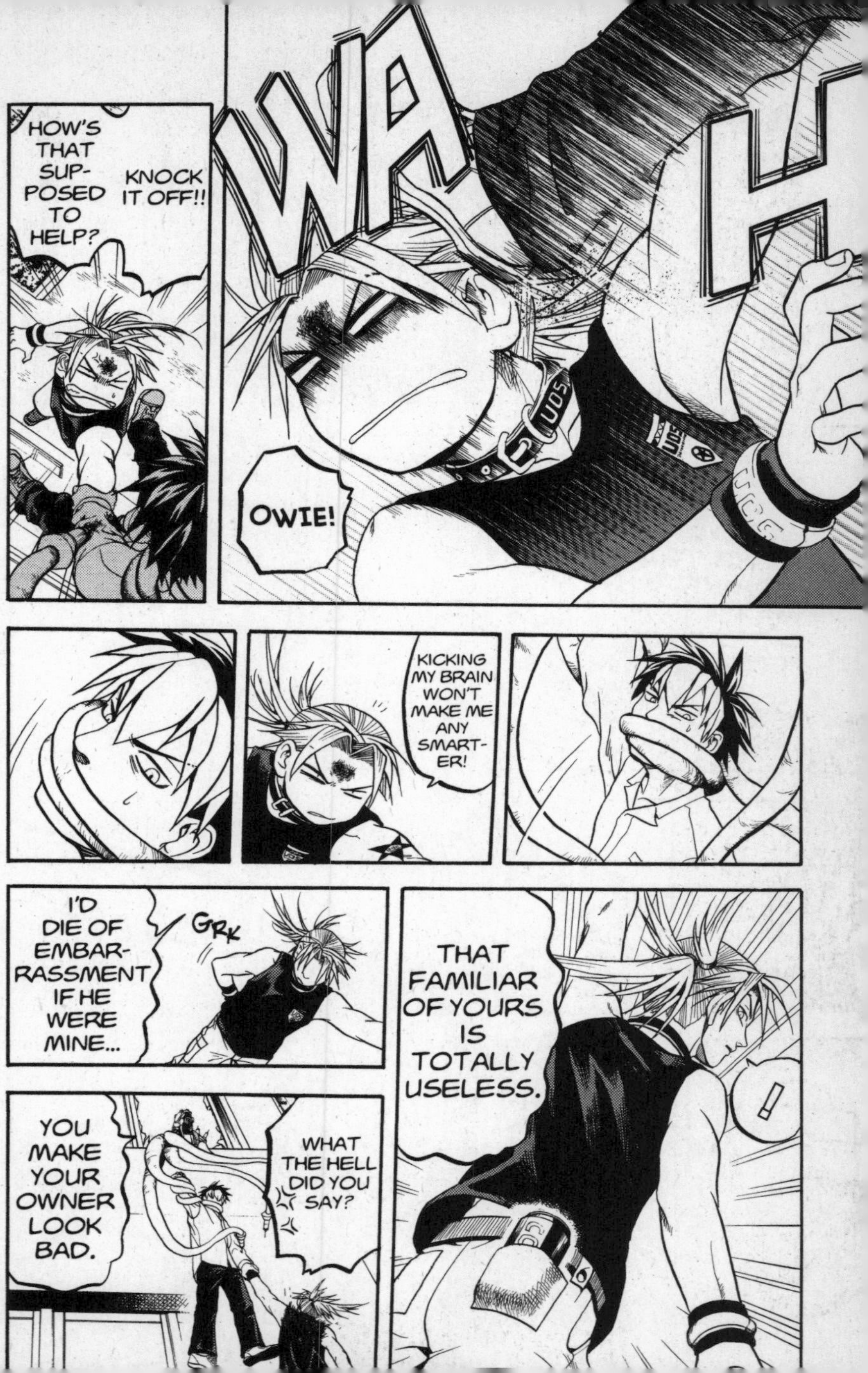
WA
H
OWIE!
KNOCK IT OFF!!
HOW'S THAT SUP-POSED TO HELP?
KICKING MY BRAIN WON'T MAKE ME ANY SMART-ER!
THAT FAMILIAR OF YOURS IS TOTALLY USELESS.
!
GRK
I'D DIE OF EMBAR-RASSMENT IF HE WERE MINE...
YOU MAKE YOUR OWNER LOOK BAD.
WHAT THE HELL DID YOU SAY?

READ THIS WAY

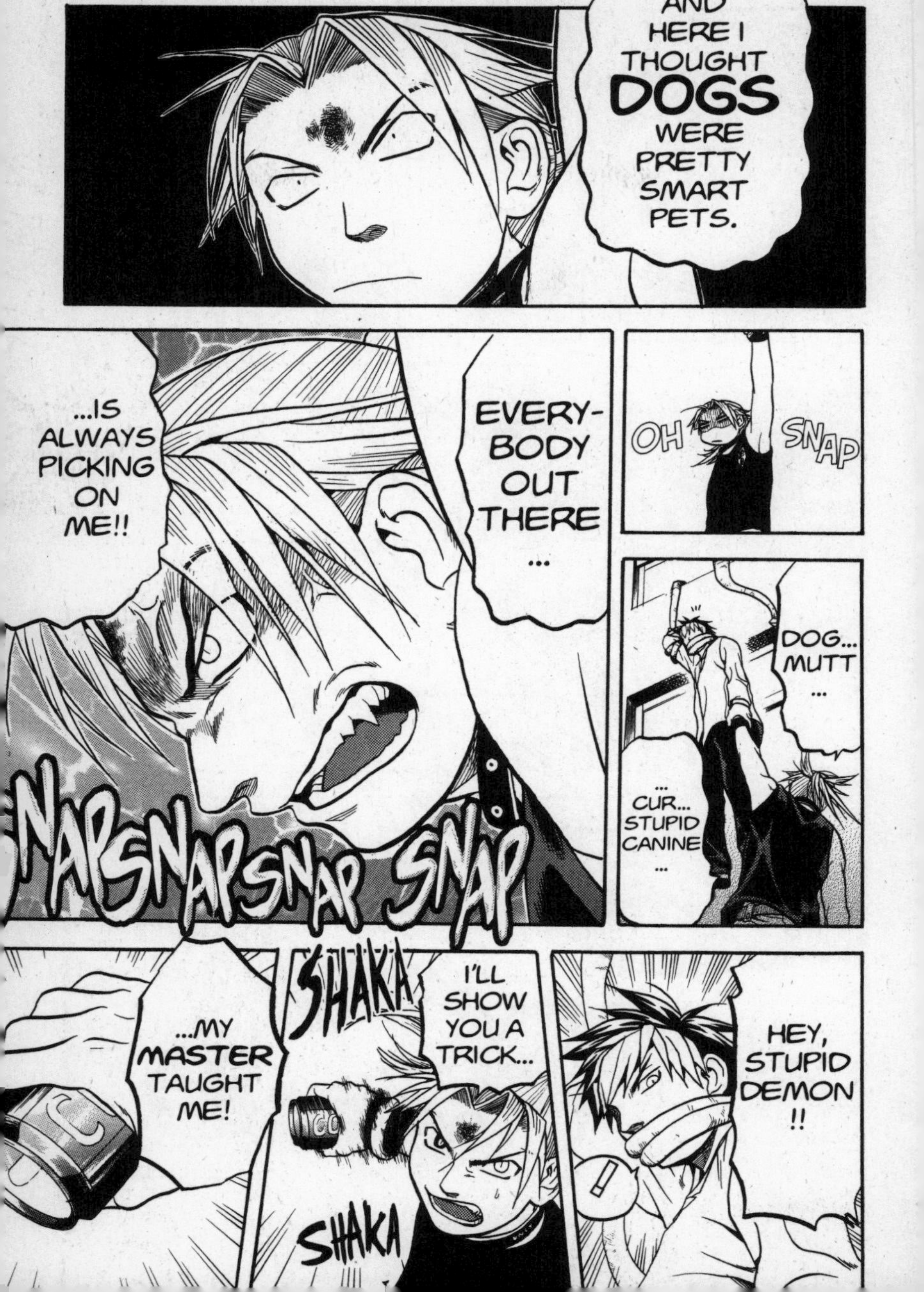
AND HERE I THOUGHT DOGS WERE PRETTY SMART PETS.
SNAP
OH
DOG... MUTT ...
... CUR... STUPID CANINE ...
EVERY-BODY OUT THERE ...
...IS ALWAYS PICKING ON ME!!
SNAPSNAPSNAP SNAP
HEY, STUPID DEMON !!
!
I'LL SHOW YOU A TRICK...
SHAKA
SHAKA
...MY MASTER TAUGHT ME!

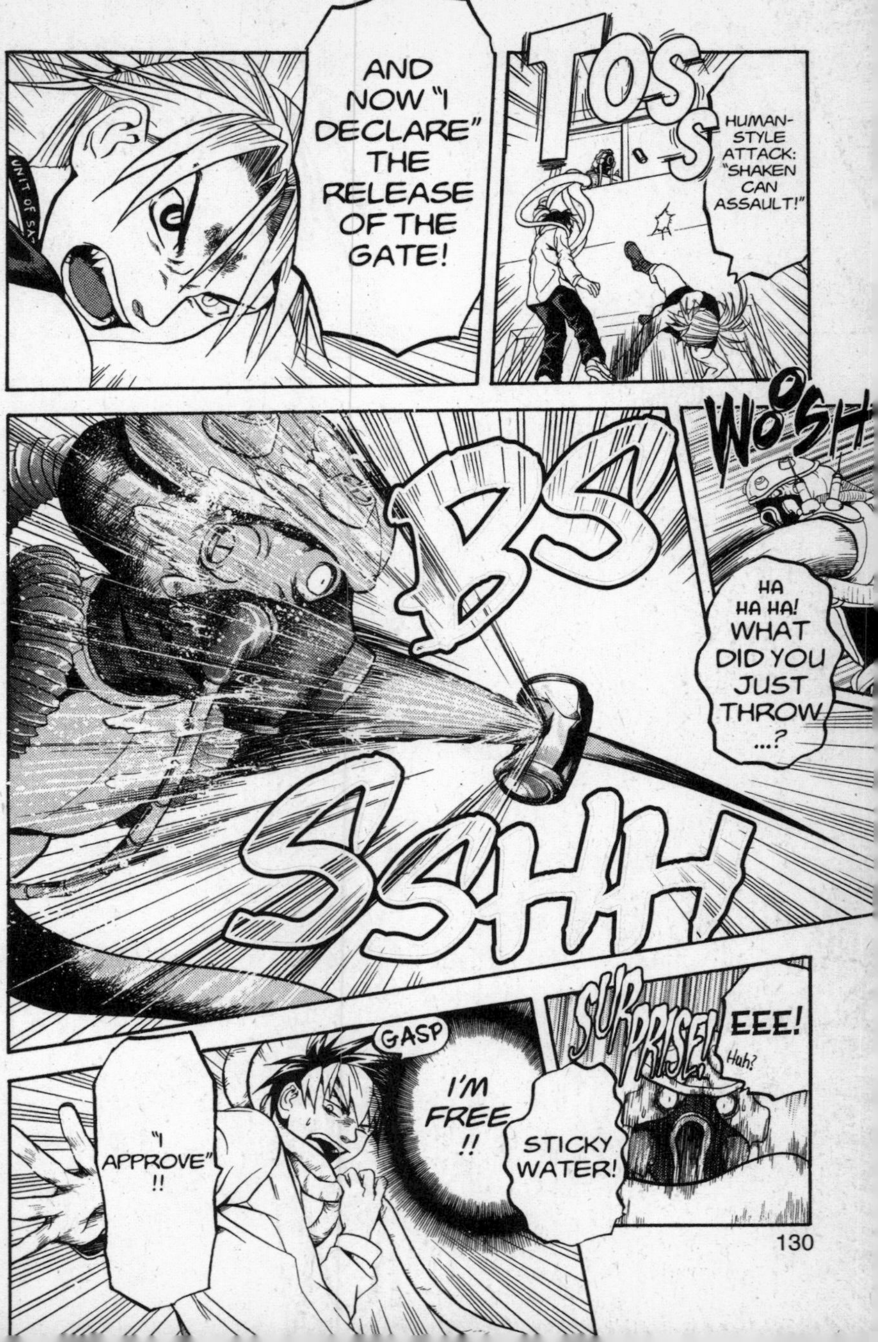
TOSS
HUMAN-STYLE ATTACK: "SHAKEN CAN ASSAULT!"
AND NOW "I DECLARE" THE RELEASE OF THE GATE!
WOOSH
HA HA HA! WHAT DID YOU JUST THROW ...?
BS
SSHH
SURPRISE!!
EEE!
Huh?
STICKY WATER!
I'M FREE !!
GASP
"I APPROVE" !!

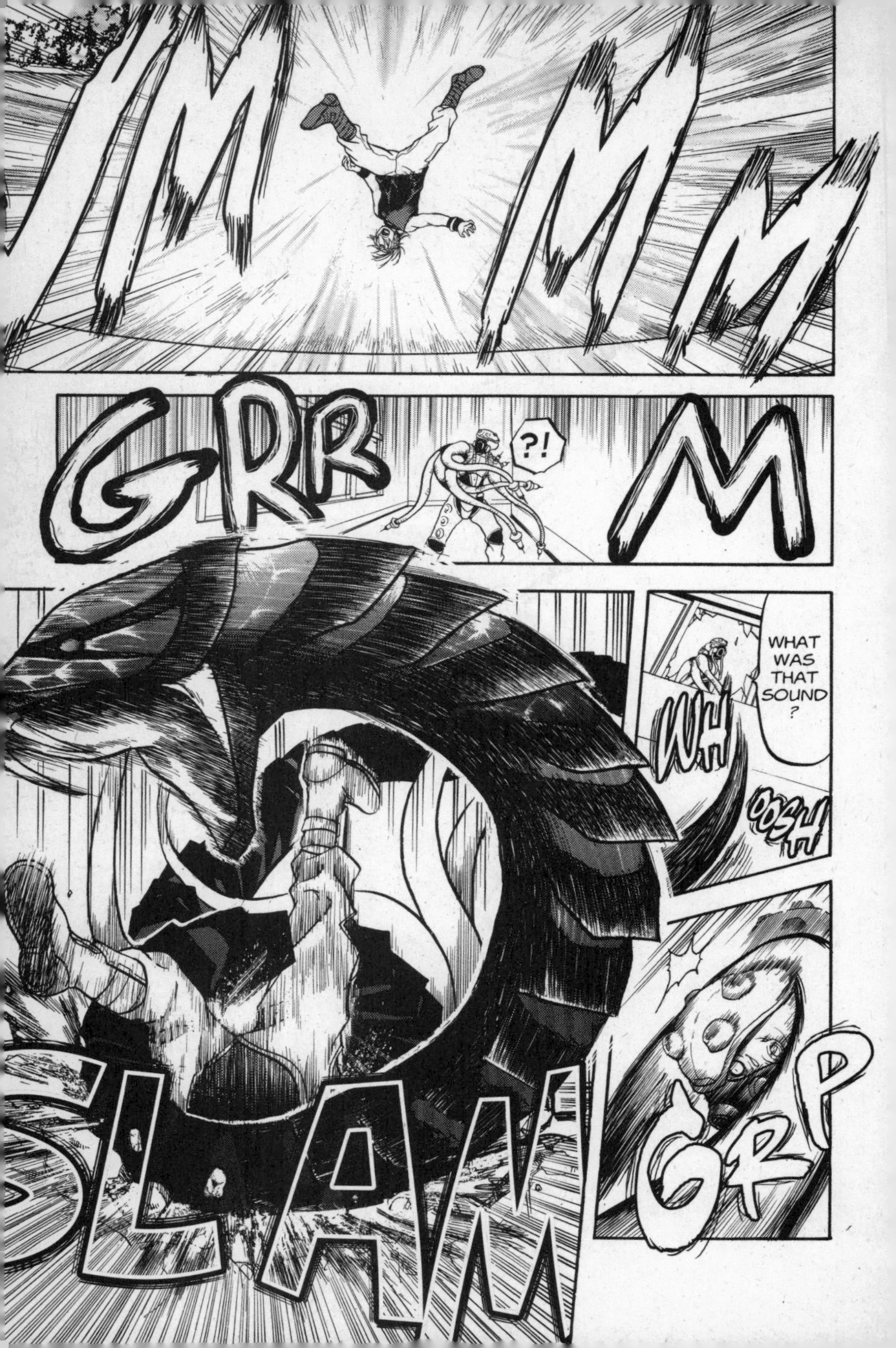
MMMMM
?!
GRR M
WHAT WAS THAT SOUND ?
WH OOSH
SLAM
GRP

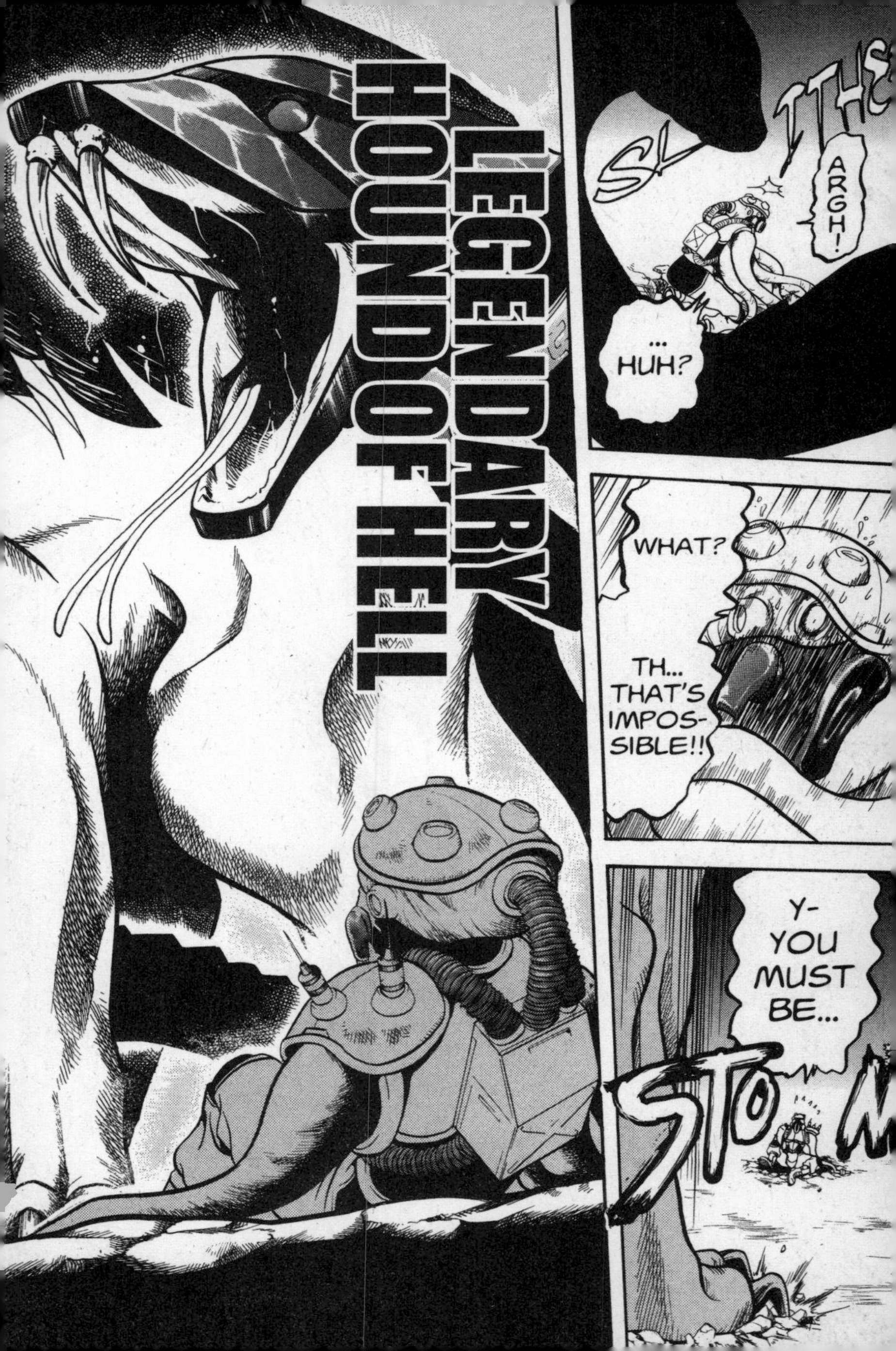
ARGH!
... HUH?
WHAT?
TH... THAT'S IMPOSSIBLE!!
Y-YOU MUST BE...
LEGENDARY HOUND OF HELL

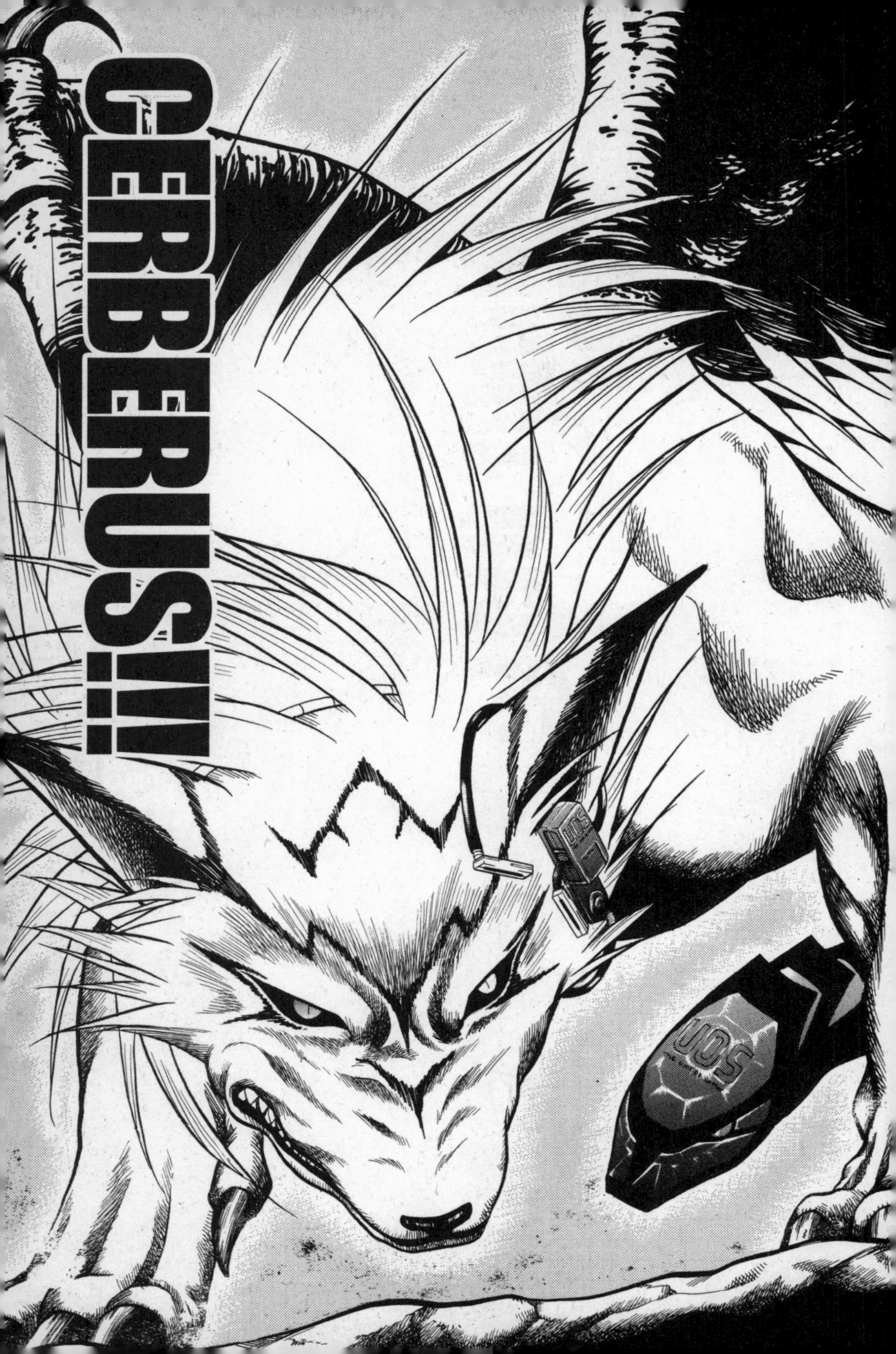
CERBERUS!!!

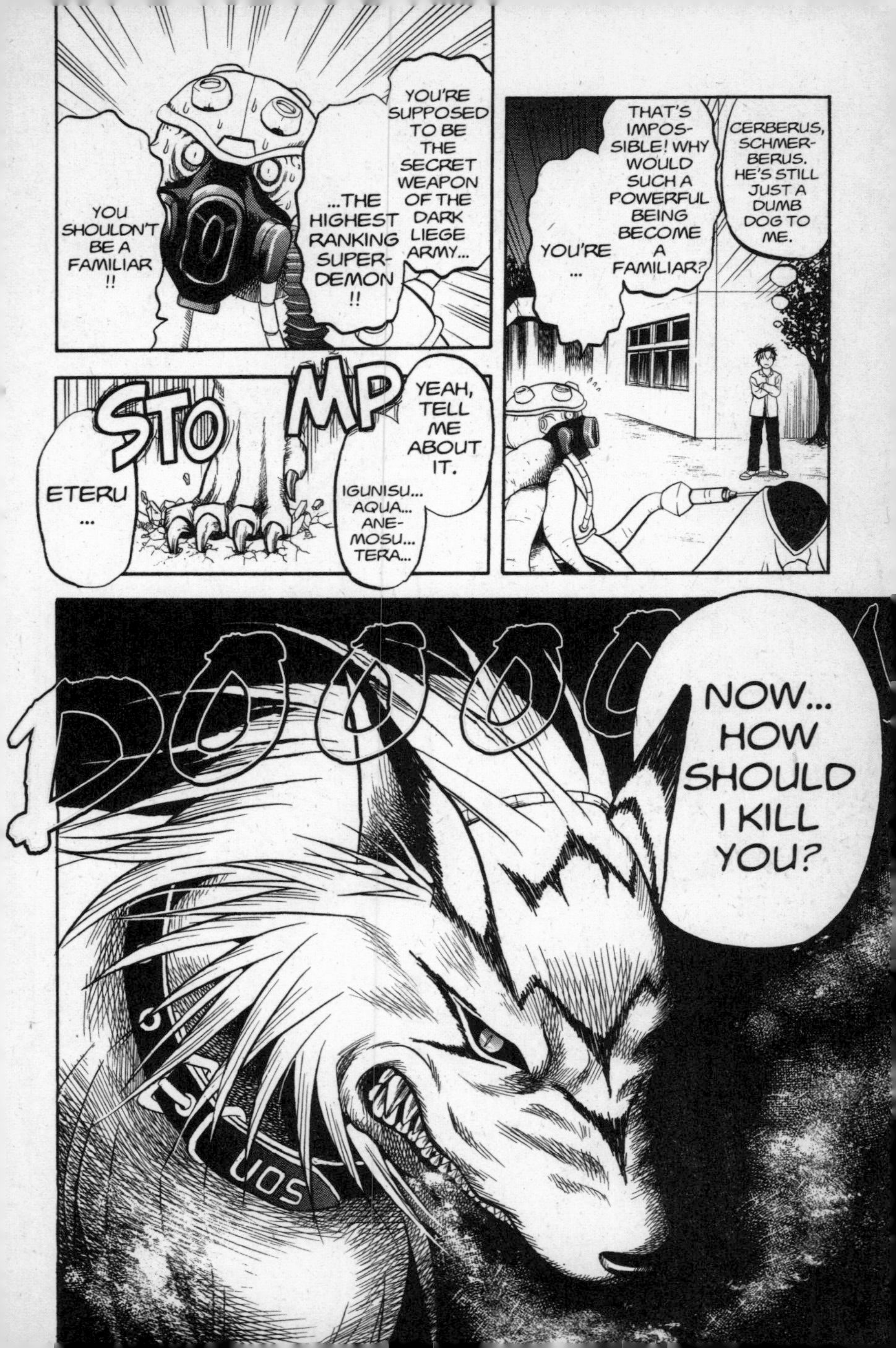
CERBERUS, SCHMER-BERUS. HE'S STILL JUST A DUMB DOG TO ME.
THAT'S IMPOS-SIBLE! WHY WOULD SUCH A POWERFUL BEING BECOME A FAMILIAR?
YOU'RE ...
YOU'RE SUPPOSED TO BE THE SECRET WEAPON OF THE DARK LIEGE ARMY...
...THE HIGHEST RANKING SUPER-DEMON !!
YOU SHOULDN'T BE A FAMILIAR !!
YEAH, TELL ME ABOUT IT.
STOMP
IGUNISU... AQUA... ANE-MOSU... TERA...
ETERU ...
NOW... HOW SHOULD I KILL YOU?
DOOOO

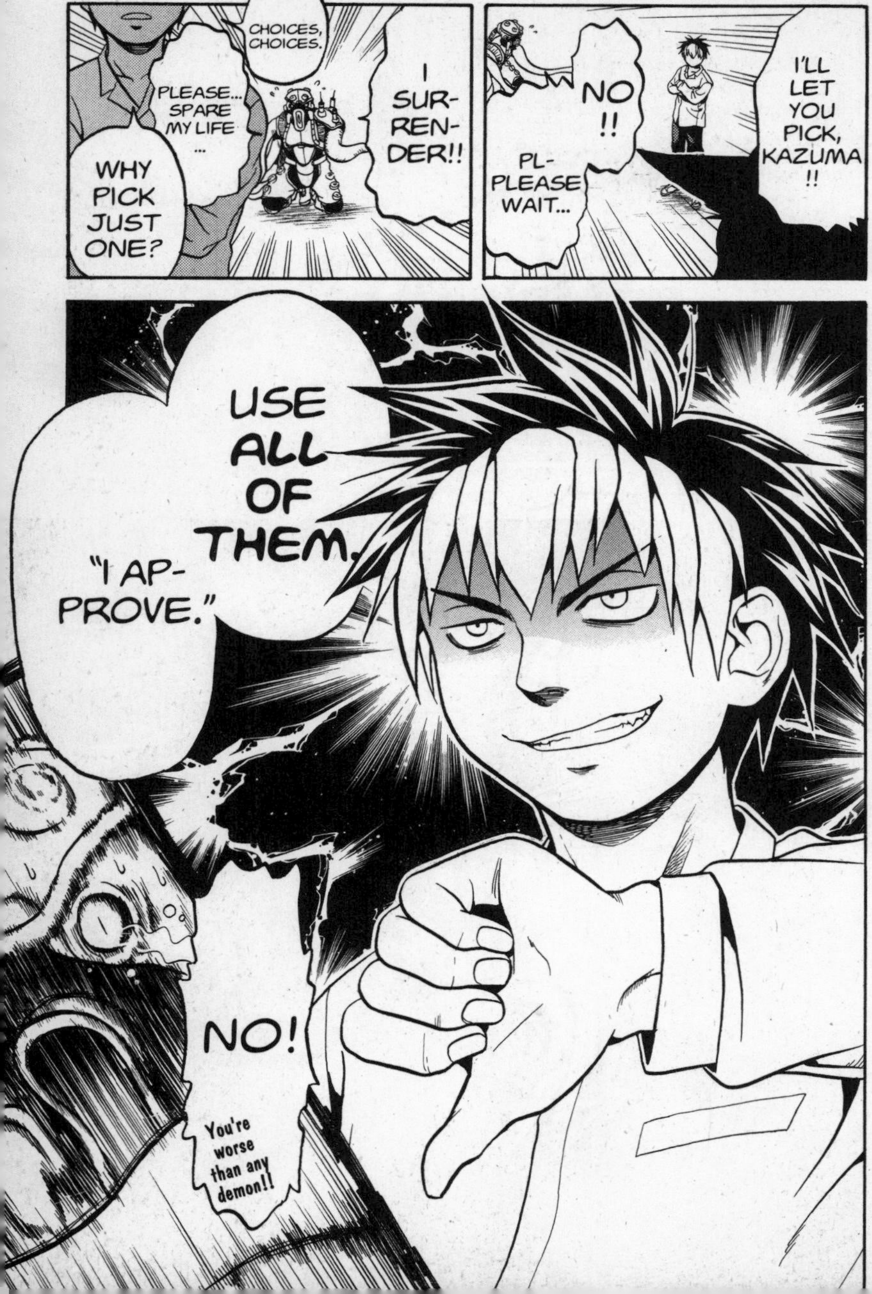

I'LL LET YOU PICK, KAZUMA!!
NO!!
PL- PLEASE WAIT...
I SUR- REN- DER!!
CHOICES, CHOICES.
PLEASE... SPARE MY LIFE ...
WHY PICK JUST ONE?
USE ALL OF THEM.
"I AP- PROVE."
NO!
You're worse than any demon!!

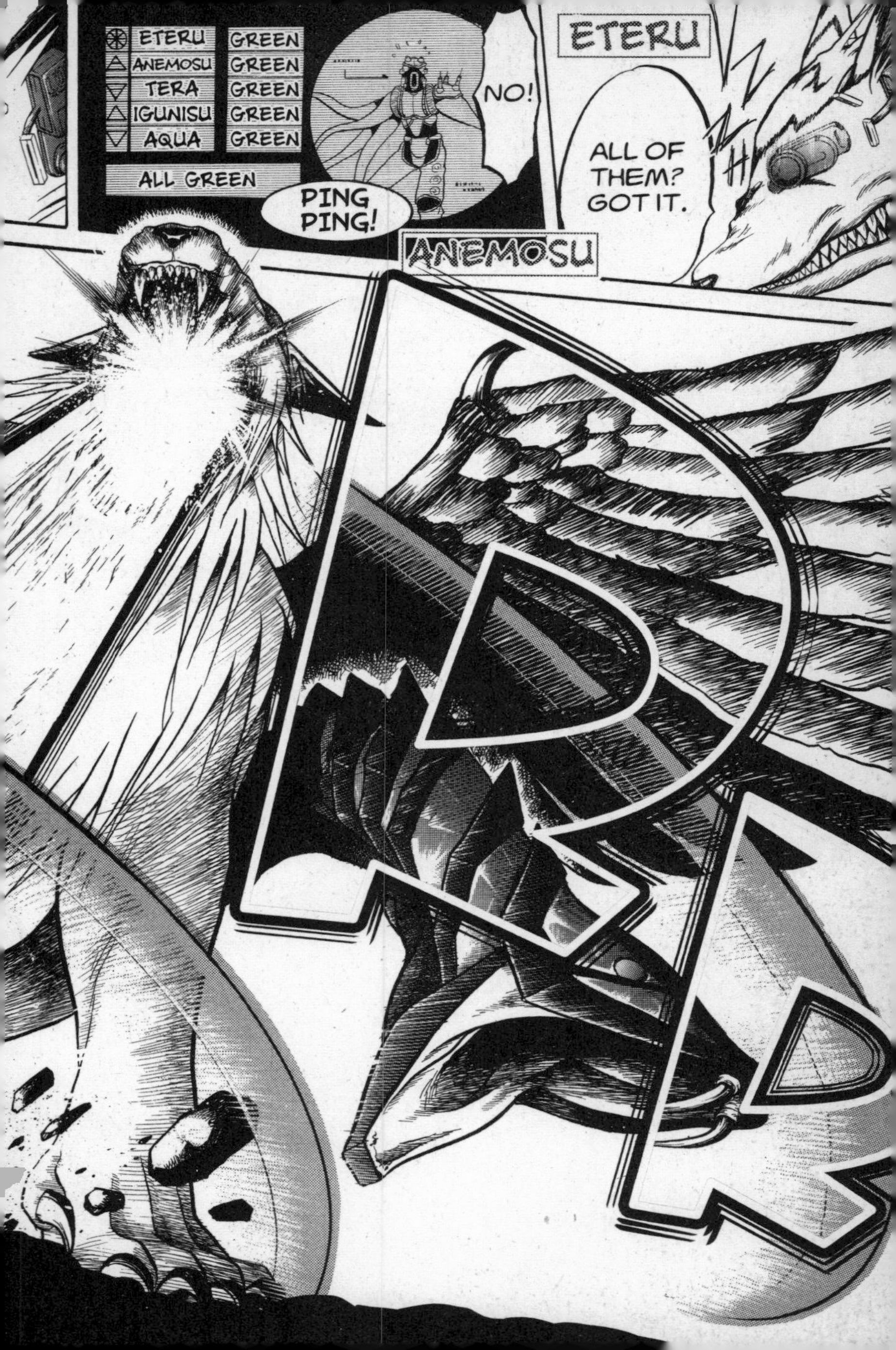
ETERU
ALL OF THEM? GOT IT.
NO!
PING PING!
ETERU GREEN
ANEMOSU GREEN
TERA GREEN
IGUNISU GREEN
AQUA GREEN
ALL GREEN
ANEMOSU

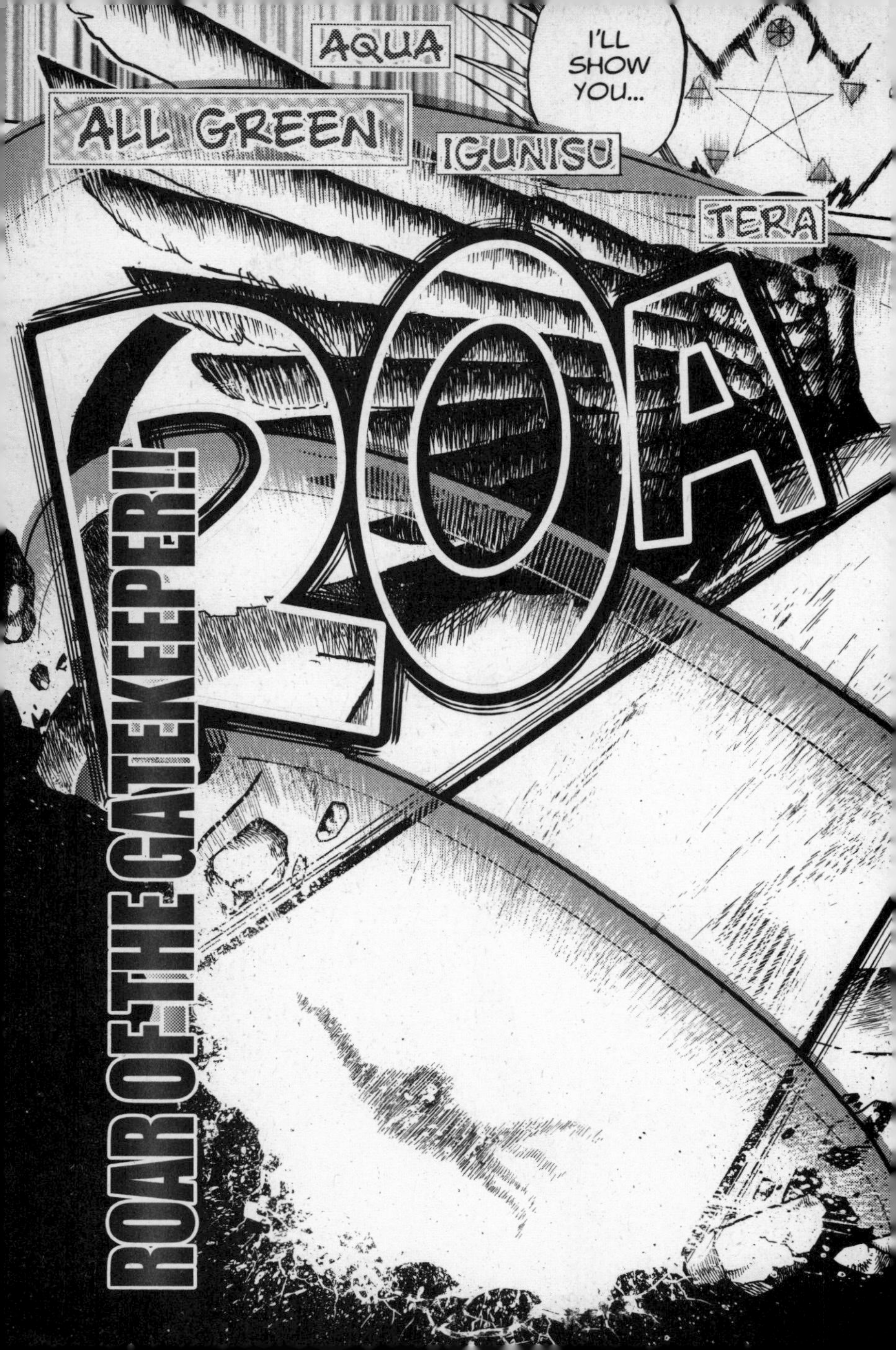
I'LL SHOW YOU...
AQUA
ALL GREEN
IGUNISU
TERA
20A
ROAR OF THE GATEKEEPER!!

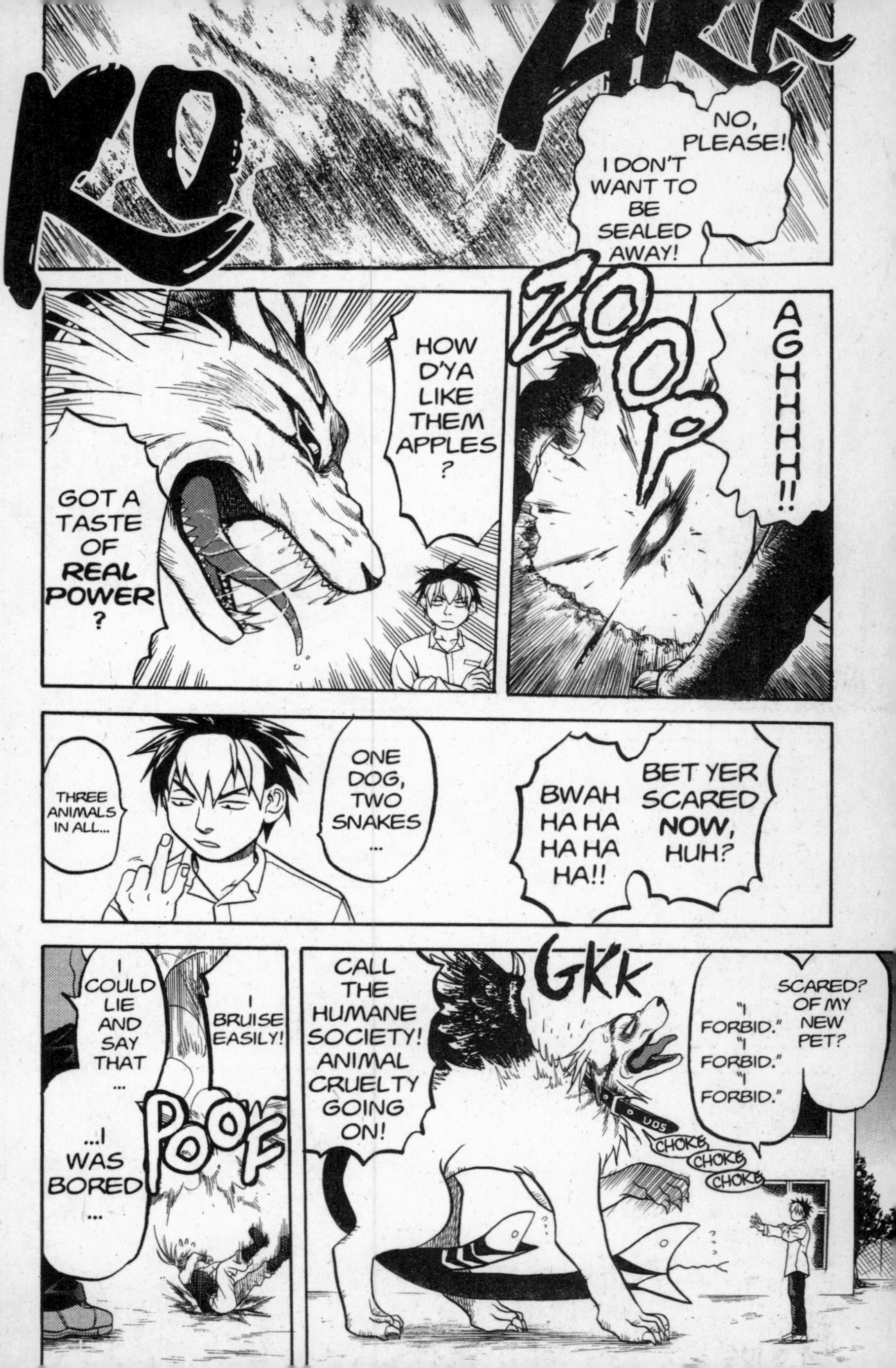
NO, PLEASE! I DON'T WANT TO BE SEALED AWAY!
ZOOOP
AGHHHH!!
HOW D'YA LIKE THEM APPLES?
GOT A TASTE OF **REAL POWER**?
BWAH HA HA HA HA HA!!
BET YER SCARED **NOW**, HUH?
ONE DOG, TWO SNAKES...
THREE ANIMALS IN ALL...
GKK
SCARED? OF MY NEW PET?
"I FORBID." "I FORBID." "I FORBID."
CHOKE
CHOKE
CHOKE
CALL THE HUMANE SOCIETY! ANIMAL CRUELTY GOING ON!
I COULD LIE AND SAY THAT...
I BRUISE EASILY!
POOF
...I WAS BORED...

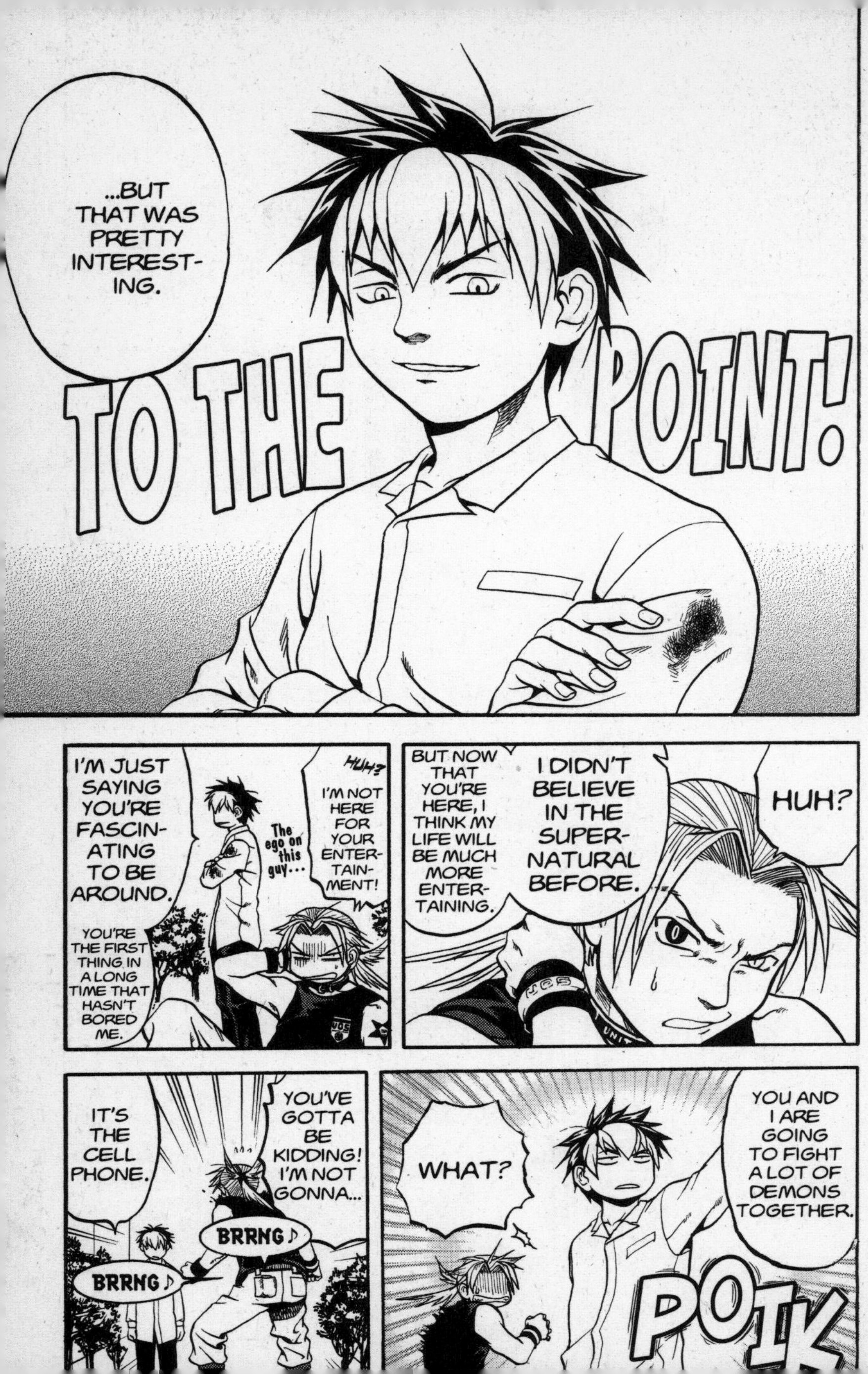
...BUT THAT WAS PRETTY INTEREST-ING.
TO THE POINT!
HUH?
I DIDN'T BELIEVE IN THE SUPER-NATURAL BEFORE.
BUT NOW THAT YOU'RE HERE, I THINK MY LIFE WILL BE MUCH MORE ENTER-TAINING.
HUH?
I'M NOT HERE FOR YOUR ENTER-TAIN-MENT!
The ego on this guy...
I'M JUST SAYING YOU'RE FASCIN-ATING TO BE AROUND.
YOU'RE THE FIRST THING IN A LONG TIME THAT HASN'T BORED ME.
YOU AND I ARE GOING TO FIGHT A LOT OF DEMONS TOGETHER.
WHAT?
POIK
YOU'VE GOTTA BE KIDDING! I'M NOT GONNA...
IT'S THE CELL PHONE.
BRRNG♪
BRRNG♪

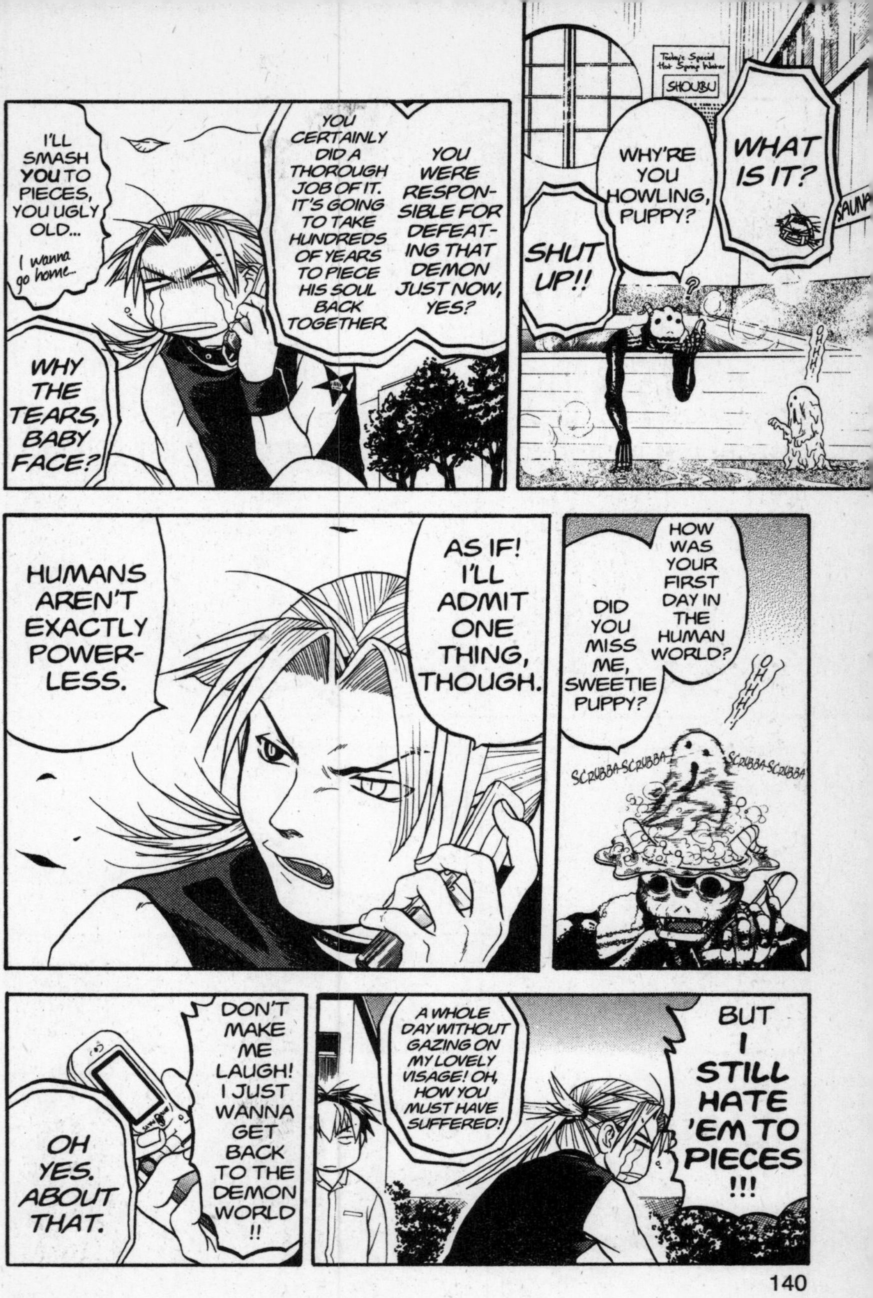
Today's Special
Hot Spring Water
SHOUBU
WHAT IS IT?
WHY'RE YOU HOWLING, PUPPY?
SHUT UP!!
SAUNA
OHHH
YOU WERE RESPONSIBLE FOR DEFEATING THAT DEMON JUST NOW, YES?
YOU CERTAINLY DID A THOROUGH JOB OF IT. IT'S GOING TO TAKE HUNDREDS OF YEARS TO PIECE HIS SOUL BACK TOGETHER.
I'LL SMASH YOU TO PIECES, YOU UGLY OLD...
I wanna go home...
WHY THE TEARS, BABY FACE?
HOW WAS YOUR FIRST DAY IN THE HUMAN WORLD?
DID YOU MISS ME, SWEETIE PUPPY?
OHHH
SCRUBBA-SCRUBBA
SCRUBBA-SCRUBBA
AS IF! I'LL ADMIT ONE THING, THOUGH.
HUMANS AREN'T EXACTLY POWER-LESS.
BUT I STILL HATE 'EM TO PIECES!!!
A WHOLE DAY WITHOUT GAZING ON MY LOVELY VISAGE! OH, HOW YOU MUST HAVE SUFFERED!
DON'T MAKE ME LAUGH! I JUST WANNA GET BACK TO THE DEMON WORLD!!
OH YES. ABOUT THAT.

READ THIS WAY

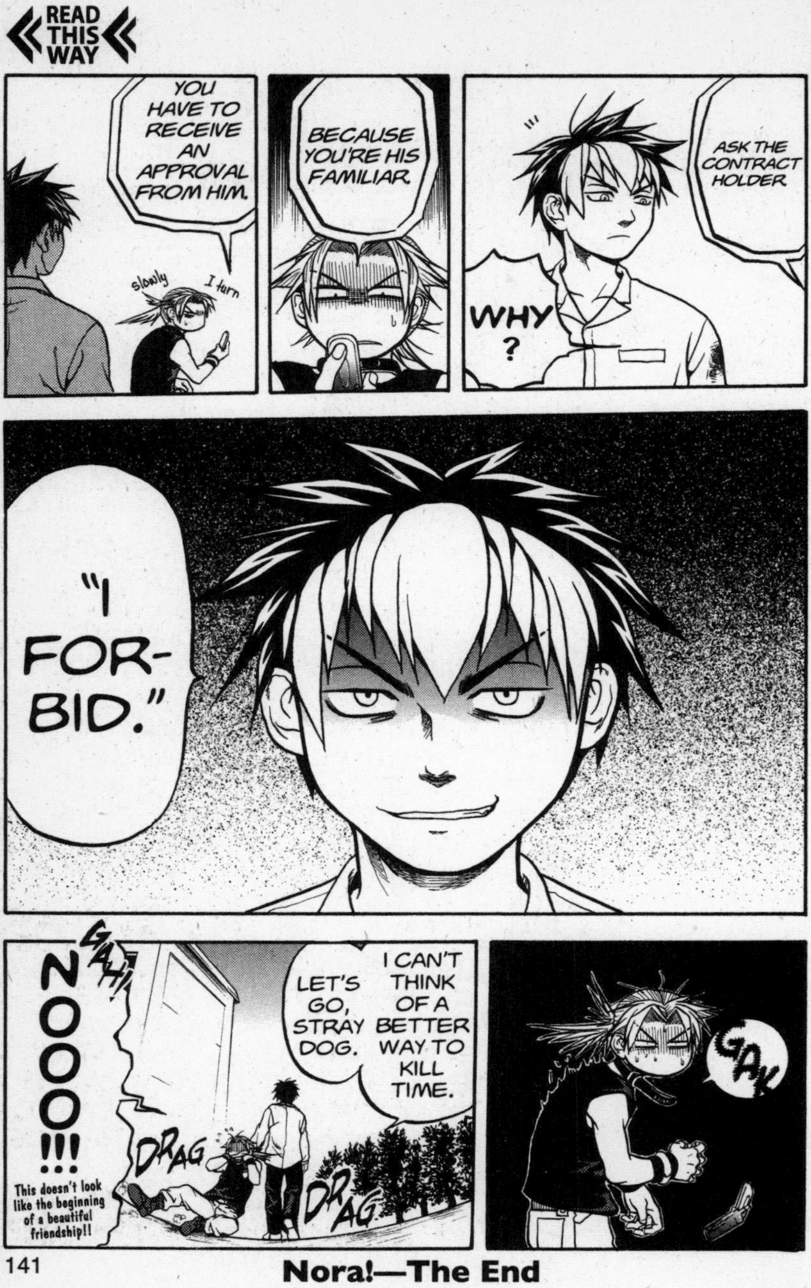

ASK THE CONTRACT HOLDER.
WHY?
BECAUSE YOU'RE HIS FAMILIAR.
YOU HAVE TO RECEIVE AN APPROVAL FROM HIM.
slowly
I turn
"I FORBID."
GAK
I CAN'T THINK OF A BETTER WAY TO KILL TIME.
LET'S GO, STRAY DOG.
GAH!
NOOOO!!!
DRAG
DRAG
This doesn't look like the beginning of a beautiful friendship!!

Nora!—The End

ABOUT THE SHORT STORY "SEVERER REITO"

I CAN'T REREAD THIS STORY EITHER, FOR DIFFERENT REASONS. I DIDN'T ADD ANY CORRECTIONS OR REVISIONS TO THIS ONE EITHER. I WAS ON A REALLY TIGHT DEADLINE; IT AMAZES ME THAT I GOT IT DRAWN SO QUICKLY. I REALLY DIDN'T HAVE ENOUGH TIME, EVEN WITHOUT ANY DAYS OFF... I HAVE NO IDEA HOW I WAS ABLE TO DO IT.

THIS IS AN IMMATURE WORK IN MANY WAYS (EVEN SOMEONE FROM MY OWN FAMILY WAS LIKE, "WHAT THE HECK IS THIS?"). BUT I DO LIKE HOW THE MAIN CHARACTER AND HIS DAD CAME OUT. I'D LIKE TO USE SOME ELEMENTS FROM THIS COMIC IN A FUTURE PROJECT.

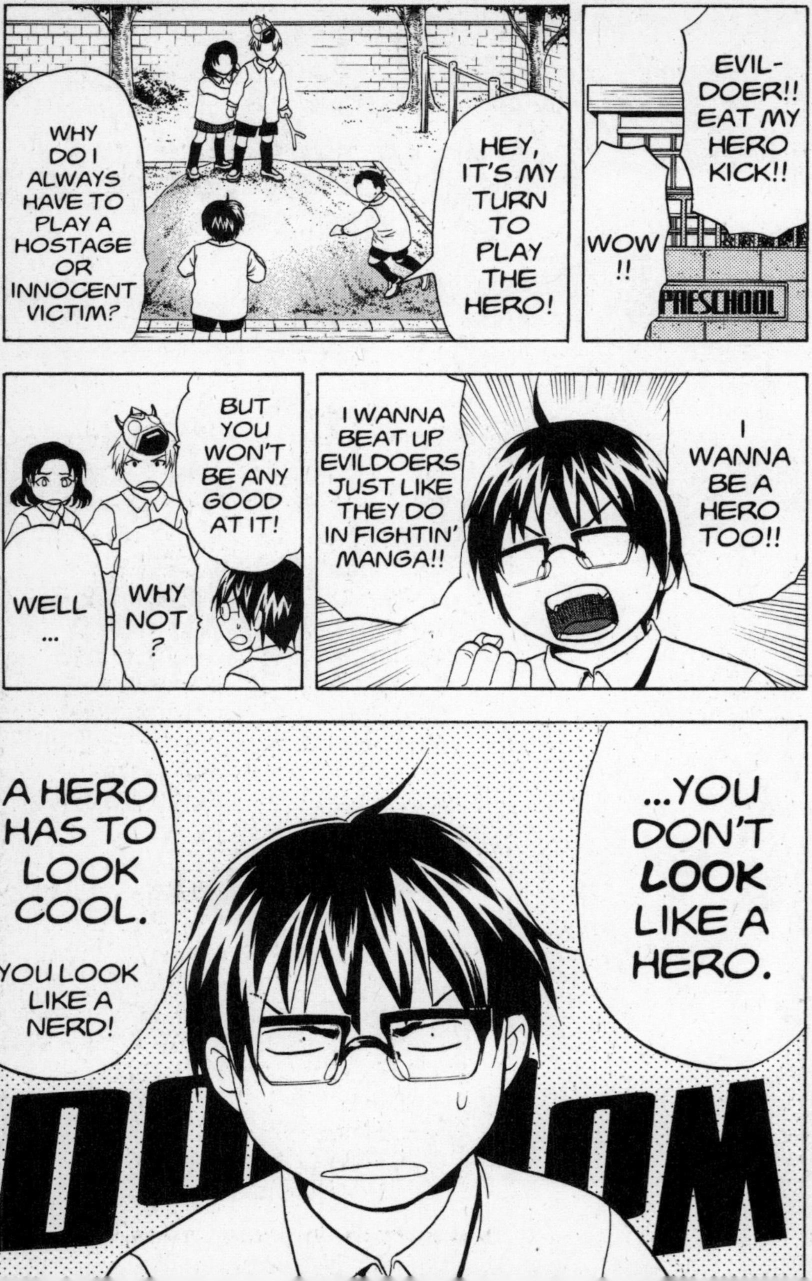
EVIL-DOER!! EAT MY HERO KICK!!
WOW !!
PRESCHOOL
HEY, IT'S MY TURN TO PLAY THE HERO!
WHY DO I ALWAYS HAVE TO PLAY A HOSTAGE OR INNOCENT VICTIM?
I WANNA BE A HERO TOO!!
I WANNA BEAT UP EVILDOERS JUST LIKE THEY DO IN FIGHTIN' MANGA!!
BUT YOU WON'T BE ANY GOOD AT IT!
WHY NOT ?
WELL ...
...YOU DON'T LOOK LIKE A HERO.
A HERO HAS TO LOOK COOL.
YOU LOOK LIKE A NERD!

SPECIAL
SHORT STORY

SEVERER REITO

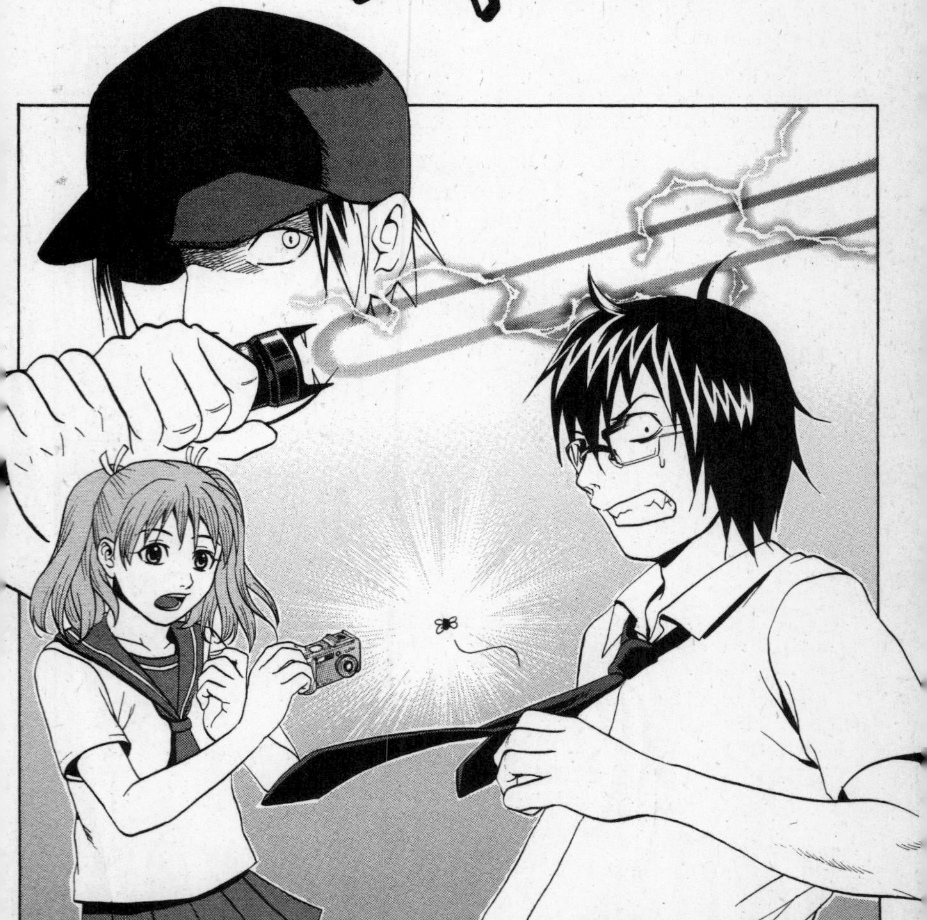

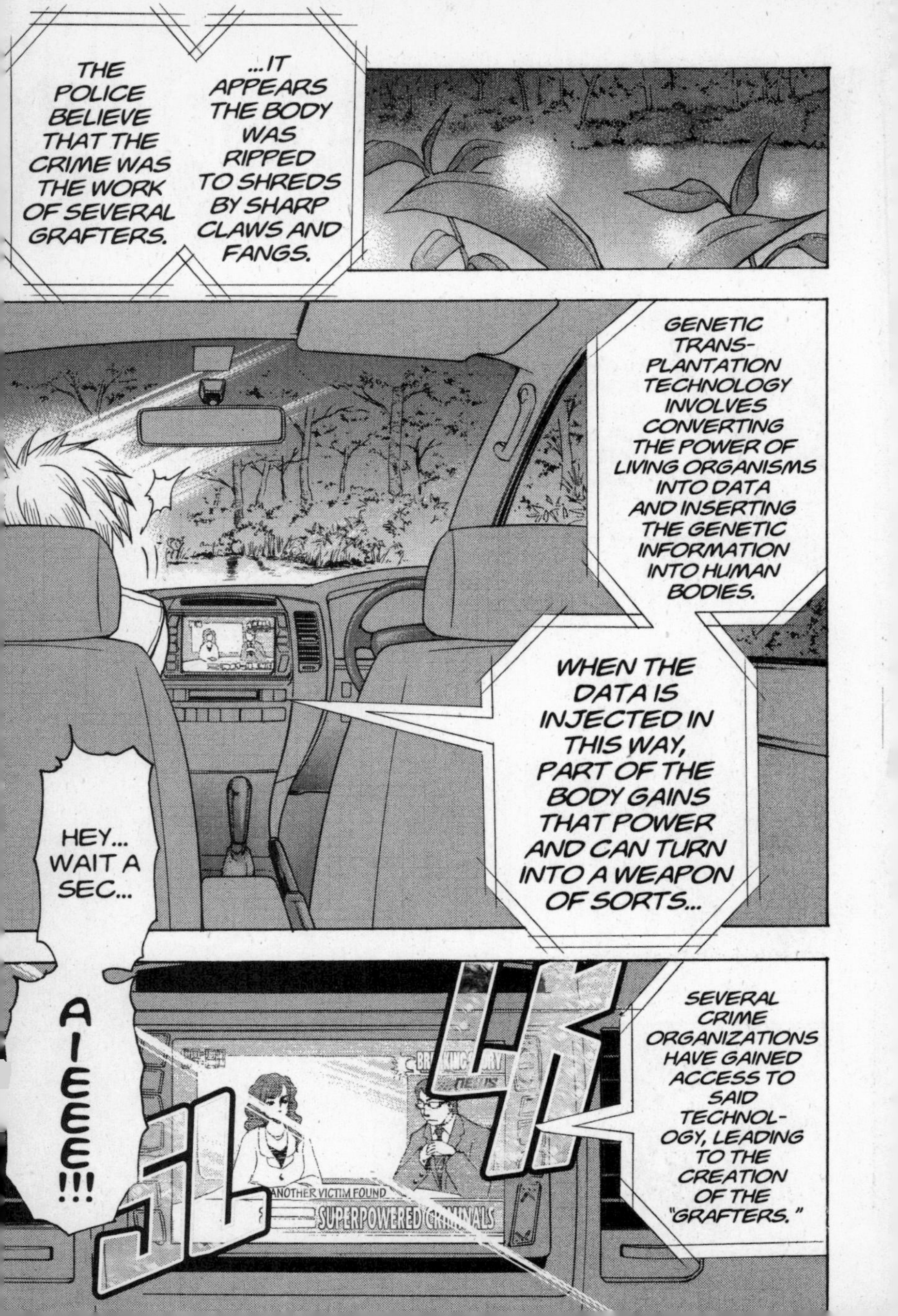
...IT APPEARS THE BODY WAS RIPPED TO SHREDS BY SHARP CLAWS AND FANGS.
THE POLICE BELIEVE THAT THE CRIME WAS THE WORK OF SEVERAL GRAFTERS.
GENETIC TRANS-PLANTATION TECHNOLOGY INVOLVES CONVERTING THE POWER OF LIVING ORGANISMS INTO DATA AND INSERTING THE GENETIC INFORMATION INTO HUMAN BODIES.
WHEN THE DATA IS INJECTED IN THIS WAY, PART OF THE BODY GAINS THAT POWER AND CAN TURN INTO A WEAPON OF SORTS...
HEY... WAIT A SEC...
SEVERAL CRIME ORGANIZATIONS HAVE GAINED ACCESS TO SAID TECHNOL-OGY, LEADING TO THE CREATION OF THE "GRAFTERS."
ANOTHER VICTIM FOUND
SUPERPOWERED CRIMINALS
AIEEE!!!

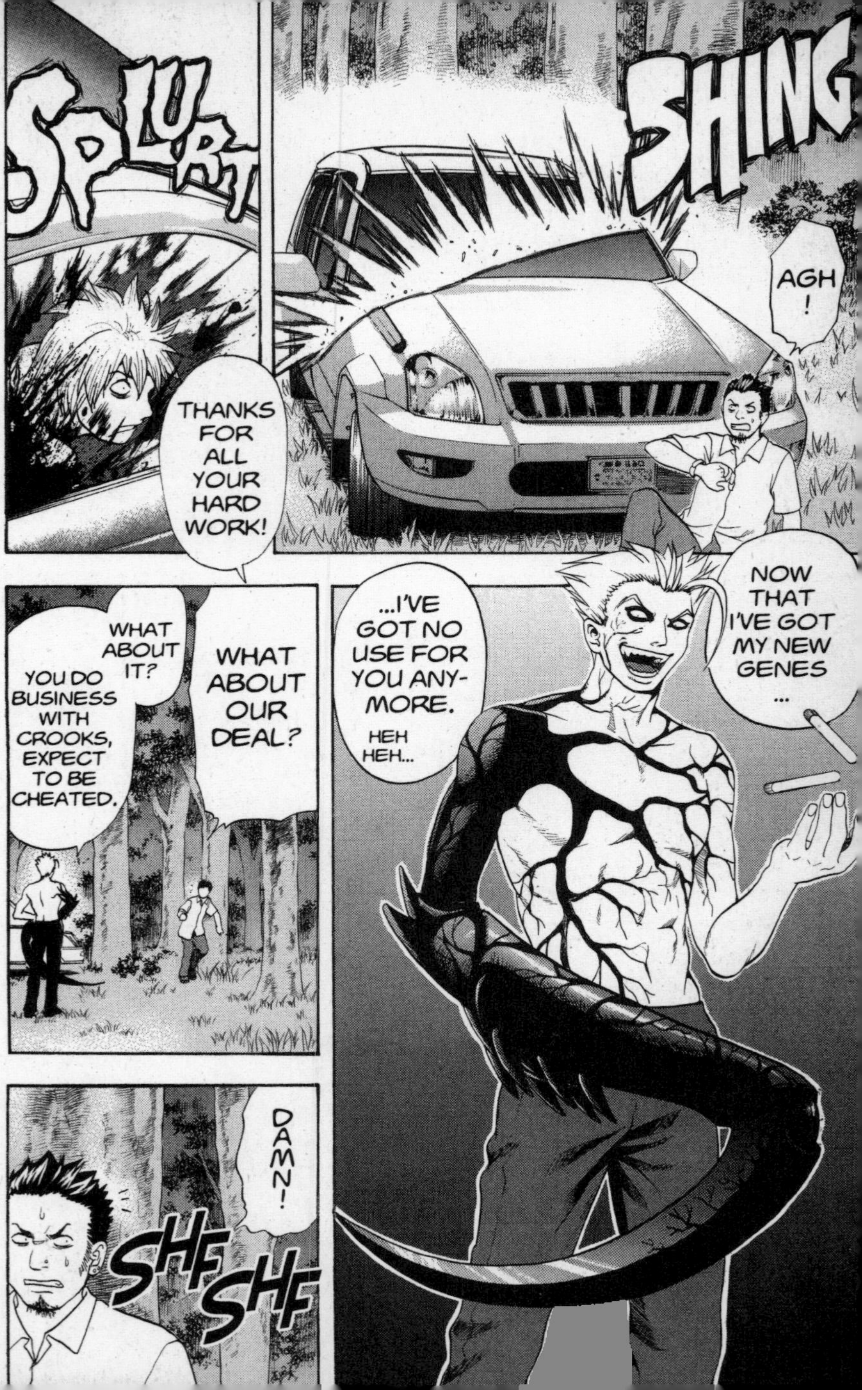
SHING
AGH!
SPLURT
THANKS FOR ALL YOUR HARD WORK!
NOW THAT I'VE GOT MY NEW GENES...
...I'VE GOT NO USE FOR YOU ANY-MORE.
HEH HEH...
WHAT ABOUT OUR DEAL?
WHAT ABOUT IT?
YOU DO BUSINESS WITH CROOKS, EXPECT TO BE CHEATED.
DAMN!
SHF SHF

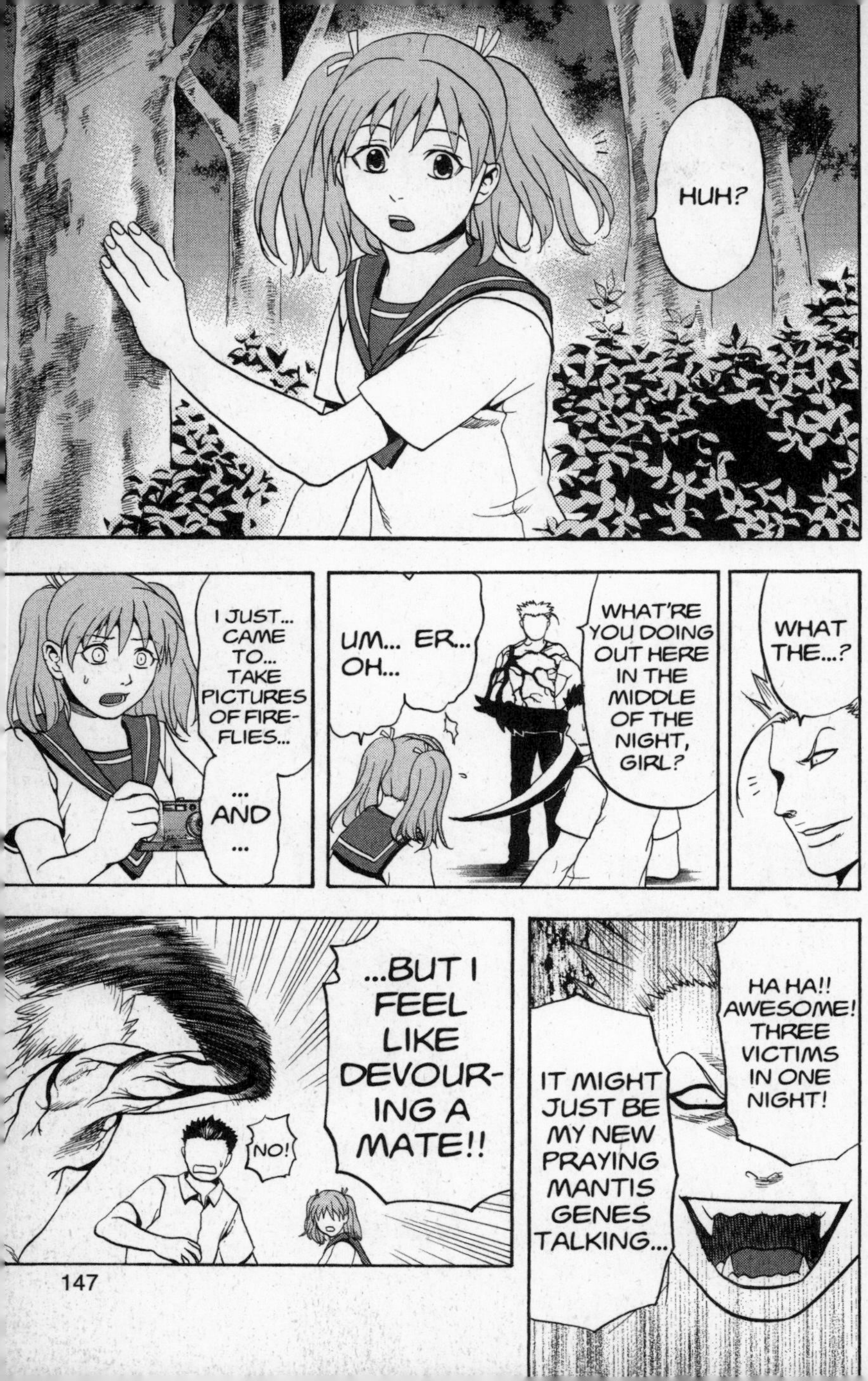

HUH?
WHAT THE...?
WHAT'RE YOU DOING OUT HERE IN THE MIDDLE OF THE NIGHT, GIRL?
UM... ER... OH...
I JUST... CAME TO... TAKE PICTURES OF FIRE-FLIES...
... AND ...
HA HA!! AWESOME! THREE VICTIMS IN ONE NIGHT!
IT MIGHT JUST BE MY NEW PRAYING MANTIS GENES TALKING...
...BUT I FEEL LIKE DEVOURING A MATE!!
NO!

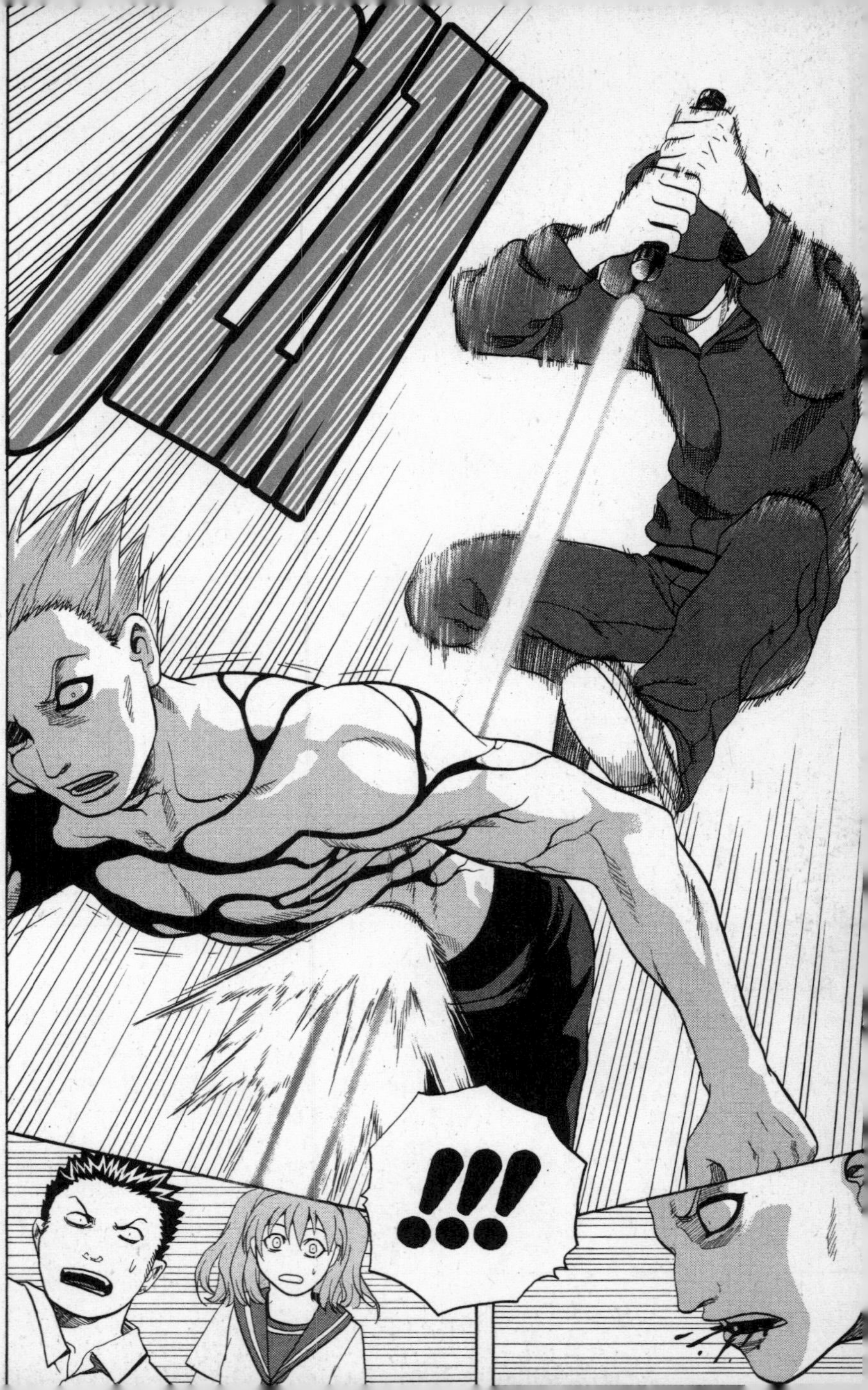
!!!

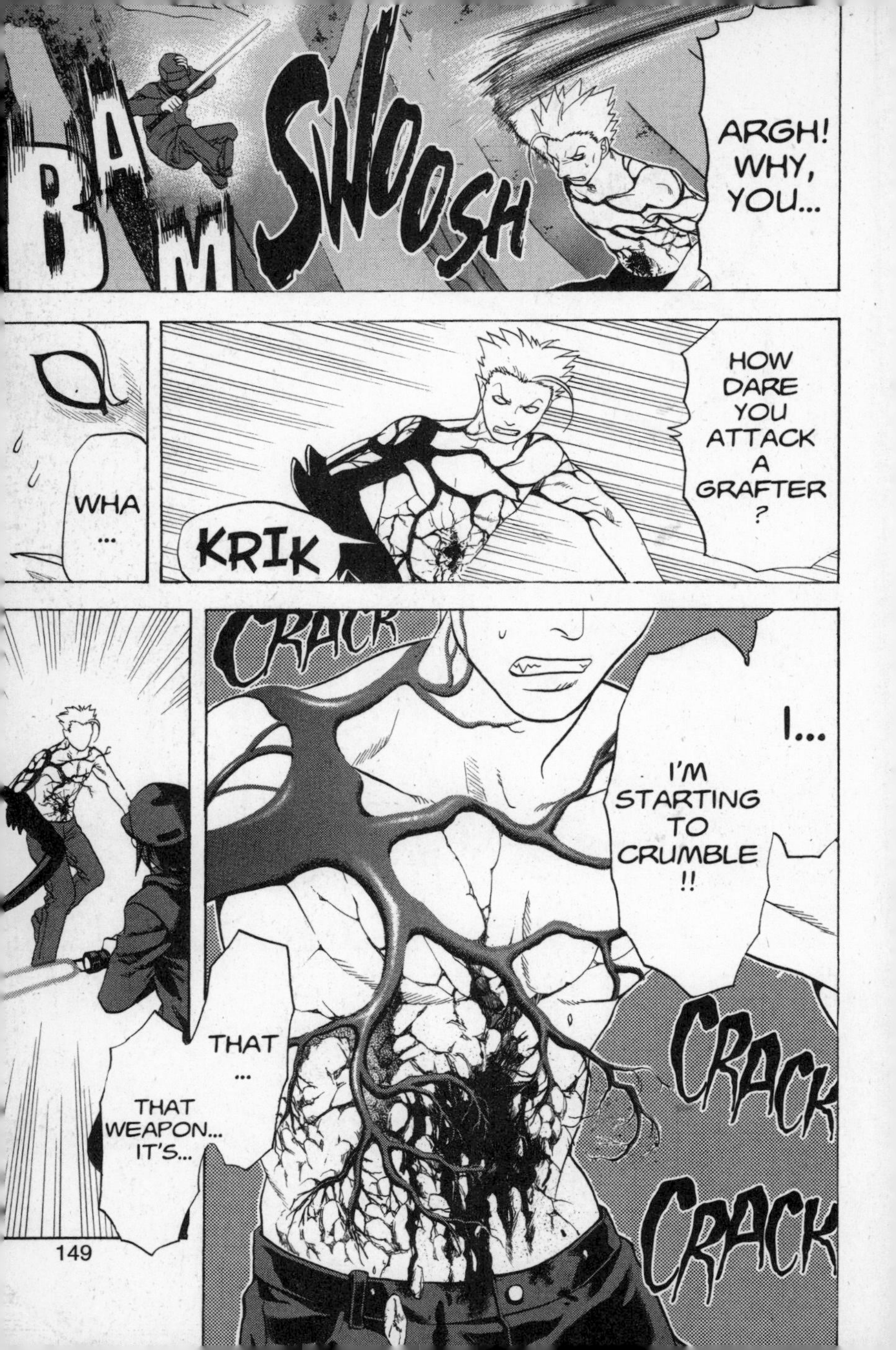
ARGH! WHY, YOU...
SWOOSH
BAM
HOW DARE YOU ATTACK A GRAFTER?
KRIK
WHA...
CRACK
I...
I'M STARTING TO CRUMBLE!!
CRACK
CRACK
THAT...
THAT WEAPON... IT'S...

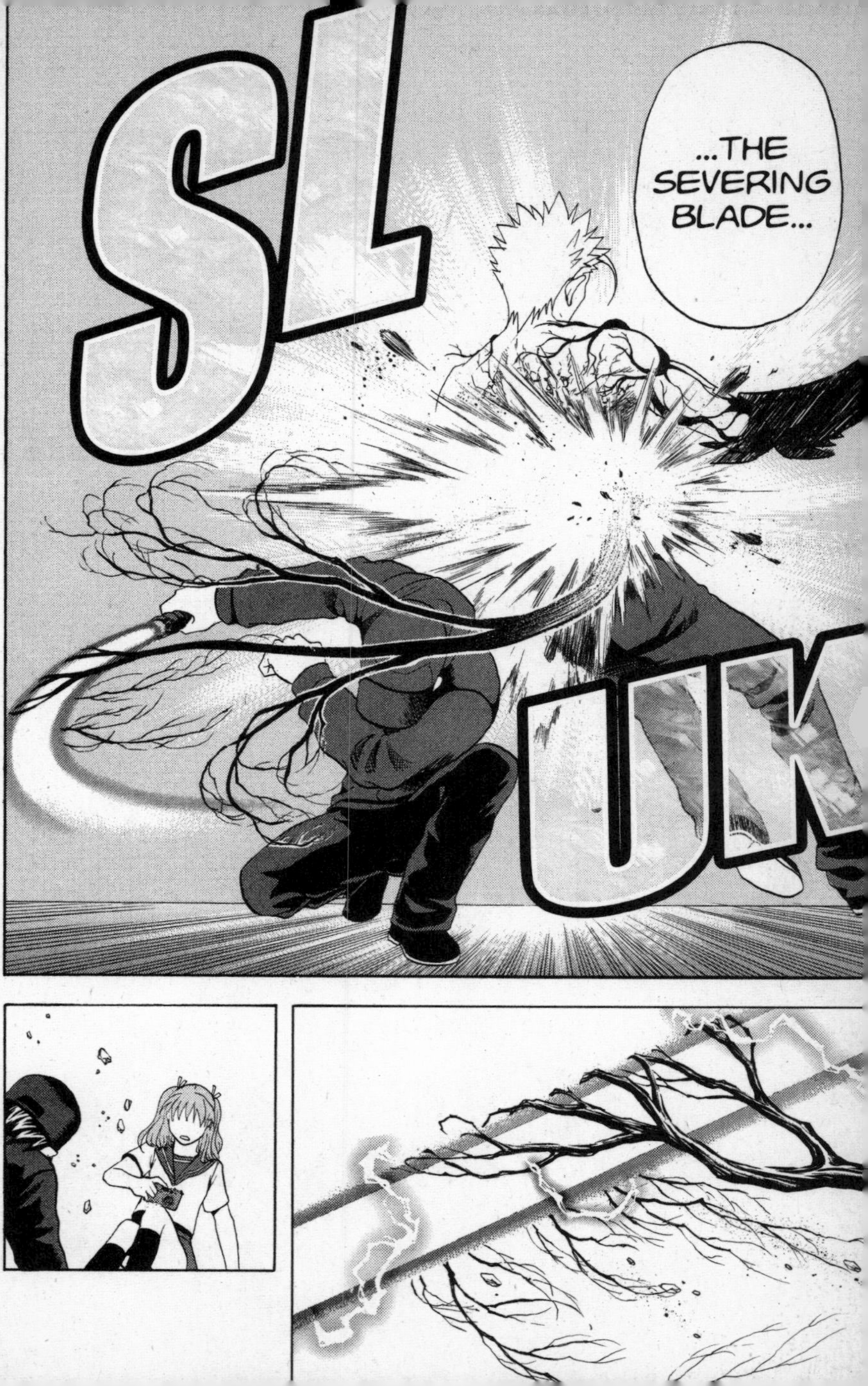
...THE SEVERING BLADE...
SL
UK

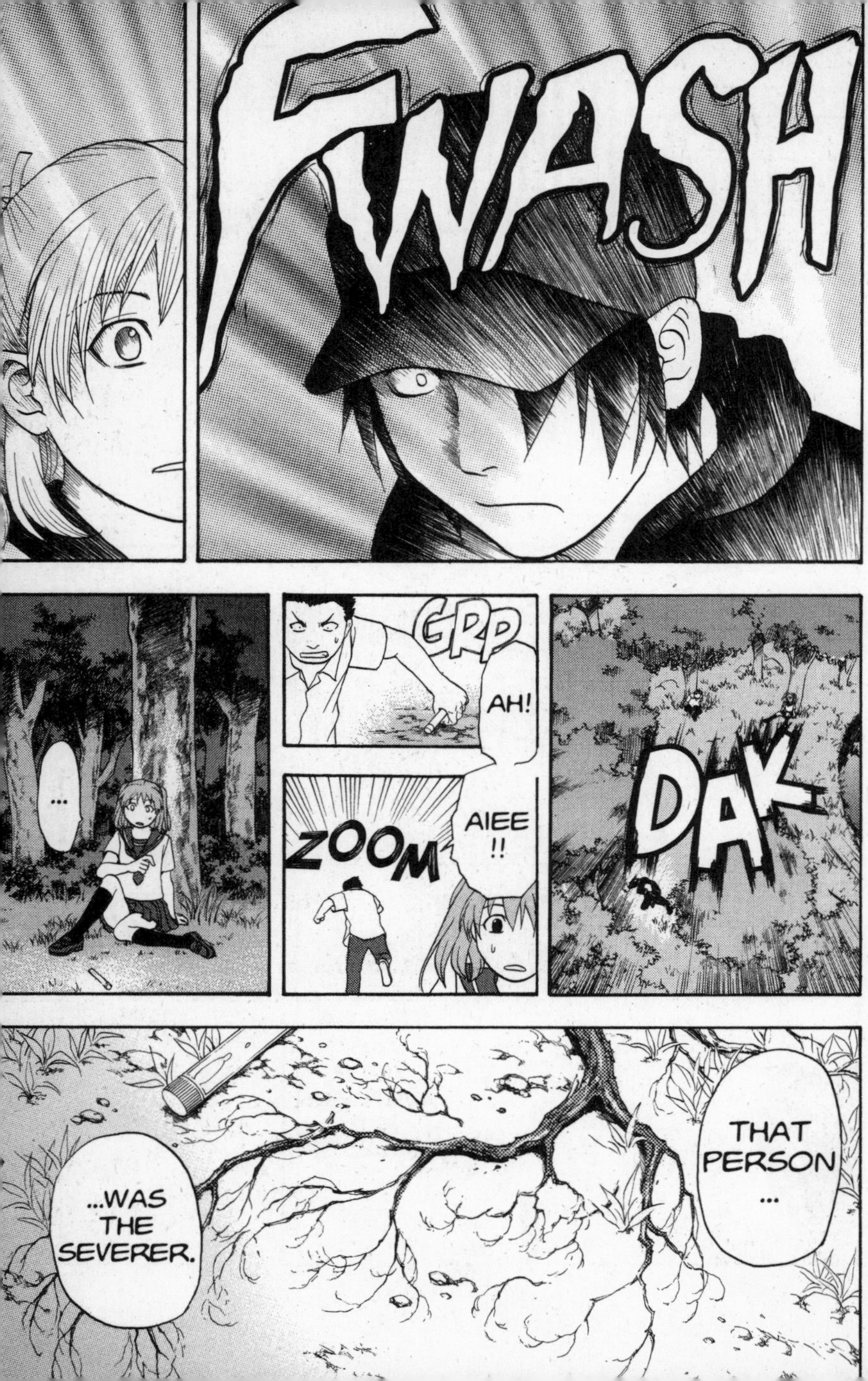
FWASH
DAK
GRP
AH!
AIEE !!
ZOOM
...
THAT PERSON ...
...WAS THE SEVERER.

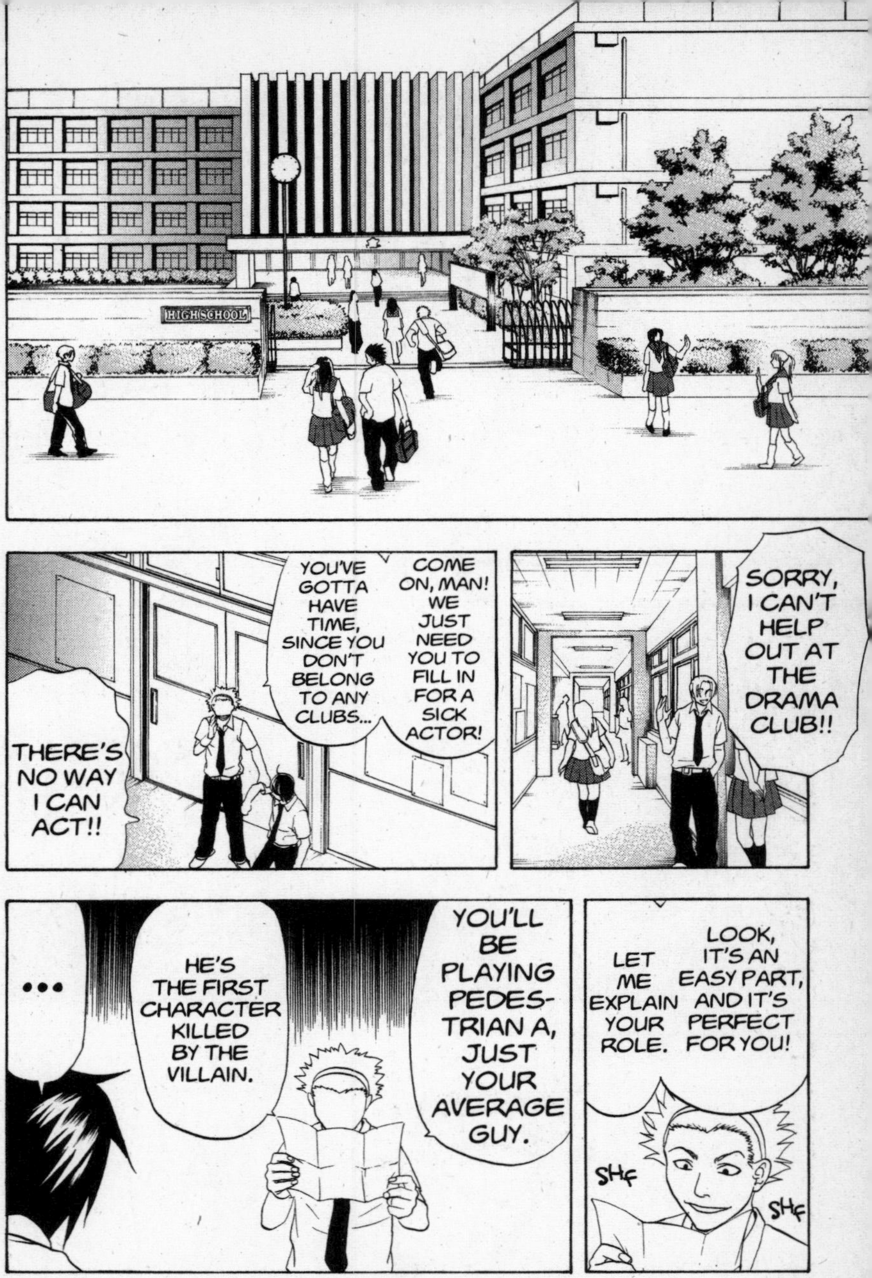
HIGHSCHOOL
SORRY, I CAN'T HELP OUT AT THE DRAMA CLUB!!
COME ON, MAN! WE JUST NEED YOU TO FILL IN FOR A SICK ACTOR!
YOU'VE GOTTA HAVE TIME, SINCE YOU DON'T BELONG TO ANY CLUBS...
THERE'S NO WAY I CAN ACT!!
LOOK, IT'S AN EASY PART, AND IT'S PERFECT FOR YOU!
LET ME EXPLAIN YOUR ROLE.
SHF
SHF
YOU'LL BE PLAYING PEDES-TRIAN A, JUST YOUR AVERAGE GUY.
HE'S THE FIRST CHARACTER KILLED BY THE VILLAIN.
...

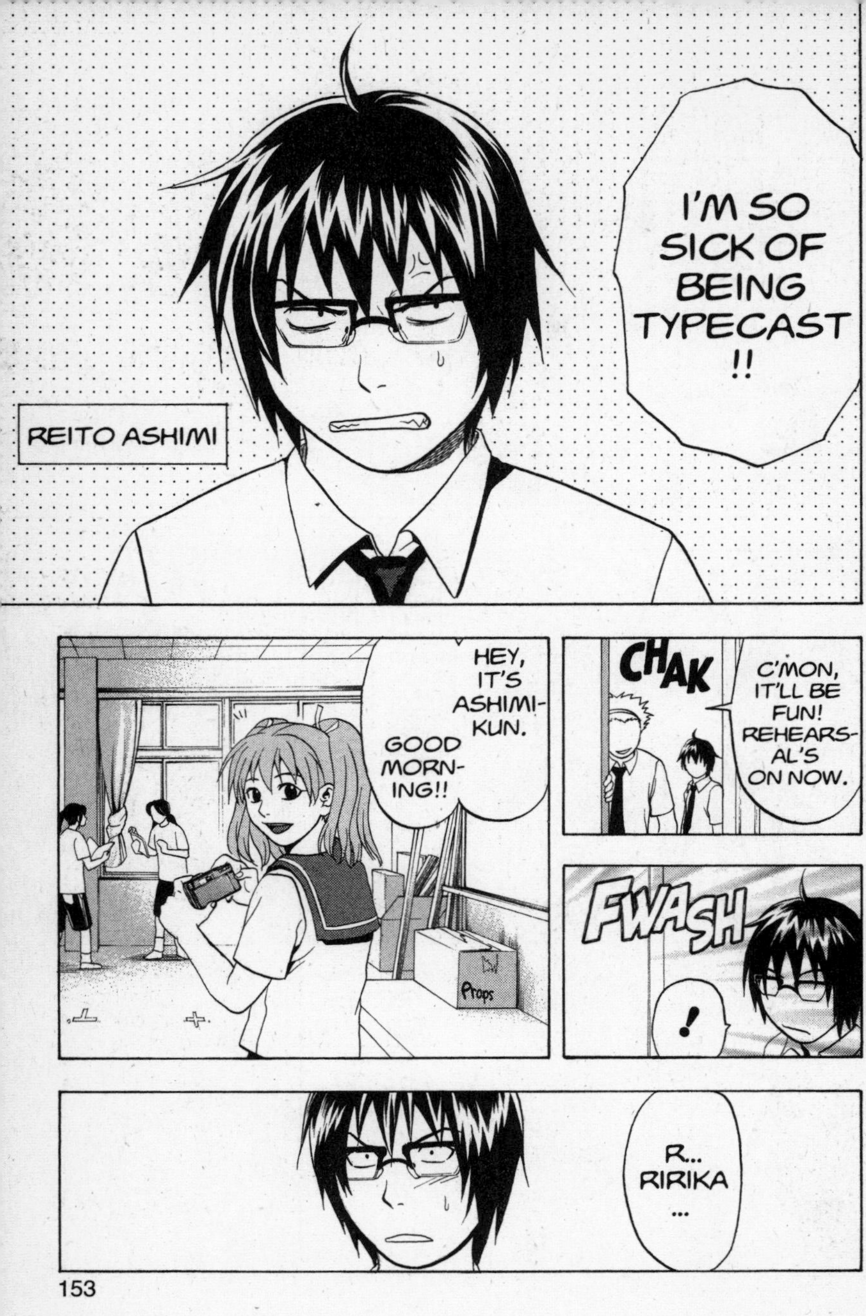
I'M SO SICK OF BEING TYPECAST!!
REITO ASHIMI
CHAK
C'MON, IT'LL BE FUN! REHEARSAL'S ON NOW.
FWASH
!
HEY, IT'S ASHIMI-KUN.
GOOD MORNING!!
Props
R... RIRIKA...

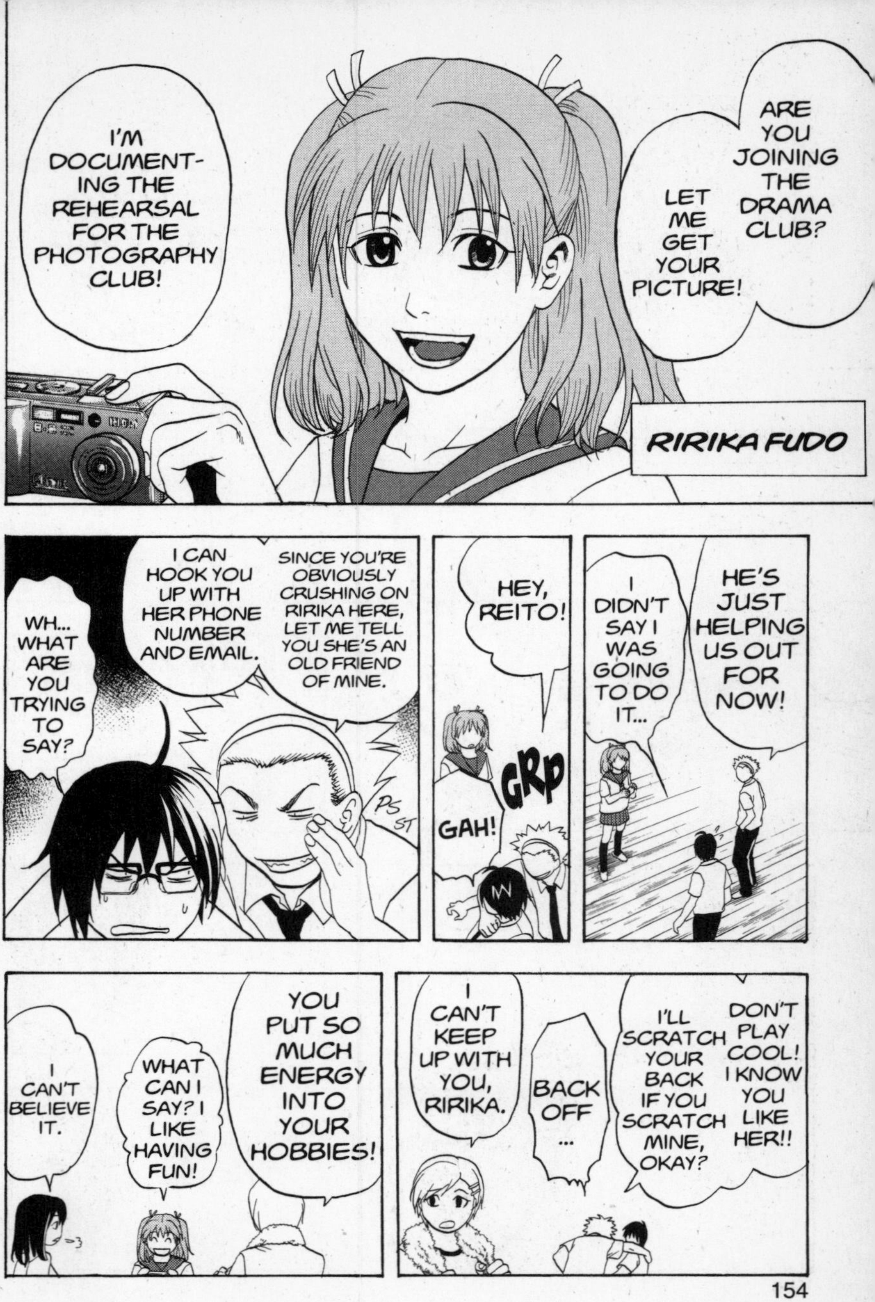
ARE YOU JOINING THE DRAMA CLUB?
LET ME GET YOUR PICTURE!
I'M DOCUMENTING THE REHEARSAL FOR THE PHOTOGRAPHY CLUB!
RIRIKA FUDO
HE'S JUST HELPING US OUT FOR NOW!
I DIDN'T SAY I WAS GOING TO DO IT...
HEY, REITO!
GRP
GAH!
SINCE YOU'RE OBVIOUSLY CRUSHING ON RIRIKA HERE, LET ME TELL YOU SHE'S AN OLD FRIEND OF MINE.
I CAN HOOK YOU UP WITH HER PHONE NUMBER AND EMAIL.
PSST
WH... WHAT ARE YOU TRYING TO SAY?
DON'T PLAY COOL! I KNOW YOU LIKE HER!!
I'LL SCRATCH YOUR BACK IF YOU SCRATCH MINE, OKAY?
BACK OFF...
I CAN'T KEEP UP WITH YOU, RIRIKA.
YOU PUT SO MUCH ENERGY INTO YOUR HOBBIES!
WHAT CAN I SAY? I LIKE HAVING FUN!
I CAN'T BELIEVE IT.

READ THIS WAY

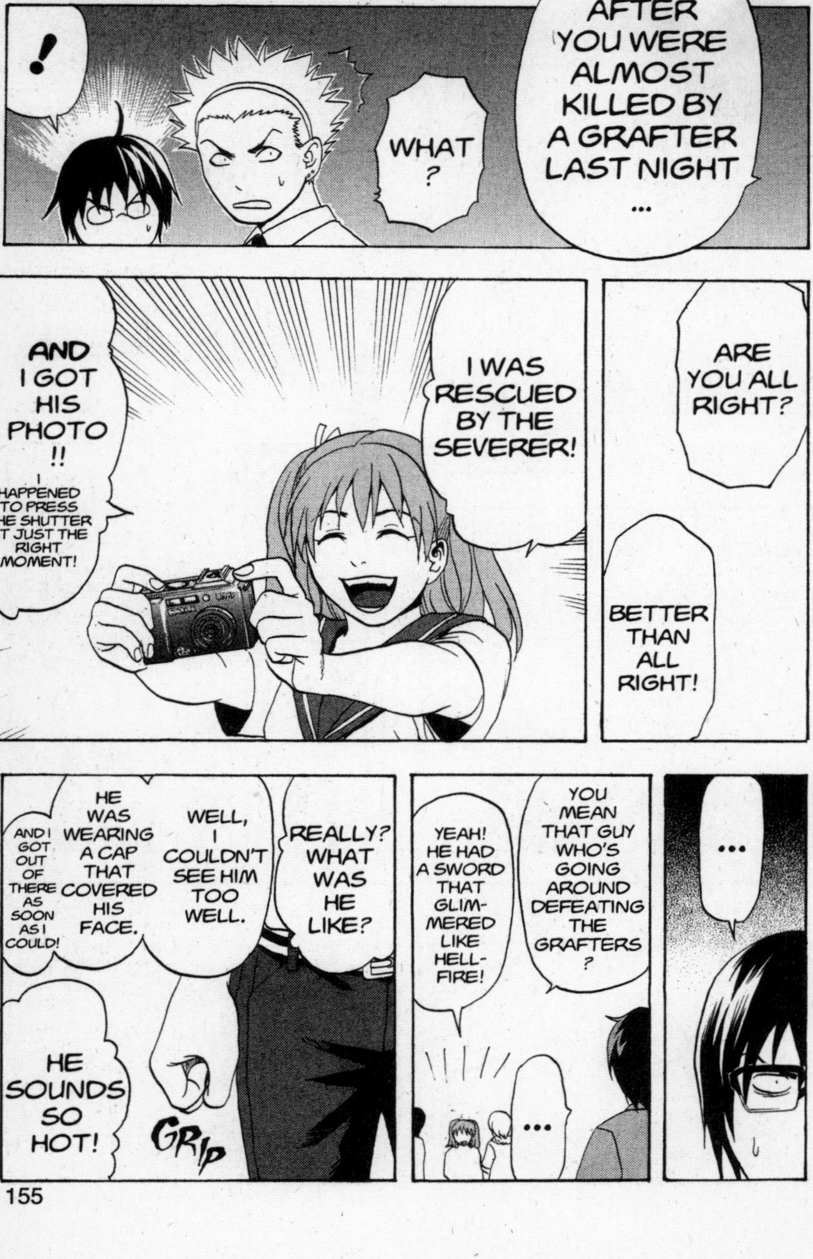
AFTER YOU WERE ALMOST KILLED BY A GRAFTER LAST NIGHT ...
WHAT ?
!
ARE YOU ALL RIGHT?
BETTER THAN ALL RIGHT!
I WAS RESCUED BY THE SEVERER!
AND I GOT HIS PHOTO !!
I HAPPENED TO PRESS THE SHUTTER AT JUST THE RIGHT MOMENT!
...
YOU MEAN THAT GUY WHO'S GOING AROUND DEFEATING THE GRAFTERS ?
YEAH! HE HAD A SWORD THAT GLIM-MERED LIKE HELL-FIRE!
...
REALLY? WHAT WAS HE LIKE?
WELL, I COULDN'T SEE HIM TOO WELL.
HE WAS WEARING A CAP THAT COVERED HIS FACE.
AND I GOT OUT OF THERE AS SOON AS I COULD!
HE SOUNDS SO HOT!
GRIP

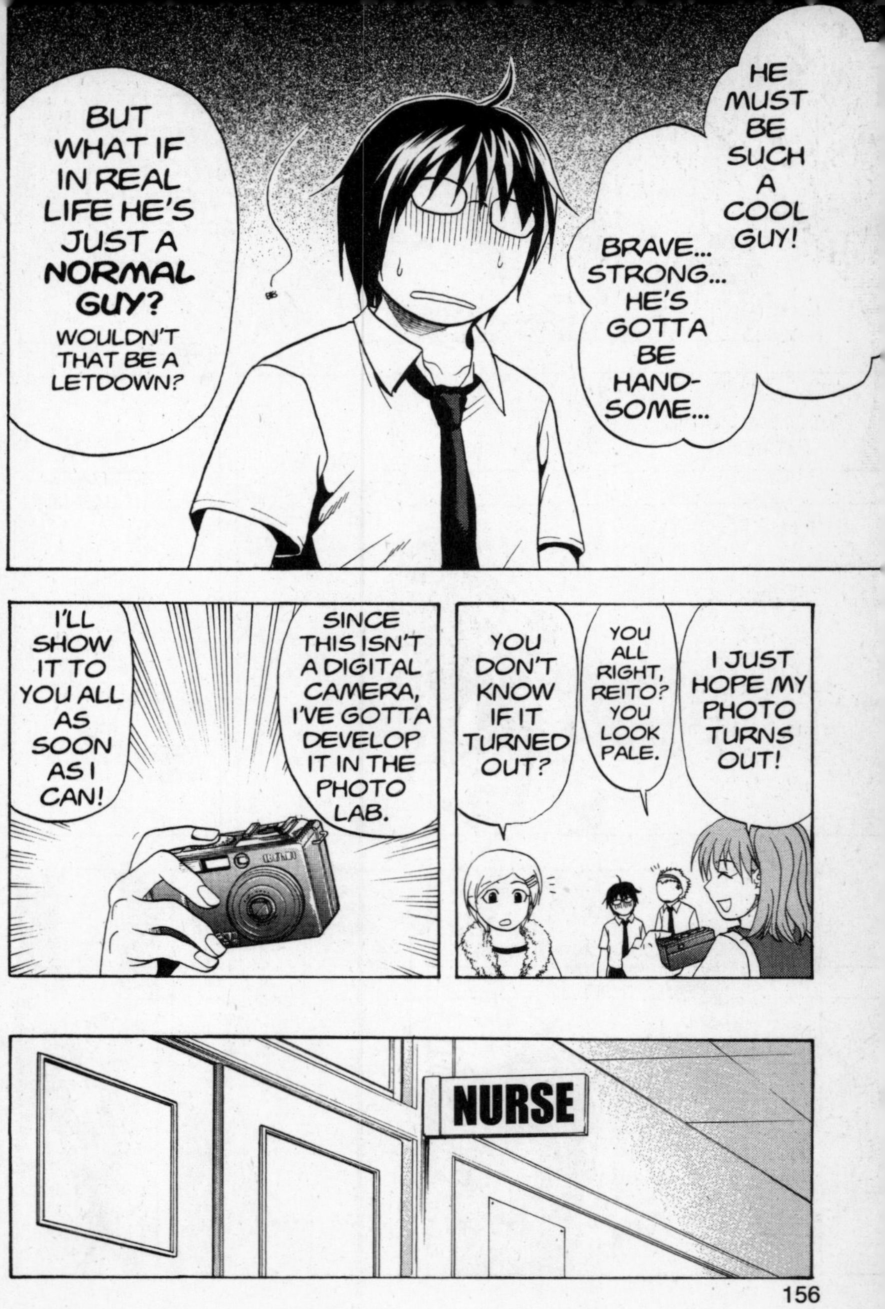
HE MUST BE SUCH A COOL GUY!
BRAVE... STRONG... HE'S GOTTA BE HAND-SOME...
BUT WHAT IF IN REAL LIFE HE'S JUST A **NORMAL GUY?** WOULDN'T THAT BE A LETDOWN?
I JUST HOPE MY PHOTO TURNS OUT!
YOU ALL RIGHT, REITO? YOU LOOK PALE.
YOU DON'T KNOW IF IT TURNED OUT?
SINCE THIS ISN'T A DIGITAL CAMERA, I'VE GOTTA DEVELOP IT IN THE PHOTO LAB.
I'LL SHOW IT TO YOU ALL AS SOON AS I CAN!
NURSE

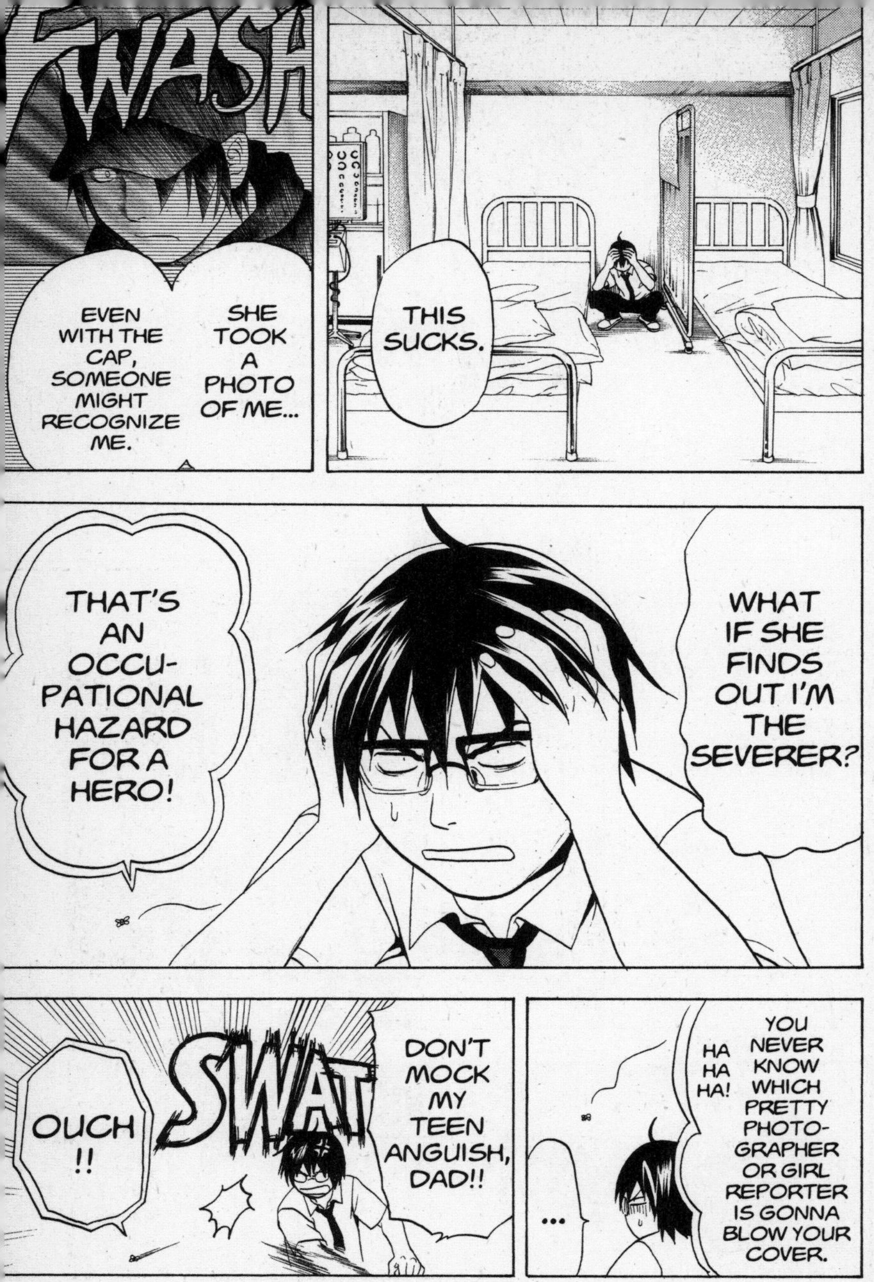
THIS SUCKS.
SHE TOOK A PHOTO OF ME...
EVEN WITH THE CAP, SOMEONE MIGHT RECOGNIZE ME.
WHAT IF SHE FINDS OUT I'M THE SEVERER?
THAT'S AN OCCU-PATIONAL HAZARD FOR A HERO!
YOU NEVER KNOW WHICH PRETTY PHOTO-GRAPHER OR GIRL REPORTER IS GONNA BLOW YOUR COVER.
HA HA HA!
...
DON'T MOCK MY TEEN ANGUISH, DAD!!
SWAT
OUCH!!

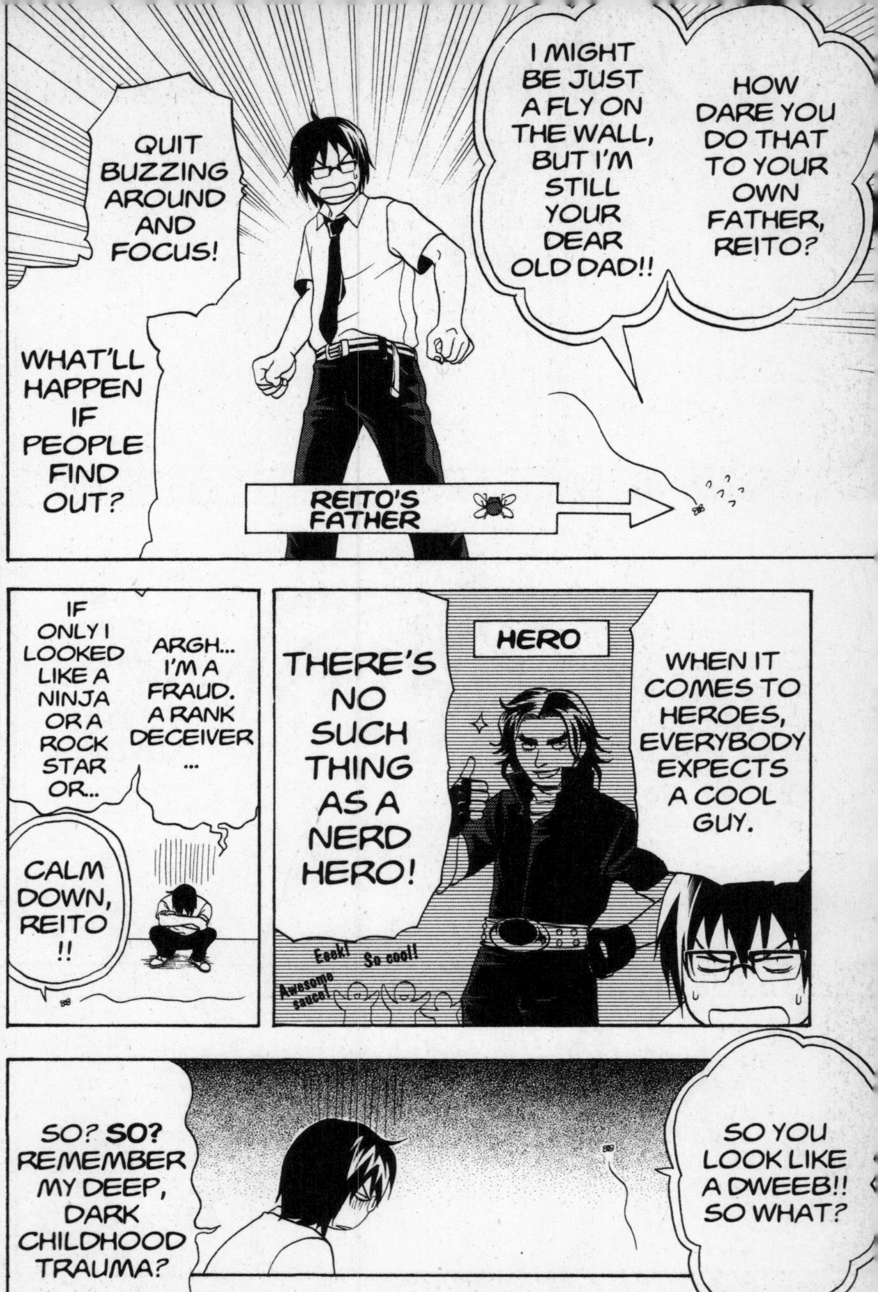
HOW DARE YOU DO THAT TO YOUR OWN FATHER, REITO?
I MIGHT BE JUST A FLY ON THE WALL, BUT I'M STILL YOUR DEAR OLD DAD!!
QUIT BUZZING AROUND AND FOCUS!
WHAT'LL HAPPEN IF PEOPLE FIND OUT?
REITO'S FATHER
WHEN IT COMES TO HEROES, EVERYBODY EXPECTS A COOL GUY.
HERO
THERE'S NO SUCH THING AS A NERD HERO!
So cool!
Eeek!
Awesome sauce!
ARGH... I'M A FRAUD. A RANK DECEIVER...
IF ONLY I LOOKED LIKE A NINJA OR A ROCK STAR OR...
CALM DOWN, REITO!!
SO YOU LOOK LIKE A DWEEB!! SO WHAT?
SO? SO? REMEMBER MY DEEP, DARK CHILDHOOD TRAUMA?

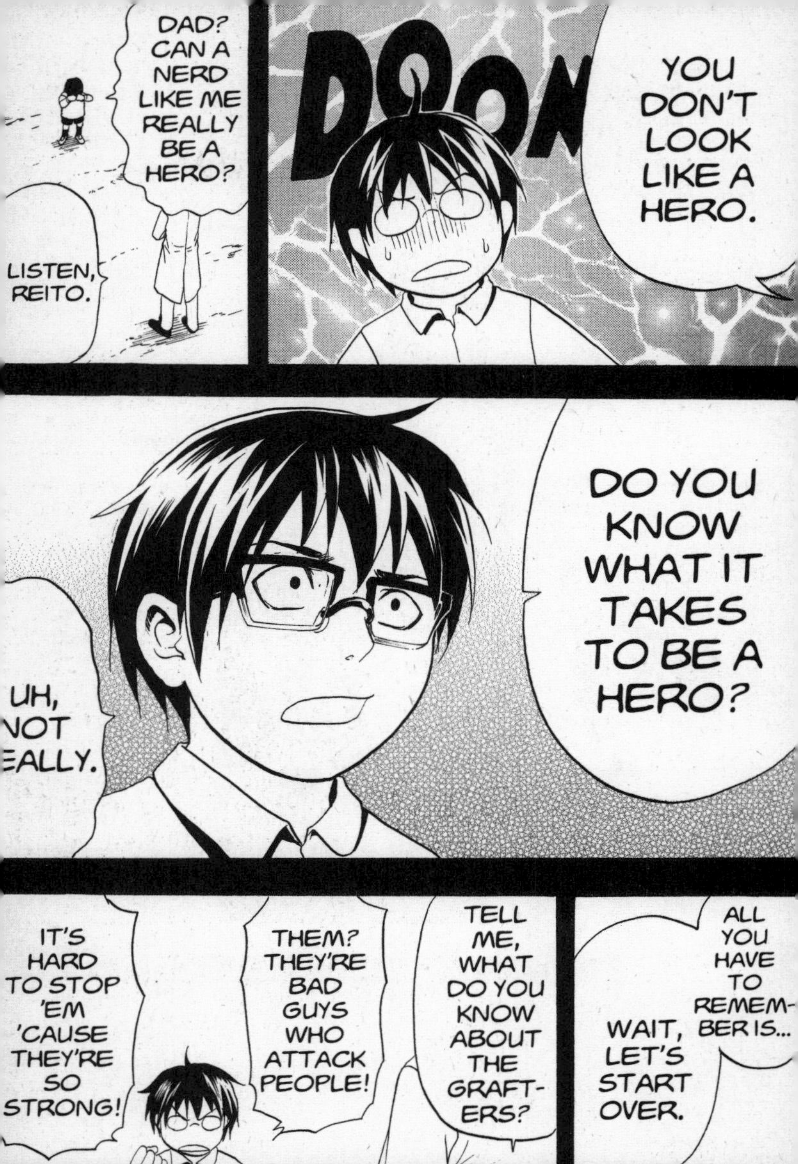
YOU DON'T LOOK LIKE A HERO.
DOOM
DAD? CAN A NERD LIKE ME REALLY BE A HERO?
LISTEN, REITO.
DO YOU KNOW WHAT IT TAKES TO BE A HERO?
UH, NOT EALLY.
ALL YOU HAVE TO REMEMBER IS...
WAIT, LET'S START OVER.
TELL ME, WHAT DO YOU KNOW ABOUT THE GRAFTERS?
THEM? THEY'RE BAD GUYS WHO ATTACK PEOPLE!
IT'S HARD TO STOP 'EM 'CAUSE THEY'RE SO STRONG!

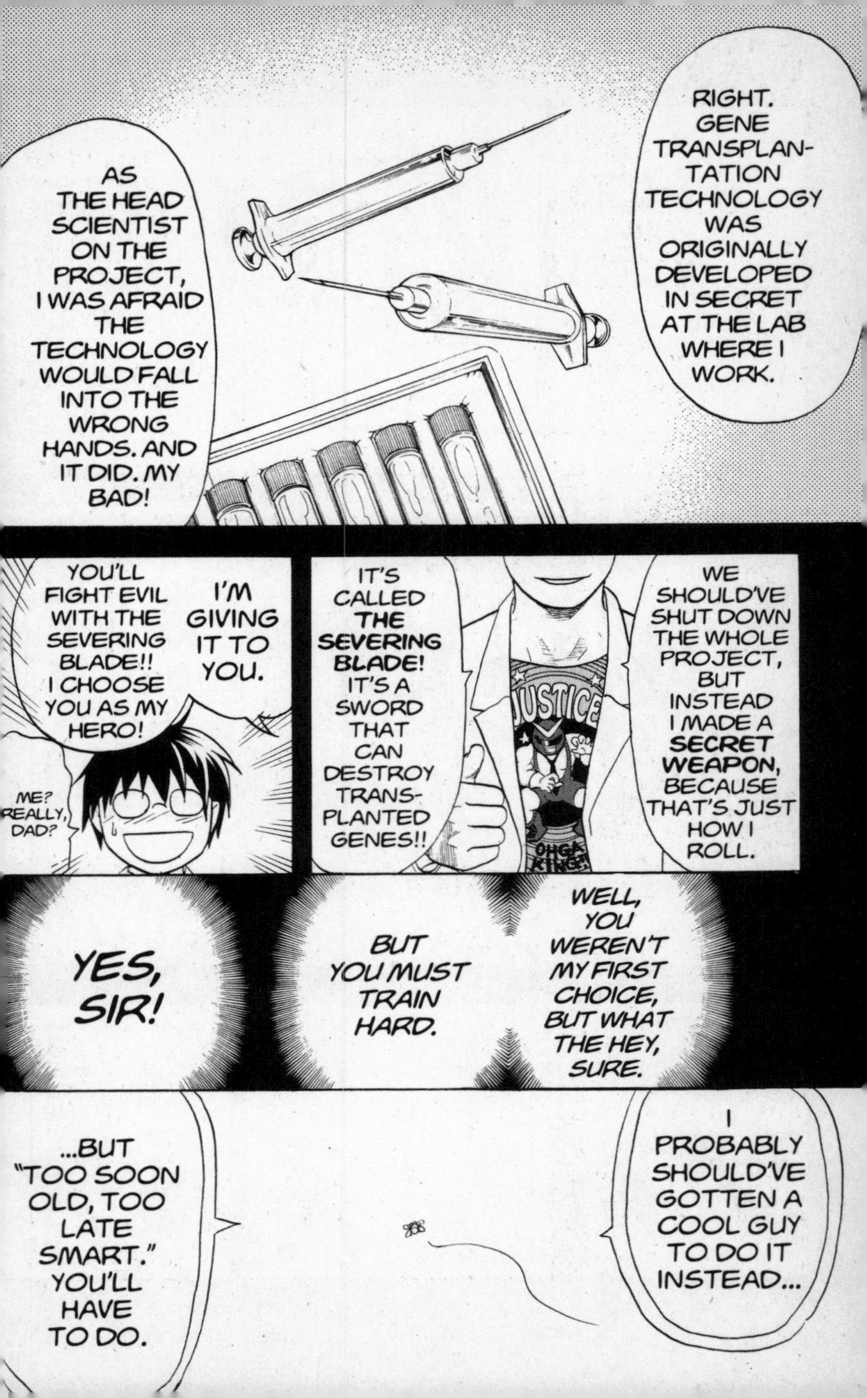
RIGHT. GENE TRANSPLANTATION TECHNOLOGY WAS ORIGINALLY DEVELOPED IN SECRET AT THE LAB WHERE I WORK.
AS THE HEAD SCIENTIST ON THE PROJECT, I WAS AFRAID THE TECHNOLOGY WOULD FALL INTO THE WRONG HANDS. AND IT DID. MY BAD!
WE SHOULD'VE SHUT DOWN THE WHOLE PROJECT, BUT INSTEAD I MADE A **SECRET WEAPON**, BECAUSE THAT'S JUST HOW I ROLL.
IT'S CALLED **THE SEVERING BLADE!** IT'S A SWORD THAT CAN DESTROY TRANSPLANTED GENES!!
JUSTICE
OHGA KING!!
I'M GIVING IT TO YOU.
YOU'LL FIGHT EVIL WITH THE SEVERING BLADE!! I CHOOSE YOU AS MY HERO!
ME? REALLY, DAD?
WELL, YOU WEREN'T MY FIRST CHOICE, BUT WHAT THE HEY, SURE.
BUT YOU MUST TRAIN HARD.
YES, SIR!
I PROBABLY SHOULD'VE GOTTEN A COOL GUY TO DO IT INSTEAD...
...BUT "TOO SOON OLD, TOO LATE SMART." YOU'LL HAVE TO DO.

READ THIS WAY

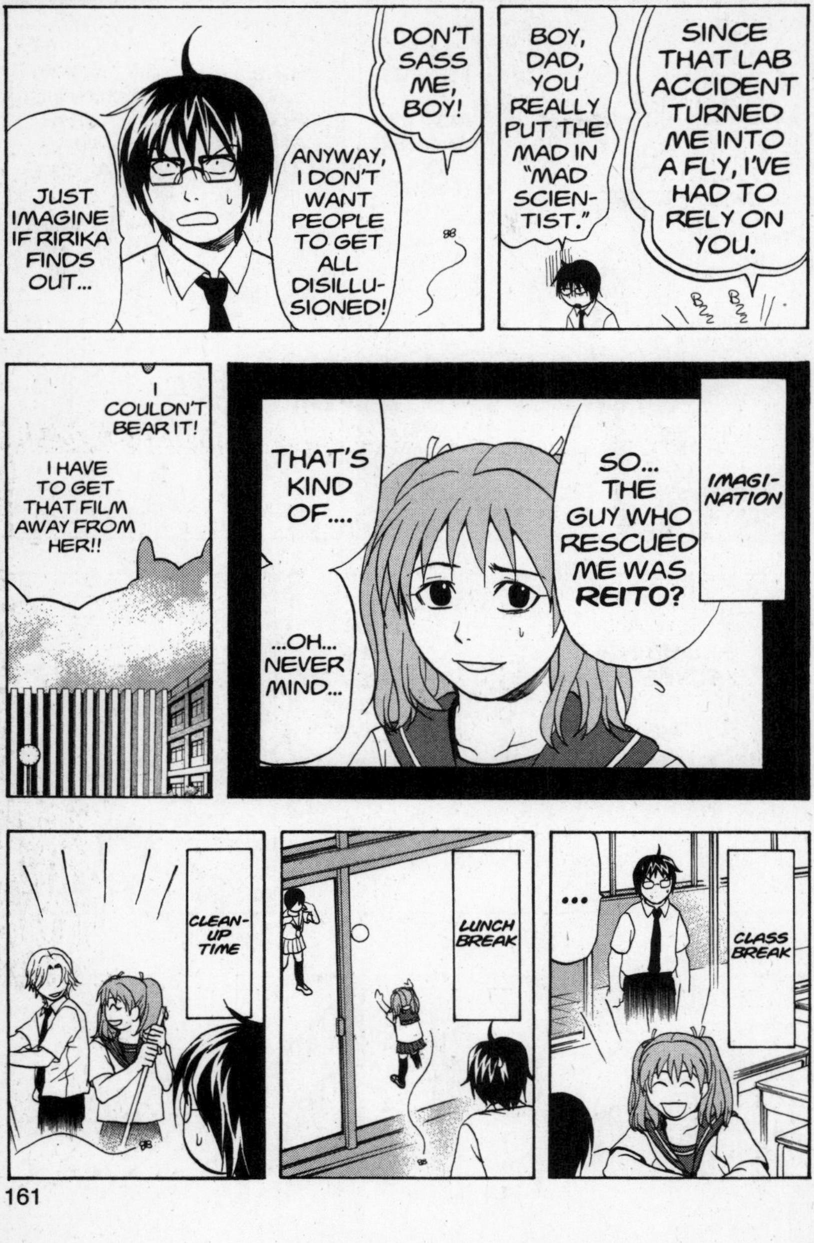
SINCE THAT LAB ACCIDENT TURNED ME INTO A FLY, I'VE HAD TO RELY ON YOU.
BOY, DAD, YOU REALLY PUT THE MAD IN "MAD SCIENTIST."
DON'T SASS ME, BOY!
ANYWAY, I DON'T WANT PEOPLE TO GET ALL DISILLUSIONED!
JUST IMAGINE IF RIRIKA FINDS OUT...
IMAGINATION
SO... THE GUY WHO RESCUED ME WAS REITO?
THAT'S KIND OF....
...OH... NEVER MIND...
I COULDN'T BEAR IT!
I HAVE TO GET THAT FILM AWAY FROM HER!!
CLASS BREAK
...
LUNCH BREAK
CLEAN-UP TIME

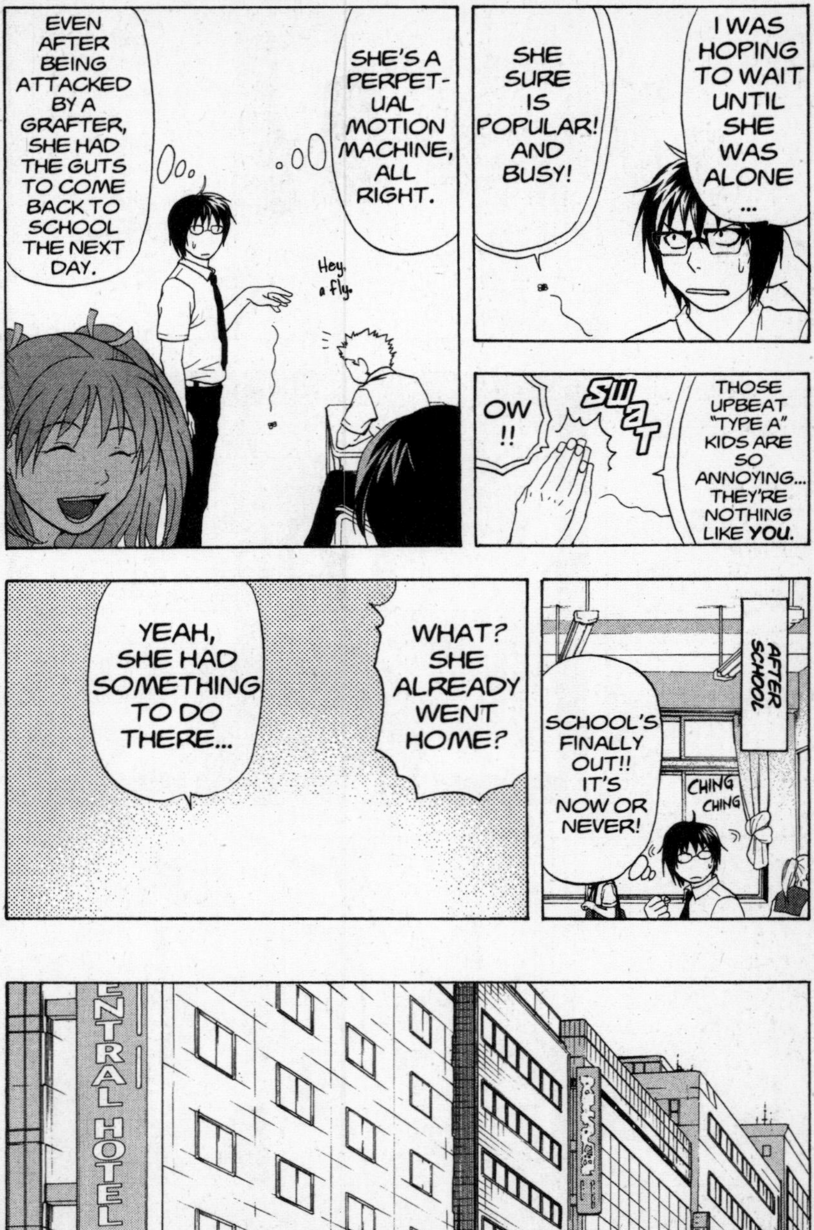
I WAS HOPING TO WAIT UNTIL SHE WAS ALONE ...
SHE SURE IS POPULAR! AND BUSY!
THOSE UPBEAT "TYPE A" KIDS ARE SO ANNOYING... THEY'RE NOTHING LIKE **YOU**.
SWAT
OW !!
SHE'S A PERPETUAL MOTION MACHINE, ALL RIGHT.
EVEN AFTER BEING ATTACKED BY A GRAFTER, SHE HAD THE GUTS TO COME BACK TO SCHOOL THE NEXT DAY.
Hey, a fly.
AFTER SCHOOL
SCHOOL'S FINALLY OUT!! IT'S NOW OR NEVER!
CHING CHING
WHAT? SHE ALREADY WENT HOME?
YEAH, SHE HAD SOMETHING TO DO THERE...
NTRAL HOTEL

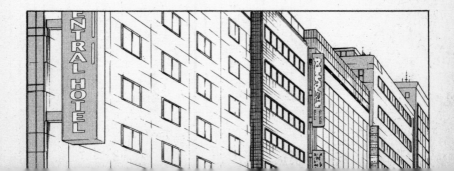

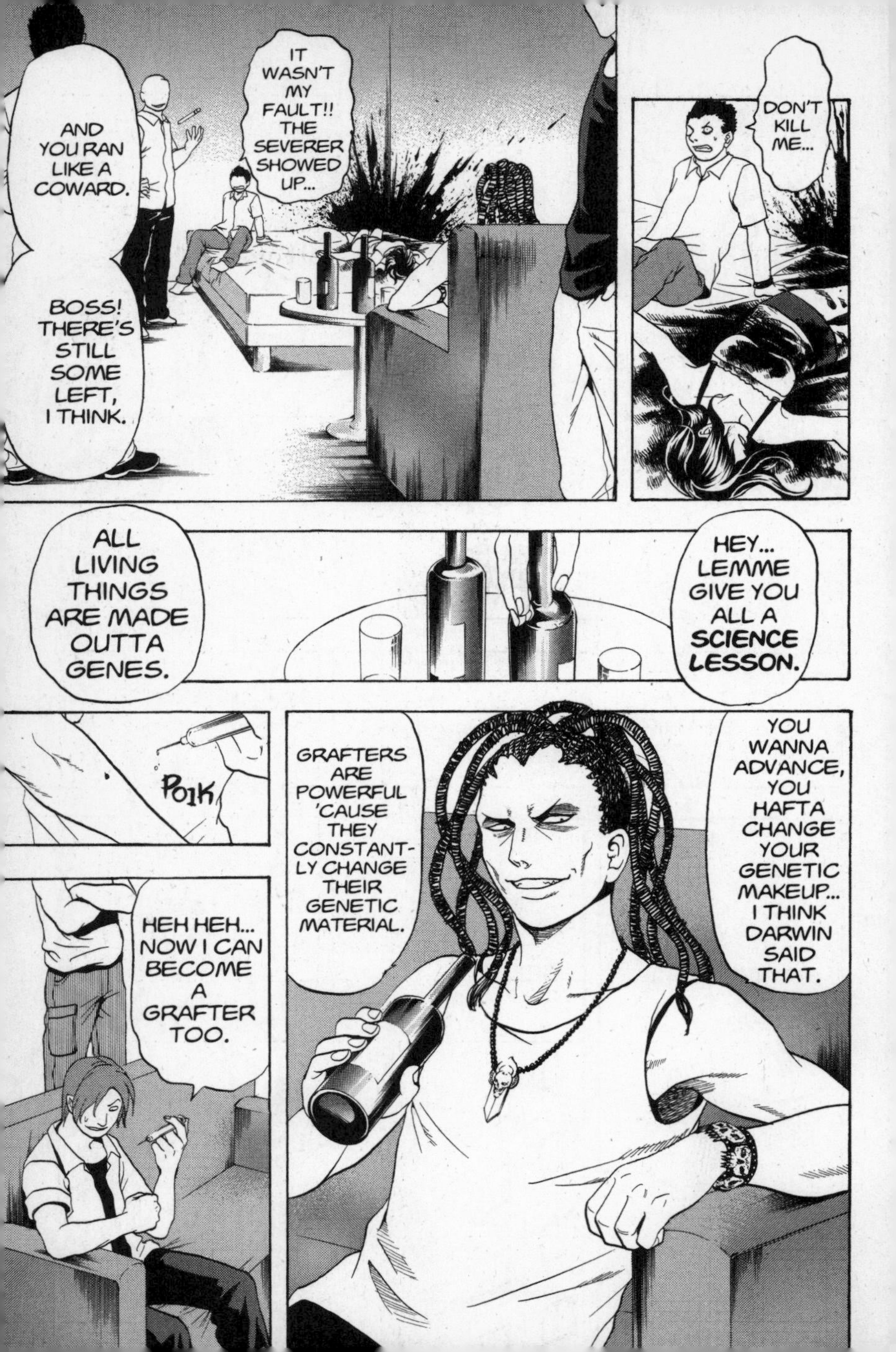
DON'T KILL ME...
IT WASN'T MY FAULT!! THE SEVERER SHOWED UP...
AND YOU RAN LIKE A COWARD.
BOSS! THERE'S STILL SOME LEFT, I THINK.
HEY... LEMME GIVE YOU ALL A **SCIENCE LESSON.**
ALL LIVING THINGS ARE MADE OUTTA GENES.
YOU WANNA ADVANCE, YOU HAFTA CHANGE YOUR GENETIC MAKEUP... I THINK DARWIN SAID THAT.
GRAFTERS ARE POWERFUL 'CAUSE THEY CONSTANT-LY CHANGE THEIR GENETIC MATERIAL.
POIK
HEH HEH... NOW I CAN BECOME A GRAFTER TOO.

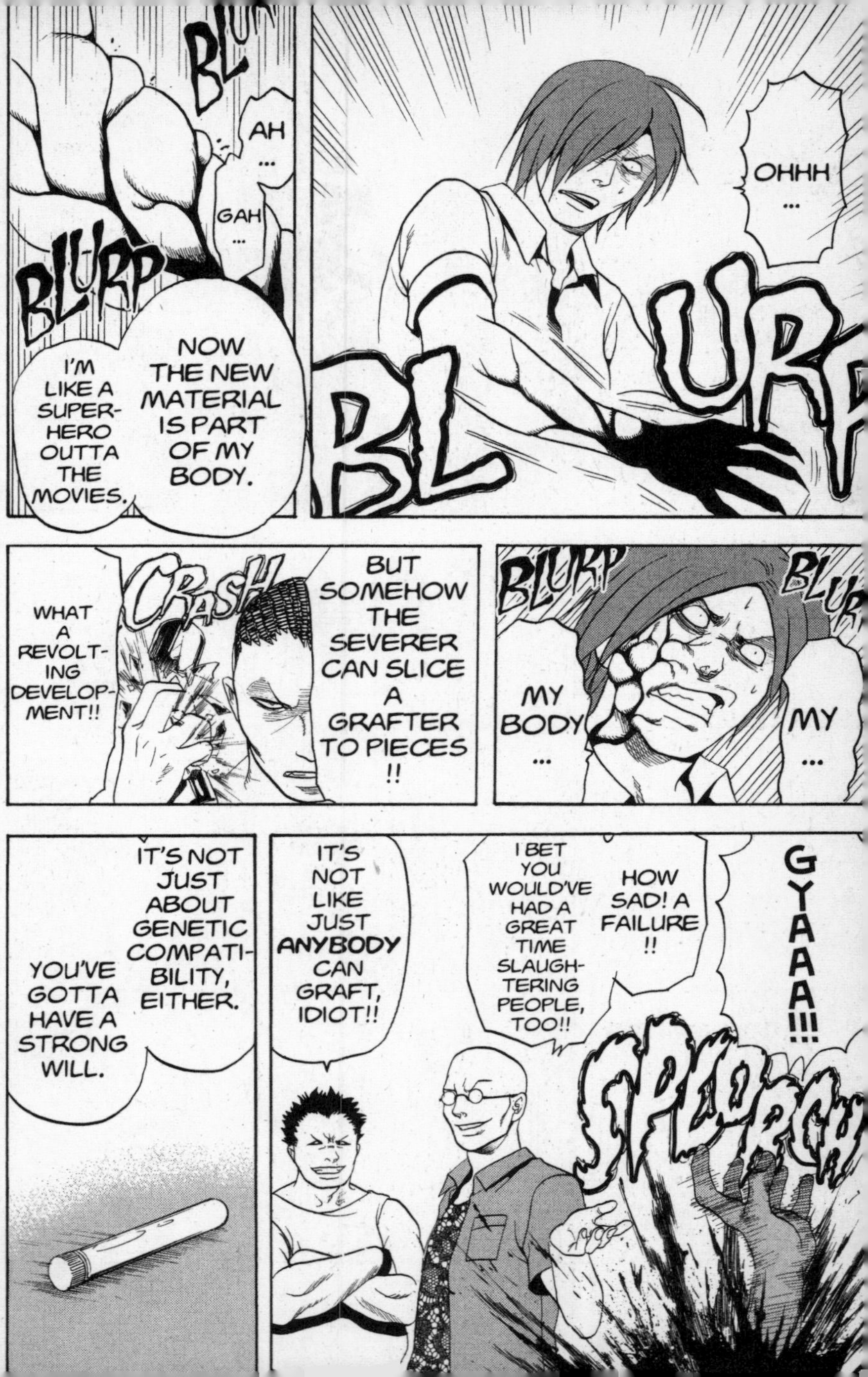
OHHH...
BLURP
AH...
GAH...
BLURP
NOW THE NEW MATERIAL IS PART OF MY BODY.
I'M LIKE A SUPERHERO OUTTA THE MOVIES.
BLURP
BLURP
MY...
MY BODY...
BUT SOMEHOW THE SEVERER CAN SLICE A GRAFTER TO PIECES!!
CRASH
WHAT A REVOLTING DEVELOPMENT!!
GYAAAA!!!
SPLORCH
HOW SAD! A FAILURE!!
I BET YOU WOULD'VE HAD A GREAT TIME SLAUGHTERING PEOPLE, TOO!!
IT'S NOT LIKE JUST **ANYBODY** CAN GRAFT, IDIOT!!
IT'S NOT JUST ABOUT GENETIC COMPATIBILITY, EITHER.
YOU'VE GOTTA HAVE A STRONG WILL.

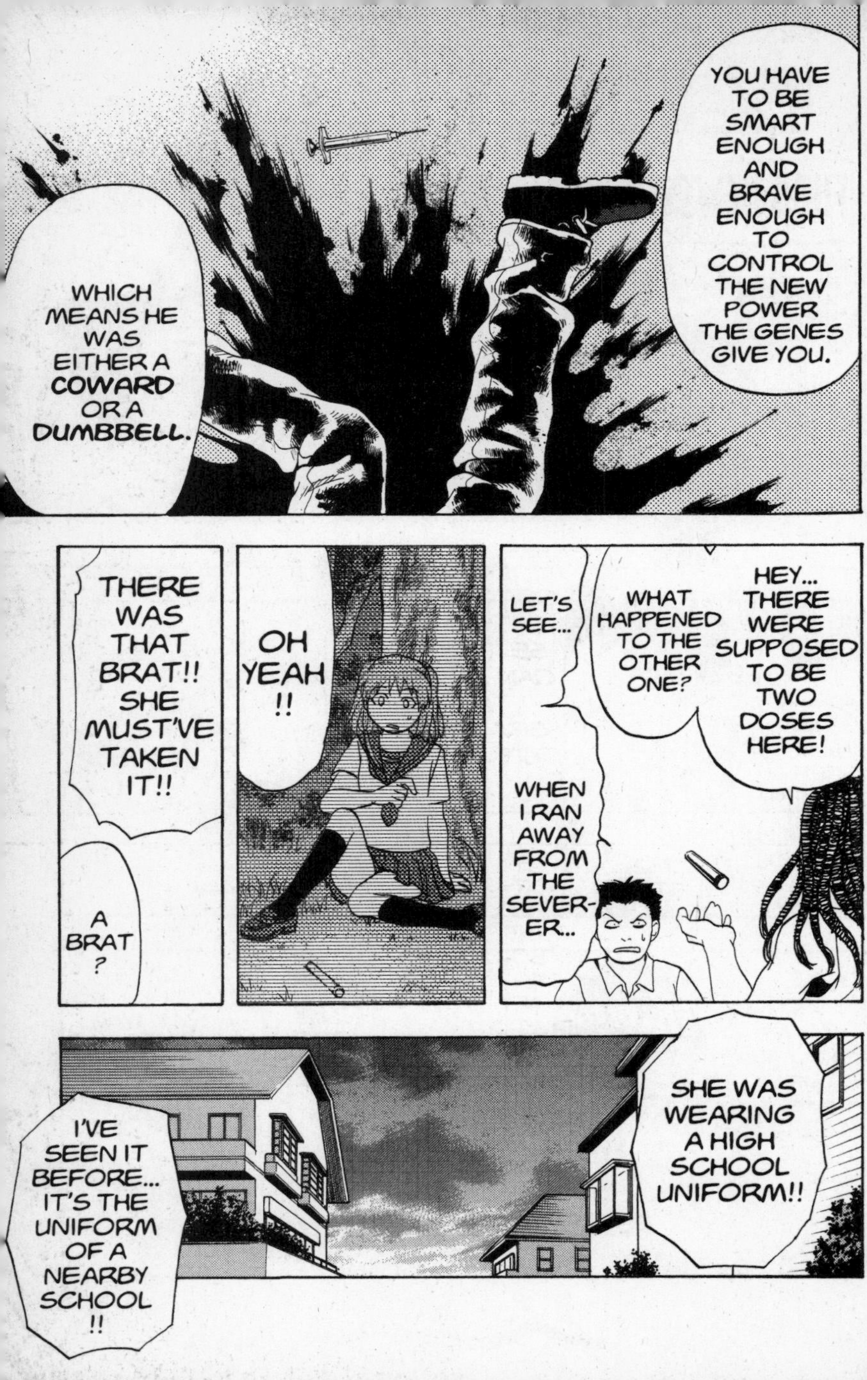
YOU HAVE TO BE SMART ENOUGH AND BRAVE ENOUGH TO CONTROL THE NEW POWER THE GENES GIVE YOU.
WHICH MEANS HE WAS EITHER A **COWARD** OR A **DUMBBELL.**
HEY... THERE WERE SUPPOSED TO BE TWO DOSES HERE!
WHAT HAPPENED TO THE OTHER ONE?
LET'S SEE...
WHEN I RAN AWAY FROM THE SEVER-ER...
OH YEAH !!
THERE WAS THAT BRAT!! SHE MUST'VE TAKEN IT!!
A BRAT ?
SHE WAS WEARING A HIGH SCHOOL UNIFORM!!
I'VE SEEN IT BEFORE... IT'S THE UNIFORM OF A NEARBY SCHOOL !!

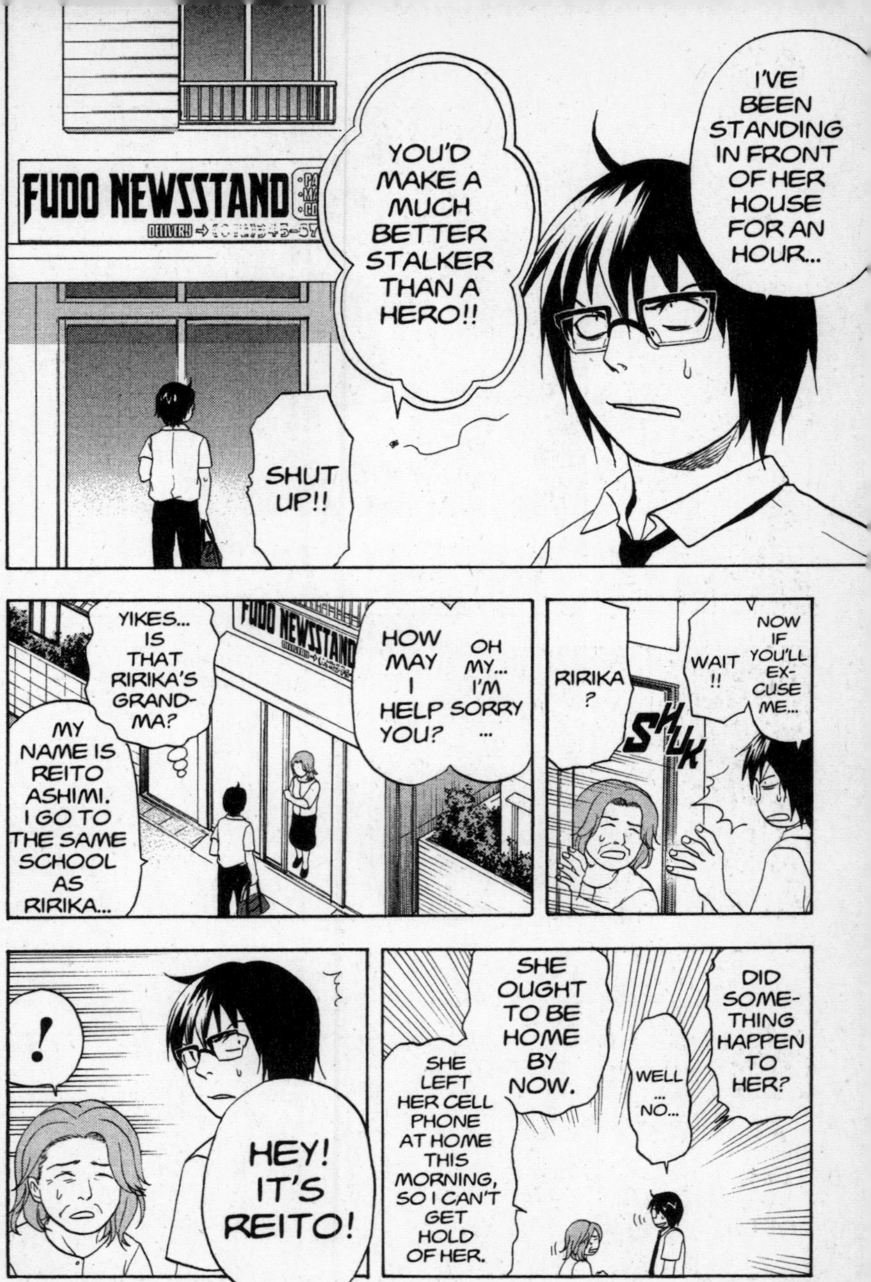
I'VE BEEN STANDING IN FRONT OF HER HOUSE FOR AN HOUR...
YOU'D MAKE A MUCH BETTER STALKER THAN A HERO!!
FUDO NEWSSTAND
DELIVERY
SHUT UP!!
NOW IF YOU'LL EX-CUSE ME...
WAIT!!
RIRIKA?
SHUK
OH MY... I'M SORRY...
HOW MAY I HELP YOU?
FUDO NEWSSTAND
YIKES... IS THAT RIRIKA'S GRAND-MA?
MY NAME IS REITO ASHIMI. I GO TO THE SAME SCHOOL AS RIRIKA...
DID SOME-THING HAPPEN TO HER?
WELL... NO...
SHE OUGHT TO BE HOME BY NOW.
SHE LEFT HER CELL PHONE AT HOME THIS MORNING, SO I CAN'T GET HOLD OF HER.
!
HEY! IT'S REITO!

READ THIS WAY

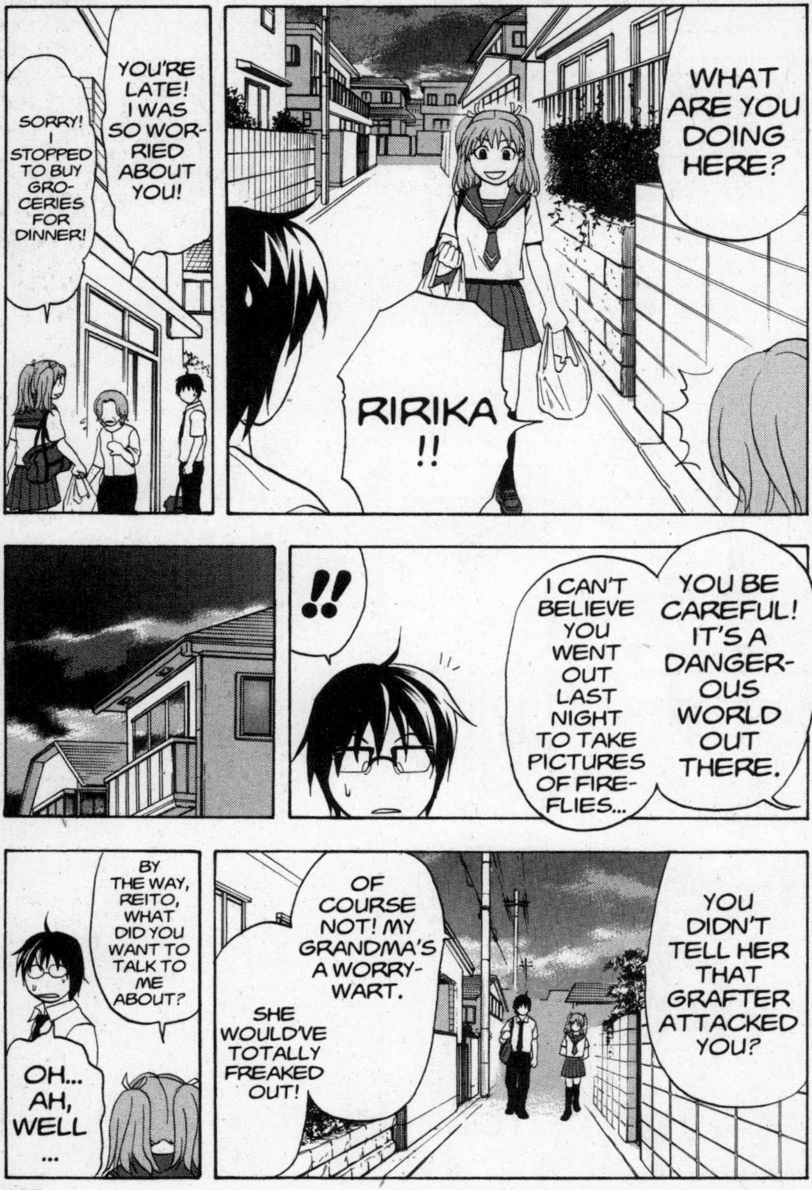
WHAT ARE YOU DOING HERE?
RIRIKA !!
YOU'RE LATE! I WAS SO WORRIED ABOUT YOU!
SORRY! I STOPPED TO BUY GROCERIES FOR DINNER!
YOU BE CAREFUL! IT'S A DANGEROUS WORLD OUT THERE.
I CAN'T BELIEVE YOU WENT OUT LAST NIGHT TO TAKE PICTURES OF FIREFLIES...
!!
YOU DIDN'T TELL HER THAT GRAFTER ATTACKED YOU?
OF COURSE NOT! MY GRANDMA'S A WORRYWART.
SHE WOULD'VE TOTALLY FREAKED OUT!
BY THE WAY, REITO, WHAT DID YOU WANT TO TALK TO ME ABOUT?
OH... AH, WELL ...

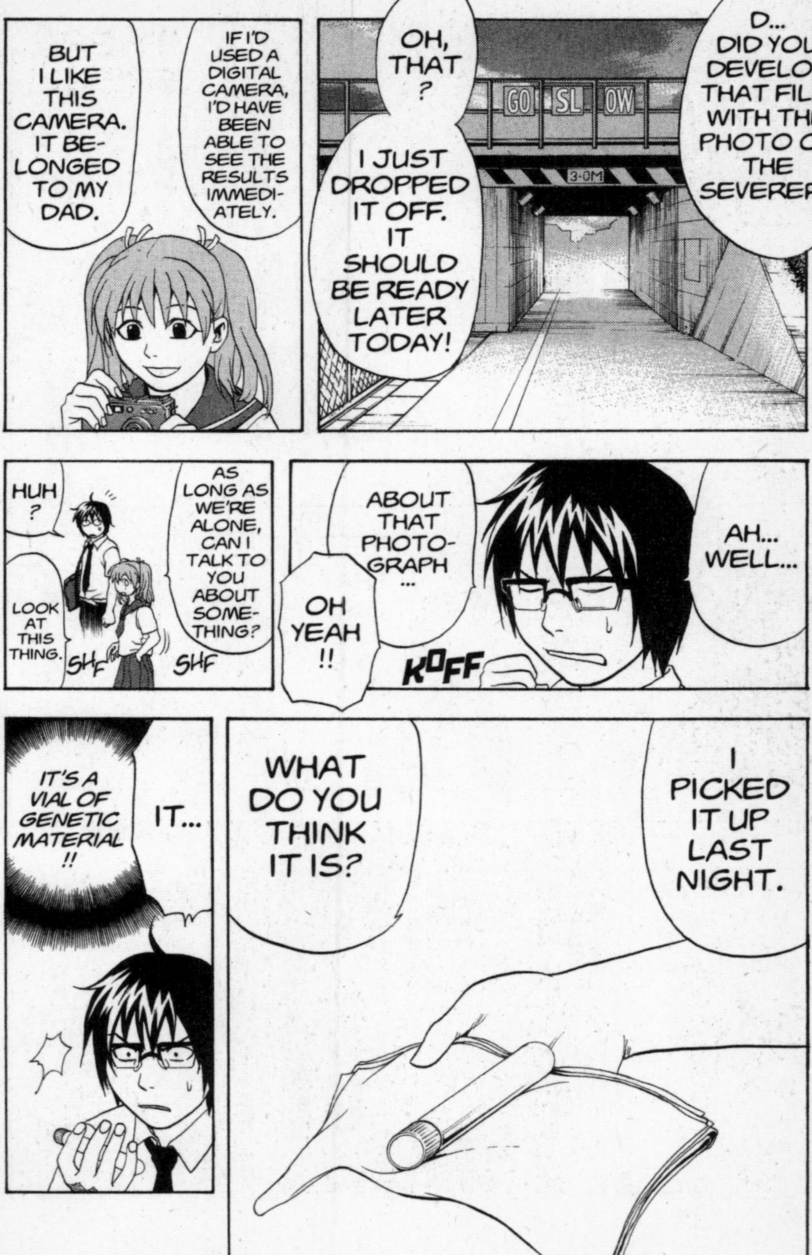
D... DID YOU DEVELOP THAT FILM WITH THE PHOTO OF THE SEVERER?
OH, THAT?
I JUST DROPPED IT OFF. IT SHOULD BE READY LATER TODAY!
GO SLOW
3.0M
IF I'D USED A DIGITAL CAMERA, I'D HAVE BEEN ABLE TO SEE THE RESULTS IMMEDIATELY.
BUT I LIKE THIS CAMERA. IT BE-LONGED TO MY DAD.
AH... WELL...
ABOUT THAT PHOTOGRAPH...
OH YEAH!!
KOFF
AS LONG AS WE'RE ALONE, CAN I TALK TO YOU ABOUT SOMETHING?
HUH?
LOOK AT THIS THING.
SHF
SHF
I PICKED IT UP LAST NIGHT.
WHAT DO YOU THINK IT IS?
IT...
IT'S A VIAL OF GENETIC MATERIAL!!

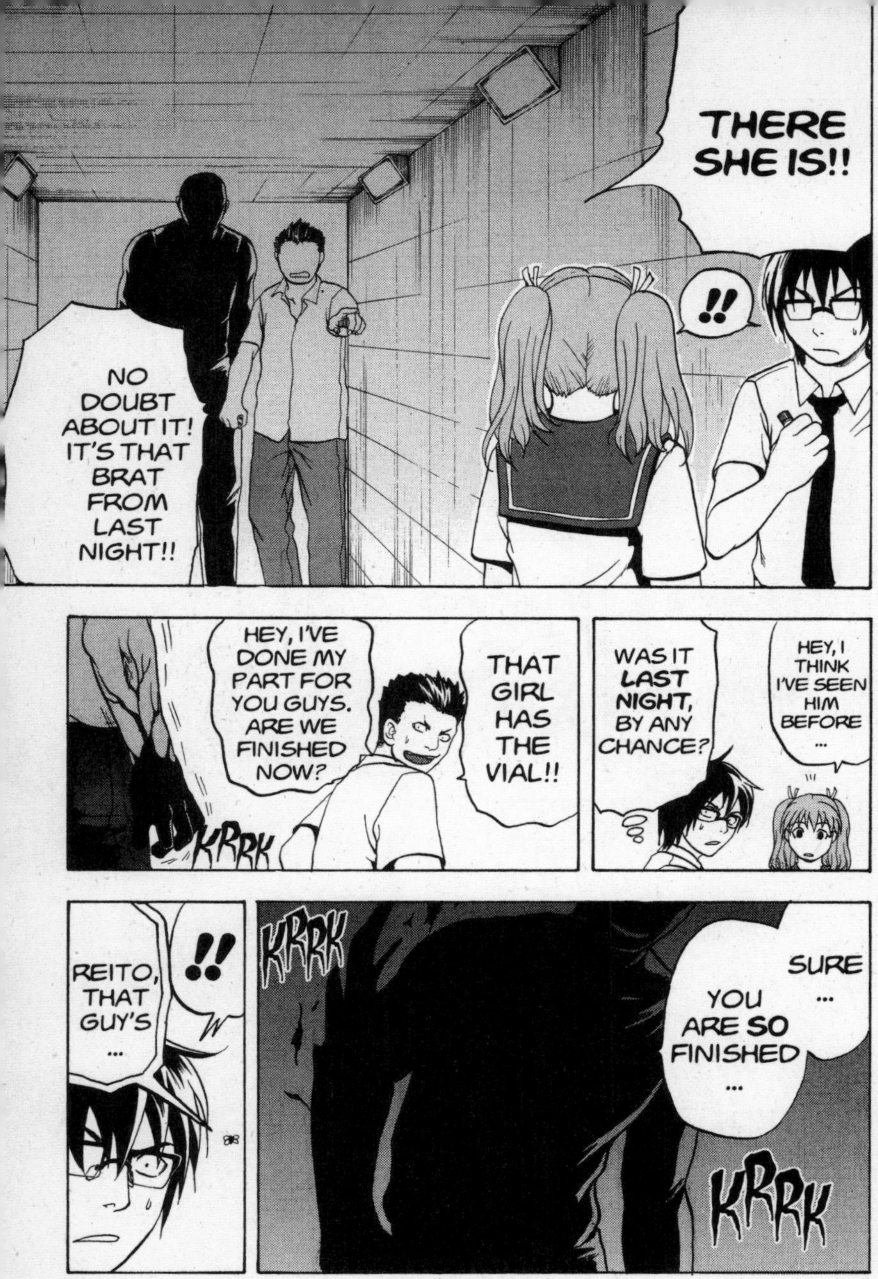
THERE SHE IS!!
!!
NO DOUBT ABOUT IT! IT'S THAT BRAT FROM LAST NIGHT!!
HEY, I THINK I'VE SEEN HIM BEFORE ...
WAS IT LAST NIGHT, BY ANY CHANCE?
THAT GIRL HAS THE VIAL!!
HEY, I'VE DONE MY PART FOR YOU GUYS. ARE WE FINISHED NOW?
KRRK
KRRK
SURE ...
YOU ARE SO FINISHED ...
KRRK
!!
REITO, THAT GUY'S ...

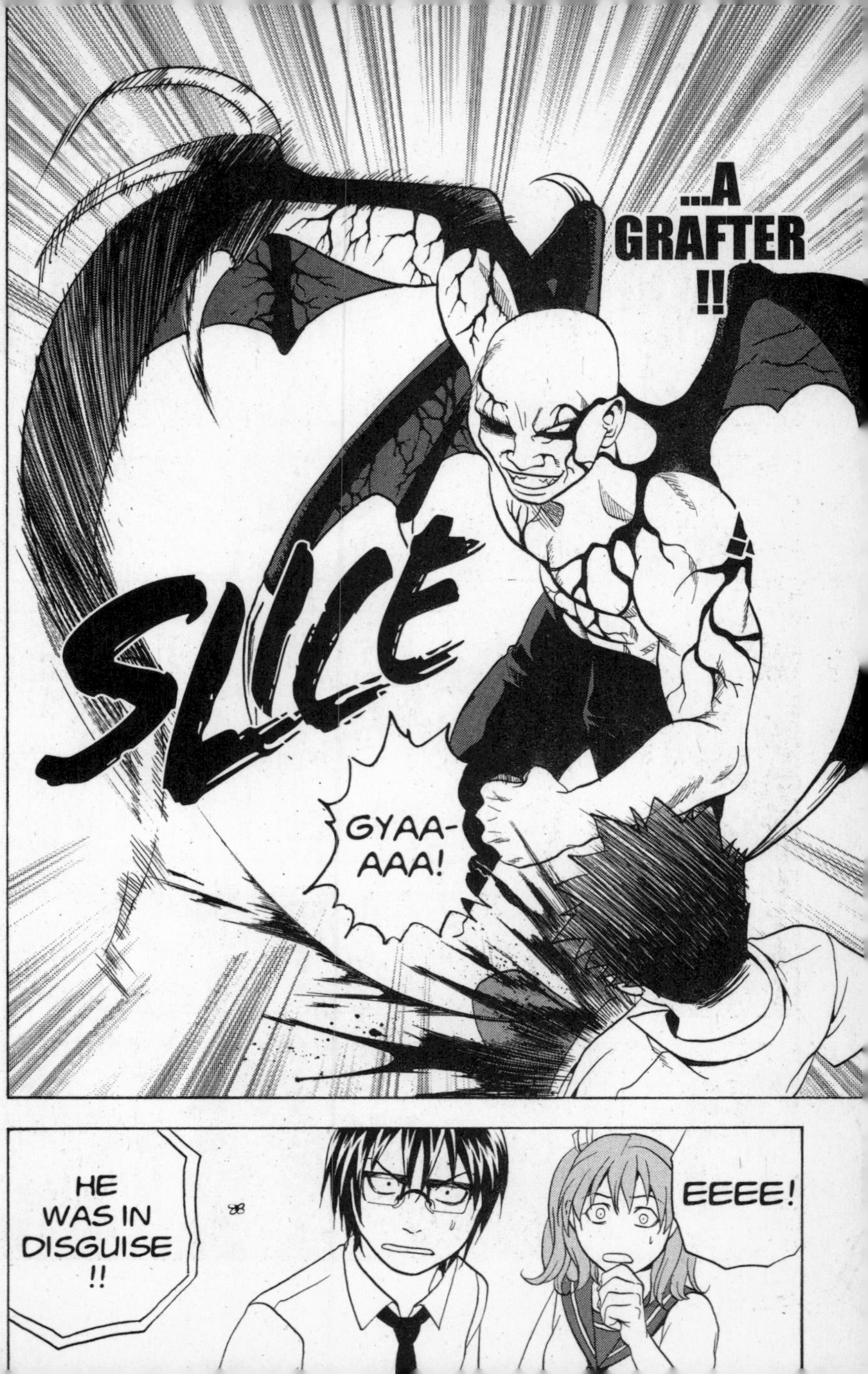
...A GRAFTER !!
SLICE
GYAA-AAA!
EEEEE!
HE WAS IN DISGUISE !!

READ THIS WAY

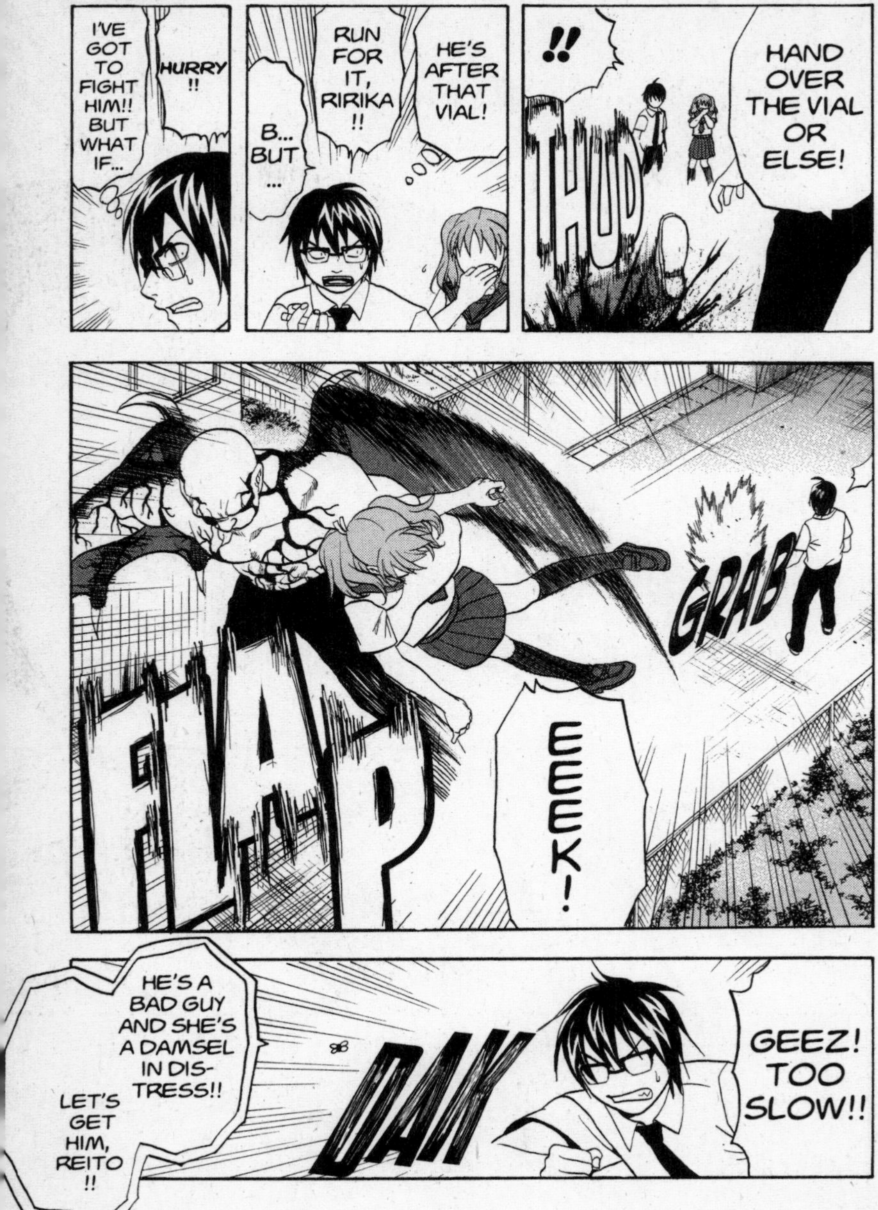
HAND OVER THE VIAL OR ELSE!
!!
THUD
HE'S AFTER THAT VIAL!
RUN FOR IT, RIRIKA!!
B... BUT ...
HURRY!!
I'VE GOT TO FIGHT HIM!! BUT WHAT IF...
GRAB
FLAP
EEEK!
GEEZ! TOO SLOW!!
DAH
HE'S A BAD GUY AND SHE'S A DAMSEL IN DIS-TRESS!!
LET'S GET HIM, REITO!!

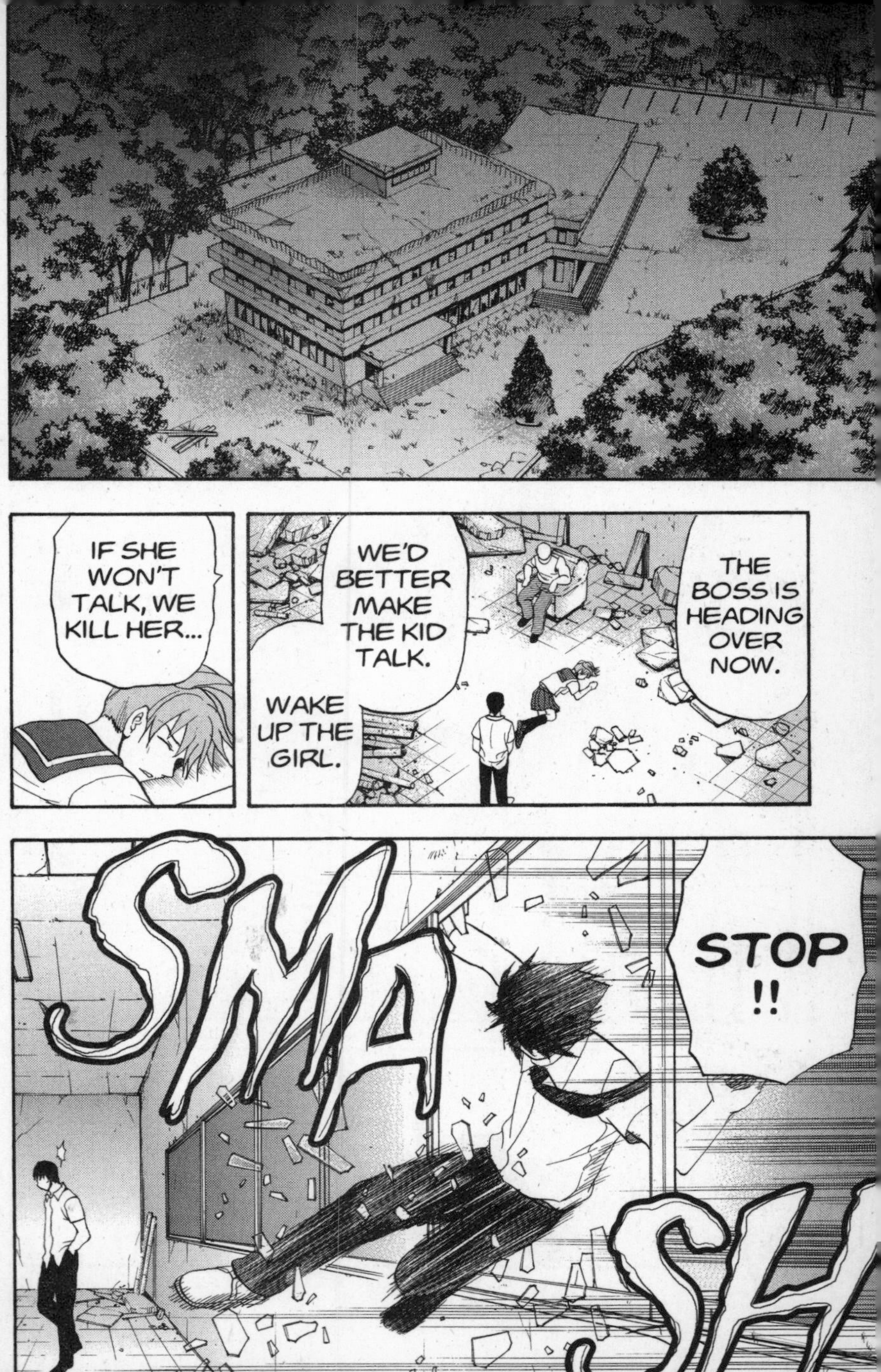
THE BOSS IS HEADING OVER NOW.
WE'D BETTER MAKE THE KID TALK.
WAKE UP THE GIRL.
IF SHE WON'T TALK, WE KILL HER...
STOP !!
SMA
SH

READ THIS WAY

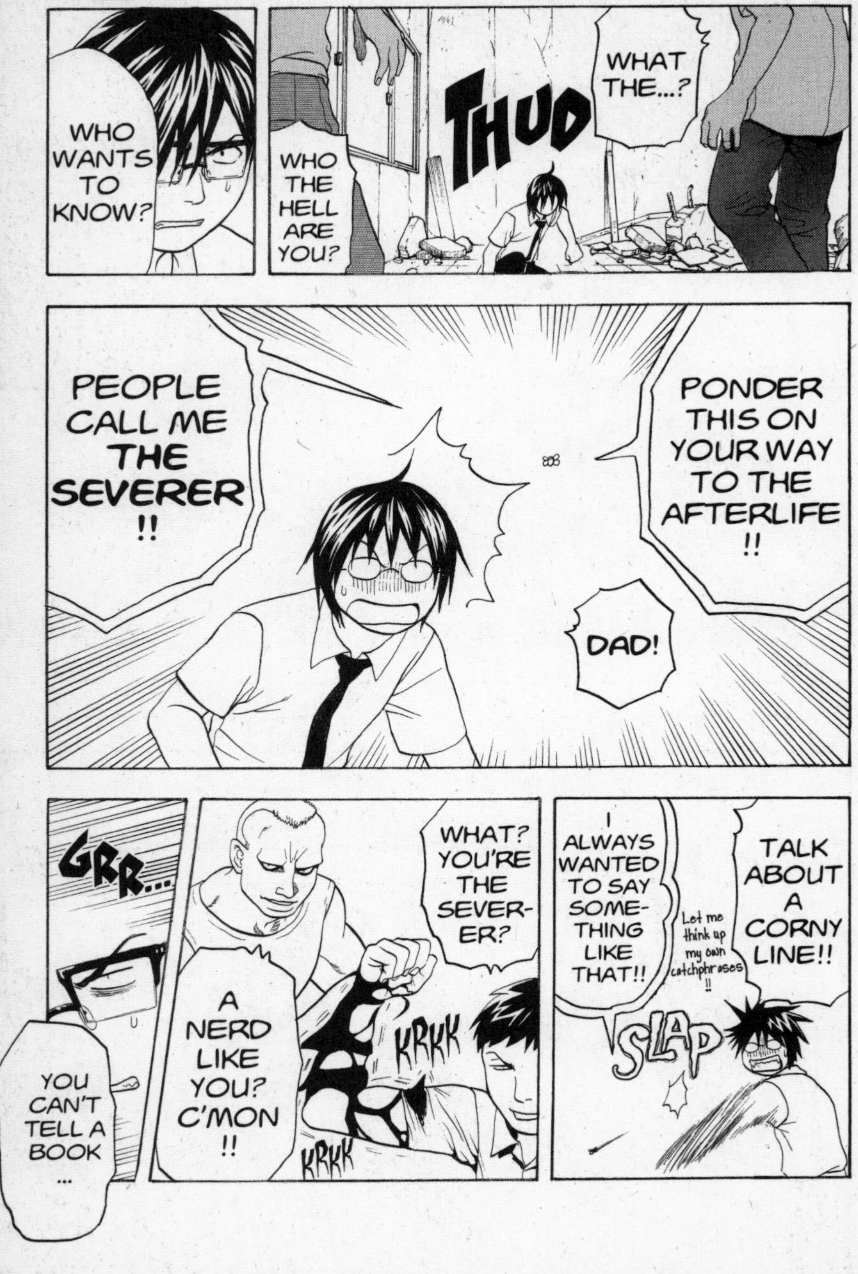

WHAT THE...?
THUD
WHO THE HELL ARE YOU?
WHO WANTS TO KNOW?
PONDER THIS ON YOUR WAY TO THE AFTERLIFE!!
PEOPLE CALL ME THE SEVERER!!
DAD!
TALK ABOUT A CORNY LINE!!
I ALWAYS WANTED TO SAY SOMETHING LIKE THAT!!
Let me think up my own catchphrases!!
SLAP
WHAT? YOU'RE THE SEVER-ER?
A NERD LIKE YOU? C'MON!!
KRKK
KRKK
GRR...
YOU CAN'T TELL A BOOK...

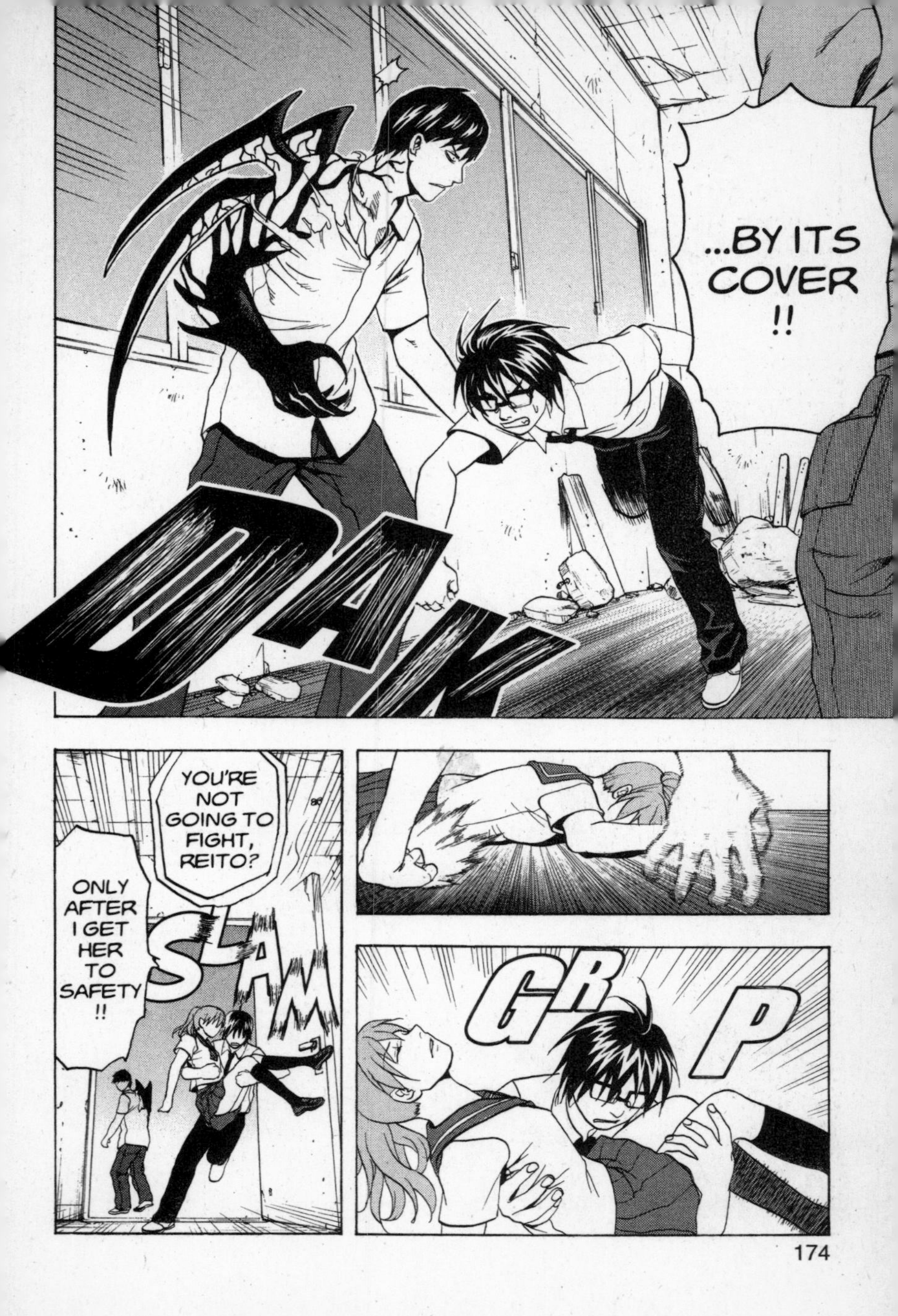
...BY ITS COVER !!
DAN
GR P
YOU'RE NOT GOING TO FIGHT, REITO?
ONLY AFTER I GET HER TO SAFETY !!
SLAM

READ THIS WAY

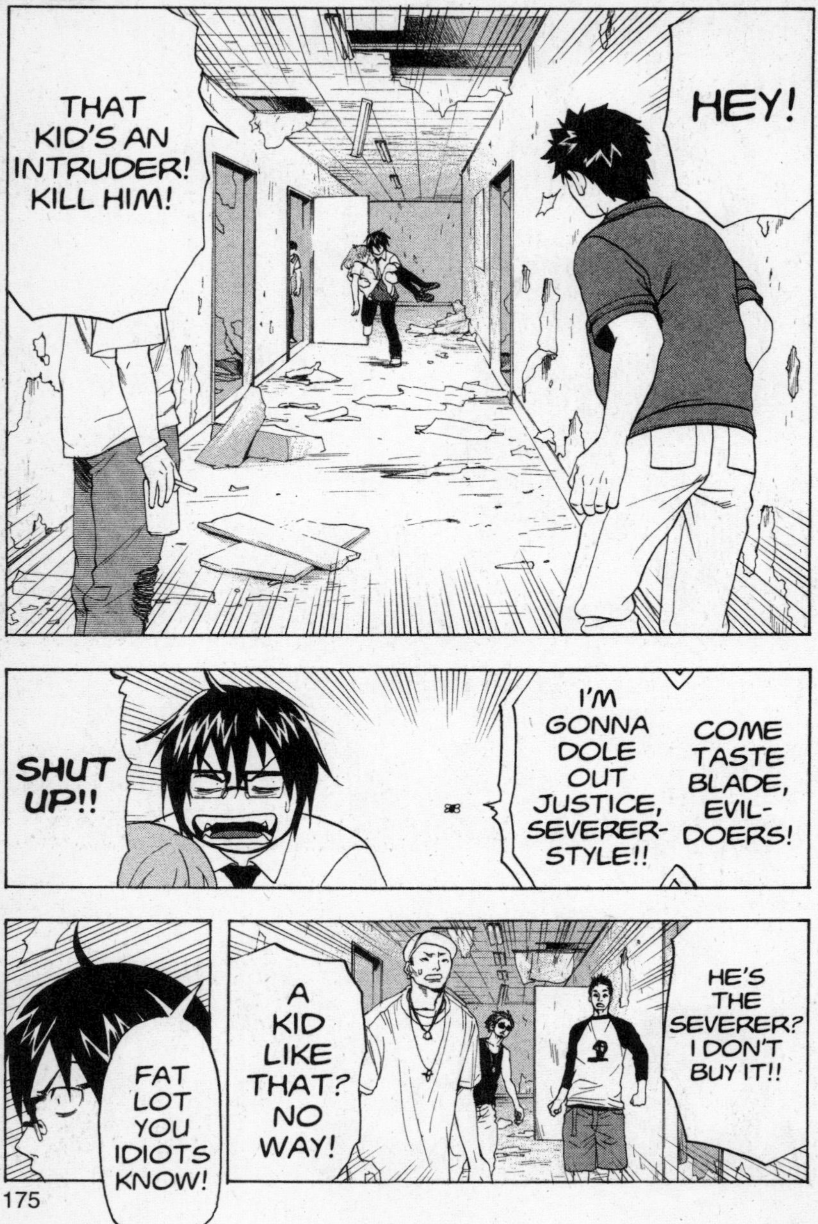
HEY!
THAT KID'S AN INTRUDER! KILL HIM!
COME TASTE BLADE, EVIL-DOERS!
I'M GONNA DOLE OUT JUSTICE, SEVERER-STYLE!!
SHUT UP!!
HE'S THE SEVERER? I DON'T BUY IT!!
A KID LIKE THAT? NO WAY!
FAT LOT YOU IDIOTS KNOW!

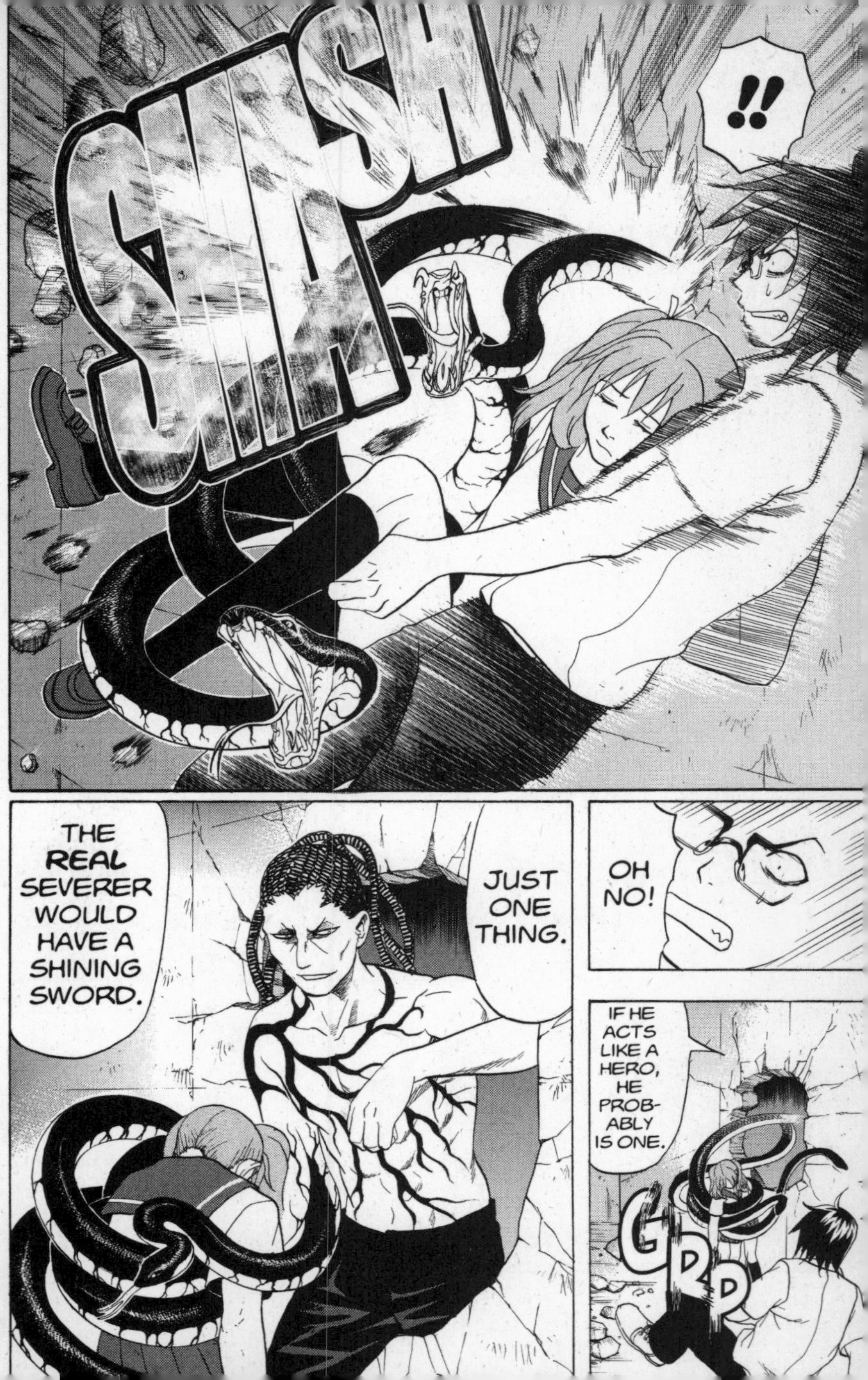
!!
SMASH
OH NO!
IF HE ACTS LIKE A HERO, HE PROBABLY IS ONE.
GRIP
JUST ONE THING.
THE REAL SEVERER WOULD HAVE A SHINING SWORD.

READ THIS WAY

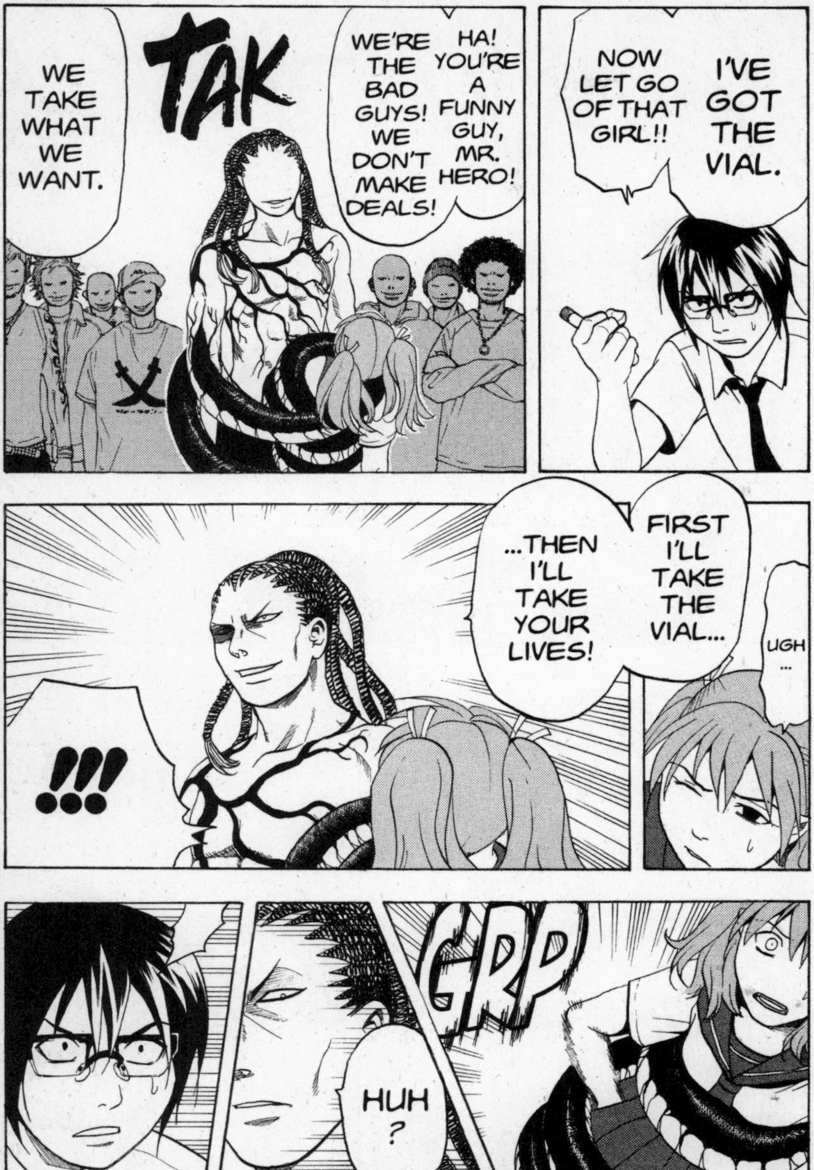
I'VE GOT THE VIAL.
NOW LET GO OF THAT GIRL!!
HA! YOU'RE A FUNNY GUY, MR. HERO!
WE'RE THE BAD GUYS! WE DON'T MAKE DEALS!
TAK
WE TAKE WHAT WE WANT.
UGH ...
FIRST I'LL TAKE THE VIAL...
...THEN I'LL TAKE YOUR LIVES!
!!!
GRP
HUH ?

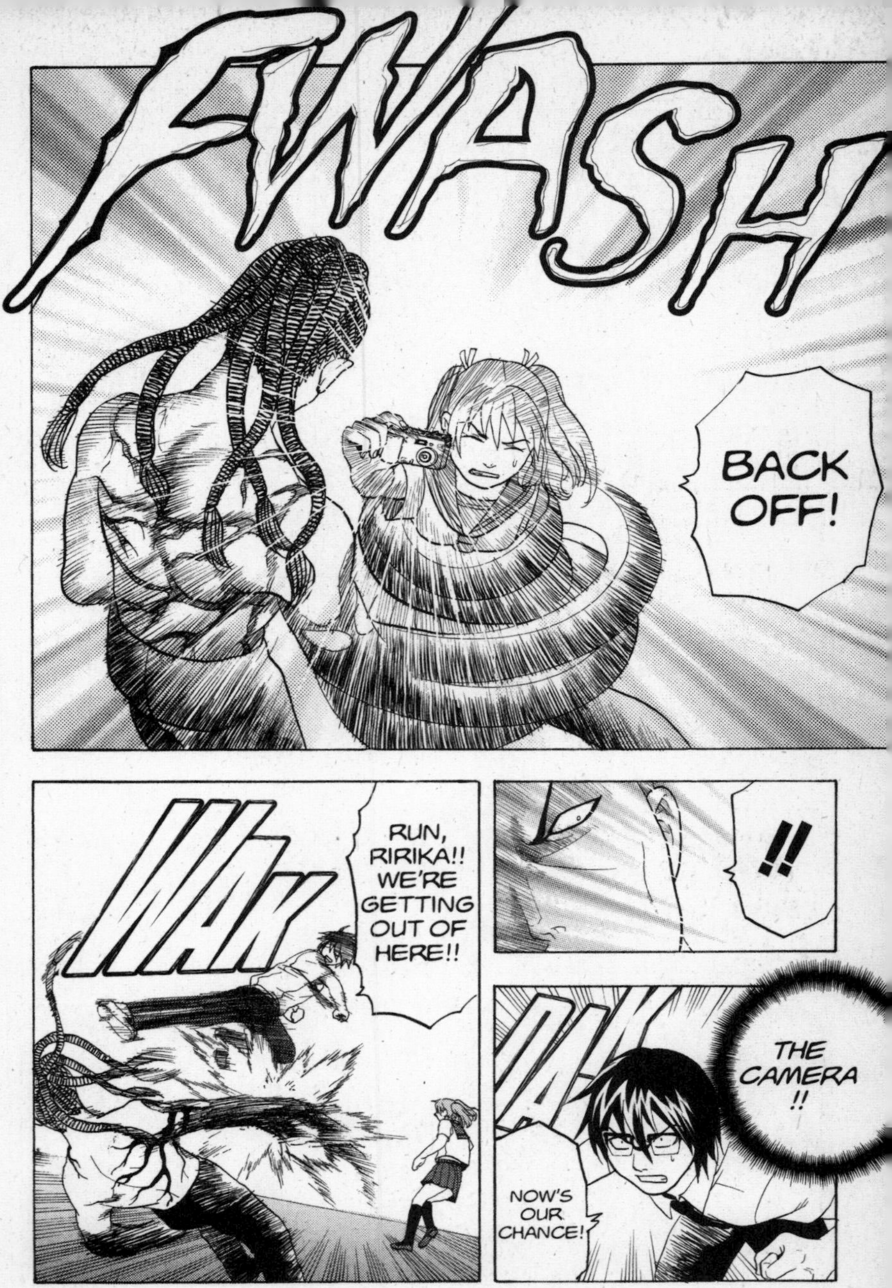
FWASH
BACK OFF!
!!
DAK
THE CAMERA !!
NOW'S OUR CHANCE!
WAK
RUN, RIRIKA!! WE'RE GETTING OUT OF HERE!!

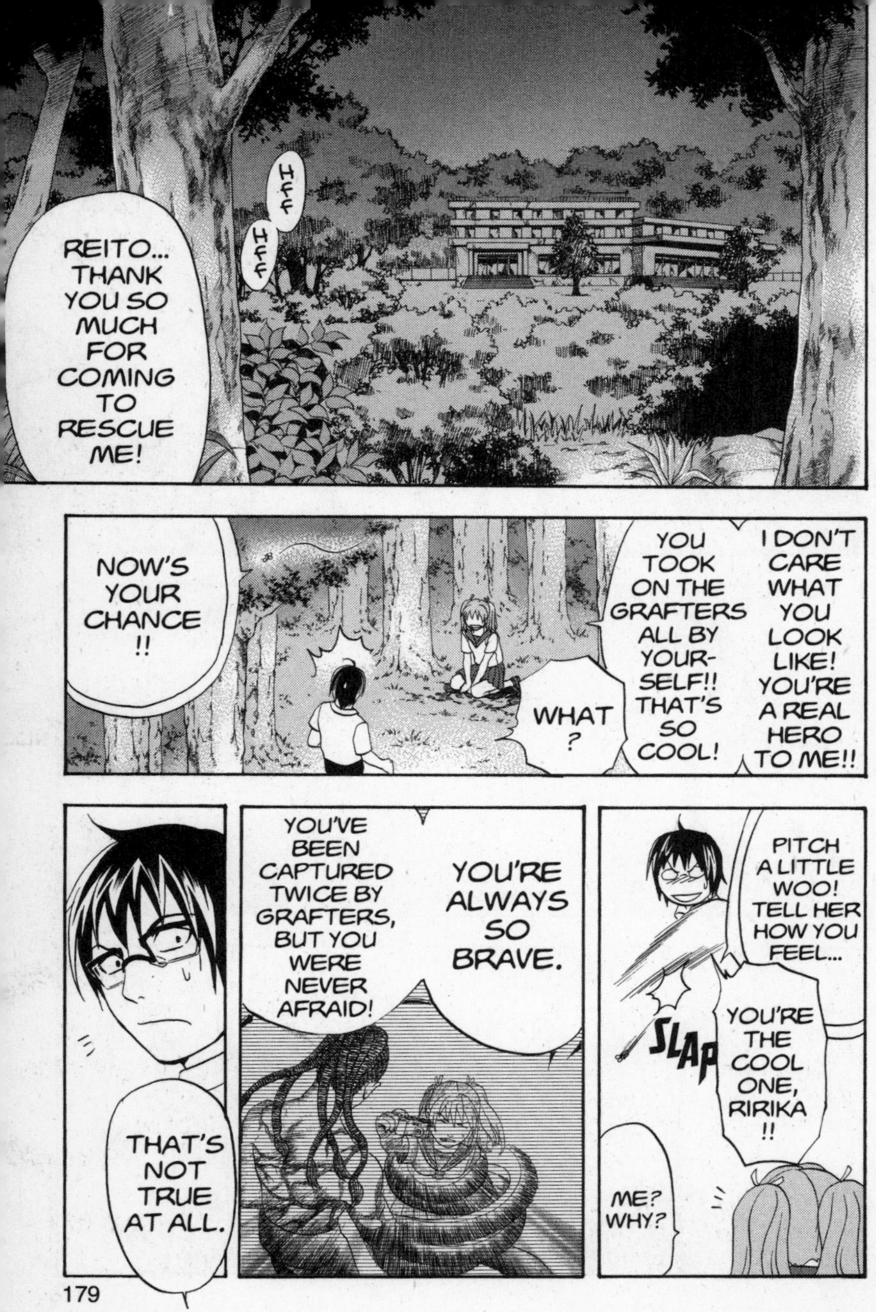
Hff Hff
REITO... THANK YOU SO MUCH FOR COMING TO RESCUE ME!
I DON'T CARE WHAT YOU LOOK LIKE! YOU'RE A REAL HERO TO ME!!
YOU TOOK ON THE GRAFTERS ALL BY YOURSELF!! THAT'S SO COOL!
WHAT?
NOW'S YOUR CHANCE!!
PITCH A LITTLE WOO! TELL HER HOW YOU FEEL...
SLAP
YOU'RE THE COOL ONE, RIRIKA!!
ME? WHY?
YOU'RE ALWAYS SO BRAVE.
YOU'VE BEEN CAPTURED TWICE BY GRAFTERS, BUT YOU WERE NEVER AFRAID!
THAT'S NOT TRUE AT ALL.

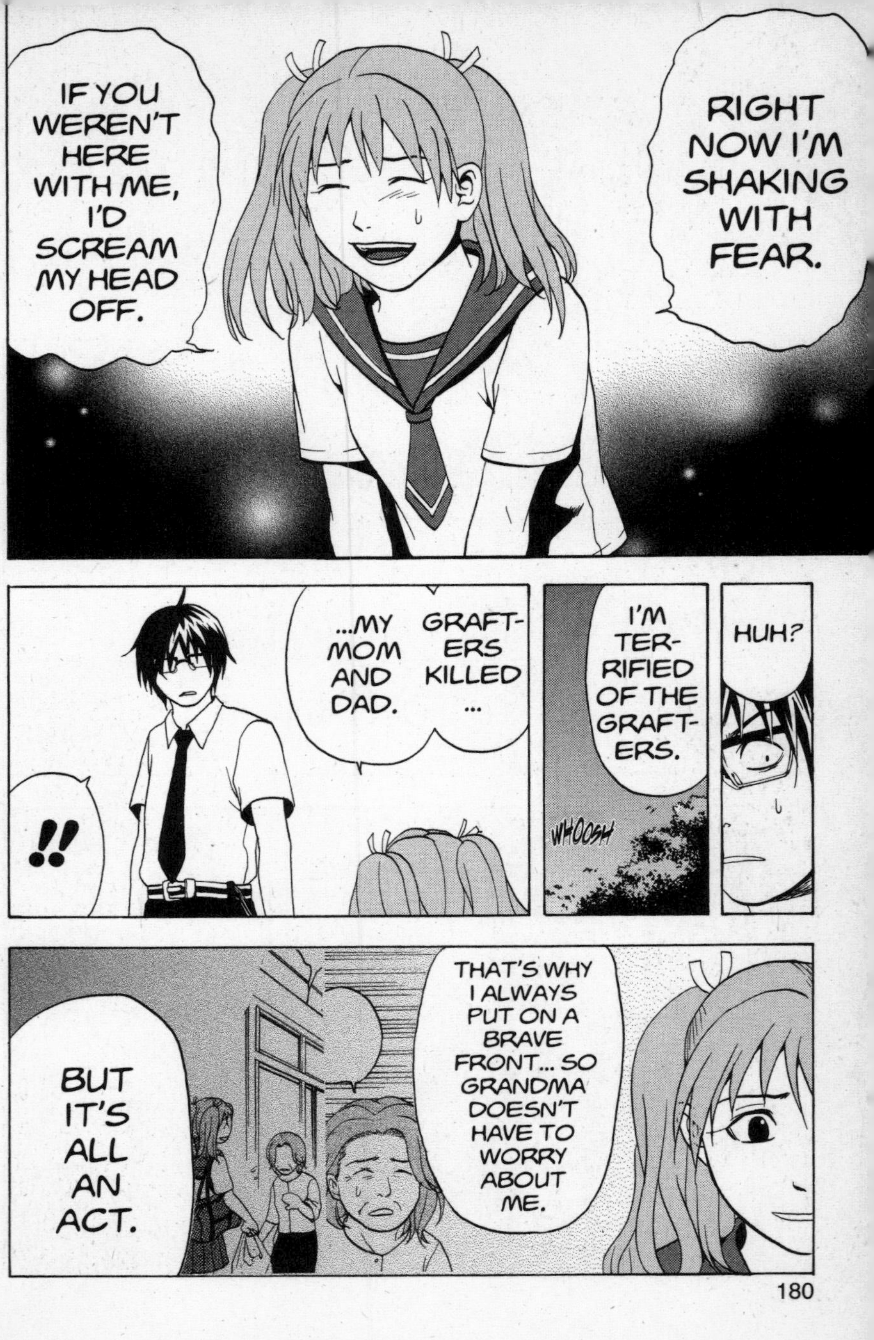
RIGHT NOW I'M SHAKING WITH FEAR.
IF YOU WEREN'T HERE WITH ME, I'D SCREAM MY HEAD OFF.
HUH?
I'M TER-RIFIED OF THE GRAFT-ERS.
WHOOSH
GRAFT-ERS KILLED...
...MY MOM AND DAD.
!!
THAT'S WHY I ALWAYS PUT ON A BRAVE FRONT... SO GRANDMA DOESN'T HAVE TO WORRY ABOUT ME.
BUT IT'S ALL AN ACT.

READ THIS WAY

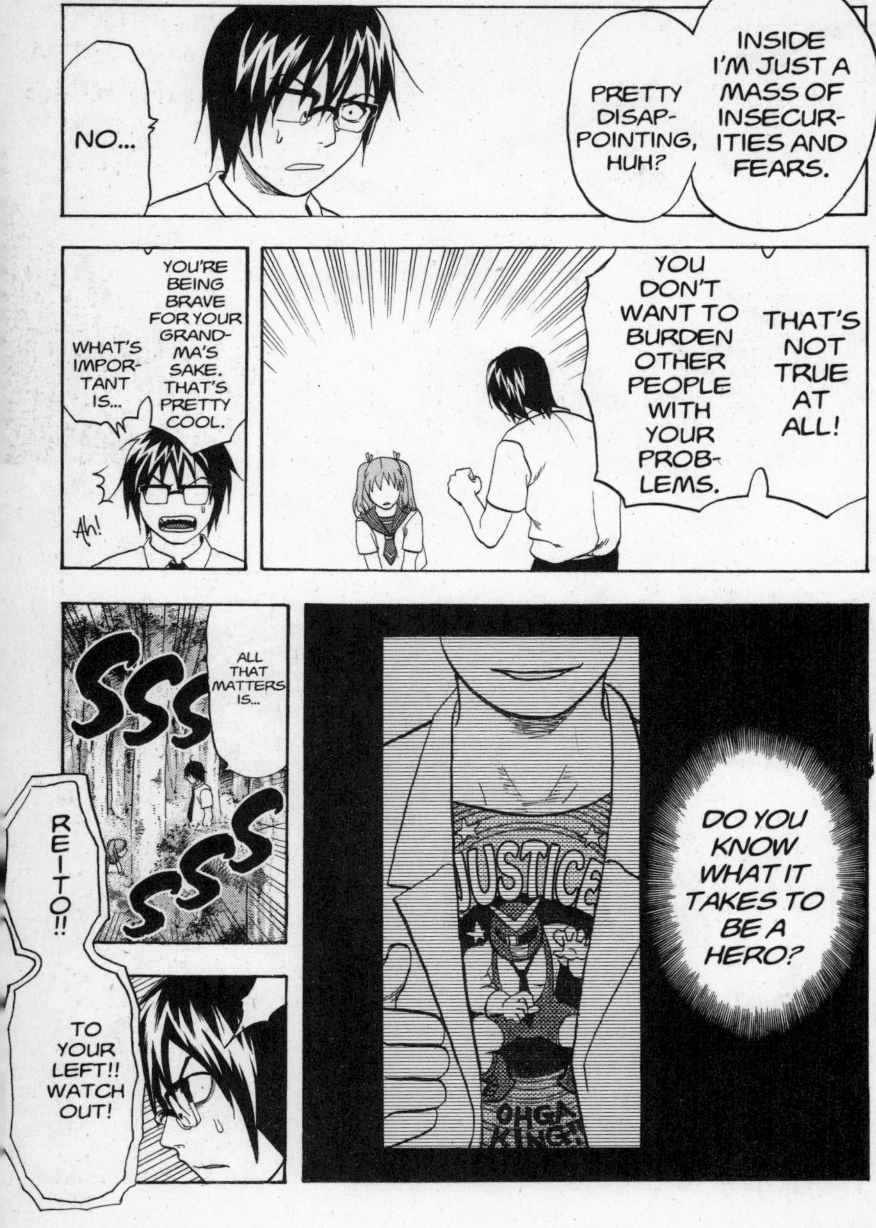

INSIDE I'M JUST A MASS OF INSECURITIES AND FEARS.
PRETTY DISAPPOINTING, HUH?
NO...
THAT'S NOT TRUE AT ALL!
YOU DON'T WANT TO BURDEN OTHER PEOPLE WITH YOUR PROBLEMS.
YOU'RE BEING BRAVE FOR YOUR GRANDMA'S SAKE. THAT'S PRETTY COOL.
WHAT'S IMPORTANT IS...
Ah!
DO YOU KNOW WHAT IT TAKES TO BE A HERO?
JUSTICE
ALL THAT MATTERS IS...
SSSS
SSSS
REITO!!
TO YOUR LEFT!! WATCH OUT!

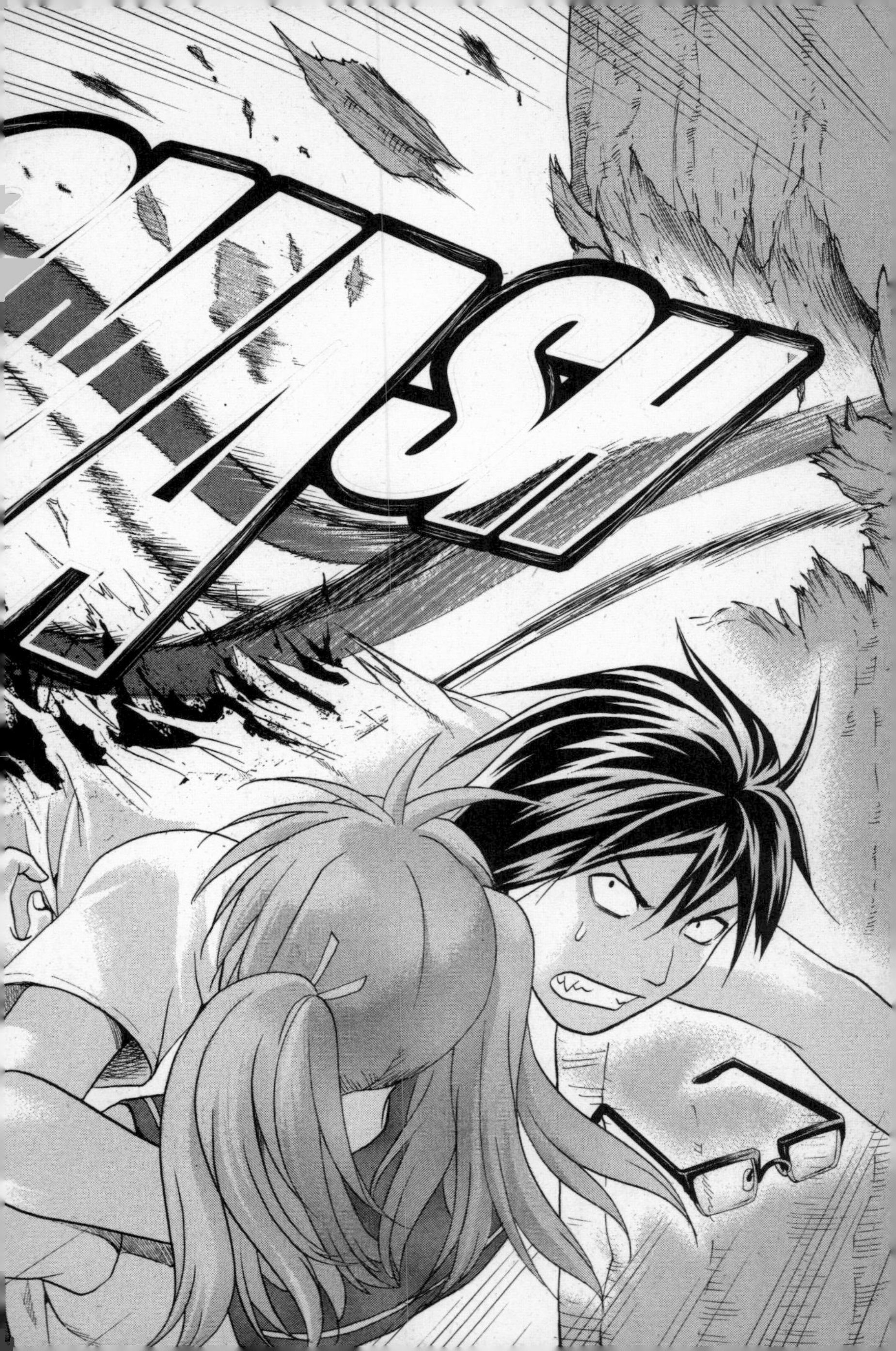

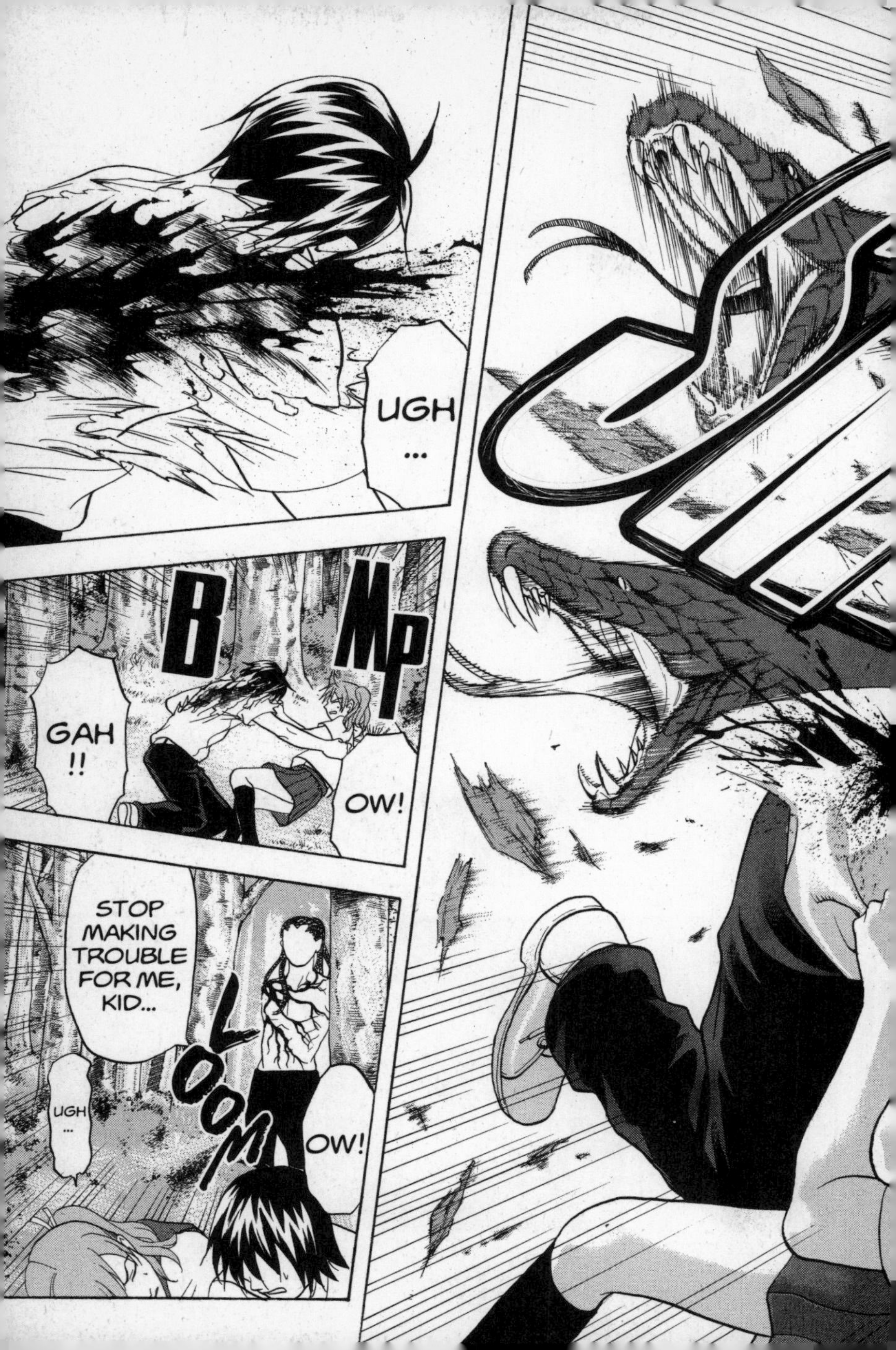
UGH ...
BMP
GAH !!
OW!
STOP MAKING TROUBLE FOR ME, KID...
VOOOM
OW!
UGH ...

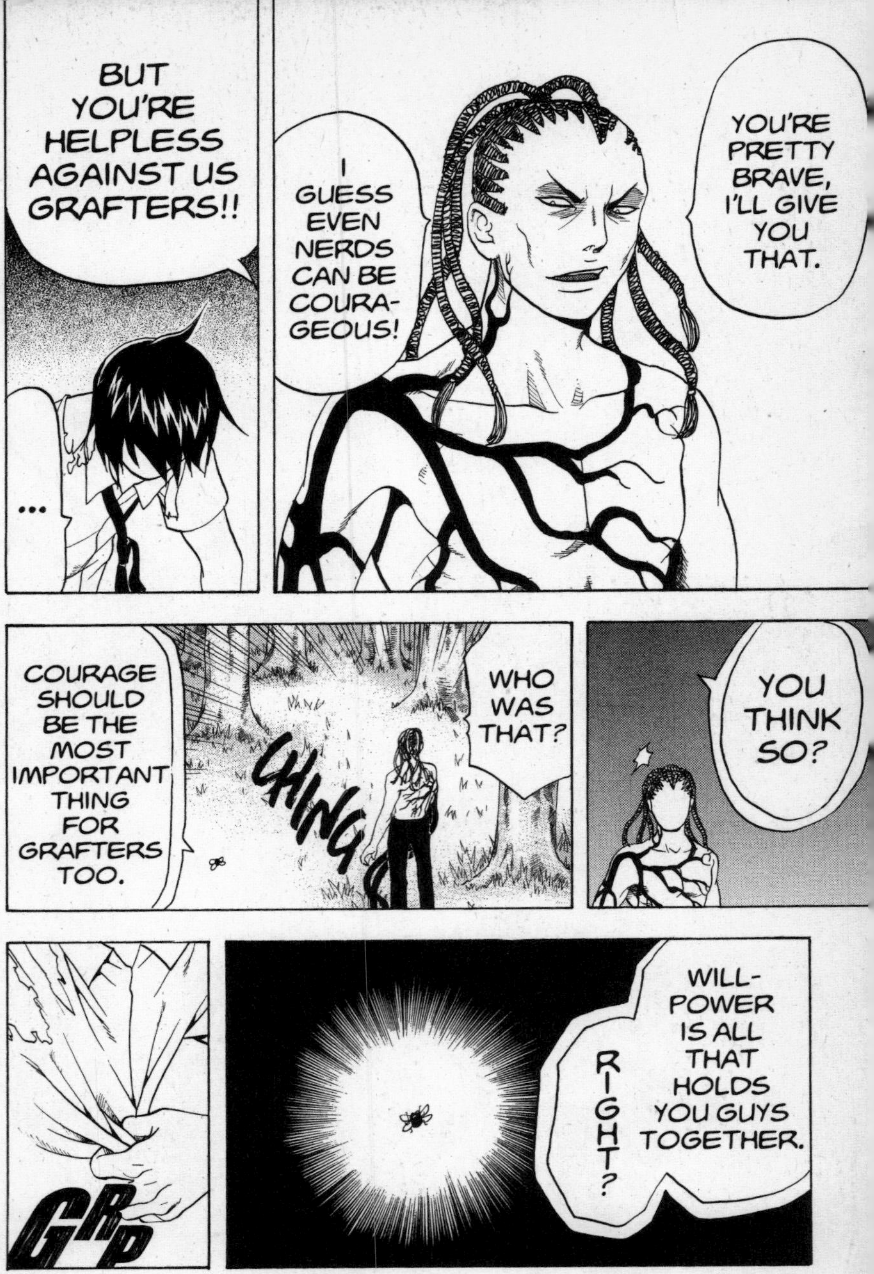
YOU'RE PRETTY BRAVE, I'LL GIVE YOU THAT.
I GUESS EVEN NERDS CAN BE COURAGEOUS!
BUT YOU'RE HELPLESS AGAINST US GRAFTERS!!
...
YOU THINK SO?
WHO WAS THAT?
CHING
COURAGE SHOULD BE THE MOST IMPORTANT THING FOR GRAFTERS TOO.
WILL-POWER IS ALL THAT HOLDS YOU GUYS TOGETHER.
RIGHT?
GRIP

READ THIS WAY

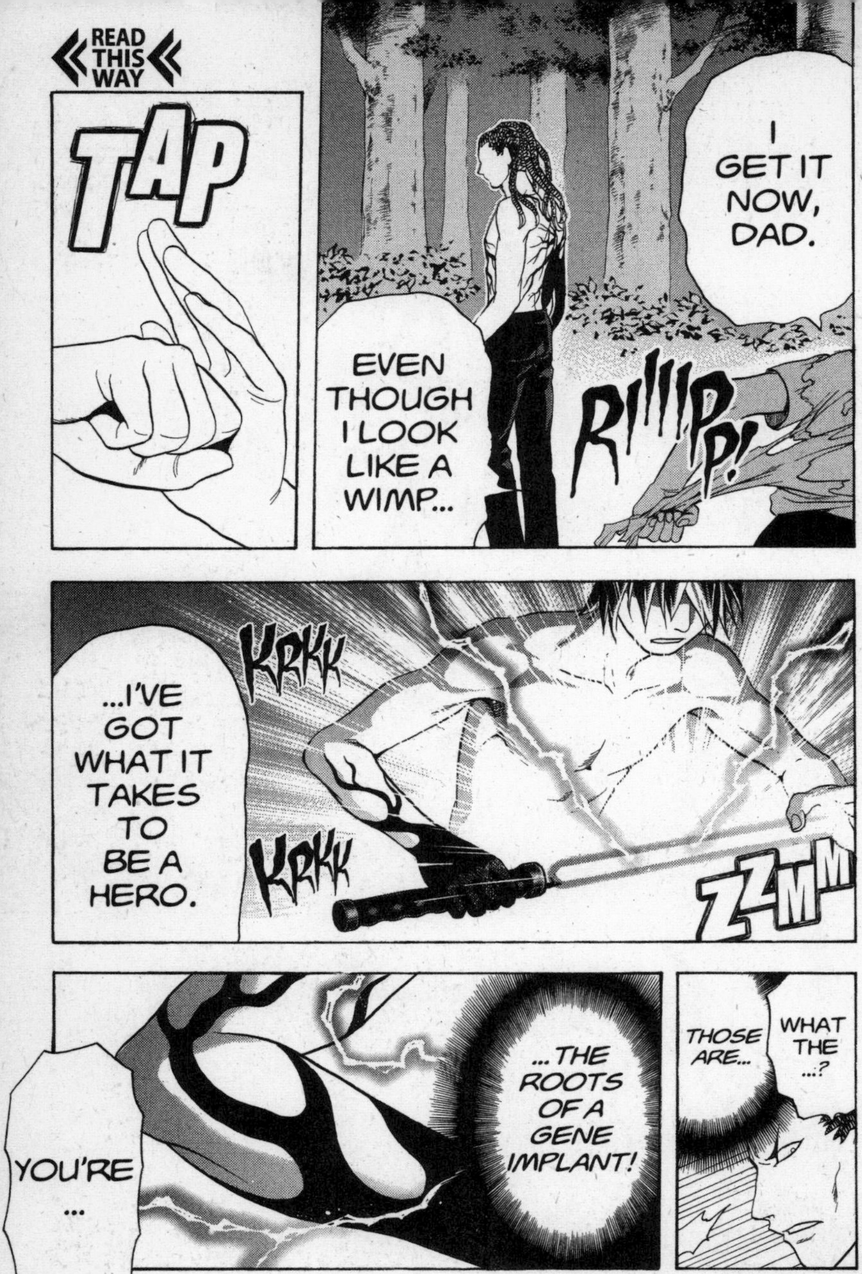
I GET IT NOW, DAD.
EVEN THOUGH I LOOK LIKE A WIMP...
RIIIPP!
TAP
KRKK
...I'VE GOT WHAT IT TAKES TO BE A HERO.
KRKK
ZZMMM
WHAT THE ...?
THOSE ARE...
...THE ROOTS OF A GENE IMPLANT!
YOU'RE ...

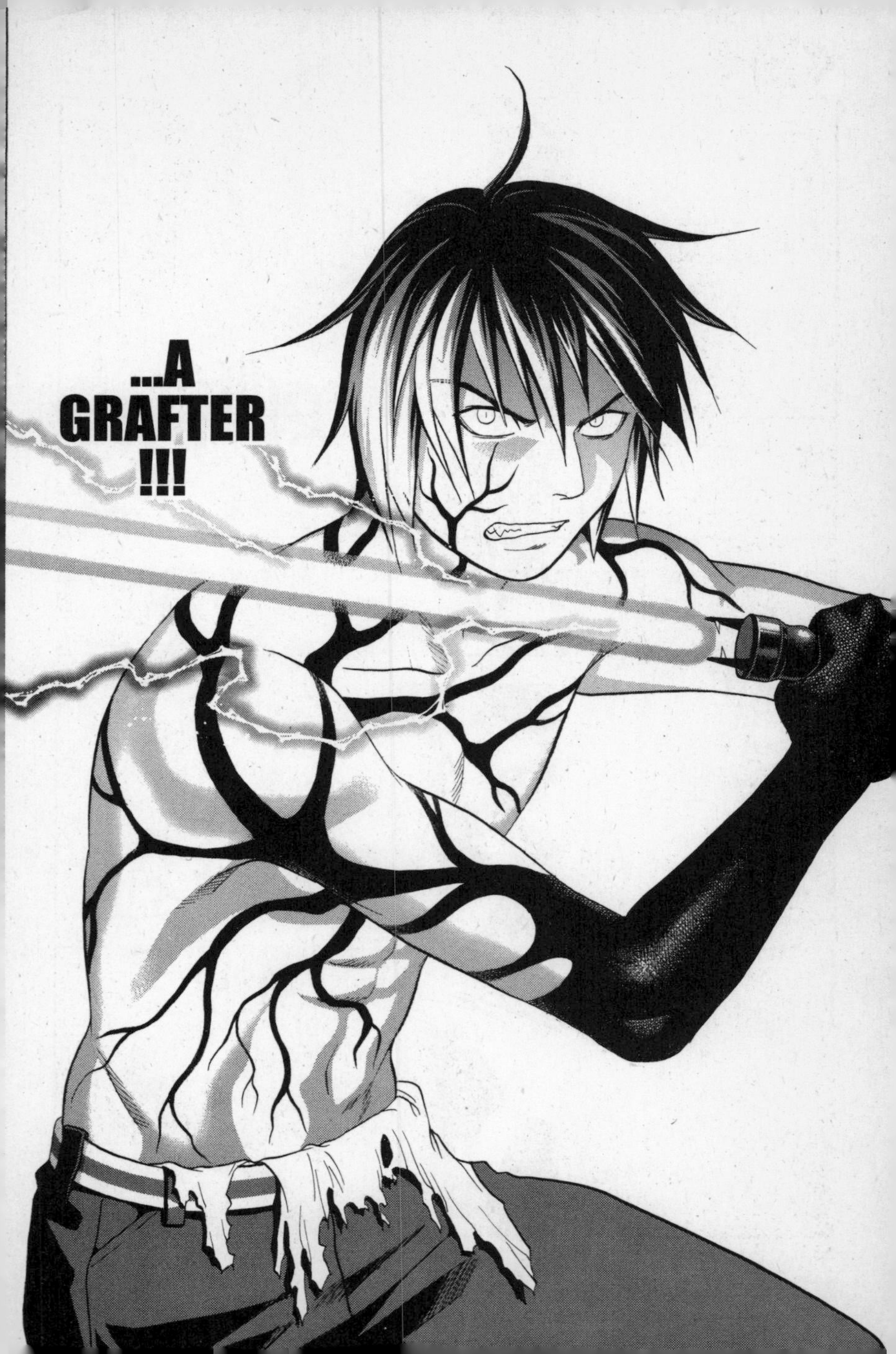
...A GRAFTER !!!

READ THIS WAY

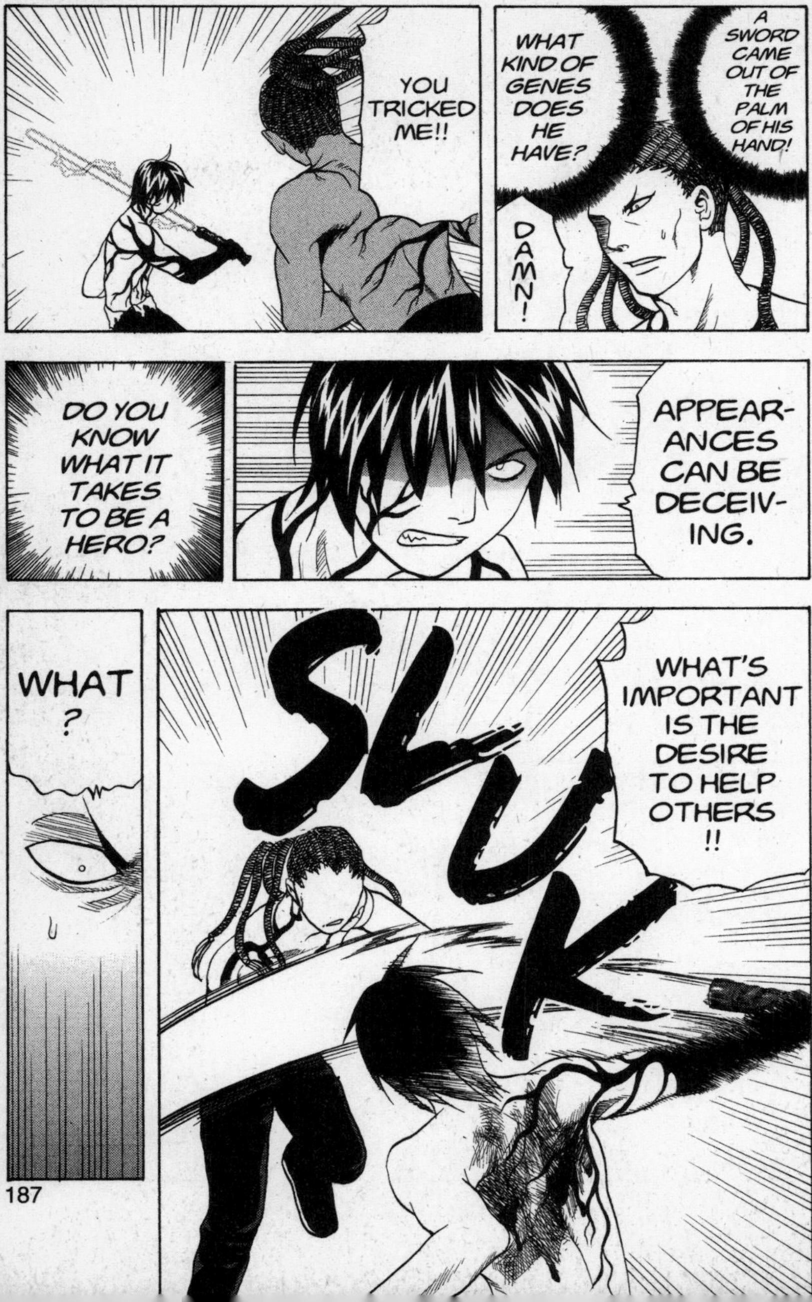
A SWORD CAME OUT OF THE PALM OF HIS HAND!
WHAT KIND OF GENES DOES HE HAVE?
DAMN!
YOU TRICKED ME!!
APPEARANCES CAN BE DECEIVING.
DO YOU KNOW WHAT IT TAKES TO BE A HERO?
WHAT'S IMPORTANT IS THE DESIRE TO HELP OTHERS!!
WHAT?

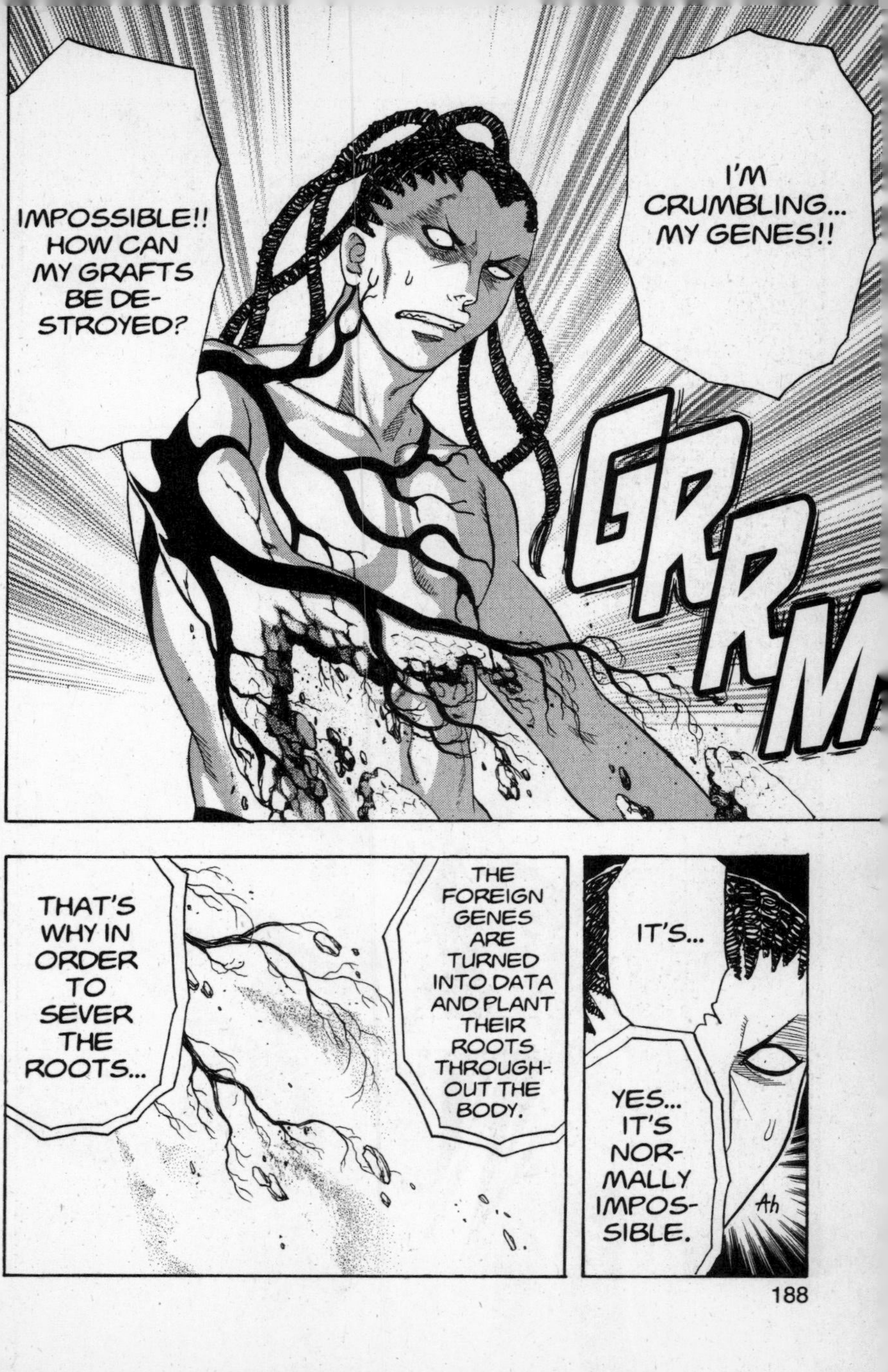
I'M CRUMBLING... MY GENES!!
IMPOSSIBLE!! HOW CAN MY GRAFTS BE DE-STROYED?
GRRM
IT'S...
YES... IT'S NOR-MALLY IMPOS-SIBLE.
Ah
THE FOREIGN GENES ARE TURNED INTO DATA AND PLANT THEIR ROOTS THROUGH-OUT THE BODY.
THAT'S WHY IN ORDER TO SEVER THE ROOTS...

READ THIS WAY

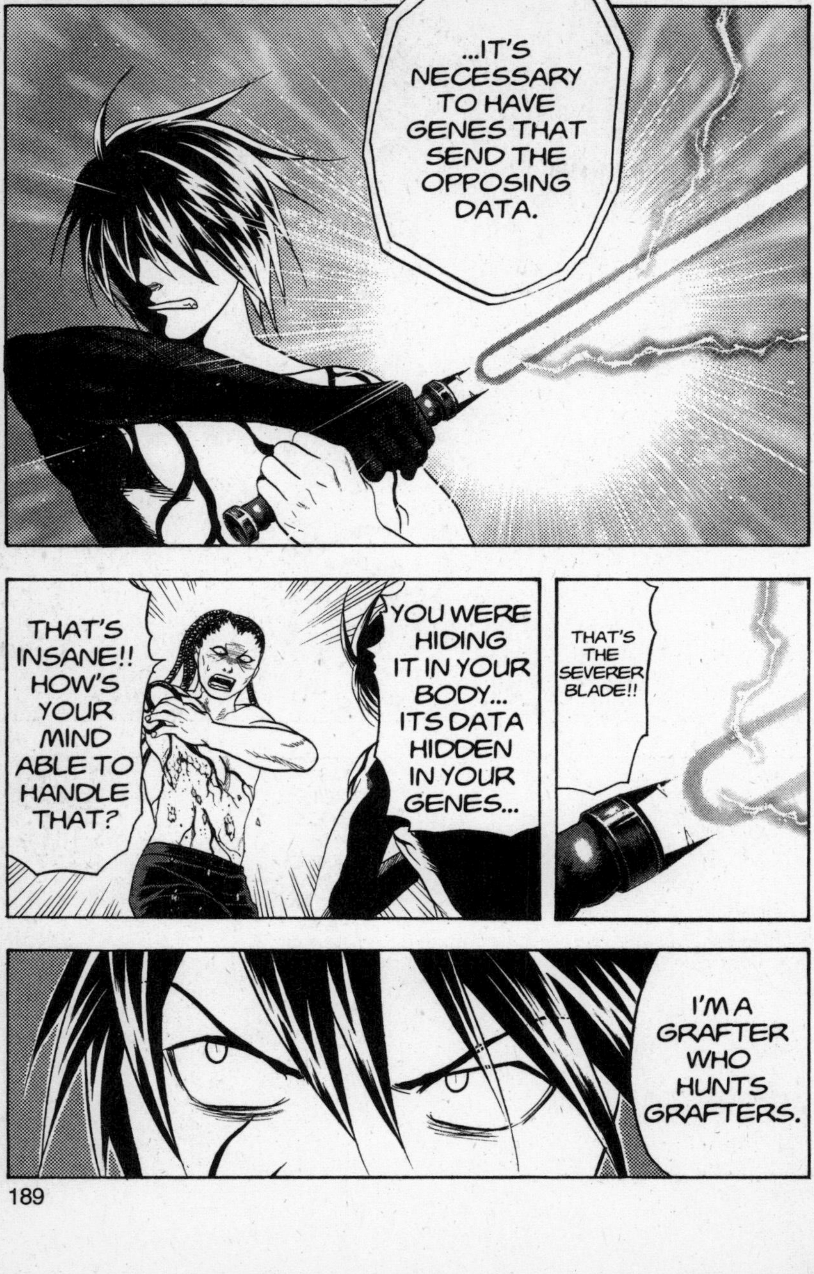
...IT'S NECESSARY TO HAVE GENES THAT SEND THE OPPOSING DATA.
THAT'S THE SEVERER BLADE!!
YOU WERE HIDING IT IN YOUR BODY... ITS DATA HIDDEN IN YOUR GENES...
THAT'S INSANE!! HOW'S YOUR MIND ABLE TO HANDLE THAT?
I'M A GRAFTER WHO HUNTS GRAFTERS.

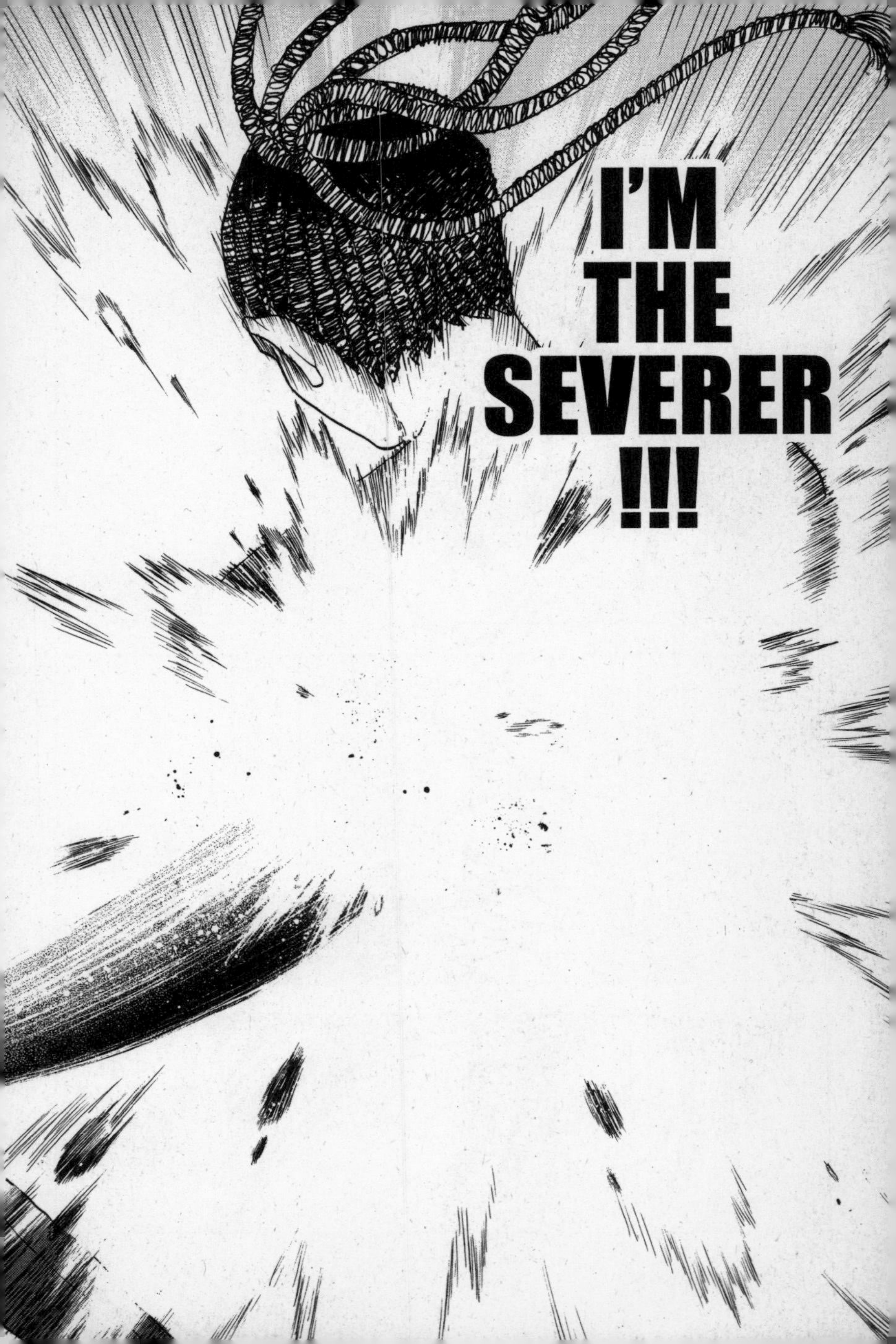
I'M THE SEVERER !!!

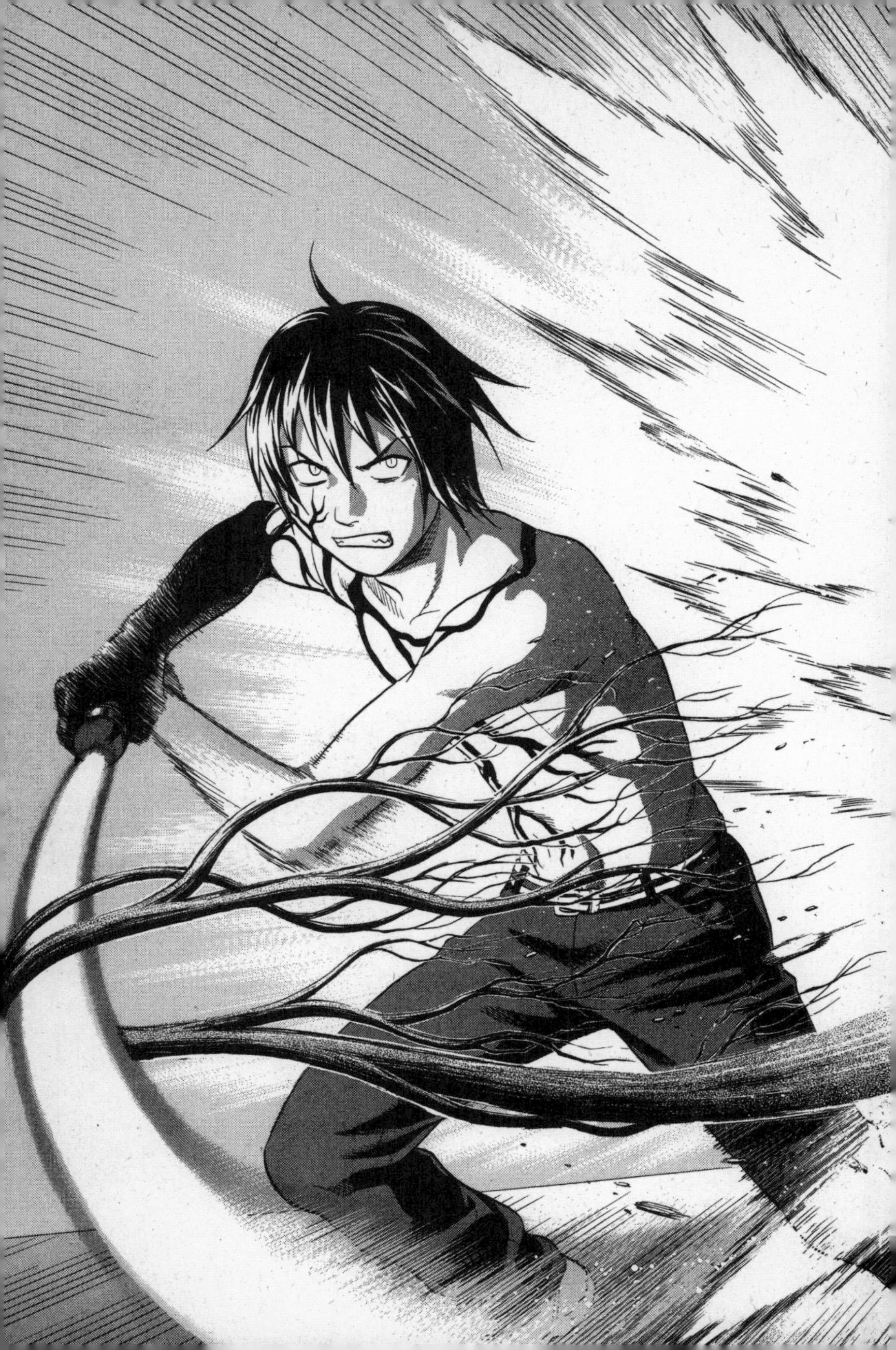

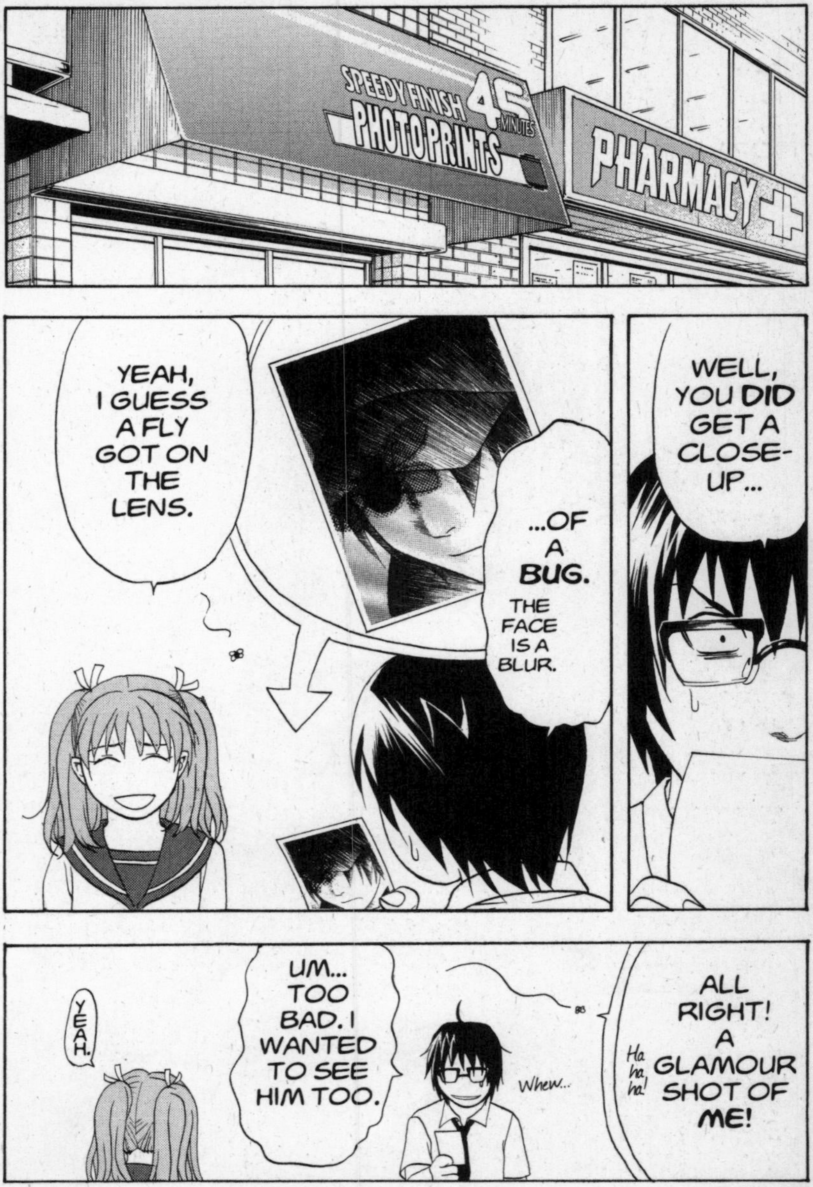
SPEEDY FINISH 45 MINUTES
PHOTO PRINTS
PHARMACY
WELL, YOU DID GET A CLOSE-UP...
...OF A BUG.
THE FACE IS A BLUR.
YEAH, I GUESS A FLY GOT ON THE LENS.
Ha ha ha!
ALL RIGHT! A GLAMOUR SHOT OF ME!
Whew...
UM... TOO BAD. I WANTED TO SEE HIM TOO.
YEAH.

READ THIS WAY

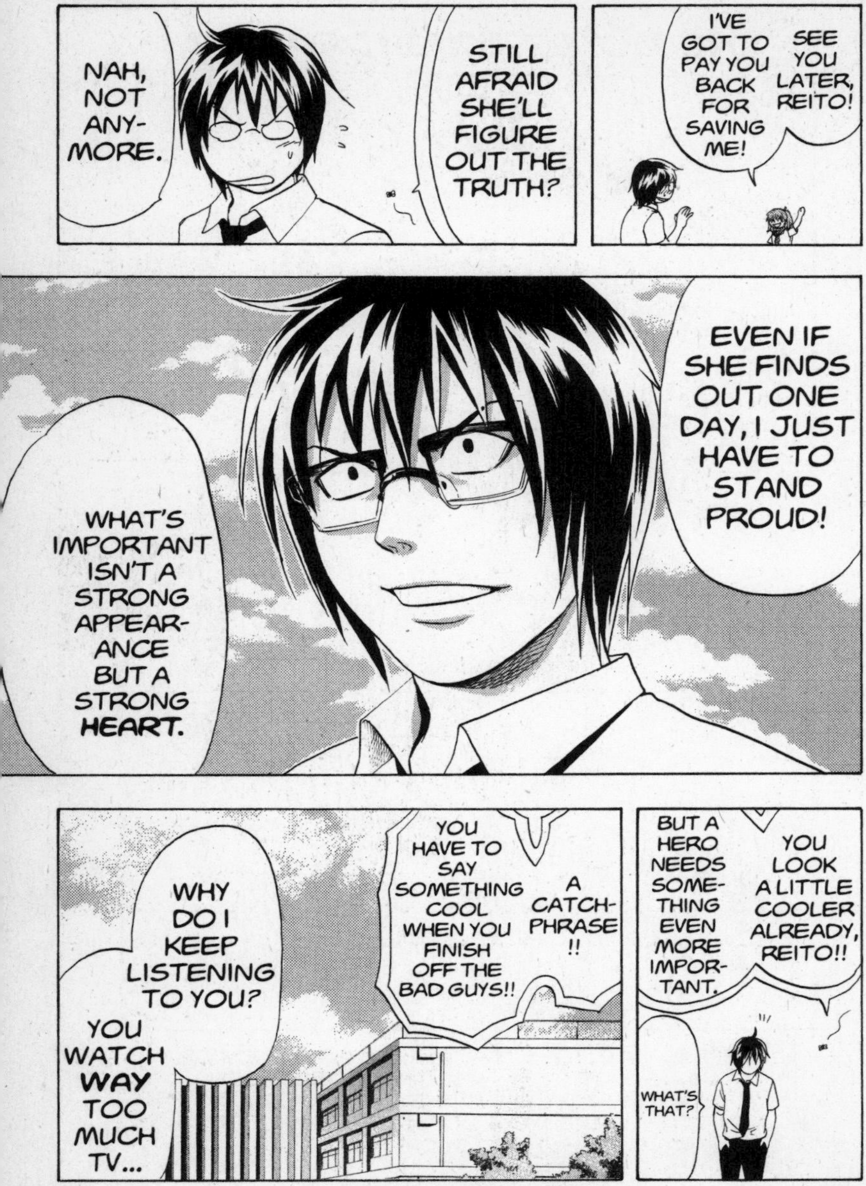
SEE YOU LATER, REITO!
I'VE GOT TO PAY YOU BACK FOR SAVING ME!
STILL AFRAID SHE'LL FIGURE OUT THE TRUTH?
NAH, NOT ANY-MORE.
EVEN IF SHE FINDS OUT ONE DAY, I JUST HAVE TO STAND PROUD!
WHAT'S IMPORTANT ISN'T A STRONG APPEAR-ANCE BUT A STRONG HEART.
YOU LOOK A LITTLE COOLER ALREADY, REITO!!
BUT A HERO NEEDS SOME-THING EVEN MORE IMPOR-TANT.
WHAT'S THAT?
YOU HAVE TO SAY SOMETHING COOL WHEN YOU FINISH OFF THE BAD GUYS!!
A CATCH-PHRASE!!
WHY DO I KEEP LISTENING TO YOU?
YOU WATCH WAY TOO MUCH TV...

Severer Reito—The End

REJECTED ROUGH DRAFT #1

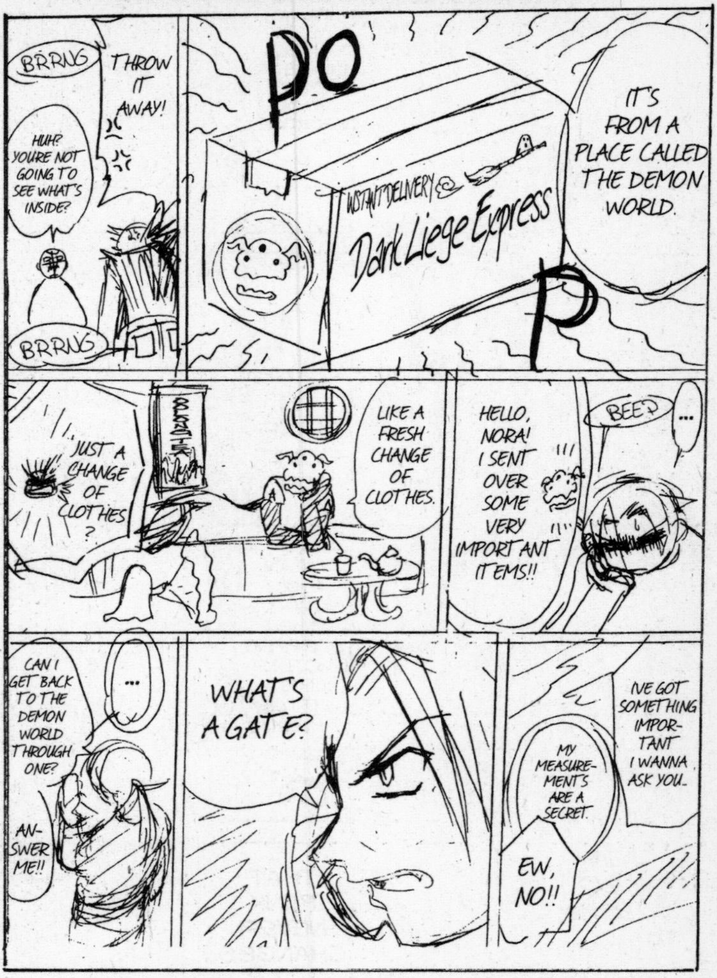
IT'S FROM A PLACE CALLED THE DEMON WORLD.
PO
INSTANT DELIVERY
Dark Liege Express
P
THROW IT AWAY!
BRRNG
HUH? YOU'RE NOT GOING TO SEE WHAT'S INSIDE?
BRRNG
BEEP
...
HELLO, NORA! I SENT OVER SOME VERY IMPORTANT ITEMS!!
LIKE A FRESH CHANGE OF CLOTHES.
JUST A CHANGE OF CLOTHES?
I'VE GOT SOMETHING IMPORTANT I WANNA ASK YOU..
MY MEASUREMENTS ARE A SECRET.
EW, NO!!
WHAT'S A GATE?
...
CAN I GET BACK TO THE DEMON WORLD THROUGH ONE?
ANSWER ME!!

AT THIS TIME, THE STORY MOSTLY INVOLVED NORA CLOSING GATES THAT HAD OPENED BETWEEN THE DEMON WORLD AND THE HUMAN WORLD. I WROTE NORA'S NAME IN ENGLISH HERE, JUST LIKE I DID IN THE SHORT STORY.

KAZUMA AND NORA

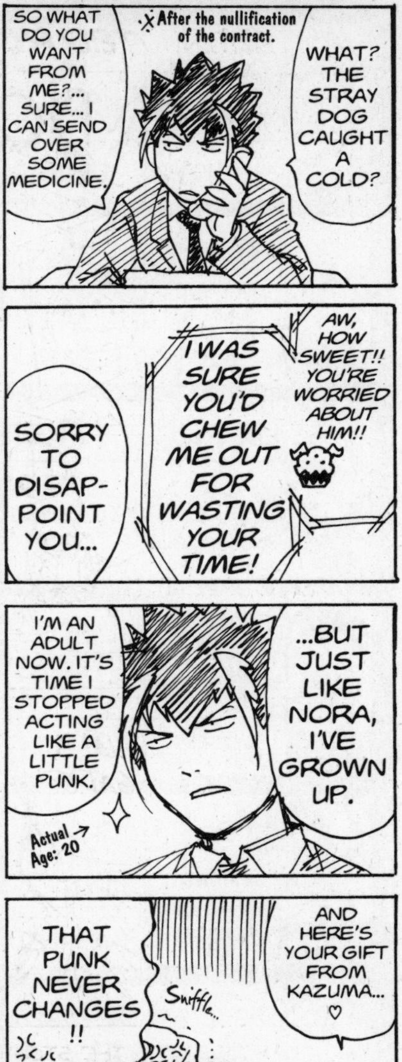
※After the nullification of the contract.
WHAT? THE STRAY DOG CAUGHT A COLD?
SO WHAT DO YOU WANT FROM ME?... SURE... I CAN SEND OVER SOME MEDICINE.
AW, HOW SWEET!! YOU'RE WORRIED ABOUT HIM!!
I WAS SURE YOU'D CHEW ME OUT FOR WASTING YOUR TIME!
SORRY TO DISAP-POINT YOU...
...BUT JUST LIKE NORA, I'VE GROWN UP.
I'M AN ADULT NOW. IT'S TIME I STOPPED ACTING LIKE A LITTLE PUNK.
Actual Age: 20
AND HERE'S YOUR GIFT FROM KAZUMA... ♡
THAT PUNK NEVER CHANGES!!
Sniffle...
WOOF! WOOF! Dog Pills

CAN YOU PLAY ROCK-PAPER-SCISSORS?

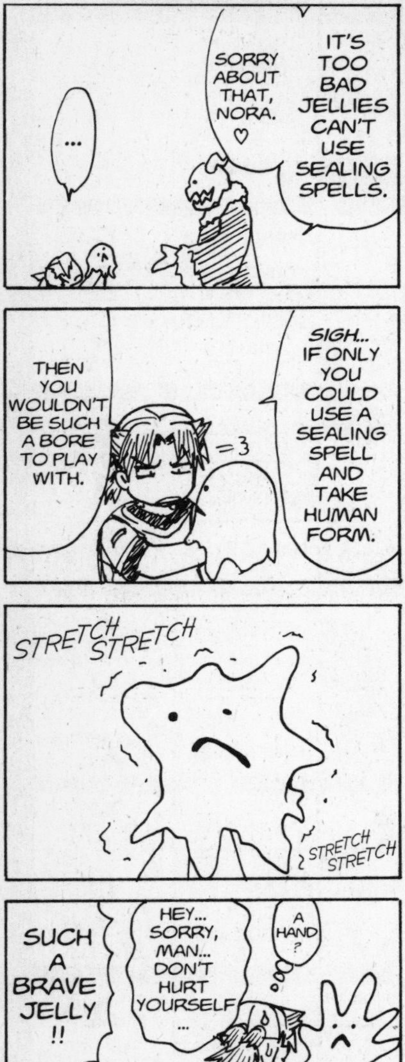
IT'S TOO BAD JELLIES CAN'T USE SEALING SPELLS.
SORRY ABOUT THAT, NORA. ♡
...
SIGH... IF ONLY YOU COULD USE A SEALING SPELL AND TAKE HUMAN FORM.
THEN YOU WOULDN'T BE SUCH A BORE TO PLAY WITH.
STRETCH STRETCH
STRETCH STRETCH
A HAND?
HEY... SORRY, MAN... DON'T HURT YOURSELF...
SUCH A BRAVE JELLY!!
SOB

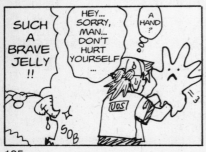

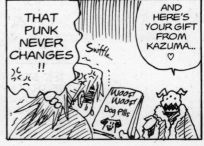

STAFF STATS BY TAKESHI HITOUJI

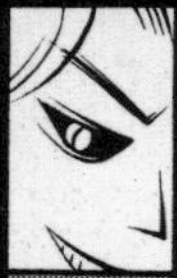 HIRAKAWA	NATURAL GOOFINESS	A
	REACTION	F
	APPEARANCE	THUG
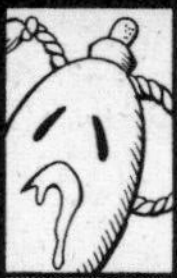 KAKEI	HUMAN NATURE	A
	APPETITE	A
	MOTIVATION	F
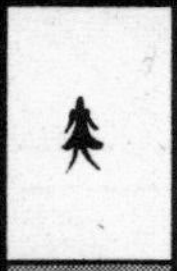 SHIBA	KNOWLEDGE	B
	NINTENDO SKILLS	A
	SIZE	SMALL
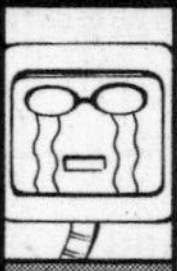 YUNOKI	PERSONALITY	B
	ABILITY TO MAKE SNAPPY COMEBACKS	C
	QUALITY OF HAIR	A
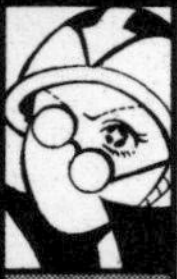 YANO	BASEBALL	B
	SAKE	F
	UNBALANCED DIET	A
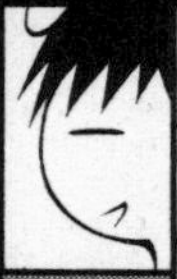 KOBA	TECHNIQUES	A
	SENSE OF RESPONSIBILITY	A
	PRIVATE LIFE	A MYSTERY
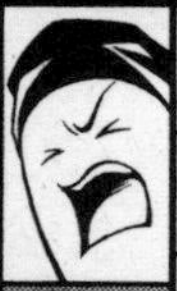 FUJIWARA	QUALITY OF VOICE	B
	INDIFFERENCE TO SOCIETY	A
	USELESS KNOWLEDGE	A+
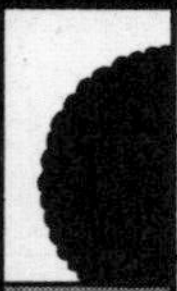 SEJIMA	LIFE EXPERIENCE	A
	TV TALENT QUALITY	B
	FINAL FORM	AEGAGROPILA
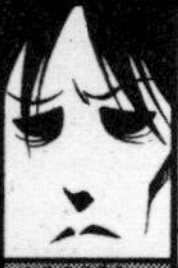 KAMIMURA	IMPRESSION	BLACK
	HEART	PURE
	PERSONALITY	WEIRDO
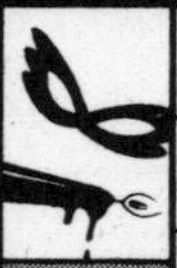 YOSHI	MUSCLES	LOVES THEM
	ANTIQUENESS	B
	PERSONALITY	VERY SMALL
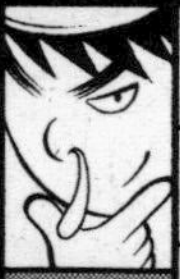 HITOUJI	WAY OF LIFE	CLUMSY
	FAVORITE MOVE	MEMORY LOSS
	FAVORITE PHRASE	"YOU MADE ME MAD..."
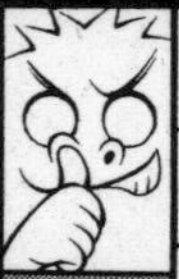 OHGAKI	COOKING	A
	PERSONALITY	HANDSOME
	STOMACH	COMES OUT

WITH LOVE

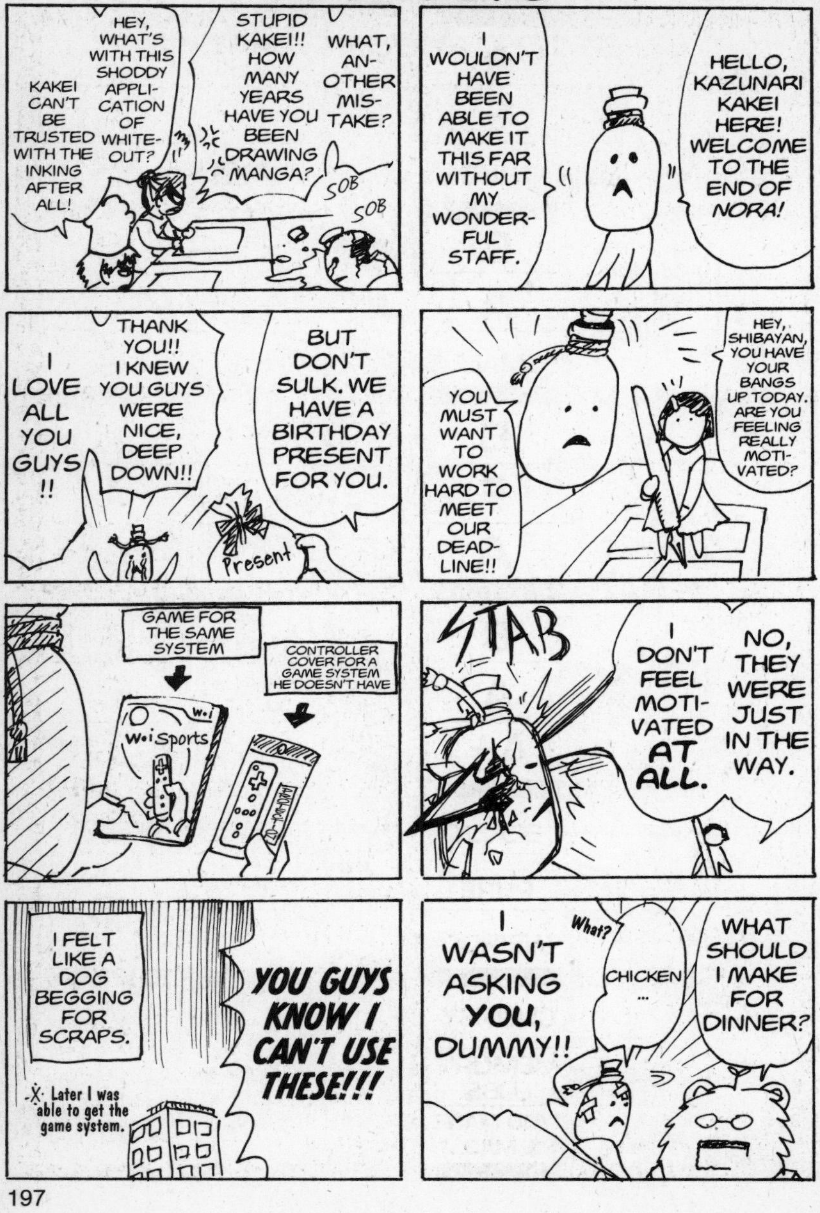

HELLO, KAZUNARI KAKEI HERE! WELCOME TO THE END OF *NORA!*
I WOULDN'T HAVE BEEN ABLE TO MAKE IT THIS FAR WITHOUT MY WONDERFUL STAFF.
WHAT, ANOTHER MISTAKE?
STUPID KAKEI!! HOW MANY YEARS HAVE YOU BEEN DRAWING MANGA?
HEY, WHAT'S WITH THIS SHODDY APPLICATION OF WHITE-OUT?
KAKEI CAN'T BE TRUSTED WITH THE INKING AFTER ALL!
SOB
SOB
HEY, SHIBAYAN, YOU HAVE YOUR BANGS UP TODAY. ARE YOU FEELING REALLY MOTIVATED?
YOU MUST WANT TO WORK HARD TO MEET OUR DEADLINE!!
BUT DON'T SULK. WE HAVE A BIRTHDAY PRESENT FOR YOU.
THANK YOU!! I KNEW YOU GUYS WERE NICE, DEEP DOWN!!
I LOVE ALL YOU GUYS!!
Present
NO, THEY WERE JUST IN THE WAY.
I DON'T FEEL MOTIVATED AT ALL.
STAB
CONTROLLER COVER FOR A GAME SYSTEM HE DOESN'T HAVE
GAME FOR THE SAME SYSTEM
W·i Sports
WHAT SHOULD I MAKE FOR DINNER?
CHICKEN ...
What?
I WASN'T ASKING YOU, DUMMY!!
YOU GUYS KNOW I CAN'T USE THESE!!!
I FELT LIKE A DOG BEGGING FOR SCRAPS.
※ Later I was able to get the game system.

REJECTED ROUGH DRAFT #2

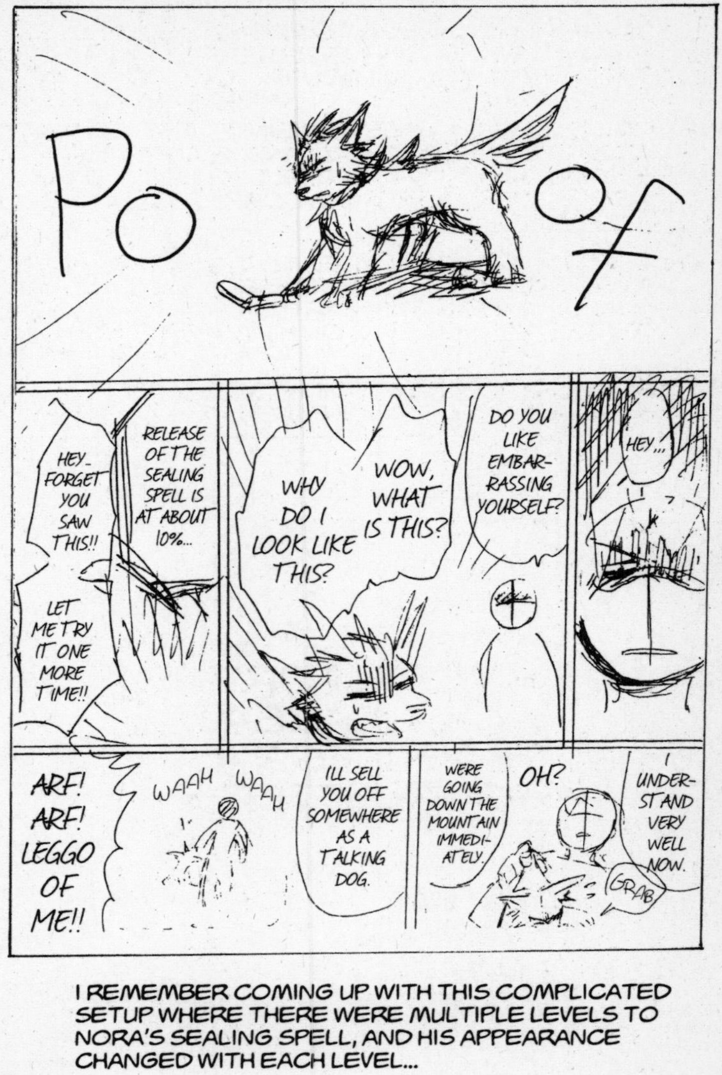
POOF
HEY...
DO YOU LIKE EMBARRASSING YOURSELF?
WOW, WHAT IS THIS?
WHY DO I LOOK LIKE THIS?
RELEASE OF THE SEALING SPELL IS AT ABOUT 10%...
HEY_ FORGET YOU SAW THIS!!
LET ME TRY IT ONE MORE TIME!!
I UNDERSTAND VERY WELL NOW.
OH?
WERE GOING DOWN THE MOUNTAIN IMMEDIATELY.
GRAB
ILL SELL YOU OFF SOMEWHERE AS A TALKING DOG.
WAAAH
WAAAH
ARF! ARF! LEGGO OF ME!!

I REMEMBER COMING UP WITH THIS COMPLICATED SETUP WHERE THERE WERE MULTIPLE LEVELS TO NORA'S SEALING SPELL, AND HIS APPEARANCE CHANGED WITH EACH LEVEL...

NORA MAILBAG

KAZUNARI KAKEI ANSWERS YOUR QUESTIONS

Q: I'D LIKE TO KNOW HOW TO PRONOUNCE THE NAMES OF THE CHARACTERS, ESPECIALLY BARIK, LEONARD AND MELFIA.

(SORACHIKA, TOKYO)

A: I BELIEVE THE NAMES WERE INTENDED TO BE READ AS *BARIK, LEONARD,* AND *MELFIA*... BUT SINCE I WASN'T VERY CAREFUL ABOUT IT, I MAY NOT HAVE SPELLED THEM CORRECTLY IN JAPANESE.

Q: WHEN KAZUMA RETURNED TO THE HUMAN WORLD AT AGE 19, THE DARK LIEGE USED MAGIC TO MAKE HIM LOOK LIKE A REGULAR HIGH SCHOOLER AGAIN. DID THAT MAGIC WORK ON HIRASAKA TOO?

(CHIBA PREFECTURE, BUDOU)

A: FOR SOME REASON IT DIDN'T WORK ON HIRASAKA OR KAZUMA'S PARENTS.

THAT'S IT FOR THE
NORA MAILBAG!
THANKS FOR ALL
YOUR LETTERS!

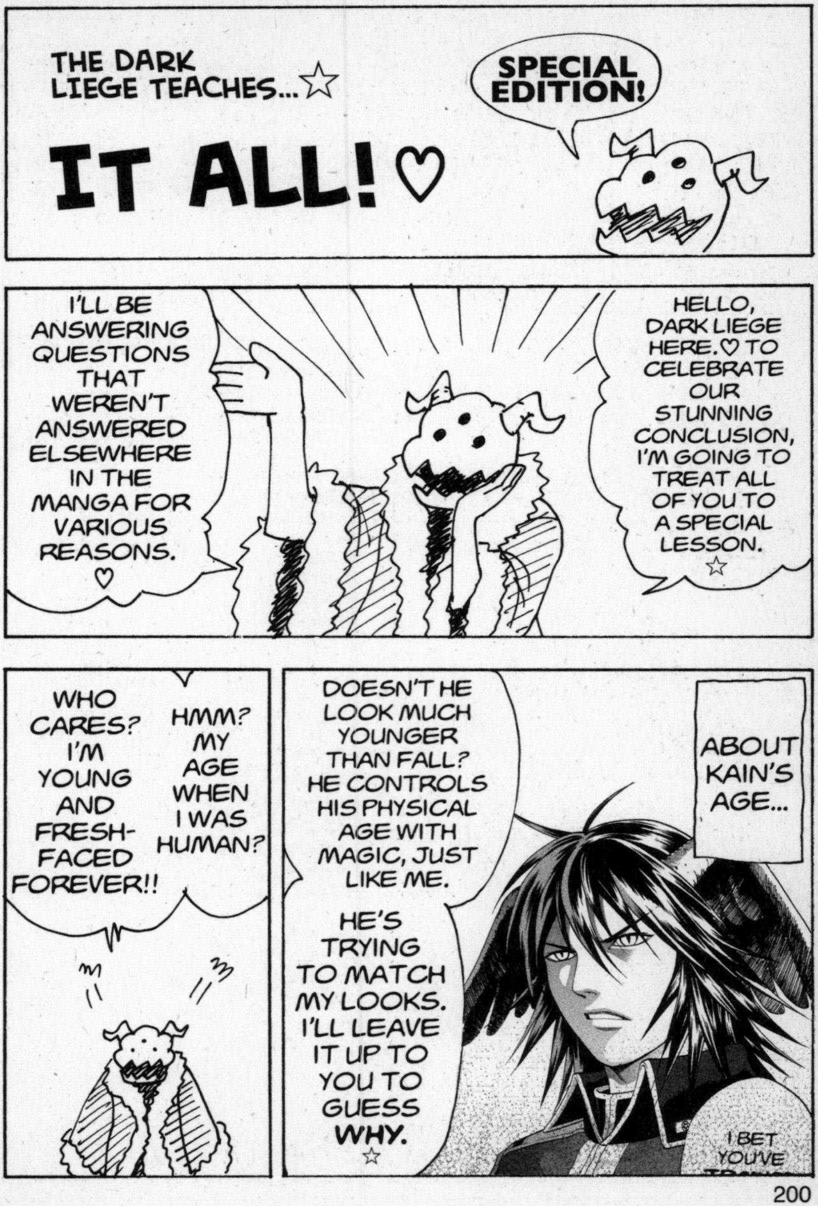
SPECIAL EDITION!
THE DARK LIEGE TEACHES...☆
IT ALL!♡
HELLO, DARK LIEGE HERE.♡ TO CELEBRATE OUR STUNNING CONCLUSION, I'M GOING TO TREAT ALL OF YOU TO A SPECIAL LESSON. ☆
I'LL BE ANSWERING QUESTIONS THAT WEREN'T ANSWERED ELSEWHERE IN THE MANGA FOR VARIOUS REASONS. ♡
ABOUT KAIN'S AGE...
DOESN'T HE LOOK MUCH YOUNGER THAN FALL? HE CONTROLS HIS PHYSICAL AGE WITH MAGIC, JUST LIKE ME.
HE'S TRYING TO MATCH MY LOOKS. I'LL LEAVE IT UP TO YOU TO GUESS WHY. ☆
HMM? MY AGE WHEN I WAS HUMAN?
WHO CARES? I'M YOUNG AND FRESH-FACED FOREVER!!

ABOUT THE MEMBERS OF THE ANCIENT RACES BESIDES DAHLIA...

THEY DISAPPEARED WHEN FALL TOOK OVER THE MAIN HEADQUARTERS.

...SO WE'RE STILL SEARCHING FOR THE MISSING INDIVIDUALS INCLUDING SOME FROM THE ELITE CLASS.

THEY DIDN'T GET ALONG WELL WITH NORA IN THE FIRST PLACE. IT DOES MAKE ME WORRY...

ABOUT NICKS'S ACCENT...

JAPANESE READERS MAY HAVE GUESSED THAT NICKS LIVED IN THE KANSAI REGION IN THE HUMAN WORLD BEFORE JOINING THE RESISTANCE.

ABOUT OSERU'S APPEARANCE WHEN HE USES A SEALING SPELL...

HE'S BAD AT SEALING SPELLS, SO HE'S NEVER ASSUMED HUMAN FORM.

ABOUT THE POWER BALANCE BETWEEN THE FOUR GENERALS...

PEOPLE KEEP WRITING TO ASK WHICH OF THEM IS THE STRONGEST.

WHEN IT COMES TO OVERALL BALANCE OF ABILITIES, LEONARD IS THE BEST.

RIVAN HAS THE MOST EXPLOSIVE ATTACK POWER AND BAJEE HAS THE GREATEST STRENGTH AND STAMINA.

MELFIA IS THE MOST PROFICIENT AT USING TECHNIQUES AND TACTICS.

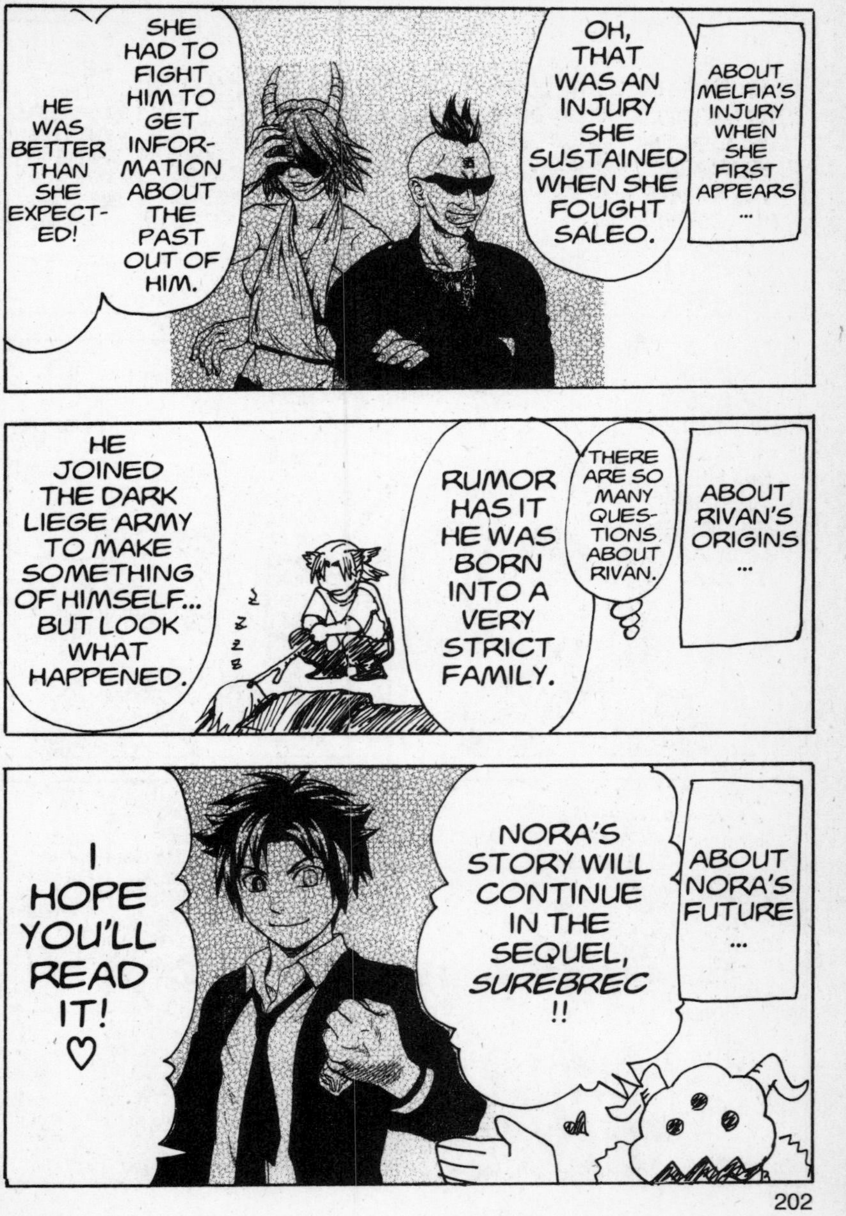
ABOUT MELFIA'S INJURY WHEN SHE FIRST APPEARS ...
OH, THAT WAS AN INJURY SHE SUSTAINED WHEN SHE FOUGHT SALEO.
SHE HAD TO FIGHT HIM TO GET INFOR-MATION ABOUT THE PAST OUT OF HIM.
HE WAS BETTER THAN SHE EXPECT-ED!
ABOUT RIVAN'S ORIGINS ...
THERE ARE SO MANY QUES-TIONS ABOUT RIVAN.
RUMOR HAS IT HE WAS BORN INTO A VERY STRICT FAMILY.
HE JOINED THE DARK LIEGE ARMY TO MAKE SOMETHING OF HIMSELF... BUT LOOK WHAT HAPPENED.
ABOUT NORA'S FUTURE ...
NORA'S STORY WILL CONTINUE IN THE SEQUEL, *SUREBREC* !!
I HOPE YOU'LL READ IT! ♡

WITH THE CONCLUSION OF *NORA*, I'VE FINISHED A LONG JOURNEY FROM THAT FIRST SHORT STORY. I COULDN'T HAVE COME THIS FAR WITHOUT THE SUPPORT OF ALL MY FANS. PLEASE KEEP READING MY WORK IN THE FUTURE!!

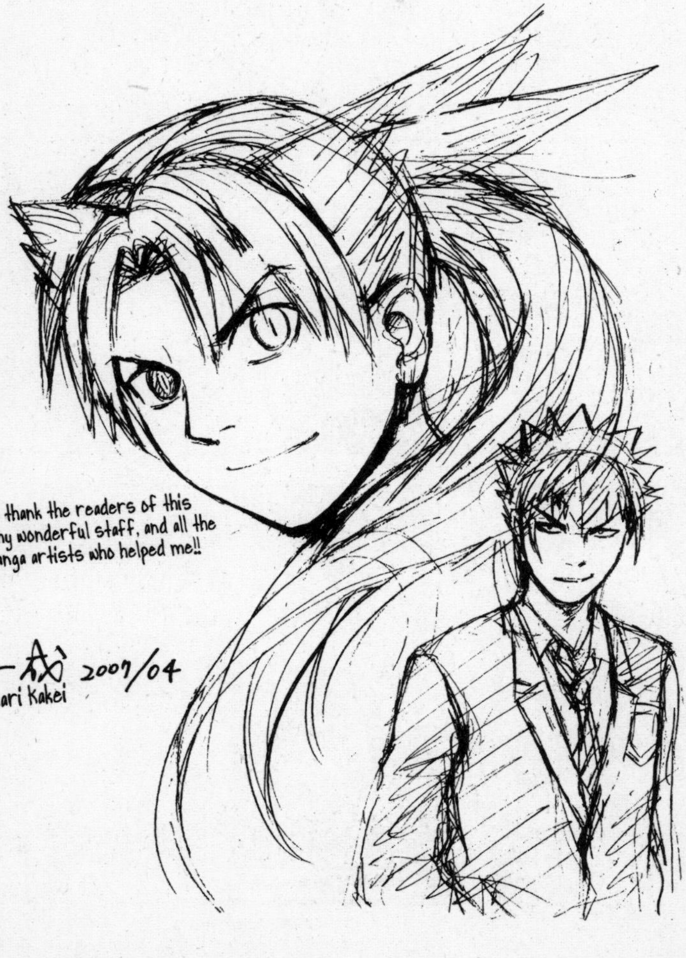

I want to thank the readers of this series, my wonderful staff, and all the other manga artists who helped me!!

筧一成 2007/04
Kazunari Kakei

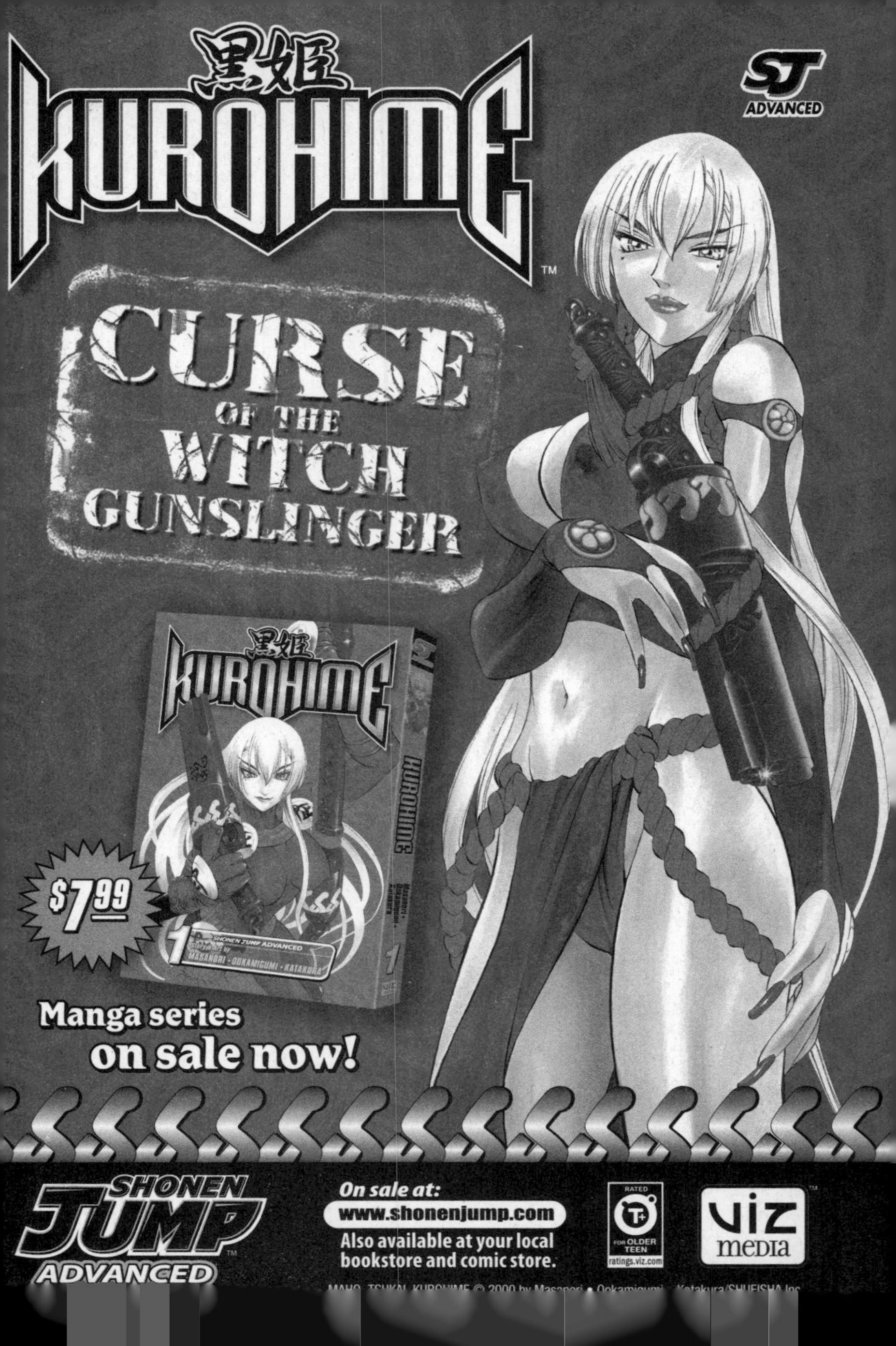

黒姫
KUROHIME™
SJ ADVANCED
CURSE OF THE WITCH GUNSLINGER
$7.99
Manga series on sale now!
SHONEN JUMP ADVANCED
On sale at:
www.shonenjump.com
Also available at your local bookstore and comic store.
RATED T+ FOR OLDER TEEN ratings.viz.com
VIZ MEDIA
MAHO TSUKAI KUROHIME © 2000 by Masanori • Ookamigumi • Katakura/SHUEISHA Inc.

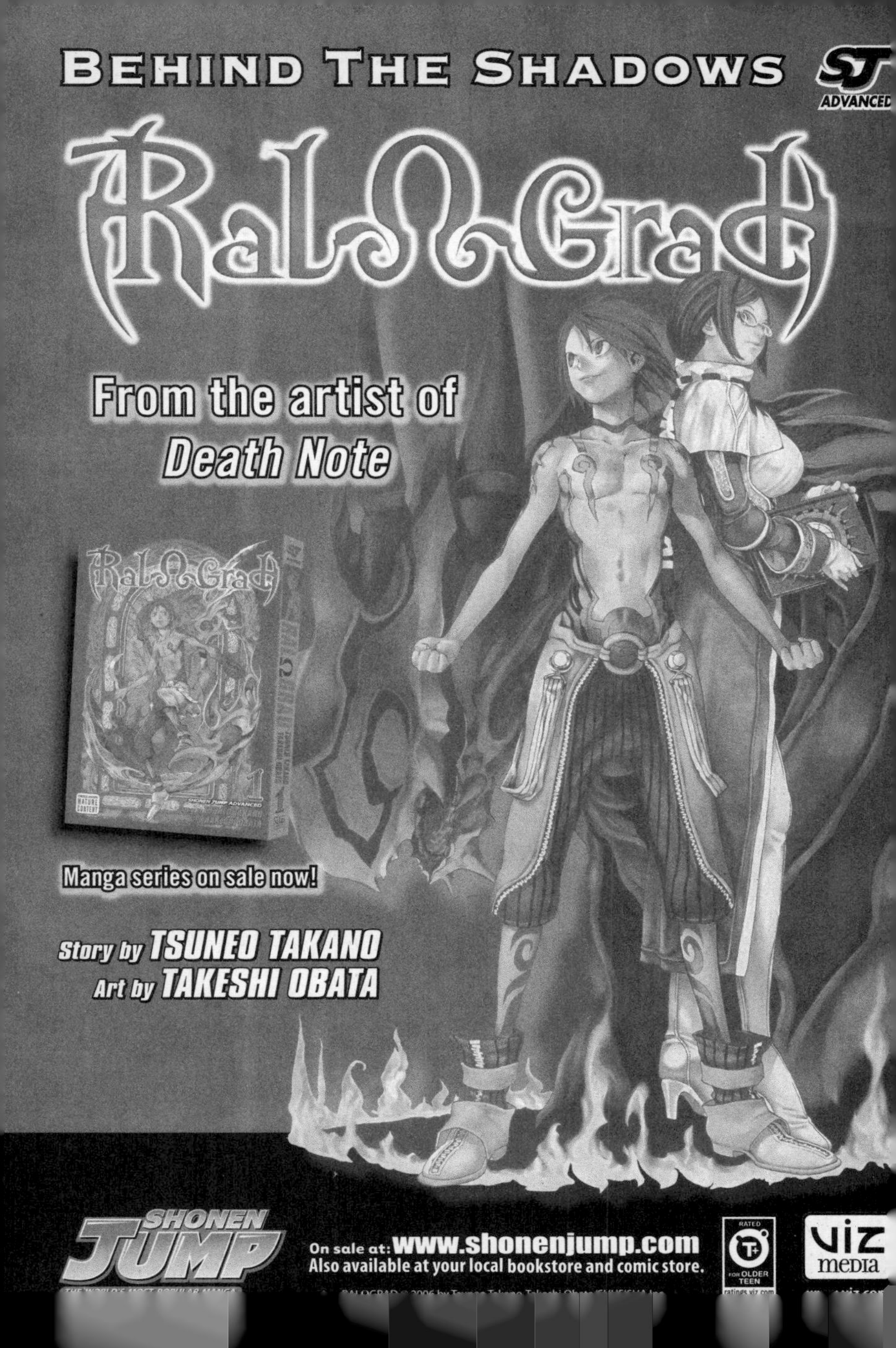

BEHIND THE SHADOWS
SJ ADVANCED
RaL Ω Grad
From the artist of
Death Note
Manga series on sale now!
Story by TSUNEO TAKANO
Art by TAKESHI OBATA
SHONEN JUMP
On sale at: www.shonenjump.com
Also available at your local bookstore and comic store.
RATED T+ FOR OLDER TEEN
ratings.viz.com
VIZ media